Pathology, Toxicogenetics, and Criminalistics of Drug Abuse

Pathology, Toxicogenetics, and Criminalistics of Drug Abuse

Edited by
Steven B. Karch, MD, FFFLM

Consultant Pathologist and Toxicologist
Berkeley, California

CRC Press is an imprint of the
Taylor & Francis Group, an informa business

CRC Press
Taylor & Francis Group
6000 Broken Sound Parkway NW, Suite 300
Boca Raton, FL 33487-2742

© 2008 by Taylor & Francis Group, LLC
CRC Press is an imprint of Taylor & Francis Group, an Informa business

No claim to original U.S. Government works
Printed in the United States of America on acid-free paper
10 9 8 7 6 5 4 3 2 1

International Standard Book Number-13: 978-1-4200-5455-2 (Hardcover)

This book contains information obtained from authentic and highly regarded sources. Reprinted material is quoted with permission, and sources are indicated. A wide variety of references are listed. Reasonable efforts have been made to publish reliable data and information, but the author and the publisher cannot assume responsibility for the validity of all materials or for the consequences of their use.

Except as permitted under U.S. Copyright Law, no part of this book may be reprinted, reproduced, transmitted, or utilized in any form by any electronic, mechanical, or other means, now known or hereafter invented, including photocopying, microfilming, and recording, or in any information storage or retrieval system, without written permission from the publishers.

For permission to photocopy or use material electronically from this work, please access www.copyright.com (http://www.copyright.com/) or contact the Copyright Clearance Center, Inc. (CCC) 222 Rosewood Drive, Danvers, MA 01923, 978-750-8400. CCC is a not-for-profit organization that provides licenses and registration for a variety of users. For organizations that have been granted a photocopy license by the CCC, a separate system of payment has been arranged.

Trademark Notice: Product or corporate names may be trademarks or registered trademarks, and are used only for identification and explanation without intent to infringe.

Visit the Taylor & Francis Web site at
http://www.taylorandfrancis.com

and the CRC Press Web site at
http://www.crcpress.com

Contents

Chapter 1 The Criminalistics of Controlled Substances 1
Joseph P. Bono, M.A.

Chapter 2 Overview of Pathology of Drug Abuse: Scene of Death and the Autopsy 71
Charles V. Wetli, M.D.

Chapter 3 Heart Disease 79
Renu Virmani, M.D., F.A.C.C., Allen P. Burke, M.D., and Andrew Farb, M.D.

Chapter 4 Vascular Effects of Substance Abuse 97
Frank D. Kolodgie, Ph.D., Allen P. Burke, M.D., Jagat Narula, M.D., Ph.D., Florabel G. Mullick, M.D., and Renu Virmani, M.D., F.A.C.C.

Chapter 5 Myocardial Alterations in Drug Abusers...115
Steven B. Karch, M.D., FFFLM

Chapter 6 Valvular Heart Disease...123
Michael D. Bell, M.D.

Chapter 7 Lung Disease..129
Michael D. Bell, M.D.

Chapter 8 Disorders of the Central Nervous System..137
Michael D. Bell, M.D.

Chapter 9 Toxicogenetics in Drug Abuse: Pharmacogenomics for Toxicology...................153
Robert M. White, Sr., Ph.D. and Steven H.Y. Wong, Ph.D.

Chapter 10 Toxicogenetics in Drug Abuse: Heritable Channelopathies and Myopathies 165
Kathryn A. Glatter, M.D., Jonica Calkins, M.D., and Sanjay J. Ayirookuzhi, M.D.

Index 185

Preface

In a very broad sense, the criminalistics and pathology of drug abuse are determined by the particular drugs abused, the ways those drugs are used and administered, their toxic effects, and the behavioral modifications they produce. This volume begins with a basic overview of the identification and analysis of physical evidence derived from drugs and drug users. The discussion continues with an examination of pathological changes resulting from the pharmacologic effects of various drugs that are abused and from the ways that these drugs are administered: in short, a review of the changes one would likely encounter at the autopsy table. Much of this book focuses on emerging concepts and newly discovered phenomena, with an emphasis on death scene investigation, evaluation of the drug abuse victim (living or deceased), and cardiovascular pathology. In many instances, the authors have relied on their own academic and investigative experiences to provide a practical approach to evaluating these drug abuse victims.

Much of what is known about the pathology of drug abuse has been derived from thorough and carefully performed autopsies. Much of this book deals with the autopsy and will be of particular interest to pathologists; however, far from this being an academic exercise, it is hoped that the reader will discern applications to clinical situations. This, in fact, has been accomplished over the years as clinicians have come to better appreciate the pathophysiology of diseases resulting from drug abuse.

The final two chapters explore exciting new methods and advances in molecular biology and DNA technology that now make it possible to explain instances of sudden death that previously were unexplained. Emerging evidence suggests that the underlying cause of death in many is genetic, and that heart and liver abnormalities may play a role. The problem is that death from a wide variety of genetic defects leaves no histological markers. The ability to identify these "invisible diseases" with postmortem genetic testing has become a reality far more quickly than anyone had ever imagined. It may not yet be "standard of care" to test for cardiac channelopathies or P450 polymorphisms, but it will be in the not-too-distant future.

The Editor

Steven B. Karch, M.D., FFFLM, received his undergraduate degree from Brown University. He attended graduate school in anatomy and cell biology at Stanford University. He received his medical degree from Tulane University School of Medicine. Dr. Karch did postgraduate training in neuropathology at the Royal London Hospital and in cardiac pathology at Stanford University. For many years he was a consultant cardiac pathologist to San Francisco's Chief Medical Examiner.

In the U.K., Dr. Karch served as a consultant to the Crown and helped prepare the cases against serial murderer Dr. Harold Shipman, who was subsequently convicted of murdering 248 of his patients. He has testified on drug abuse–related matters in courts around the world. He has a special interest in cases of alleged euthanasia, and in episodes where mothers are accused of murdering their children by the transference of drugs, either *in utero* or by breast feeding.

Dr. Karch is the author of nearly 100 papers and book chapters, most of which are concerned with the effects of drug abuse on the heart. He has published seven books. He is currently completing the fourth edition of *Pathology of Drug Abuse*, a widely used textbook. He is also working on a popular history of Napoleon and his doctors.

Dr. Karch is forensic science editor for Humana Press, and he serves on the editorial boards of the *Journal of Cardiovascular Toxicology*, the *Journal of Clinical Forensic Medicine* (London), *Forensic Science, Medicine and Pathology*, and *Clarke's Analysis of Drugs and Poisons*.

Dr. Karch was elected a fellow of the Faculty of Legal and Forensic Medicine, Royal College of Physicians (London) in 2006. He is also a fellow of the American Academy of Forensic Sciences, the Society of Forensic Toxicologists (SOFT), the National Association of Medical Examiners (NAME), the Royal Society of Medicine in London, and the Forensic Science Society of the U.K. He is a member of The International Association of Forensic Toxicologists (TIAFT).

Contributors

Sanjay J. Ayirookuzhi, M.D.
Department of Cardiology and Internal
  Medicine
University of California
Davis, California

Michael D. Bell, M.D.
District Medical Examiner
Palm Beach Medical Examiner Office
West Palm Beach, Florida

Joseph P. Bono, M.A.
Supervisory Chemist
Drug Enforcement Administration
Special Testing and Research Laboratory
McLean, Virginia

Allen P. Burke, M.D.
Professor of Pathology and Medical Director
Kernan Hospital Pathology Laboratory
University of Maryland Medical Center
Baltimore, Maryland

Jonica Calkins, M.D.
Department of Cardiology and Internal
  Medicine
University of California
Davis, California

Andrew Farb, M.D.
U.S. Food and Drug Administration
Rockville, Maryland

Kathryn A. Glatter, M.D.
Department of Cardiology and Internal
  Medicine
University of California
Davis, California

Steven B. Karch, M.D., FFFLM
Consultant Pathologist/Toxicologist
Berkeley, California

Frank D. Kolodgie, Ph.D.
Armed Forces Institute of Pathology
Washington, D.C.

Florabel G. Mullick, M.D.
Armed Forces Institute of Pathology
Washington, D.C.

Jagat Narula, M.D., Ph.D.
University of California, Irvine
School of Medicine and Medical Center
Irvine, California

Renu Virmani, M.D., F.A.C.C.
Medical Director
CVPath
International Registry of Pathology
Gaithersburg, Maryland

Charles V. Wetli, M.D.
Chief Medical Examiner
Office of the Suffolk County Medical Examiner
Hauppage, New York

Robert M. White, Sr., Ph.D.
Technical Director
DSI Laboratories
Fort Myers, Florida

Steven H.Y. Wong, Ph.D.
Professor of Pathology
and
Director
Clinical Chemistry/Toxicology
TDM, Pharmacogenomics, Proteomics
Medical College of Wisconsin
and
Scientific Director
Toxicology Department
Milwaukee County Medical Examiner's Office
Milwaukee, Wisconsin

CHAPTER **1**

The Criminalistics of Controlled Substances

Joseph P. Bono, M.A.
Supervisory Chemist, Drug Enforcement Administration, Special Testing and Research Laboratory, McLean, Virginia

CONTENTS

Introduction 3
1.1 Definition and Scheduling of Controlled Substances...3
1.2 Scheduling of Controlled Substances 3
1.3 Controlled Substance Analogue Enforcement Act of 1986...4
1.4 Controlled Substances 5
    1.4.1 Heroin 5
        1.4.1.1 Heroin Sources by Region...6
        1.4.1.2 Isolation of Morphine and Heroin Production 7
    References...9
    1.4.2 Cocaine 9
        1.4.2.1 Sources of Cocaine 10
        1.4.2.2 Historical Considerations..11
        1.4.2.3 Isolation and Purification 11
        1.4.2.4 Conversion to "Crack" 12
        1.4.2.5 Other Coca Alkaloids..13
        1.4.2.6 Cocaine Adulterants 14
        1.4.2.7 Conclusion...14
    References...14
    1.4.3 Marijuana...15
        1.4.3.1 History and Terminology 15
        1.4.3.2 Laboratory Analysis 16
    1.4.4 Peyote 17
    1.4.5 Psilocybin Mushrooms 18
    References...19
    1.4.6 Lysergic Acid Diethylamide..20
    1.4.7 Phencyclidine...20
    1.4.8 Fentanyl 21
    1.4.9 Phenethylamines 22

1.4.10 Methcathinone 28
1.4.11 *Catha edulis* (Khat) 29
References..29
1.4.12 Anabolic Steroids 30
        1.4.12.1 Regulatory History 30
        1.4.12.2 Structure–Activity Relationship...32
        1.4.12.3 Forensic Analysis 33
Acknowledgment..34
References..34
1.5 Legitimate Pharmaceutical Preparations 35
1.5.1 Benzodiazepines 35
1.5.2 Other Central Nervous System Depressants...35
1.5.3 Narcotic Analgesics..36
1.5.4 Central Nervous System Stimulants 37
1.5.5 Identifying Generic Products 37
Reference 37
1.6 Unique Identifying Factors..37
1.6.1 Packaging Logos 37
1.6.2 Tablet Markings and Capsule Imprints...38
1.6.3 Blotter Paper LSD...39
References..40
1.7 Analyzing Drugs in the Forensic Science Laboratory 40
1.7.1 Screening Tests 40
        1.7.1.1 Physical Characteristics 40
        1.7.1.2 Color Tests 41
        1.7.1.3 Thin-Layer Chromatography 41
1.7.2 Confirmatory Chemical Tests...42
        1.7.2.1 Microcrystal Identifications 42
        1.7.2.2 Gas Chromatography 42
        1.7.2.3 High-Performance Liquid Chromatography...43
        1.7.2.4 Capillary Electrophoresis..44
        1.7.2.5 Infrared Spectrophotometry 44
        1.7.2.6 Gas Chromatography/Mass Spectrometry 45
        1.7.2.7 Nuclear Magnetic Resonance Spectroscopy..46
References..47
1.7.3 Controlled Substances Examinations...47
        1.7.3.1 Identifying and Quantitating Controlled Substances...............................48
        1.7.3.2 Identifying Adulterants and Diluents...50
        1.7.3.3 Quantitating Controlled Substances...51
        1.7.3.4 Reference Standards...52
References..53
1.8 Comparative Analysis..53
1.8.1 Determining Commonality of Source...53
1.8.2 Comparing Heroin Exhibits 54
1.8.3 Comparing Cocaine Exhibits 54
References..55
1.9 Clandestine Laboratories...55
1.9.1 Safety Concerns..57
1.9.2 Commonly Encountered Chemicals in the Clandestine Laboratory 58
Reference 60

THE CRIMINALISTICS OF CONTROLLED SUBSTANCES

1.9.3   Tables of Controlled Substances..60
          1.9.3.1   Generalized List by Category of Physiological Effects and Medical
                     Uses of Controlled Substances 60
          1.9.3.2   Listing of Controlled Substances by Schedule Number 62

INTRODUCTION

This chapter is concerned with the identification and analysis of physical evidence derived from drugs and drug users. The chapter begins with an introduction to the most popular synthetic routes preferred by clandestine drug makers. Sections are devoted to brief regulatory histories and overviews of the most common drugs (heroin, cocaine, and marijuana) as well as some of the lesser known licit and illicit drug agents. An overview is provided of what information is required to make a defensible forensic identification. This includes an introduction to drug logos, tablet markings and capsule imprints, and blotter acid. The remaining sections provide introductions to the various field and laboratory screening and confirmatory testing procedures. Techniques of comparative analysis are explained, and methods for comparing cocaine and heroin courtroom exhibits are presented. The trade names of commonly encountered chemicals are listed. The chapter concludes with tabular listings of controlled substances by schedule number.

1.1 DEFINITION AND SCHEDULING OF CONTROLLED SUBSTANCES

A "controlled substance" is a drug or substance of which the use, sale, or distribution is regulated by the federal government or a state government entity. These controlled substances are listed specifically or by classification on the federal level in the Controlled Substances Act (CSA) or in Part 1308 of the Code of Federal Regulations. The purpose of the CSA is to minimize the quantity of usable substances available to those who are likely to abuse them. At the same time, the CSA provides for the legitimate medical, scientific, and industrial needs of these substances in the U.S.

1.2 SCHEDULING OF CONTROLLED SUBSTANCES

Eight factors are considered when determining whether or not to schedule a drug as a controlled substance:

1. Actual or relative potential for abuse
2. Scientific evidence of pharmacological effect
3. State of current scientific knowledge
4. History of current pattern of abuse
5. Scope, duration, and significance of abuse
6. Risk to the public health
7. Psychic or physiological dependence liability
8. Immediate precursor

The definition of potential for abuse is based on individuals taking a drug of their own volition in sufficient amounts to cause a health hazard to themselves or to others in the community. Data are then collected to evaluate three factors: (1) actual abuse of the drug; (2) the clandestine manufacture of the drug; (3) trafficking and diversion of the drug or its precursors from legitimate channels into clandestine operations. Preclinical abuse liability studies are then conducted on animals to evaluate physiological responses to the drug. At this point, clinical abuse liability studies can be conducted with human subjects, which evaluate preference studies and epidemiology.

Accumulating scientific evidence of a drug's pharmacological effects involves examining the scientific data concerning whether the drug elicits a stimulant, depressant, narcotic, or hallucinogenic response. A determination can then be made regarding how closely the pharmacology of the drug resembles that of other drugs that are already controlled.

Evidence is also accumulated about the scientific data on the physical and chemical properties of the drug. This can include determining which salts and isomers are possible and which are available. There is also a concern for the ease of detection and identification using analytical chemistry. Because many controlled substances have the potential for clandestine synthesis, there is a requirement for evaluating precursors, possible synthetic routes, and theoretical yields in these syntheses. At this phase of the evaluation, medical uses are also evaluated.

The next three factors — (1) history and patterns of abuse; (2) scope, duration, and significance of abuse; and (3) risks to public health — all involve sociological and medical considerations. The results of these studies focus on data collection and population studies. Psychic and physiological dependence liability studies must be satisfied for a substance to be placed on Schedules II through V. This specific finding is not necessary to place a drug on Schedule I. A practical problem here is that it is not always easy to prove a development of dependence.

The last factor is one that can involve the forensic analyst. Under the law, an "immediate precursor" is defined as a substance that is an immediate chemical intermediary used or likely to be used in the manufacture of a specific controlled substance. Defining synthetic pathways in the clandestine production of illicit controlled substances requires knowledge possessed by the experienced analyst.

A controlled substance will be classified and named in one of five schedules. Schedule I includes drugs or other substances that have a high potential for abuse, no currently accepted use in the treatment of medical conditions, and little, if any, accepted safety criteria under the supervision of a medical professional. Use of these substances will almost always lead to abuse and dependence. Some of the more commonly encountered Schedule I controlled substances are heroin, marijuana, lysergic acid diethylamide (LSD), 3,4-methylenedioxy-amphetamine (MDA), and psilocybin mushrooms.

Progressing from Schedule II to Schedule V, abuse potential decreases. Schedule II controlled substances also include drugs or other substances that have a high potential for abuse, but also have some currently accepted, but severely restricted, medical uses. Abuse of Schedule II substances may lead to dependence, which can be both physical and psychological. Because Schedule II controlled substances do have some recognized medical uses, they are usually available to health professionals in the form of legitimate pharmaceutical preparations. Cocaine hydrochloride is still used as a topical anesthetic in some surgical procedures. Methamphetamine, up until a few years ago, was used in the form of Desoxyn to treat hyperactivity in children. Raw opium is included in Schedule II. Amobarbital and secobarbital, which are used as central nervous system depressants, are included, as is phencyclidine (PCP), which was used as a tranquilizer in veterinary pharmaceutical practices. In humans, PCP acts as a hallucinogen. Although many of the substances seized under Schedule II were not prepared by legitimate pharmaceutical entities, cocaine hydrochloride and methamphetamine are two examples of Schedule II drugs that, when confiscated as white to off-white powder or granules in plastic or glassine packets, have almost always been prepared on the illicit market for distribution. As one progresses from Schedules III through V, most legitimate pharmaceutical preparations are encountered.

1.3 CONTROLLED SUBSTANCE ANALOGUE ENFORCEMENT ACT OF 1986

In recent years, the phenomenon of controlled substance analogues and homologues has presented a most serious challenge to the control of drug trafficking and successful prosecution of clandestine laboratory operators. These homologues and analogues are synthesized drugs that are

THE CRIMINALISTICS OF CONTROLLED SUBSTANCES

chemically and pharmacologically similar to substances that are listed in the Controlled Substances Act, but which themselves are not specifically controlled by name. (The term "designer drug" is sometimes used to describe these substances.) The concept of synthesizing controlled substance analogues in an attempt to circumvent existing drug law was first noticed in the late 1960s. At about this time there were seizures of clandestine laboratories engaged in the production of analogues of controlled phenethylamines. In the 1970s variants of methaqualone and phencyclidine were being seized in clandestine laboratories. By the 1980s, Congress decided that the time had come to deal with this problem with a federal law enforcement initiative. The Controlled Substance Analogue Enforcement Act of 1986 amends the Comprehensive Drug Abuse Prevention and Control Act of 1970 by including the following section:

Section 203. A controlled substance analogue shall to the extent intended for human consumption, be treated, for the purposes of this title and title III as a controlled substance in schedule I.

The 99th Congress went on to define the meaning of the term "controlled substance analogue" as a substance:

(i) the chemical structure of which is substantially similar to the chemical structure of a controlled substance in schedule I or II;

(ii) which has a stimulant, depressant, or hallucinogenic effect on the central nervous system that is substantially similar to or greater than the stimulant, depressant, or hallucinogenic effect on the central nervous system of a controlled substance in schedule I or II; or

(iii) with respect to a particular person, which person represents or intends to have a stimulant, depressant, or hallucinogenic effect on the central nervous system of a controlled substance in schedule I or II.

The Act goes on to exclude:

(i) a controlled substance

(ii) any substance for which there is an approved new drug application

(iii) with respect to a particular person any substance, if an exemption is in effect for investigational use, for that person, under section 505 ... to the extent conduct with respect to such substance is pursuant to such exemption; or

(iv) any substance to the extent not intended for human consumption before such an exemption takes effect with respect to that substance.

Treatment of exhibits falling under the purview of the federal court system is described in Public Law 91-513 or Part 1308 of the Code of Federal Regulations. Questions relating to controlled substance analogues and homologues can usually be answered by reference to the Controlled Substances Analogue and Enforcement Act of 1986.

1.4 CONTROLLED SUBSTANCES

1.4.1 Heroin

Whenever one thinks about drugs of abuse and addiction, heroin is one of the most recognized drugs. Heroin is a synthetic drug, produced from the morphine contained in the sap of the opium poppy. The abuse of this particular controlled substance has been known for many years. The correct chemical nomenclature for heroin is O^3,O^6-diacetylmorphine. Heroin is synthesized from morphine in a relatively simple process. The first synthesis of diacetylmorphine reported in the literature was in 1875 by two English chemists, G.H. Beckett and C.P. Alder Wright.[1] In 1898 in Elberfeld, Germany, the Farbenfabriken vorm. Friedrich Bayer & Co. produced the drug commercially. An employee of the company, H. Dresser, named the morphine product "heroin."[2] There is no definitive documentation as to where the name "heroin" originated. However, it probably had its origin in the "heroic remedies" class of drugs of the day.

Heroin was used in place of codeine and morphine for patients suffering from lung diseases such as tuberculosis. Additionally, the Bayer Company advertised heroin as a cure for morphine addiction. The analgesic properties of the drug were very effective. However, the addictive properties were quite devastating. In 1924, Congress amended the Narcotic Drug Import and Export Act to prohibit the importation of opium for the manufacture of heroin. However, stockpiles were still available and could be legally prescribed by physicians. The 1925 International Opium Convention imposed drug controls that began to limit the supply of heroin from Europe. Shortly thereafter, the clandestine manufacture of heroin was reported in China. The supplies of opium in the Far East provided a ready source of morphine — the starting material for the synthesis. The medical use of heroin in the U.S. was not banned until July 19, 1956 with the passage of Public Law 728, which required all inventories to be surrendered to the federal government by November 19, 1956.

In the past 50 or so years, the source countries for opium used in clandestine heroin production have increased dramatically. Political and economic instability in many areas of the world accounts for much of the increased production of heroin. The opium that is used to produce the heroin that enters the U.S. today has four principal sources. Geographically all of these regions are characterized by a temperate climate with appropriate rainfall and proper soil conditions. However, there are differences in the quality of opium, the morphine content, and the number of harvests from each of these areas. Labor costs are minimal and the profit margins are extremely high for those in the upper echelons of heroin distribution networks.

1.4.1.1 *Heroin Sources by Region*

Southeast Asia — The "Golden Triangle" areas of Burma, China, and Laos are the three major source countries in this part of the world for the production of illicit opium. Of these three countries, 60 to 80% of the total world supply of heroin comes from Burma. Heroin destined for the U.S. transits a number of countries including Thailand, Hong Kong, Japan, Korea, the Philippines, Singapore, and Taiwan. Southeast Asian heroin is usually shipped to the U.S. in significant quantities by bulk cargo carriers. The techniques for hiding the heroin in the cargo are quite ingenious. The shipment of Southeast Asian (SEA) heroin in relatively small quantities is also commonplace. Criminal organizations in Nigeria have been deeply involved in the small-quantity smuggling of SEA heroin into the U.S. The "body carry" technique and ingestion are two of the better known methods of concealment by the Nigerians. SEA heroin is high quality and recognized by its white crystalline appearance. Although the cutting agents are numerous, caffeine and acetaminophen appear quite frequently.

Southwest Asia — Turkey, Iraq, Iran, Afghanistan, Pakistan, India, Lebanon, and the newly independent states of the former Soviet Union (NIS) are recognized as source countries in this part of the world. Trafficking of Southwest Asian heroin has been on the decline in the U.S. since the end of 1994. Southwest Asian heroin usage is more predominant in Europe than in the U.S. The Southwest Asian heroin that does arrive in the U.S. is normally transshipped through Europe, Africa, and the NIS. The political and economic conditions of the NIS and topography of the land make these countries ideal as transit countries for heroin smuggling. The rugged mountainous terrain and the absence of significant enforcement efforts enable traffickers to proceed unabated. Most Southwest Asian heroin trafficking groups in the originating countries, the transiting countries, and the U.S. are highly cohesive ethnic groups. These groups rely less on the bulk shipment and more on smaller

THE CRIMINALISTICS OF CONTROLLED SUBSTANCES

quantity commercial cargo smuggling techniques. Southwest Asian heroin is characterized by its off-white to tan powdery appearance as compared to the white SEA heroin. The purity of Southwest Asian heroin is only slightly lower than that of SEA heroin. The cutting agents are many: phenobarbital, caffeine, acetaminophen, and calcium carbonate appear quite frequently.

Central America — Mexico and Guatemala are the primary source countries for heroin in Central America. Mexico's long border with the U.S. provides easy access for smuggling and distribution networks. Smuggling is usually small scale and often involves illegal immigrants and migrant workers crossing into the U.S. Heroin distribution in the U.S. is primarily the work of Mexican immigrants from the States of Durango, Michoacan, Nuevo Leon, and Sinaloa. Concealment in motor vehicles, public transportation, external body carries, and commercial package express are common. This heroin usually ranges from a dark brown powder to a black tar. The most commonly encountered adulterants are amorphous (formless and indeterminate) materials and sugars. The dark color of Mexican heroin is attributed to processing by-products. The purity of Mexican heroin varies greatly from seizure to seizure.

South America — Heroin production in this part of the world is a relatively new phenomenon. Cultivation of opium has been documented along the Andean mountain range within Colombia in the areas of Cauca, Huila, Tolima, and Santaner. There have been a number of morphine base and heroin processing facilities seized in Colombia in the past few years. Smuggling of South American heroin into the U.S. increased dramatically in 1994 and 1995. The primary method of smuggling has been by Colombian couriers aboard commercial airliners using false-sided briefcases and luggage, hollowed out shoes, or by ingestion. Miami and New York are the primary ports of entry into the U.S. One advantage that the traffickers from South America have is the importation networks that are already in place for the distribution of cocaine into the U.S. Transshipment of this heroin through other South American countries and the Caribbean is also a common practice. South American heroin has many of the same physical characteristics of Southwest Asian heroin. However, the purity of South American heroin is higher, with fewer adulterants than Southwest Asian heroin. Cocaine in small quantities is oftentimes encountered in South American heroin exhibits. In such cases, it is not always clear whether the cocaine is present as a contaminant introduced due to common packaging locations of cocaine and heroin, or whether it has been added as an adulterant.

1.4.1.2 Isolation of Morphine and Heroin Production

There are some very specific methods for producing heroin. However, all involve the same four steps: (1) The opium poppy (*Papaver somniferum* L.) is cultivated; (2) the poppy head is scored and the opium latex is collected; (3) the morphine is then isolated from the latex; and (4) the morphine is treated with an acetylating agent. Isolation of the morphine in Step 3 is accomplished using a rendition of one of the following five methods:

1. **Thiboumery and Mohr Process (TMP)** — This is the best known of the reported methods for isolating morphine followed by the acetylation to heroin. Dried opium latex is dissolved in three times its weight of hot water. The solution is filtered hot, which removes undissolved botanical substances. These undissolved botanicals are washed with hot water and filtered. This is done to ensure a maximized yield of morphine in the final product. The filtrate is reduced to half its volume by boiling off the water. The laboratory operator then adds to the filtrate a boiling solution of calcium hydroxide, which forms the water-soluble calcium morphinate. The precipitates, which include the insoluble alkaloids from the opium, and the insoluble materials from this step are filtered. These insolubles are then washed three more times with water and filtered. The resulting filtrate, which contains calcium morphinate still in solution, is then evaporated to a weight of approximately twice the weight of the original weight of the opium and then filtered. This results in a concentrated calcium morphinate solution, which is heated to a boil. Ammonium chloride is then added to reduce the pH below 9.85. When this solution cools, morphine base precipitates and is collected by filtration. The morphine base is dissolved in a minimum volume of warm hydrochloric acid. When this solution cools the morphine hydrochloride precipitates. The precipitated morphine hydrochloride is then isolated by filtration.

2. **Robertson and Gregory Process (RGP)** — This method is similar to TMP. The laboratory operator washes the opium with five to ten times its weight of cold water. The solution is then evaporated to a syrup, which is then re-extracted with cold water and filtered. The filtrate is evaporated until the specific gravity of the solution is 1.075. The solution is boiled and calcium chloride is added. Cold water is added to the calcium morphinate solution, which is then filtered. The solution is concentrated and the calcium morphinate then precipitates out of solution as the liquid evaporates. The calcium morphinate is then redissolved in water and filtered. To the filtrate is added ammonia, which allows the morphine base to precipitate. This morphine base can then be further treated to produce the pharmaceutical quality morphine.

The TMP and RGP are used by commercial suppliers for the initial isolation of morphine from opium. In clandestine laboratories, the same methodologies and rudimentary steps are followed. However, since the operators are using "bucket chemistry," there are modifications to hasten and shortcut the processes.

Three other methods can then be utilized to convert the relatively crude morphine base through purification processes to high-quality morphine base or morphine hydrochloride crystals. Modifications of these purifications are used by clandestine laboratory operators.

3. **Barbier Purification** — The morphine base is dissolved in 80°C water. Tartaric acid is added until the solution becomes acidic to methyl orange. As the solution cools, morphine bitartrate precipitates, is filtered, washed with cold water, and dried. The morphine bitartrate is then dissolved in hot water and ammonia is added to pH 6. This results in a solution of morphine monotartrate. The laboratory operator then adds activated carbon black, sodium bisulfite, sodium acetate, and ammonium oxalate. This process results in a decolorization of the morphine. When this decolorization process is complete, ammonia is added to the solution, which results in white crystals of morphine base. These purified morphine base crystals are then filtered and dried. This high-quality morphine base is converted to morphine hydrochloride by adding 30% ethanolic HCl to a warm solution of morphine in ethanol. The morphine hydrochloride crystallizes from solution as the solution cools.
4. **Schwyzer Purification** — The acetone-insoluble morphine base (from either the TMB or RGP) is washed with acetone. The morphine base is then re-crystallized from hot ethyl alcohol.
5. **Heumann Purification** — The laboratory operator washes the morphine base (from either the TMB or RGP) with trichloroethylene, followed by a cold 40% ethanol wash. This is subsequently followed by an aqueous acetone wash.

The quality of the clandestine product is usually evaluated by the color and texture of the morphine from one of these processes. If the clandestine laboratory is producing morphine as its end product, with the intention of selling the morphine for conversion by a second laboratory, the morphine will usually be very pure. However, if the operator continues with the acetylation of the morphine to heroin, the "intermediate" morphine will frequently be relatively impure.

Heroin can be produced synthetically, but requires a ten-step process and extensive expertise in synthetic organic chemistry. The total synthesis of morphine has been reported by Gates and Tschudi in 1952 and by Elad and Ginsburg in 1954.[3,4] A more recent synthesis was reported by Rice in 1980.[5] All these methods require considerable forensic expertise and result in low yield. There are also methods reported in the literature for converting codeine to morphine using an O-demethylation. The morphine can then be acetylated to heroin. One of these procedures is referred to as "homebake" and was described in the literature by Rapoport et al.[6] This particular procedure has been reported only in New Zealand and Australia.

Acetylation of Morphine to Diacetylmorphine (Heroin) — This process involves placing dried morphine into a reaction vessel and adding excess acetic anhydride (Figure 1.1). Sometimes a co-solvent is also used. The mixture is heated to boiling and stirred for varying periods of time ranging from 30 min up to 3 or 4 h. The vessel and contents are cooled and diluted in cold water. A sodium carbonate solution is then added until precipitation of the heroin base is complete and settles to the

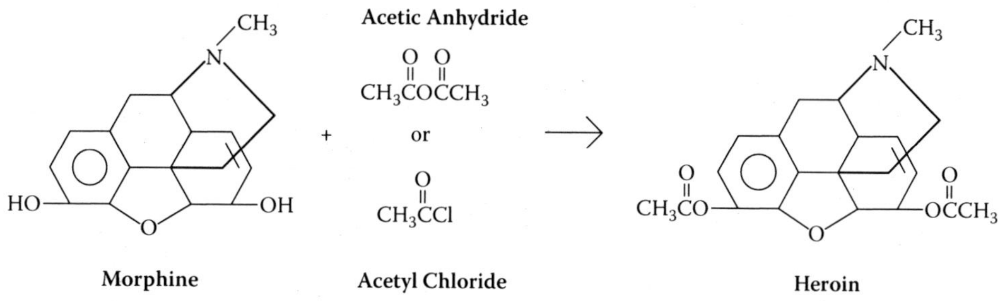

THE CRIMINALISTICS OF CONTROLLED SUBSTANCES

Figure 1.1 Clandestine laboratory synthesis of heroin.

bottom of the reaction vessel. The heroin base is then either filtered and dried or undergoes further processing to enhance the purity or to convert the base to heroin hydrochloride.

Processing By-Products and Degradation Products in Heroin — Pharmaceutical-grade heroin has a purity of greater than 99.5%. Impurities include morphine, the O-3- and O-6-monoacetylmorphines, and other alkaloidal impurities and processing by-products. The impurities found in clandestinely produced heroin include, but are certainly not limited to: the monoacetylmorphines, morphine, codeine, acetylcodeine, papaverine, noscapine, thebaine, meconine, thebaol, acetylthebaol, norlaudanosine, reticuline, and codamine. These impurities (from both quantitative and qualitative perspectives) are retained as the result of anomalies in processing methodologies.

REFERENCES

1. Anon., Heroin, *J. Chem. Soc. London,* 28, 315–318, 1875.
2. Anon., Heroin, *Arch. Ges. Physiol.,* 72, 487, 1898.
3. Gates, M. and Tschudi, G., The synthesis of morphine, *J. Am. Chem. Soc.,* 74, 1109–1110, 1952.
4. Elad, E. and Ginsburg, D., The synthesis of morphine, *J. Am. Chem. Soc.,* 76, 312–313, 1954.
5. Rice, K.C., Synthetic opium alkaloids and derivatives. A short total synthesis of (±)-dihydrothebainone, (±)-dihydrocodinone, and (±)-nordihydrocodinone as an approach to the practical synthesis of morphine, codeine, and congeners, *J. Org. Chem.,* 45, 3135–3137, 1980.
6. Rapoport, H. and Bonner, R.M., delta-7-Desoxymorphine, *J. Am. Chem. Soc.,* 73, 5485, 1951.

1.4.2 Cocaine

The social implications of cocaine abuse in the U.S. have been the subject of extensive media coverage from the 1980s to the present day. As a result, the general public has acquired some of the terminology associated with the cocaine usage. "Smoking crack" and "snorting coke" are terms that have become well understood in the American culture from elementary school through adulthood. However, there are facts associated with this drug that are not well understood by the general public. There are documented historical aspects associated with coca and cocaine abuse that go back 500 years. Recognizing some of these historical aspects enables the public to place today's problem in perspective. Cocaine addiction has been with society for well over 100 years.

There are four areas of interest this section will address: (1) Where does cocaine come from? (2) How is cocaine isolated from the coca plant? (3) What does one take into the body from cocaine purchased on the street? (4) How does the chemist analyzing the drug identify and distinguish between the different forms of cocaine?

Cocaine is a Schedule II controlled substance. The wording in Title 21, Part 1308.12(b)(4) of the Code of Federal Regulations states:

Coca leaves (9040) and any salt, compound, derivative or preparation of coca leaves (including cocaine (9041) and ecgonine (9180) and their salts, isomers, derivatives and salts of isomers and derivatives), and any salt, compound, derivative, or preparation thereof which is chemically equivalent or identical with any of these substances, except that the substances shall not include decocanized coca leaves, or extractions of coca leaves, which extractions do not contain cocaine or ecgonine.

It is significant that the term "coca leaves" is the focal point of that part of the regulation controlling cocaine. The significance of this fact will become more apparent as this discussion progresses.

1.4.2.1 Sources of Cocaine

Cocaine is just one of the alkaloidal substances present in the coca leaf. Other molecules, some of them psychoactive (norcocaine being the most prominent), are shown in Figure 1.2. Cocaine is extracted from the leaves of the coca plant. The primary of source of cocaine imported into the U.S. is South America, but the coca plant also grows in the Far East in Ceylon, Java, and India. The plant is cultivated in South America on the eastern slopes of the Andes in Peru and Bolivia. There are four varieties of coca plants — *Erythroxylon coca* var. *coca* (ECVC), *E. coca* var. *ipadu*, *E. novogranatense* var. *novogranatense*, and *E. novogranatense* var. *truxillense*.[1-3] ECVC is the variety that has been used for the manufacture of illicit cocaine. While cultivated in many countries of South America, Peru and Bolivia are the world's leading producers of the coca plant. Cocaine is present in the coca leaves from these countries at dry weight concentrations of from 0.1 to 1%. The average concentration of cocaine in the leaf is 0.7%. The coca shrub has a life expectancy of 50 years and can be harvested three or four times a year.

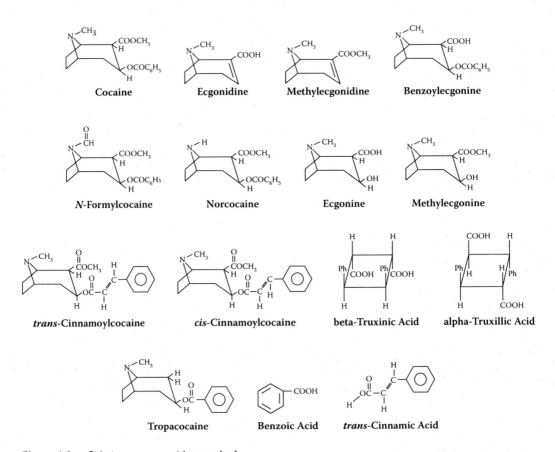

Figure 1.2 Substances present in coca leaf.

THE CRIMINALISTICS OF CONTROLLED SUBSTANCES

The method of isolating cocaine from the coca leaf does not require a high degree of technical expertise or experience. It requires no formal education or expensive scientific equipment or chemicals. In most instances the methodology is passed from one generation to the next.

1.4.2.2 *Historical Considerations*

Prior to the 1880s, the physiological properties of cocaine and the coca leaf were not readily distinguishable in the literature. During that year, H.H. Rusby and W.G. Mortimer made the distinction between the physiological properties of "isolated" cocaine and the coca leaf. Mortimer wrote:

> [T]he properties of cocaine, remarkable as they are, lie in an altogether different direction from those of coca.[1]

In 1884, two significant papers appeared in the literature. Sigmund Freud published the first of his five papers on the medicinal properties of cocaine.[2] A few months later, Karl Koller discovered the use of cocaine as local anesthetic.[3] In 1886, Sir Arthur Conan Doyle, an eye specialist who had studied at Vienna General Hospital, where Freud and Koller made their discoveries, made reference to Sherlock Holmes's use of cocaine in *The Sign of Four.*[4] That same year in Atlanta, Georgia, John Pemberton introduced to this country, caught up in the frenzy of alcohol prohibition, a beverage consisting of coca leaf extracts, African kola nuts, and a sweet carbonated syrup. The product was named "Coca-Cola."[5] Pemberton received his inspiration from Angelo Mariani, a Corsican pharmacist working in Paris, who had been selling a coca leaf-Bordeaux wine tincture since the early 1860s. Mariani's product was the most popular tonic of its time, and was used by celebrities, poets, popes, and presidents.[6] Patterns of coca consumption changed dramatically in the 20th century. In the 19th century, cocaine was available only in the form of a botanical product or a botanical product in solution. When chemical houses, such as Merck, began to produce significant quantities of refined cocaine, episodes of toxicity became much more frequent, the views of the medical profession changed, and physicians lost much of their enthusiasm for the drug.

Until 1923, the primary source of cocaine was from the coca leaf. In that year, Richard Willstatter was able to synthesize a mixture of D-cocaine, L-cocaine, D-pseudococaine, and L-pseudococaine. This multistep synthesis requires a high degree of technical expertise in organic chemistry and results in low yields.[7] These financial and technical factors make the extraction of cocaine from the coca leaf the method by which most, if not all, of the cocaine is isolated for distribution on both the licit and illicit markets.

1.4.2.3 *Isolation and Purification*

The extraction and isolation of cocaine from the coca leaf is not difficult. There is more than one way to do it. South American producers improvise depending on the availability of chemicals. All of the known production techniques involve three primary steps: (1) extraction of crude coca paste from the coca leaf; (2) purification of coca paste to cocaine base; and (3) conversion of cocaine base to cocaine hydrochloride. The paste and base laboratories in South America are deeply entrenched and widespread with thousands of operations, whereas the conversion laboratories are more sophisticated and centralized. They border on semi-industrial pilot-plant type laboratories involving a knowledge of chemistry and engineering.

The primary isolation method used until recently is a Solvent Extraction Technique. The essential methodology involves macerating a quantity of coca leaves with lime water, and then adding kerosene with stirring. After a while the kerosene is separated from the aqueous layer. A dilute sulfuric acid solution is added to the kerosene with stirring. This time the kerosene is separated from the aqueous layer and set aside. It is common to save the kerosene for another extraction of the leaves. The aqueous layer is retained and neutralized with limestone or some other alkaline substance. The material that precipitates after the addition of limestone is crude coca paste containing anywhere from 30 to 80% cocaine, with the remainder of the cocaine matrix composed primarily of other alkaloids, hydrolysis products, and basic inorganic salts used in the processing. This solid material is isolated by filtration for purification of the cocaine.

The coca paste is then dissolved in dilute sulfuric acid, and dilute potassium permanganate solution is added to oxidize the impurities. This solution is then filtered, and ammonium hydroxide is added to the filtrate to precipitate cocaine base. This "cocaine" is not ready for shipment to the U.S. The cocaine will first be converted to hydrochloride for easier packaging, handling, and shipment.

A second method of isolating cocaine from the leaf, which is more predominant today, is the Acid Extraction Technique. In this method, the cocaine leaves are placed directly in the maceration pit with enough sulfuric acid to cover the leaves. The pit is a hole dug into the ground and lined with heavy-duty plastic. The leaves are macerated by workers who stomp in the sulfuric acid/coca leaf pit. This stomping leaches the cocaine base from the leaf and forms an aqueous solution of cocaine sulfate. This stomping can continue for a matter of hours to ensure maximum recovery of the cocaine.

After stomping is complete, the coca solution is poured through a coarse filter to remove the insolubles including the plant material. More sulfuric acid is added to the leaves and a second or even third extraction of the remaining cocaine will take place. Maximized recovery of cocaine is important to the laboratory operators. After the extractions and filterings are completed, an excess basic lime or carbonate solution is added to the acidic solution with stirring and neutralizing the excess acid and cocaine sulfate. A very crude coca paste forms. The addition of the base is monitored until the solution is basic to an ethanolic solution of phenolphthalein. The coca paste is then back-extracted with a small volume of kerosene. The solution sets until a separation of the layers occurs. The kerosene is then back-extracted, this time with a dilute solution of sulfuric acid. Then, an inorganic base is added to precipitate the coca paste. This coca paste is essentially the same as that generated by the solvent extraction method. The advantage to this Acid Extraction Technique is that a minimal volume of organic solvent is required. And while it is more labor intensive, the cost of labor in Bolivia, the major producing country of coca paste, is very low when compared to the financial return.

The resultant cocaine base, produced by either technique, is dissolved in acetone, ether, or a mixture of both. A dilute solution of hydrochloric acid in acetone is then prepared. The two solutions are mixed and a precipitate of cocaine hydrochloride forms almost immediately and is allowed to settle to the bottom of the reaction vessel (usually an inexpensive bucket). The slurry will then be poured through clean bed sheets, filtering the cocaine hydrochloride from the solvent. The sheets are then wrung dry to eliminate excess acetone, and the high-quality cocaine hydrochloride is dried in microwave ovens, under heat lamps, or in the sunlight. It is then a simple matter to package the cocaine hydrochloride for shipment. One of the more common packaging forms encountered in laboratories analyzing seizures of illicit cocaine is the "one kilo brick." This is a brick-shaped package of cocaine wrapped in tape or plastic, sometimes labeled with a logo, with the contents weighing near 1 kg. Once the cocaine hydrochloride arrives in the U.S., drug wholesalers may add mannitol or inositol as diluents, or procaine, benzocaine, lidocaine, or tetracaine as adulterants. This cocaine can then be sold on the underground market in the U.S. either in bulk or by repackaging into smaller containers.

1.4.2.4 *Conversion to "Crack"*

"Crack" is the term used on the street and even in some courtrooms to describe the form of cocaine base that has been converted from the cocaine hydrochloride and can be smoked in a pipe.

THE CRIMINALISTICS OF CONTROLLED SUBSTANCES

This procedure of conversion from the acid to the base is usually carried out in the U.S. Cocaine base usually appears in the form of a rock-like material, and is sometimes sold in plastic packets, glass vials, or other suitable packaging. Cocaine hydrochloride is normally ingested by inhalation through a tube or straw, or by injection. Cocaine base is ingested by smoking in an improvised glass pipe. Ingestion in this manner results in the cocaine entering the bloodstream through the lungs and rushing to the brain very quickly.

Cocaine hydrochloride is converted to cocaine base in one of two ways. The first method involves dissolving the cocaine hydrochloride in water and adding sodium bicarbonate or household ammonia. The water is then boiled for a short period until all of the precipitated cocaine base melts to an oil, and ice is added to the reaction vessel. This vessel will usually be a metal cooking pan or a deep glass bowl. As the water cools, chunks of cocaine base oil will solidify at the bottom of the cooking vessel. After all the cocaine base has formed, the water can be cooled and then poured off, leaving the solid cocaine base, which is easily removed from the collection vessel. The cocaine base can be cut with a knife or broken into "rocks," which can then be dried either under a heat lamp or in a microwave oven. It is not unusual when analyzing cocaine base produced from this method to identify sodium bicarbonate mixed with the rock-like material. This cocaine base sometimes has a high moisture content due to incomplete drying.

A second method of producing cocaine base from cocaine hydrochloride involves dissolving the salt (usually cocaine hydrochloride) in water. Sodium bicarbonate or household ammonia is added to the water and mixed well. Diethyl ether is then added to the solution and stirred. The mixture then separates into two layers with the ether layer on top of the aqueous layer. The ether is decanted, leaving the water behind. The ether is then allowed to evaporate and high-quality cocaine base remains. If any of the adulterants mentioned previously (excluding sugars, which are diluents) are mixed with the cocaine hydrochloride prior to conversion, then they will also be converted to the base and will be a part of the rock-like material that results from this process. The term "free base" is used to describe this form of cocaine. Cocaine base in this form is also smoked in a glass pipe. However, residual (and sometimes substantial) amounts of ether remaining in these samples from the extraction process make ignition in a glass pipe very dangerous.

1.4.2.5 *Other Coca Alkaloids*

In the process of examining cocaine samples in the laboratory, it is not uncommon to identify other alkaloids and manufacturing by-products with the cocaine. These other alkaloids are carried over from the coca leaf in the extraction of the cocaine. Many manufacturing by-products result from the hydrolysis of the parent alkaloids (benzoylecgonine from cocaine, or truxillic acid from truxilline). As a forensic chemist, it is important to recognize the sources of these alkaloids as one progresses through an analytical scheme.

The major alkaloidal "impurities" present in the coca leaf that are carried over in the cocaine extraction are the *cis*- and *trans*-cinnamoylcocaines and the truxillines. There are 11 isomeric truxillic and truxinic acids resulting from the hydrolysis of truxilline. Another naturally occurring minor alkaloid from the coca leaf is tropacocaine. The concentration of tropacocaine will rarely, if ever, exceed 1% of the cocaine concentration and is well below the concentrations of the *cis*- and *trans*-cinnamoylcocaines and the truxillines. Two other alkaloids from the coca leaf which have been identified are cuscohygrine and hygrine. These two products are not found in cocaine, just in the leaf.

The second class of substances found in the analysis of cocaine samples is the result of degradation or hydrolysis. Ecgonine, benzoylecgonine, and methylecgonine found in cocaine samples will be the result of the hydrolysis of cocaine. It is important to recognize that some of these manufacturing by-products, such as ecgonine, can be detected by gas chromatography only if they are derivatized prior to injection. Methyl ecgonidine is a by-product of the hydrolysis of cocaine and is oftentimes identified in the laboratory by gas chromatography/mass spectrometry (GC/MS).

This artifact can also result from the thermal degradation of cocaine or the truxillines in the injection port of the GC. Benzoic acid is the other product identified when this decomposition occurs.

There are at least two substances that result directly from the permanganate oxidation of cocaine. N-Formyl cocaine results from oxidation of the N-methyl group of cocaine to an N-formyl group. Norcocaine is a hydrolysis product resulting from a Schiff's base intermediate during the permanganate oxidation. There is also evidence that norcocaine can result from the N-demethylation of cocaine, a consequence of the peroxides in diethyl ether.

1.4.2.6 Cocaine Adulterants

The primary adulterants identified in cocaine samples are procaine and benzocaine. Lidocaine is also found with less regularity. These adulterants are found in both the cocaine base and cocaine hydrochloride submissions. The primary diluents are mannitol and inositol. Many other sugars have been found, but not nearly to the same extent. Cocaine hydrochloride concentrations will usually range from 20 to 99%. The moisture content of cocaine hydrochloride is usually minimal. Cocaine base concentrations will usually range from 30 to 99%. There will usually be some moisture in cocaine base ("crack") submissions from the water/sodium bicarbonate or water/ammonia methods. The concentration of cocaine base ("free base") from the ether/sodium bicarbonate or ether/ammonia methods will usually be higher and free of water.

The methods for identifying cocaine in the laboratory include but are not limited to: infrared spectrophotometry (IR), nuclear magnetic resonance spectroscopy (NMR), mass spectrometry (MS), and gas chromatography (GC). IR and NMR will enable the analyst to distinguish between cocaine hydrochloride and cocaine base. However, it is not possible to identify the form in which the cocaine is present utilizing this instrumentation.

1.4.2.7 Conclusion

The user of either cocaine base or cocaine hydrochloride not only ingests the cocaine, but also other alkaloids from the coca plant, processing by-products, organic and inorganic reagents used in processing, diluents, and adulterants. There is no realistic way in which a cocaine user can ensure the quality of the cocaine purchases on the street, and "innocent" recreational drug use may provide more danger than the user would knowingly risk.

REFERENCES

1. Rusby, H.H., Bliss, A.R., and Ballard, C.W., *The Properties and Uses of Drugs,* Blakiston's Son & Co., Philadelphia, 1930, 125, 386, 407.
2. Byck, R., Ed., *Cocaine Papers by Sigmund Freud,* Stonehill, New York, 1975.
3. Pendergrast, M., *For God, Country, and Coca-Cola; The Definitive History of the Great American Soft Drink and the Company That Makes It,* Basic Books, New York, 2000.
4. Musto, D., A study in cocaine: Sherlock Holmes and Sigmund Freud, *J. Am. Med. Assoc.,* 204, 125, 1968.
5. Brecher, E. and the Editors of Consumer Reports, *Licit and Illicit Drugs,* Little, Brown, Boston, 1972, 33–36, 270.
6. Mariani, A., Ed., *Album Mariani, Les Figures Contemporaines. Contemporary Celebrities from the Album Mariani, etc.,* various publishers for Mariani & Co., 13 Vols., 1891–1913.
7. Willstatter, R., Wolfes, O., and Mader, H., Synthese des Naturlichen Cocains, *Justus Liebigs's Ann. Chim.,* 434, 111–139, 1923.
8. Casale, J.F. and Klein, R.F.X., Illicit cocaine production, *Forensic Sci. Rev,* 5, 96–107, 1993.

1.4.3 Marijuana

1.4.3.1 *History and Terminology*

Marijuana is a Schedule I controlled substance. In botanical terms, "marijuana" is defined as *Cannabis sativa* L. Legally, marijuana is defined as all parts of the plant *C. sativa* L. (and any of its varieties) whether growing or not, the seeds thereof, the resin extracted from any part of the plant, and every compound, manufacture, salt, derivative, mixture, or preparation of such plant; its seeds and resins. Such terms do not include the mature stalk of the plants, fibers produced from such plants, oils or cakes made from the pressed seeds of such plants, any other compound, manufacture, salt derivative, mixture or preparation of such mature stalks (except the resin extracted therefrom), fiber, oil or cake, pressed seed, or the sterilized seed which is incapable of germination.[1] Pharmaceutical preparations that contained the resinous extracts of cannabis were available on the commercial market from the 1900s to 1937. These products were prescribed for their analgesic and sedative effects. In 1937 the U.S. Food and Drug Administration declared these products to be of little medical utility, and they were removed from the market. Cannabis, in the forms of the plant material, hashish, and hashish oil, is the most abused illicit drug in the world.

Cannabis is cultivated in many areas of the world. Commercial *C. sativa* L. is referred to as "hemp." The plant is cultivated for cloth and rope from its fiber. A valuable drying oil used in art and a substitute for linseed oil is available from the seeds. Bird seed mixtures are also found to contain sterilized marijuana seeds. In the early days of the U.S., hemp was grown in the New England colonies. Its cultivation spread south into Pennsylvania and Virginia. From there it spread south and west, most notably into Kentucky and Missouri. Its abundance in the early days of the country is still evident by the fact that it still grows wild in many fields and along many roadways. The plant is now indigenous to many areas, and adapts easily to most soil and moderate climatic conditions.

Marijuana is classified as a hallucinogenic substance. The primary active constituents in the plant are cannabinol, cannabidiol, and the tetrahydrocannabinols, illustrated in Figure 1.3. The tetrahydrocannabinols (THCs) are the active components responsible for the hallucinogenic properties of marijuana. The THC of most interest is the Δ^9 tetrahydrocannabinol. The other THCs of interest in marijuana are the Δ^1 *cis*- and *trans*-tetrahydrocannabinols, the Δ^6 *cis*- and *trans*-tetrahydrocannabinols, and the Δ^3 and Δ^4 tetrahydrocannabinols. The concentrations vary dramatically from geographic area to geographic area, from field to field, and from sample to sample. This concentration range varies from less than 1% to as high as 30%. In recent hash oil exhibits, the highest official reported concentration of Δ^9-THC is 43%.[2] Five other terms associated with marijuana are as follows:

Hashish: Resinous material removed from cannabis. Hashish is usually found in the form of a brown to black cake of resinous material. The material is ingested by smoking in pipes or by consuming in food.

Hashish oil: Extract of the marijuana plant which has been heated to remove the extracting solvents. The material exists as a colorless to brown or black oil or tar-like substance.

Sinsemilla: The flowering tops of the unfertilized female cannabis plant. (There are no seeds on such a plant.) Sinsemilla is usually considered a "gourmet" marijuana because of its appearance and relatively high concentrations of the THCs.

Thai sticks: Marijuana leaves tied around stems or narrow-diameter bamboo splints. Thai sticks are considered a high-quality product by the drug culture. The THC concentrations of the marijuana leaves on Thai sticks are higher than domestic marijuana. Unlike hashish and sinsemilla, seeds and small pieces of stalks and stems are found in Thai sticks.

Brick or **Kilo:** Marijuana compressed into a brick-shaped package with leaves, stems, stalk, and seeds. The pressed marijuana is usually tightly wrapped in paper and tape. This is the form of marijuana encountered in most large-scale seizures. These large-scale seizure packages weigh approximately

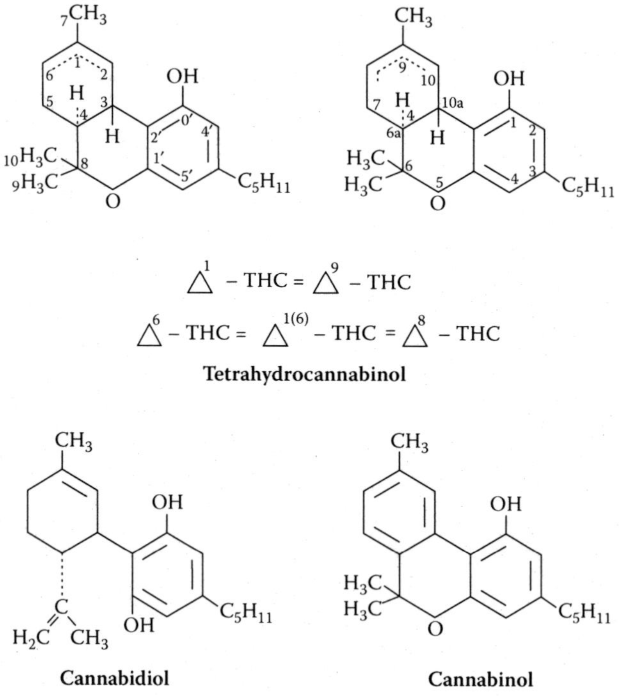

Figure 1.3 The primary active constituents in marijuana.

$$\triangle^1 - THC = \triangle^9 - THC$$

$$\triangle^6 - THC = \triangle^{1(6)} - THC = \triangle^8 - THC$$

Tetrahydrocannabinol

Cannabidiol

Cannabinol

1000 g (1 kg). This is the packaging form of choice for clandestine operators because of the ease of handling, packaging, shipping, and distribution.

1.4.3.2 Laboratory Analysis

The specificity of a marijuana analysis is still a widely discussed topic among those in the forensic and legal communities. In the course of the past 25 years, the consensus of opinion concerning the analysis of marijuana has remained fairly consistent. In those situations where plant material is encountered, the marijuana is first examined using a stereomicroscope. The presence of the bear claw cystolithic hairs and other histological features are noted using a compound microscope. The plant material is then examined chemically using Duquenois–Levine reagent in a modified Duquenois–Levine testing sequence. These two tests are considered to be conclusive within the realm of existing scientific certainty in establishing the presence of marijuana.[3–5]

The modified Duquenois–Levine test is conducted using Duquenois reagent, concentrated hydrochloric acid, and chloroform. The Duquenois reagent is prepared by dissolving 2 g of vanillin and 0.3 ml of acetaldehyde in 100 ml of ethanol. Small amounts (25 to 60 mg is usually sufficient) of suspected marijuana leaf are placed in a test tube and approximately 2 ml of Duquenois reagent is added. After 1 min, approximately 1 ml of concentrated hydrochloric acid is added. Small bubbles rise from the leaves in the liquid. These are carbon dioxide bubbles produced by the reaction of the hydrochloric acid with the calcium carbonate at the base of the cystolithic hair of the marijuana. A blue to blue-purple color forms very quickly in the solution. Approximately 1 ml of chloroform is then added to the Duquenois reagent/hydrochloric acid mixture. Because chloroform is not miscible with water, and because it is heavier than water, two liquid layers are visible in the tube — the Duquenois reagent/hydrochloric acid layer is on top, and the chloroform layer is on the bottom. After mixing with a vortex stirrer and on settling, the two layers are again clearly distin-

THE CRIMINALISTICS OF CONTROLLED SUBSTANCES 17

guishable. However, the chloroform layer has changed from clear to the blue to blue-purple color of the Duquenois reagent/hydrochloric acid mixture.

One variation in this testing process involves pouring off the Duquenois reagent sitting in the tube with the leaves before adding the hydrochloric acid. The remainder of the test is conducted using only the liquid. Another variation involves conducting the test in a porcelain spot plate. This works, although some analysts find the color change a bit more difficult to detect. A third variation involves extracting the cannabis resin with ether or some other solvent, separating the solvent from the leaves, allowing the solvent to evaporate, and conducting the modified Duquenois–Levine test on the extract.

Marquis reagent is prepared by mixing 1 ml of formaldehyde solution with 9 ml of sulfuric acid. The test is done by placing a small amount of sample (1 to 5 mg) into the depression of a spot plate, adding one or two drops of reagent, and observing the color produced. This color will usually be indicative of the class of compounds, and the first color is usually the most important. A weak response may fade, and samples containing sugar will char on standing because of the sulfuric acid. Marquis reagent produces the following results:

1. Purple with opiates (heroin, codeine).
2. Orange turning to brown with amphetamine and methamphetamine.
3. Black with a dark purple halo with 3,4-methylenedioxyamphetamine (MDA) and 3,4-methylene-dioxymethamphetamine (MDMA).
4. Pink with aspirin.
5. Yellow with diphenhydramine.

A thin-layer chromatographic (TLC) analysis, which detects a systematic pattern of colored bands, can then be employed as an additional test.[6,7] Though it is not required, some analysts will run a GC/MS analysis to identify the cannabinoids in the sample.

The solvent insoluble residue of hashish should be examined with the compound microscope. Cystolythic hairs, resin glands, and surface debris should be present. However, if most of the residue is composed of green leaf fragments, the material is pulverized marijuana or imitation hashish.

1.4.4 Peyote

Peyote is a cactus plant that grows in rocky soil in the wild. Historical records document use of the plant by Indians in northern Mexico from as far back as pre-Christian times, when it was used by the Chichimaec tribe in religious rites. The plant grows as small cylinder-like "buttons." The buttons were used to relieve fatigue and hunger, and to treat victims of disease. The peyote buttons were used in group settings to achieve a trance state in tribal dances.[8]

It was used by native Americans in ritualistic ceremonies. In the U.S., peyote was cited in 1891 by James Mooney of the Bureau of American Ethnology.[9] Mooney talked about the use of peyote by the Kiowa Indians, the Comanche Indians, and the Mescalero Apache Indians, all in the southern part of the country. In 1918, he came to the aid of the Indians by incorporating the "Native American Church" in Oklahoma to ensure their rights in the use of peyote in religious ceremonies. Although several bills have been introduced over the years, the U.S. Congress has never passed a law prohibiting the Indians' religious use of peyote. Both mescaline and peyote are listed as Schedule I controlled substances in the Comprehensive Drug Abuse Prevention and Control Act of 1970.

The principal alkaloid of peyote responsible for its hallucinogenic response is mescaline, a derivative of β-phenethylamine. Chemically, mescaline is 3,4,5-trimethoxyphenethylamine. As illustrated in Figure 1.4, its structure is similar to the amphetamine group in general. Mescaline was first isolated from the peyote plant in 1894 by the German chemist A. Heffter.[10] The first complete synthesis of mescaline was in 1919 by E. Späth.[11] The extent of abuse of illicit mescaline has not been accurately determined. The use of peyote buttons became popular in the 1950s and

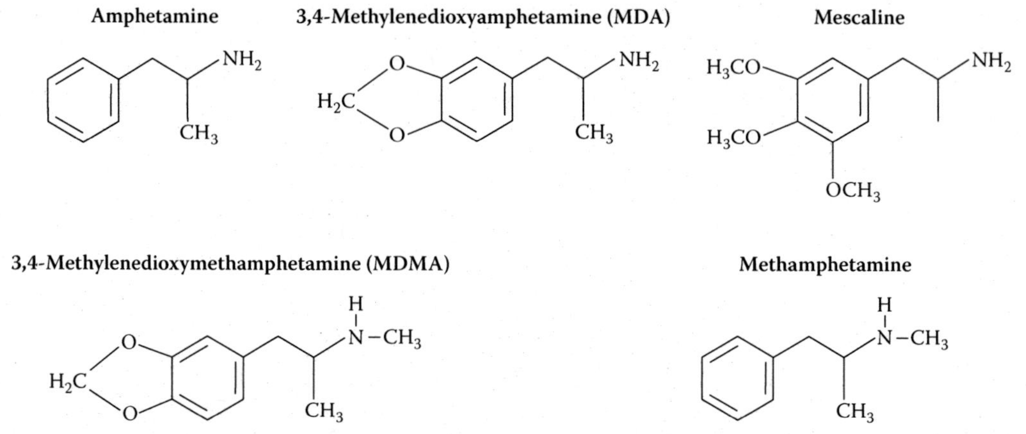

Amphetamine 3,4-Methylenedioxyamphetamine (MDA) Mescaline

3,4-Methylenedioxymethamphetamine (MDMA) Methamphetamine

Figure 1.4 Chemical structure of mescaline.

again in the period from 1967 to 1970. These two periods showed a dramatic increase in experimentation with hallucinogens in general.

1.4.5 Psilocybin Mushrooms

The naturally occurring indoles responsible for the hallucinogen properties in some species of mushrooms are psilocybin (Figure 1.5) and psilocin.[12] The use of hallucinogenic mushrooms dates to the 16th century, occurring during the coronation of Montezuma in 1502.[8] In 1953, R.G. Wassen and V.P. Wasson were credited with the rediscovery of the ritual of the Indian cultures of Mexico and Central America.[13] They were able to obtain samples of these mushrooms. The identification of the mushrooms as the species *Psilocybe* is credited to the French mycologist, Roger Heim.[14]

Albert Hofmann (the discoverer of lysergic acid diethylamine) and his colleagues at Sandoz Laboratories in Switzerland are credited with the isolation and identification of psilocybin (phosphorylated 4-hydroxydimethyltryptamine) and psilocin (4-hydroxydimethyltryptamine).[15] Psilocybin was the major component in the mushrooms, and psilocin was found to be a minor component. However, psilocybin is very unstable and is readily metabolized to psilocin in the body. This phenomenon of phosphate cleavage from the psilocybin to form the psilocin occurs quite easily in the forensic science laboratory. This can be a concern in ensuring the specificity of identification.

The availability of the mushroom has existed worldwide wherever proper climactic conditions exist — that means plentiful rainfall. In the U.S., psilocybin mushrooms are reported to be plentiful in Florida, Hawaii,[16] the Pacific Northwest, and Northern California.[17] Mushrooms analyzed in the forensic science laboratory confirm the fact that the mushrooms spoil easily. The time factor between harvesting the mushrooms and the analysis proves to be the greatest detriment to successfully identifying the psilocybin or psilocin. Storage prior to shipment is best accomplished by drying the mushrooms. Entrepreneurs reportedly resort to storage of mushrooms in honey to preserve the psychedelic properties.[18]

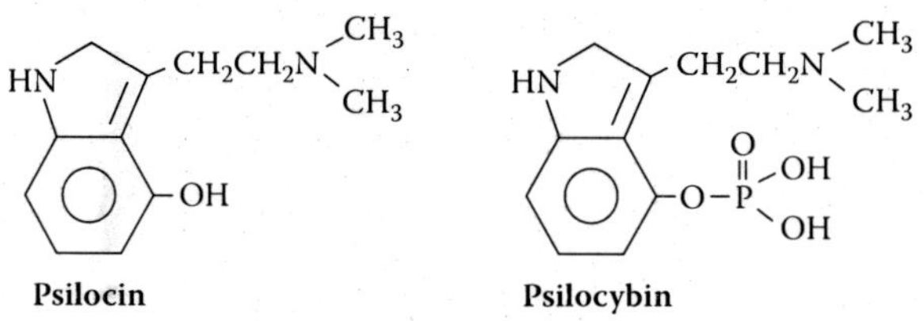

Psilocin Psilocybin

Figure 1.5 Chemical structure of psilocin and psilocybin.

THE CRIMINALISTICS OF CONTROLLED SUBSTANCES

Progressing through the analytical scheme of separating and isolating the psilocybin and psilocin from the mushroom matrix, cleavage of the phosphate occurs quite easily. Prior to beginning the analysis, drying the mushrooms in a desiccator with phosphorus pentoxide ensures a dry starting material. In many instances, the clean-up procedure involves an extraction process carried out through a series of chloroform washes from a basic extract and resolution of the components by TLC. The spots or, more probably, streaks are then scraped from the plate, separated by a back-extraction, and then analyzed by IR. Direct analysis by GC is very difficult because both psilocybin and psilocin are highly polar and not suitable for direct GC analysis. Derivatization followed by GC/MS is an option except in those instances where the mushrooms have been preserved in sugar.[19] With the development and availability of high-performance liquid chromatography (HPLC), the identification and quantitation of psilocybin and psilocyn in mushrooms are becoming more feasible for many forensic science laboratories.[20]

REFERENCES

1. Section 102 (15), Public Law 91-513.
2. ElSohly, M.A. and Ross, S.A., Quarterly Report Potency Monitoring Project, Report 53, January 1, 1995 to March 31, 1995.
3. Nakamura, G.R., Forensic aspects of cystolithic hairs of cannabis and other plants, *J. Assoc. Off. Anal. Chem.*, 52, 5–16, 1969.
4. Thornton, J.I. and Nakamura, G.R., The identification of marijuana, *J. Forensic Sci. Soc.*, 24, 461–519, 1979.
5. Hughes, R.B. and Warner, V.J., A study of false positives in the chemical identification of marijuana, *J. Forensic Sci.*, 23, 304–310, 1978.
6. Hauber, D.J., Marijuana analysis with recording of botanical features present with and without the environmental pollutants of the Duquenois-Levine test, *J. Forensic Sci.*, 37, 1656–1661, 1992.
7. Hughes, R.B. and Kessler, R.R., Increased safety and specificity in the thin-layer chromatographic identification of marijuana, *J. Forensic Sci.*, 24, 842–846, 1979.
8. Report Series, National Clearinghouse for Drug Abuse Information, Mescaline, Series 15, No. 1, May 1973.
9. Mooney, J., The mescal plant and ceremony, *Ther. Gaz.*, 12, 7–11, 1896.
10. Heffter, A., Ein Beitrag zur pharmakologishen Kenntniss der Cacteen, *Arch. Exp Pathol. Pharmakol.*, 34, 65–86, 1894.
11. Spath, E., Über die Anhalonium-Alkaloide, Anhalin und Mescalin, *Monatsh. Chem. Verw. TL*, 40, 1929, 1919.
12. Hofman, A., Heim, R., Brack, A., and Kobel, H., Psilocybin, ein psychotroper Wirkstoff aus dem mexikanishen Rauschpitz *Psilocybe mexicana* Heim, *Experiencia*, 14, 107–109, 1958.
13. Wasson, V.P. and Wasson, R.G., *Mushrooms, Russia, and History.* Pantheon Books, New York, 1957.
14. Heim, R., Genest, K., Hughes, D.W., and Belec, G., Botanical and chemical characterisation of a forensic mushroom specimen of the genus psilocybe, *Forensic Sci. Soc. J.*, 6, 192–201, 1966.
15. Hofmann, A., Chemical aspects of psilocybin, the psychotropic principle from the Mexican fungus, *Psilocybe mexicana* Heim, in Bradley, P.B., Deniker, P., and Radouco-Thomas, C., Eds. *Neuropsychopharmacology*, Elsevier, Amsterdam, 1959, 446–448.
16. Pollock, S.H., A novel experience with Panaeolus: a case study from Hawaii, *J. Psychedelic Drugs*, 6, 85–90, 1974.
17. Weil, H., Mushroom hunting in Oregon, *J. Psychedelic Drugs*, 7, 89–102, 1975.
18. Pollock, S.H., Psilocybin mycetismus with special reference to *Panaeolus*, *J. Psychedelic Drugs*, 8(1), 50, 1976.
19. Repke, D.B., Leslie, D.T., Mandell, D.M., and Kish, N.G., GLC-mass spectral analysis of psilocin and psilocybin, *J. Psychedelic Drugs*, 66, 743–744, 1977.
20. Thomas, B.M., Analysis of psilocybin and psilocin in mushroom extracts by reversed-phase high performance liquid chromatography, *J. Forensic Sci.*, 25, 779–785, 1980.

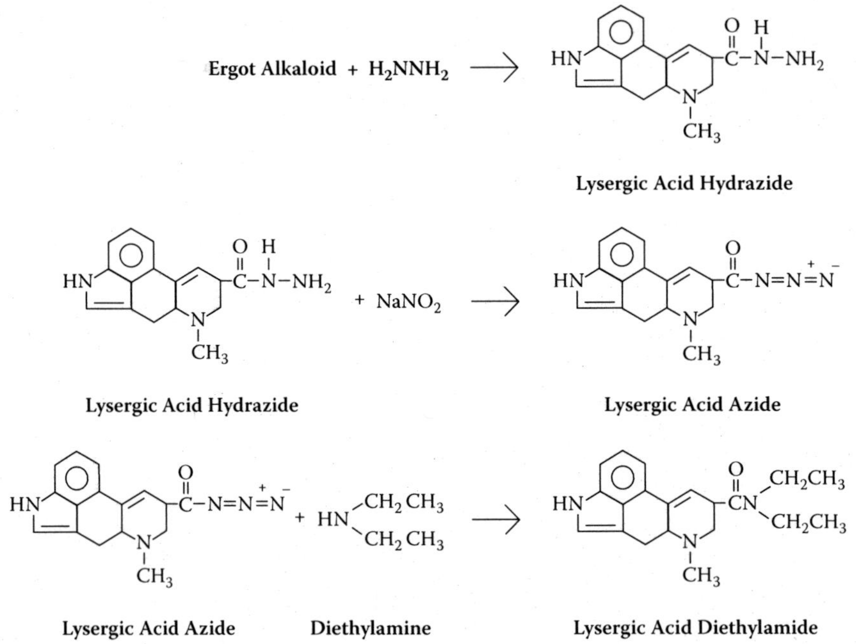

Figure 1.6 Synthetic route utilized for the clandestine manufacture of LSD.

1.4.6 Lysergic Acid Diethylamide

LSD is a hallucinogenic substance produced from lysergic acid, a substance derived from the ergot fungus (*Clavica purpurea*), which grows on rye. It can also be derived from lysergic acid amide, which is found in morning glory seeds.[1] LSD is also referred to as LSD-25 because it was the 25th in a series of compounds produced by Dr. Albert Hofmann in Basel, Switzerland. Hofmann was interested in the chemistry of ergot compounds, especially their effect on circulation. He was trying to produce compounds that might improve circulation without exhibiting the other toxic effects associated with ergot poisoning. One of the products he produced was Methergine™, which is still in use today. When LSD-25 was first tested on animals, in 1938, the results were disappointing. Then, 5 years later, in 1943, Hofmann decided to reevaluate LSD-25. The hallucinogenic experience that ensued when he accidentally ingested some of the compound led to the start of experimentation with "psychedelic" drugs.

LSD is the most potent hallucinogenic substance known to humans. Dosages of LSD are measured in micrograms (one microgram equals one one-millionth of a gram). By comparison, dosage units of cocaine and heroin are measured in milligrams (one milligram equals one one-thousandth of a gram). LSD is available in the form of very small tablets ("microdots"), thin squares of gelatin ("window panes"), or impregnated on blotter paper ("blotter acid"). The most popular of these forms in the 1990s was blotter paper perforated into 1/4-in. squares. This paper is usually brightly colored with psychedelic designs or line drawings. There have been recent reports of LSD impregnated on sugar cubes.[2] Such LSD-laced sugar cubes were commonplace in the 1970s. The precursor to LSD, lysergic acid, is a Schedule III controlled substance. LSD is classified as a Schedule I controlled substance. The synthetic route utilized for the clandestine manufacture of LSD is shown in Figure 1.6.

1.4.7 Phencyclidine

The chemical nomenclature of phencyclidine (PCP) is phenylcyclohexylpiperidine. The term "PCP" is used most often used when referring to this drug. The acronym PCP has two origins that

THE CRIMINALISTICS OF CONTROLLED SUBSTANCES 21

are consistent. In the 1960s phencyclidine was trafficked as a peace pill ("PeaCePill"). **P**henyl**Cy**clohexyl**P**iperidine can also account for the PCP acronym.

PCP was first synthesized in 1926.[3] It was developed as a human anesthetic in 1957, and found use in veterinary medicine as a powerful tranquilizer. In 1965 human use was discontinued because, as the anesthetic wore off, confusional states and frightening hallucinations were common. Strangely, these side effects were viewed as desirable by those inclined to experiment with drugs. Today even the use of PCP as a primate anesthetic has been all but discontinued. In 1978, the commercial manufacture of PCP ceased and the drug was transferred from Schedule III to Schedule II of the Controlled Substances Act. Small amounts of PCP are manufactured for research purposes and as a drug standard.

The manufacture of PCP in clandestine laboratories is simple and inexpensive. Figure 1.7 shows three of the synthetic routes utilized for its illegal production. The first clandestinely produced PCP appeared in 1967 shortly after Parke-Davis withdrew phencyclidine as a pharmaceutical.[4] The clandestine laboratory production of PCP requires neither formal knowledge of chemistry nor a large inventory of laboratory equipment. The precursor chemicals produce phencyclidine when combined correctly using what is termed "bucket chemistry." The opportunities for a contaminated product from a clandestine PCP are greatly enhanced because of the recognized simplicity of the chemical reactions in the production processes. The final product is often contaminated with starting materials, reaction intermediates, and by-products.[5] Clandestine laboratory operators have been known to modify the manufacturing processes to obtain chemically related analogues capable of producing similar physiological responses. The most commonly encountered analogues are N-ethyl-1-phenylcyclohexylamine (PCE), 1-(1-phenylcyclohexyl)-pyrrolidine (PCPy), and 1-[1-(2-thienyl-cyclohexyl)]-piperidine (TCP).

In the 1960s, PCP was distributed as a white to off-white powder or crystalline material and ingested orally. In recent years, PCP has been encountered as the base and dissolved in diethyl ether. The liquid is then placed into small bottles that normally would hold commercial vanilla extract. This ether solution is then sprayed on leaves such as parsley and smoked. PCP is commonly encountered on long thin dark cigarettes ("Sherms") that have been dipped in the PCP/ether solution.

1.4.8 Fentanyl

Fentanyl [the technical nomenclature is N-(1-phenethyl-4-piperidyl)propionanilide] is a synthetic narcotic analgesic approximately 50 to 100 times as potent as morphine.[6] The drug had its origin in Belgium as a synthetic product of Janssen Pharmaceutica.[7] In the 1960s in Europe and in the 1970s in the U.S., it was introduced for use as an anesthetic and for the relief of post-operative pain. Almost 70% of all surgical procedures in the U.S. use fentanyl for one of these purposes.[8]

Fentanyl has been called "synthetic heroin." This is a misnomer. Victims of fentanyl overdoses were often heroin abusers with "tracks" and the typical paraphernalia. The fentanyls as a class of drugs are highly potent synthetic narcotic analgesics with all the properties of opiates and opinoids.[4] However, the fentanyl molecule does not resemble heroin. Fentanyl is strictly a synthetic product while the morphine used in heroin production is derived from the opium poppy.

Beginning in the late 1970s with α-methylfentanyl,[9] nine homologues and one analogue (excluding enantiomers) of fentanyl appeared on the illicit marketplace.[10] The degrees of potency vary among the fentanyl homologues and analogues. The potencies of the fentanyl derivatives are much higher than those of the parent compound. But the high potencies cited above explain why even dilute exhibits result in the deaths of users who believe they are dealing with heroin. Another name used by addicts when referring to fentanyl and its derivatives is "China White." This term was first used to describe substances seized and later identified as alpha-methylfentanyl in 1981.[11]

There are many fentanyl homologues and analogues. Because of the size and complexity of fentanyl derivatives, the interpretation of IR, MS, and NMR spectral data proves very valuable in elucidating specific structural information required for the identification of the material.[10]

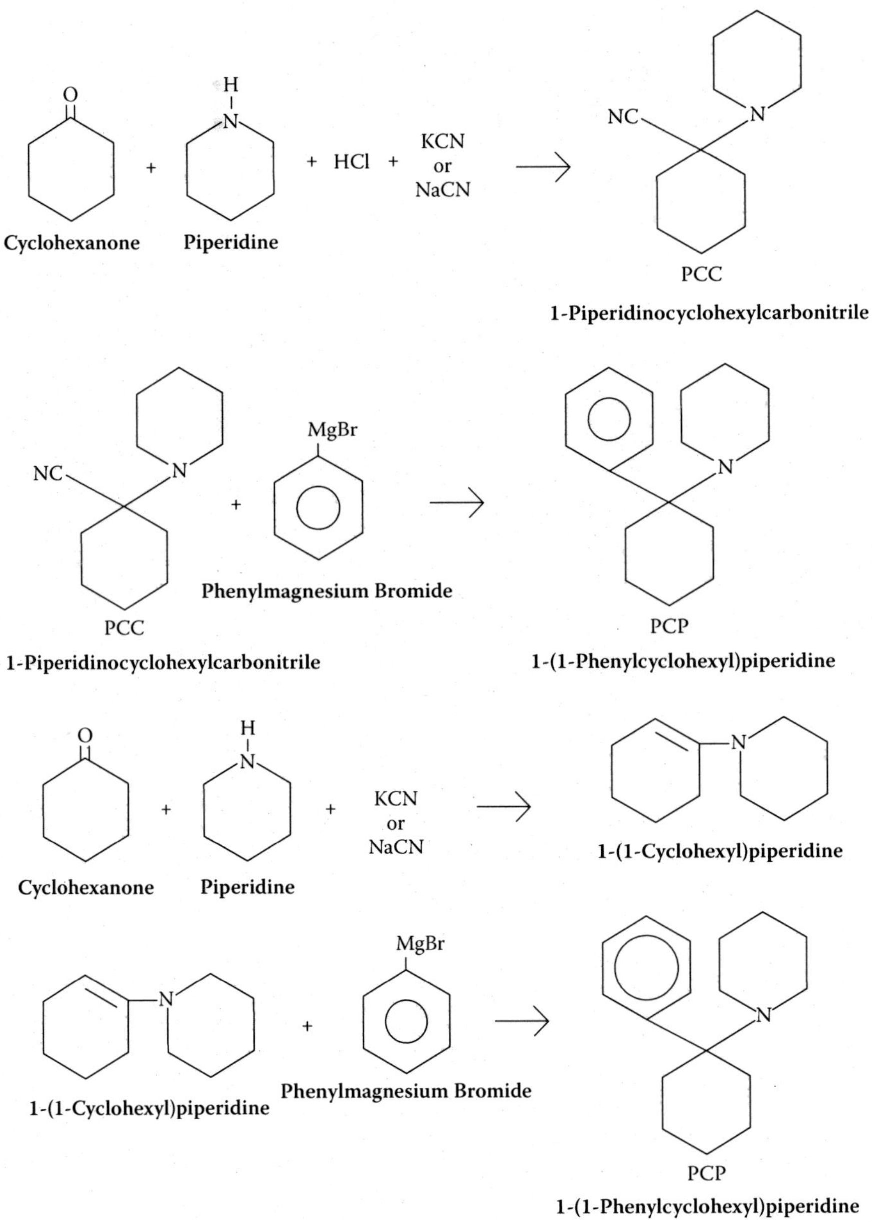

Figure 1.7 Synthetic routes utilized for illegal production of PCP. *Continued.*

Several synthetic routes are possible. As shown in Figure 1.8A and B, one of the methods requires that fentanyl precursor, *N*-(1-phenethyl)-4-piperidinyl) aniline, be produced first. Alternatively, fentanyl can be produced by reacting phenethylamine and methylacrylate to produce the phenethylamine diester (see Figure 1.9).

1.4.9 Phenethylamines

The class of compounds with the largest number of individual compounds on the illicit drug market is the phenethylamines. This class of compounds consists of a series of compounds having

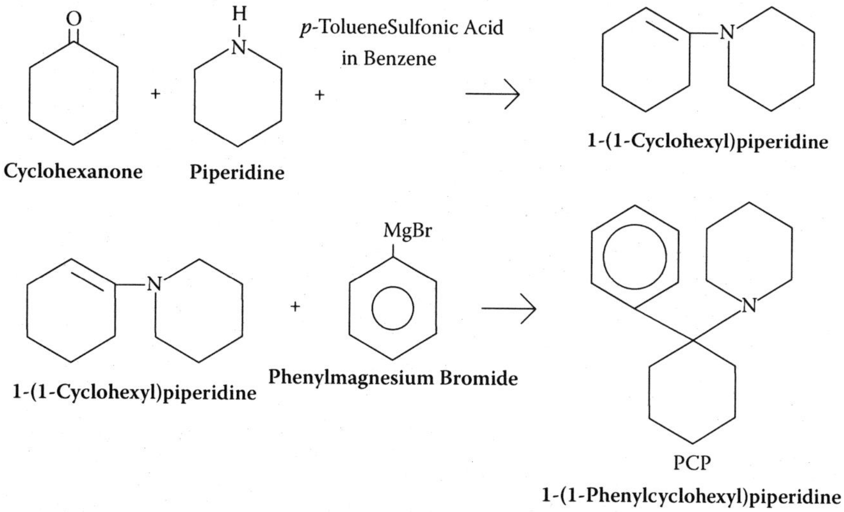

THE CRIMINALISTICS OF CONTROLLED SUBSTANCES

Figure 1.7 Continued.

a phenethylamine skeleton. Phenethylamines are easily modified chemically by adding or changing substituents at various positions on the molecule. Phenethylamines fall into one of two categories in terms of physiological effects — these compounds are either stimulants or hallucinogens. Phenethylamines are suitable for clandestine laboratory production. The parent compound in the phenethylamine series is amphetamine, a central nervous system (CNS) stimulant. With this molecule, the modifications begin by adding a methyl group to the nitrogen on the side chain. The resulting structure is the most popular clandestinely produced controlled substance in the U.S. — methamphetamine (Figure 1.10).

Like amphetamine, methamphetamine is also a CNS stimulant. It is easily produced in clandestine laboratories using two basic synthetic routes. The traditional route used by "meth cooks" began with phenyl-2-propanone; however, when bulk sales were limited by law, most clandestine chemists began using ephedrine as a precursor (Figure 1.11), although, as illustrated in Figure 1.11, some now synthesize their own supply of phenyl-2-propanone, and still other routes are possible (Figure 1.12). New legislation has now limited bulk purchases of ephedrine in the U.S., though not in neighboring countries. And the chemical structure is such that further molecular synthetic modifications are easily accomplished, resulting in a number of homologues and analogues. Few of the synthetic modifications of phenethylamines by clandestine laboratory "chemists" are novel. Most have been documented either in the scientific literature or in underground scientific literature. And the Internet now provides answers to anyone tenacious enough to search for a simple method to synthesize any analogue or homologue of a phenethylamine.

The parent compound of a second set of phenethylamine homologues and analogues (Figure 1.13) is 3,4-methylenedioxyamphetamine (MDA). This compound was first reported in the literature in 1910.[12] In the mid-1980s, the N-methyl analogue of MDA came into vogue and was known then and is still referred to as "Ecstasy." The synthesis of 3,4-methylenedioxymethamphetamine (MDMA) follows the same synthetic protocols as the less complicated phenethylamines. The clandestine laboratory operator or research chemist selectively adds one N-methyl group, an N,N-dimethyl group, an N-ethyl group, an N-propyl, an N-isopropyl group, and so on. In 1985 the N-hydroxy MDA derivative was reported.[13] This was significant because here the modification involved the addition of a hydroxyl group as opposed to an alkyl substitution on the nitrogen. Clandestine laboratory synthesis of MDA and MDMA are shown in Figure 1.13 and Figure 1.14.

The identification of the phenethylamines in the laboratory requires great care because of the chemical and molecular similarities of the exhibits. IR combined with MS and NMR spectrometry

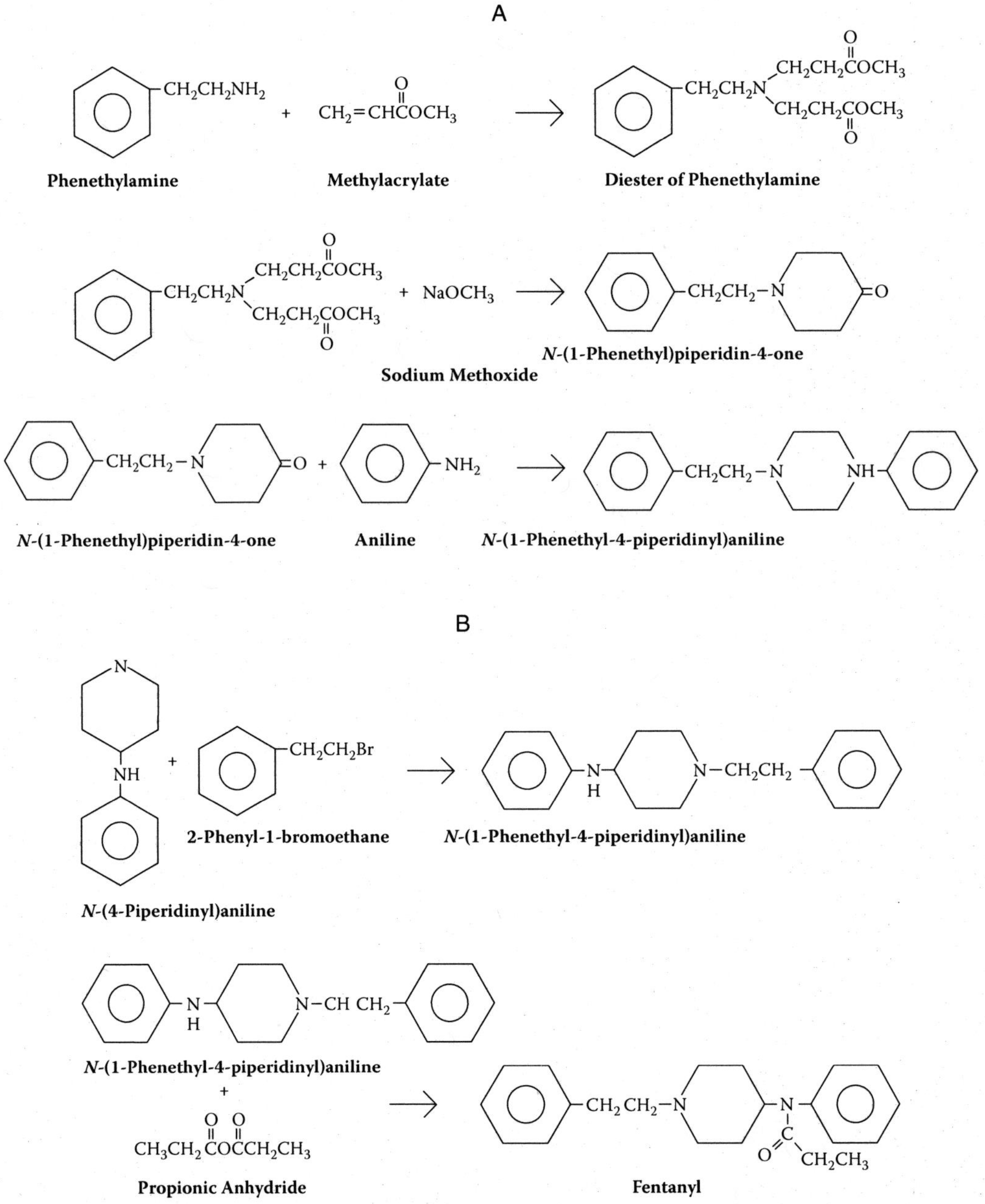

PATHOLOGY, TOXICOGENETICS, AND CRIMINALISTICS OF DRUG ABUSE

A

Phenethylamine + Methylacrylate → Diester of Phenethylamine

Diester of Phenethylamine + NaOCH₃ → N-(1-Phenethyl)piperidin-4-one

Sodium Methoxide

N-(1-Phenethyl)piperidin-4-one + Aniline → N-(1-Phenethyl-4-piperidinyl)aniline

B

N-(4-Piperidinyl)aniline + 2-Phenyl-1-bromoethane → N-(1-Phenethyl-4-piperidinyl)aniline

N-(1-Phenethyl-4-piperidinyl)aniline + Propionic Anhydride → Fentanyl

Figure 1.8 (A) Clandestine laboratory synthesis of fentanyl precursor. (B) Clandestine laboratory synthesis of fentanyl.

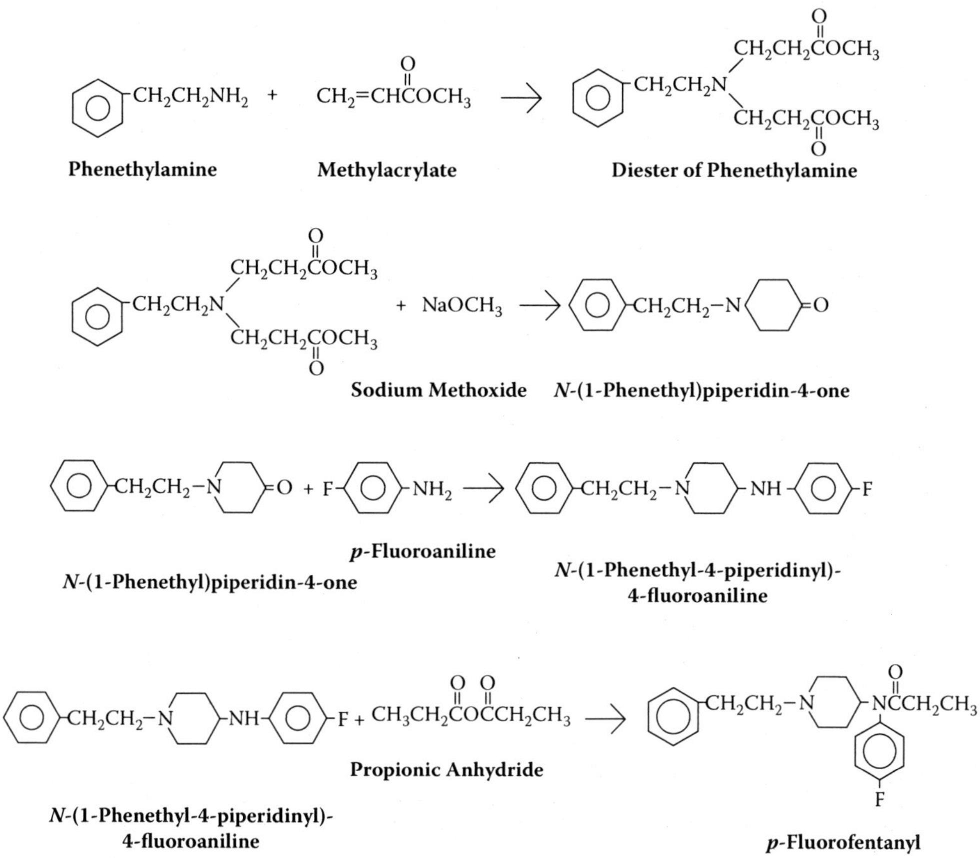

THE CRIMINALISTICS OF CONTROLLED SUBSTANCES

Figure 1.9 Clandestine laboratory synthesis of *p*-fluorofentanyl.

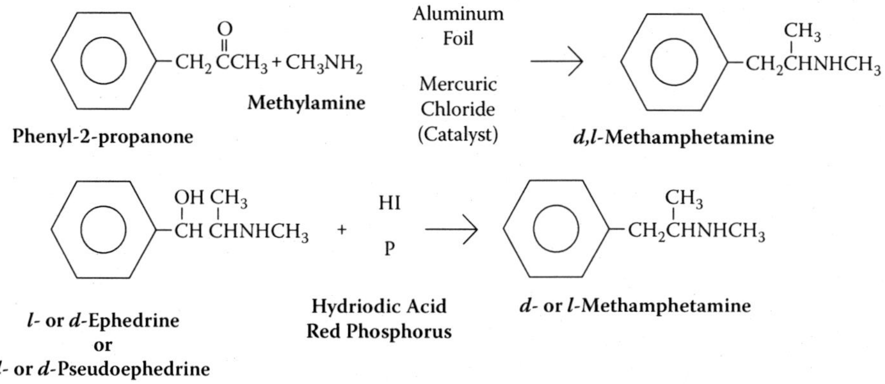

Figure 1.10 Clandestine laboratory synthesis of methamphetamine.

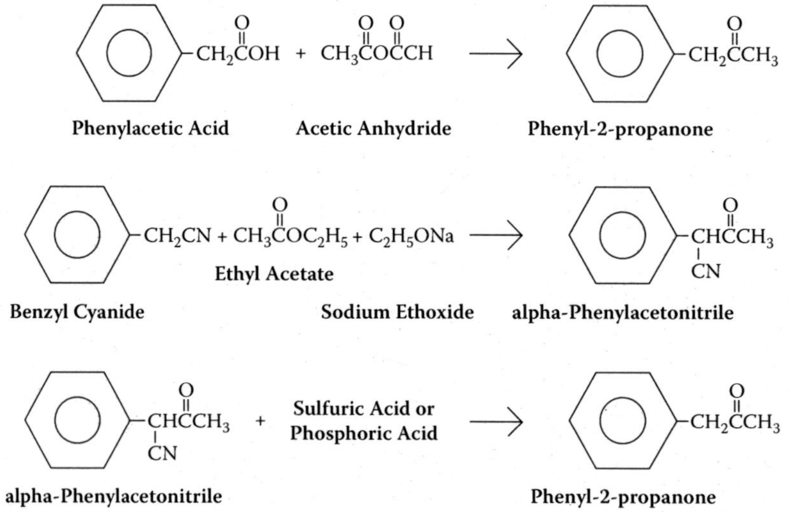

Figure 1.11 Clandestine laboratory synthesis of phenyl-2-propanone (p-2-p).

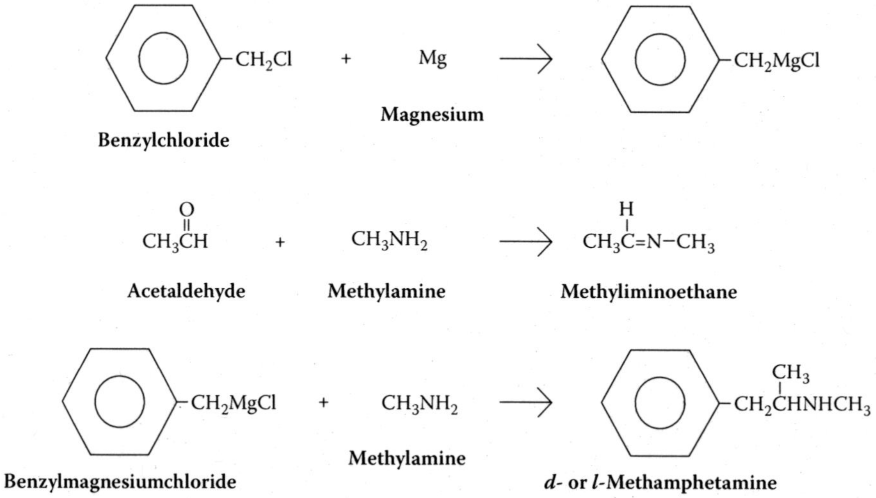

Figure 1.12 Clandestine laboratory synthesis of methamphetamine.

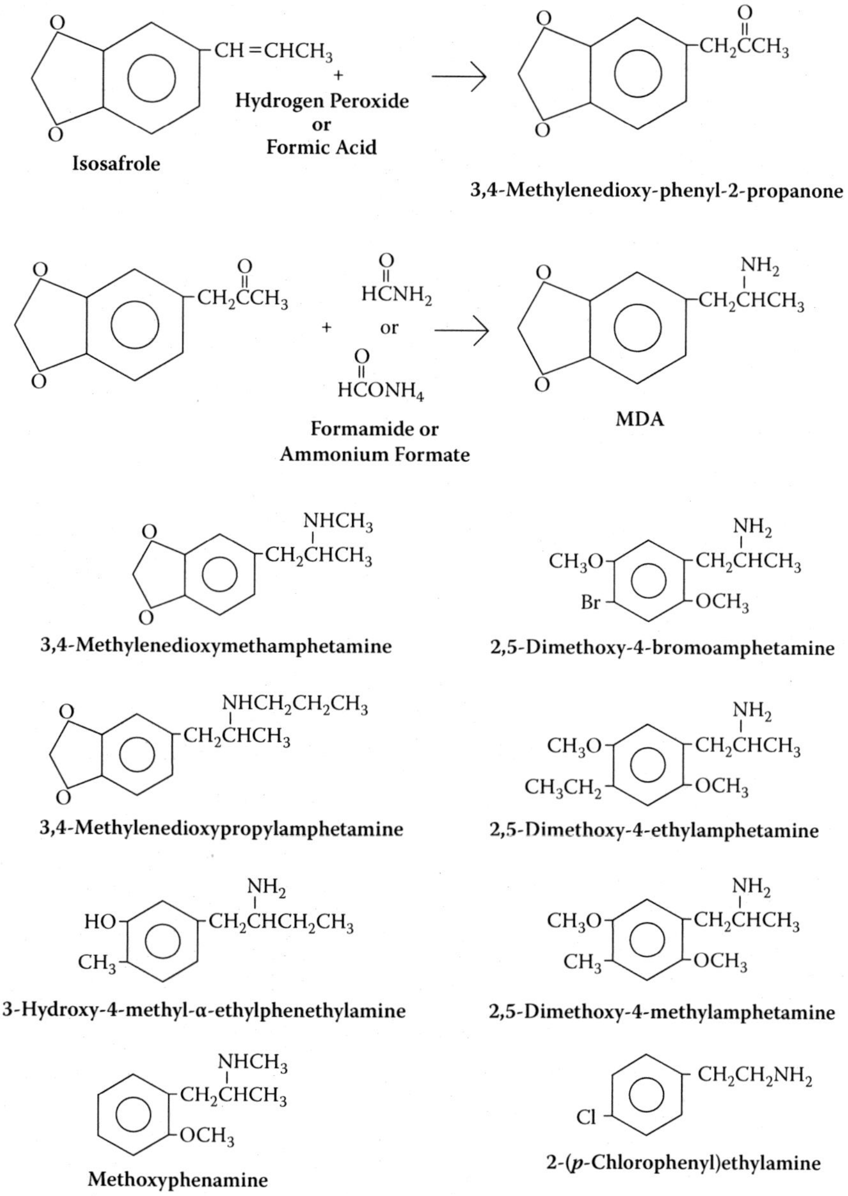

THE CRIMINALISTICS OF CONTROLLED SUBSTANCES

Figure 1.13 Clandestine laboratory synthesis of MDA.

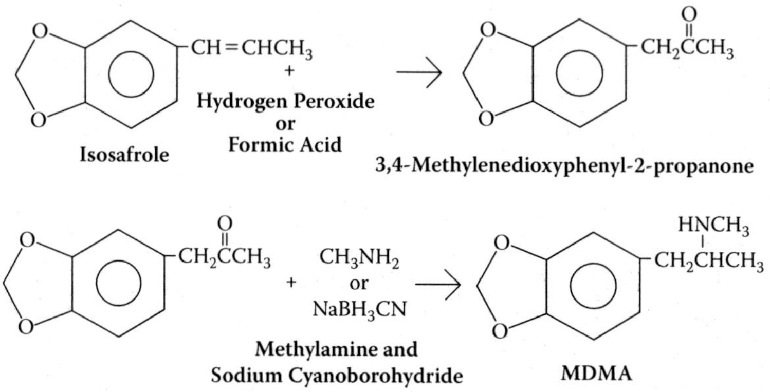

Figure 1.14 Clandestine laboratory synthesis of MDMA.

provide the most specificity in the identifications of phenethylamines in the forensic science laboratory.[13,14] From a legal perspective, the laboratory identification of the phenethylamine is part 1 in the forensic process. If prosecution is an option and the phenethylamine in question is not specified as a controlled substance under Public Law 91-513[15] or Part 1308 of the Code of Federal Regulations, another legal option is available.

In 1986, the U.S. Congress realized that the legal system was at a standstill in attempting to prosecute clandestine laboratory operators involved in molecular modification of phenethylamines and other homologues and analogues of controlled substances. The attempted closing of this loophole was the passage of the Controlled Substances Analogue and Enforcement Act of 1986.[16]

1.4.10 Methcathinone

Methcathinone (CAT) is a structural analogue of methamphetamine and cathinone (Figure 1.15 and Figure 1.16). It is potent and it, along with the parent compound, is easily manufactured. They are sold in the U.S. under the name CAT. Methcathinone is distributed as a white to off-white chunky powdered material and is sold in the hydrochloride salt form. Outside of the U.S., methcathinone is known as ephedrone and is a significant drug of abuse in Russia and some of the Baltic States.[17]

Methcathinone was permanently placed in Schedule I of the Controlled Substances Act in October 1993. Prior to its scheduling, two federal cases were effectively prosecuted in Ann Arbor and Marquette, Michigan, utilizing the analogue provision of the Controlled Substances Analogue and Enforcement Act of 1986.

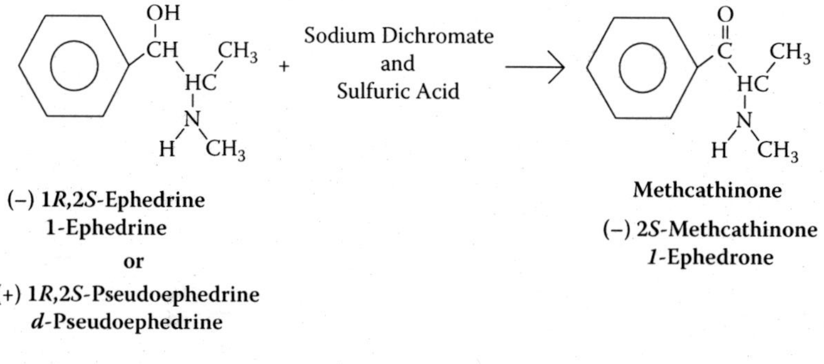

Figure 1.15 Clandestine laboratory synthesis of methcathinone.

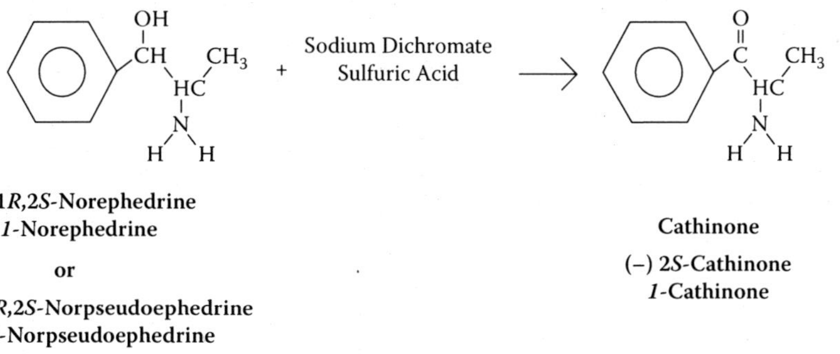

THE CRIMINALISTICS OF CONTROLLED SUBSTANCES 29

(–) 1*R*,2*S*-Norephedrine
l-Norephedrine

or

(+) 1*R*,2*S*-Norpseudoephedrine
d-Norpseudoephedrine

Cathinone

(–) 2*S*-Cathinone
l-Cathinone

Figure 1.16   Clandestine laboratory synthesis of cathinone.

1.4.11 *Catha edulis* (Khat)

Khat consists of the young leaves and tender shoots of the *Catha edulis* plant that is chewed for its stimulant properties.[18] *Catha edulis*, a species of the plant family Celastraceae, grows in eastern Africa and southern Arabia. Its effects are similar to the effects of amphetamine. The active ingredients in Khat are cathinone [(–)-a-aminopropiophenone], a Schedule I controlled substance that is quite unstable, and cathine [(+)-norpseudoephedrine], a Schedule IV controlled substance. Identification of cathinone in the laboratory presents problems because of time and storage requirements to minimize degradation.[19] Some of the decomposition or transformation products of *C. edulis* are norpseudoephedrine, norephedrine, 3,6-dimethyl-2,5-diphenylpyrazine, and 1-phenyl-1,2-propanedione.[20]

REFERENCES

1. Drugs of Abuse, U.S. Department of Justice, Drug Enforcement Administration, 1989, p. 49.
2. Kilmer, S.D., The isolation and identification of lysergic acid diethylamide (LSD) from sugar cubes and a liquid substrate, *J. Forensic Sci.*, 39, 860–862, 1994.
3. Feldman, H.W., Agar, M.H., and Beschner, G.M., Eds., *Angel Dust, An Ethnographic Study of PCP Users*, Lexington Books, Lexington, MA, 1979, 8.
4. Henderson, G.L., Designer drugs: past history and future prospects, *J. Forensic Sci.*, 33, 569–575, 1988.
5. Angelos, S.A., Raney, J.K., Skoronski, G.T., and Wagenhofer, R.J., The identification of unreacted precursors, impurities, and by-products in clandestinely produced phencyclidine preparations, *J. Forensic Sci.*, 35, 1297–1302, 1990.
6. Smialek, J.E., Levine, B., Chin, L., Wu, S.C., and Jenkins, A.J., A fentanyl epidemic in Maryland 1992, *J. Forensic Sci.*, 3, 159–164, 1994.
7. Janssen, P.A.J., U.S. patent 316400, 1965.
8. Henderson, G.L., The fentanyls, *Am. Assoc. Clin. Chem. in-Serv. Train Continuing Ed.*, 12(2), 5–17, 1990.
9. Riley, R.N. and Bagley, J.R., *J. Med. Chem.*, 22, 1167–1171.
10. Cooper, D., Jacob, M., and Allen, A., Identification of fentanyl derivatives, *J. Forensic Sci.*, 31, 511–528, 1986.
11. Kram, T.C., Cooper, D.A., and Allen, A., Behind the identification of China White, *Anal. Chem.*, 53, 1379–1386, 1981.
12. Mannich, C. and Jacobsohn, W., Hydroxyphenylalkylamines and dihydroxyphenylalkylamines, *Berichte*, 43, 189–197, 1910.
13. Dal Cason, T.A., The characterization of some 3,4-methylenedioxyphenyl-isopropylamine (MDA) analogues, *J. Forensic Sci.*, 34, 928–961, 1989.
14. Bost, R.O., 3,4-Methylenedioxymethamphetamine (MDMA) and other amphetamine derivatives, *J. Forensic Sci.*, 33, 576–587, 1988.
15. Comprehensive drug abuse prevention and control act of 1970, Public Law 91-513, 91st Congress, 27 Oct. 1970.

16. Controlled substance analogue and enforcement act of 1986, Public Law 99-570, Title I, Subtitle E, 99th Congress, 27 Oct. 1986.
17. Zhingel, K.Y., Dovensky, W., Crossman, A., and Allen, A., Ephedrone: 2-methylamino-1-phenylpropan-1-one (jell), *J. Forensic Sci.,* 36, 915–920, 1991.
18. *Catha edulis* (khat): some introductory remarks, *Bull. Narcotics,* 32, 1–3, 1980.
19. Lee, M.M., The identification of cathinone in khat (*Catha edulis*): a time study, *J. Forensic Sci.,* 40, 116–121, 1995.
20. Szendrei, K., The chemistry of khat, *Bull. Narcotics,* 32, 5–34, 1980.

1.4.12 Anabolic Steroids

1.4.12.1 *Regulatory History*

In recent years anabolic steroid abuse has become a significant problem in the U.S. There are two physiological responses associated with anabolic steroids: **androgenic activity** induces the development of male secondary sex characteristics; **anabolic activity** promotes the growth of various tissues, including muscle and blood cells. The male sex hormone testosterone is the prototype anabolic steroid. Individuals abuse these drugs in an attempt to improve athletic performance or body appearance. The more common agents are shown in Figure 1.17.

Black market availability of anabolic steroids has provided athletes and bodybuilders with a readily available supply of these drugs. Both human and veterinary steroid preparations are found in the steroid black market. Anabolic steroid preparations are formulated as tablets, capsules, and oil- and water-based injectable preparations. There is also a thriving black market for preparations that are either counterfeits of legitimate steroid preparations or are simply bogus.

Control of Steroids

In 1990, the U.S. Congress passed the Anabolic Steroid Control Act. This act placed anabolic steroids, along with their salts, esters, and isomers, as a class of drugs, into Schedule III of the Federal Controlled Substances Act (CSA). This law provided 27 names of steroids that were specifically defined under the CSA as anabolic steroids. This list, which is provided in the *Code of Federal Regulations,* is reproduced below.

1. Boldenone
2. Chlorotestosterone
3. Clostebol
4. Dehydrochlormethyltestosterone
5. Dihydrotestosterone
6. Drostanolone
7. Ethylestrenol
8. Fluoxymesterone
9. Formebolone
10. Mesterolone
11. Methandienone
12. Methandranone
13. Methandriol
14. Methandrostenolone
15. Methenolone
16. Methyltestosterone
17. Mibolerone
18. Nandrolone
19. Norethandrolone
20. Oxandrolone
21. Oxymesterone
22. Oxymetholone
23. Stanolone
24. Stanozolol
25. Testolactone
26. Testosterone
27. Trenbolone

Unfortunately, the list contains three sets of duplicate names (chlorotestosterone and Clostebol; dihydrotestosterone and stanolone; and methandrostenolone and methandienone) as well as one name (methandranone) for a drug that did not exist. So, the actual number of different steroids specifically defined under the law as anabolic steroids is 23, not 27. Realizing that the list of 23

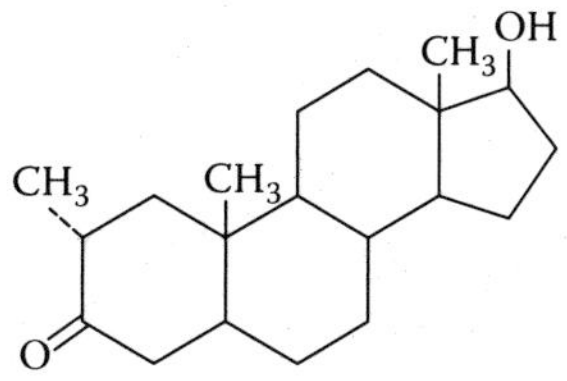

THE CRIMINALISTICS OF CONTROLLED SUBSTANCES

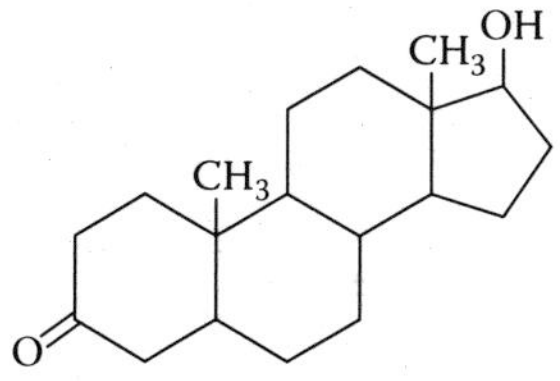

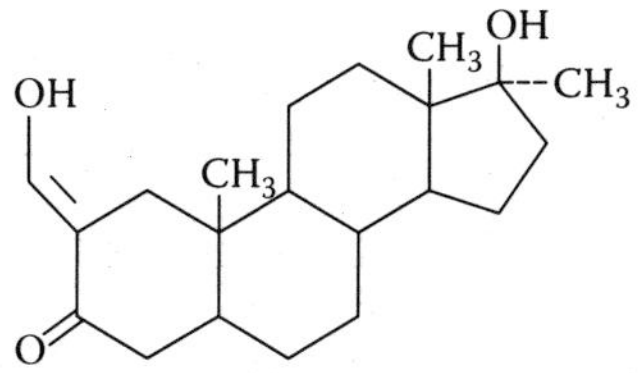

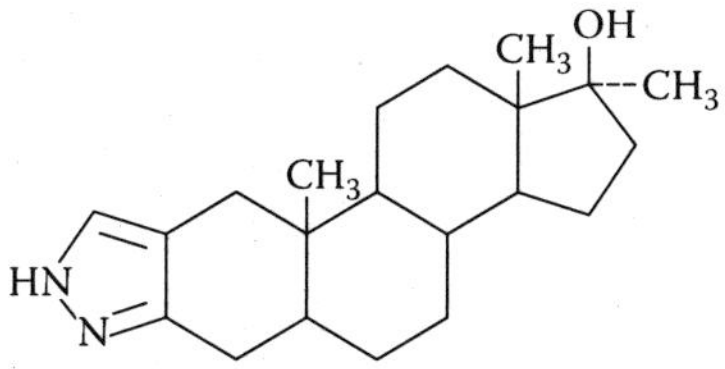

Figure 1.17 Common agents.

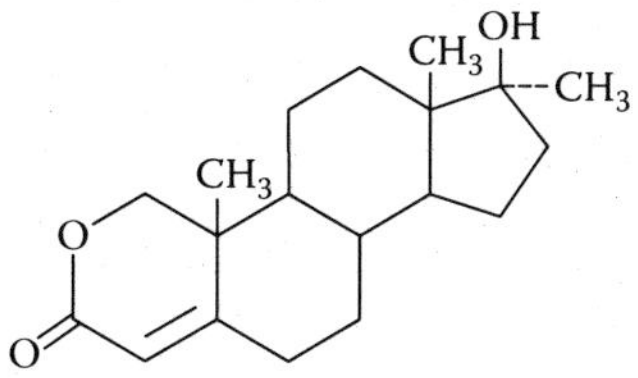

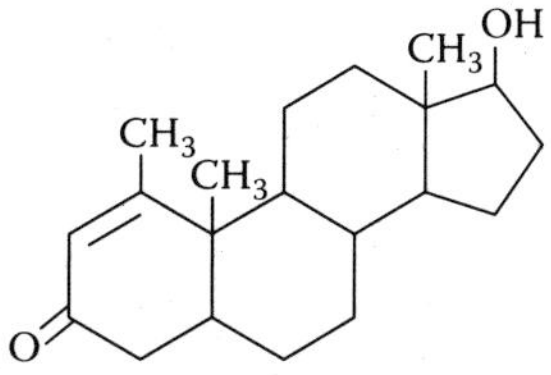

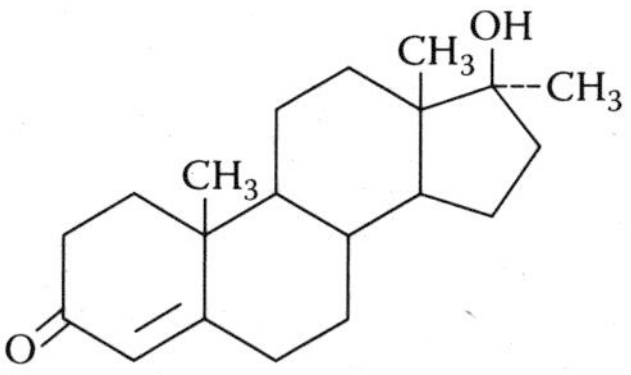

substances would not be all inclusive, Congress went on to define within the law the term "anabolic steroid" to mean "any drug or hormonal substance, chemically or pharmacologically related to testosterone (other than estrogens, progestins, and corticosteroids) and that promote muscle growth."

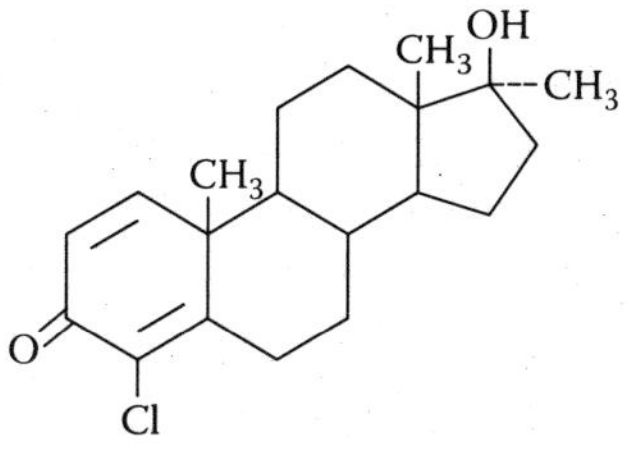

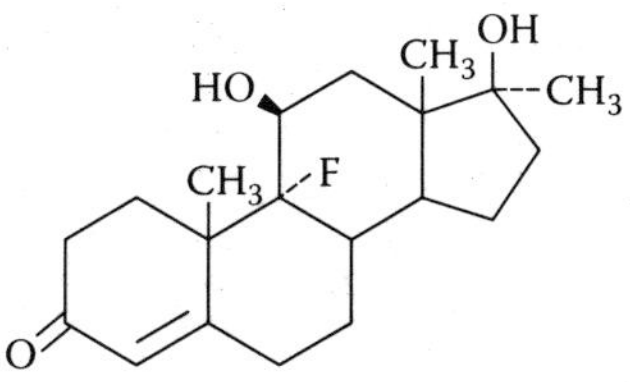

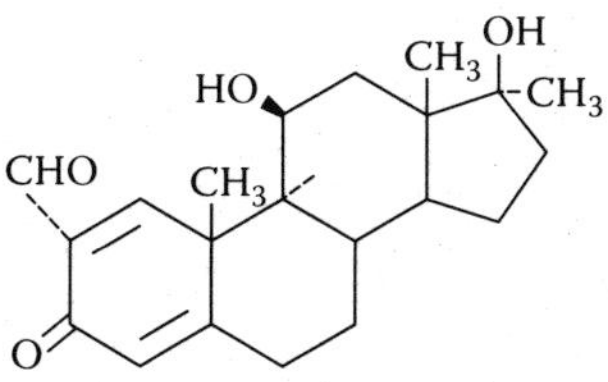

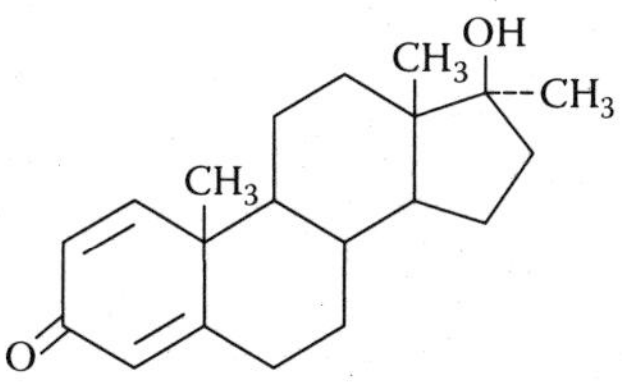

The scheduling of anabolic steroids has necessitated forensic laboratories to analyze exhibits containing steroids. In those cases involving the detection of 1 or more of the 23 steroids specifically defined as anabolic steroids under the law, questions of legality are not likely to arise. However, when a steroid is identified that is not specifically defined under the law, it becomes necessary to further examine the substance to determine if it qualifies as an anabolic steroid under the definition of such a substance under the CSA. The forensic chemist must positively identify the steroid and convey to the pharmacologist the entire structure of the steroid. It then becomes the responsibility of the pharmacologist to determine the pharmacological activity, including effects on muscle growth, of the identified steroid.

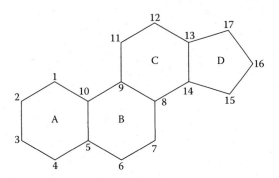

Figure 1.18 Cyclopentanoperhydrophenanthrene.

1.4.12.2 Structure–Activity Relationship

The pharmacology of the identified steroid may be evaluated in at least two ways. The first, and most important way, is to examine the scientific, medical, and patent literature for data on the pharmacological effects of the steroid. Over the years, numerous steroids have been examined in animal and/or human studies for anabolic/androgenic activity. It is possible that the identified steroid will be among that group of steroids. The second method is to evaluate possible pharmacological activity using **structure–activity relationships**. Such analysis is based on the assumption of a relationship between the structure of the steroid and its pharmacological effects. Small alterations of chemical structure may enhance, diminish, eliminate, or have no effect on the pharmacological activity of the steroid. The structure–activity relationships of androgens and anabolic steroids have been reviewed extensively.[1,2]

Extensive studies of the structure–activity relationships of anabolic/androgenic steroids have demonstrated that the following structural attributes are necessary for maximal androgenic and anabolic effects: rings A and B must be in the *trans* configuration;[3] hydroxy function at C-17 must be in the β conformational state;[5,6] and high electron density must be present in the area of C_2 and C_3.[7] The presence of a keto or hydroxl group at position 3 in the A-ring usually enhances androgenic and anabolic activity, but it is not absolutely necessary for these effects.[7] A few examples of structural alterations that enhance anabolic activity include removal of the C-19 methyl group;[8] methyl groups at the 2a and 7a positions;[9,10] a fluorine at the 9a position; or a chlorine at the 4a position.[10,11] To make it easier to visualize where these modifications are made in the ring structure, a numbered steroid skeletal ring structure, namely, the cyclopentanoperhydrophenanthrene ring, is shown in Figure 1.18.

It is essential to understand that structure–activity analysis can predict only whether or not a steroid is likely to produce androgenic/anabolic effects. It then becomes necessary to examine the steroid in the laboratory to determine whether the prediction is, in fact, true. It is also important to note that numerous studies performed over the years and designed to separate androgenic activity from anabolic activity have failed to obtain such a separation of pharmacological effect. That is, steroids found to possess androgenic activity also have anabolic activity, and vice versa. An examination of the scientific and medical literature reveals that there are, indeed, additional steroids that are not specifically listed in the law but that do, based on available data, probably produce androgenic/anabolic effects. A listing of some of these steroids is provided below.

Androisoaxazole	Mestanolone
Bolandiol	Methyltrienolone
Bolasterone	Norbolethone
Bolenol	Norclostebol
Flurazebol	Oxabolone Cypionate

Mebolazine	Quinbolone
Mesabolone	Stenbolone

1.4.12.3 *Forensic Analysis*

For the forensic chemist, when a steroid is tentatively identified, an additional problem arises, namely, obtaining an analytical standard. Many products found in the illicit U.S. market are commercially available only outside of the U.S. Locating and making contact with a foreign distributor is one problem. Requesting and then receiving a legitimate standard is another problem. The expense incurred in obtaining these standards can be quite high. Once the standard has been received, authentication then enters the analytical process. If a primary standard is unavailable, an optimized analytical process presents a real problem. Fortunately, most steroids received by forensic science laboratories are labeled directly or have labeled packaging. So a manufacturer can be identified, and there is a starting point for the chemist in confirming the material as a particular steroid.

There are no known color tests, crystal tests, or TLC methods that are specific to anabolic steroids. Screening can be accomplished by GLC or HPLC. GLC sometimes presents a problem because of thermal decomposition in the injection port, thereby resulting in several peaks. The steroid will not always be the largest peak. On-column injection will usually solve this problem. However, oil-base steroids rapidly foul or degrade GC columns. Samples in oils can be extracted with methanol/water 9:1 prior to injection onto a GC. Retention times for some anabolic steroids are quite long and nearly triple or quadruple that of heroin. Recognizing that several anabolic steroids are readily oxidized in polar, protic solvents vs. halogenated hydrocarbons, screening and analysis must be accomplished as soon as possible after isolation and dilution.

GC/MS does provide definitive spectra; however, different MS systems may provide differences in the spectra for the same steroid. These differences can be traced to the quality of the MS source and the injection liner, thermal decomposition products, and induced hydration reactions related to high source temperatures set by the MS. C^{13}NMR is the most rigorous identification technique. The limitation here is the need for pure samples and high sample concentrations. Identification by infrared alone can result in problems due to polymorphism. This can be minimized by ensuring that the sample and standard are recrystallized from the same solvent.

Ideally, all anabolic steroids should be identified using two analytical methodologies that yield the same conclusions. The collection of a library of analytical data on different anabolic steroids is essential for the subsequent identification of steroids sent to the laboratory. An ability to interpret MS data will be important in making an identification insofar as determining a molecular formula. Interpreting NMR data will be important in determining how substitutents are attached to the parent steroid ring structure.

It should be noted that selected steroids, such as testosterone, nandrolone, methenolone, boldenone, methandriol, and trenbolone, will often be encountered by the laboratory, not as the parent drug, but instead as an ester. The type of ester will be dependent on the particular steroid. For example, nandrolone is primarily found as a decanoate, laurate, or phenpropionate ester. Testosterone, although it is found as a parent drug, is actually most commonly encountered as the propionate, enanthate, cypionate, decanoate, isocaproate, or undecanoate esters. Less commonly encountered testosterone esters include the acetate, valerate, and undecylenate esters. Methenolone is almost always found in either the acetate or enanthate esterified form.

Upon reaching the forensic science laboratory, steroid preparations will be handled differently depending on the way each preparation is formulated. Tablets can be handled by finely grinding and extracting with chloroform or methanol. Aqueous suspensions can be handled by dilution/solution with methanol for HPLC screening or by extraction with chloroform for GC screening. Oils require a more specialized extraction.

What steroids have been the most predominant in the U.S. in the past few years? Although the last decade has seen the introduction of many new "designer steroids," the list of most abused steroids has changed very little in the past 10 years. From January 1990 to October 1994, the following steroids or their esters were identified by DEA laboratories. This list provides an objective evaluation of what this chemist has encountered in the not-too-distant past. The data on these particular steroids should form the basis of a reference collection for comparison with future submissions.

| | Numbers of | |
Steroids or Esters of a Steroid	Cases	Exhibits
Testosterone	260	882
Nandrolone	140	244
Methenolone	99	189
Methandrostenolone	76	158
Oxymetholone	67	103
Stanozolol	61	115
Fluoxymesterone	54	7
Methyltestosterone	48	75
Boldenone	24	28
Mesterolone	21	22
Oxandrolone	16	21
Trenbolone	13	20
Methandriol	10	8
Drostanolone	6	7
Mibolerone	4	7
Stanolone	2	2
Testolactone	1	1

Acknowledgment

The author wishes to acknowledge the assistance of Dr. James Tolliver, Pharmacologist, of the DEA Office of Diversion Control, for collaborating in the preparation of this work.

REFERENCES

1. Counsell, R.E. and Klimstra, P.D., Androgens and anabolic agents, in *Medicinal Chemistry,* 3rd ed., Burger, A., Ed., Wiley-Interscience, New York, 1970, 923.
2. Vida, J.A., *Androgens and Anabolic Agents: Chemistry and Pharmacology,* Academic Press, New York, 1969.
3. Huggins, C., Jensen, E.V., and Cleveland, A.S., Chemical structure of steroids in relation to promotion of growth of the vagina and uterus of the hypophysectomized rat, *J. Exp. Med.,* 100, 225–246, 1954.
4. Gabbard, R.B. and Segaloff, A., Facile preparation of 17 beta-hydroxy-5 beta-androstan-3-one and its 17 alpha-methyl derivative, *J. Organic Chem.,* 27, 655, 1962.
5. Kochakian, C.D., *Recent Progress in Hormonal Research,* 1, 177, 1948.
6. Kochakian, C.D., *Am. J. Physiol.,* 160, 53, 1950.
7. Bowers, A., Cross, A.D., Edwards, J.A., Carpio, H., Calzada, M.C., and Denot, E., *J. Med. Chem.,* 6, 156, 1963.
8. Hershberger, L.G., Shipley, E.G., and Meyer, R.K., *Proc. Soc. Exp. Biol. Med.,* 83, 175, 1953.
9. Counsell, R.E., Klimstra, P.D., and Colton, F.B., Anabolic agents, derivatives of 5 alpha-androst-1-ene, *J. Organic Chem.,* 27, 248, 1962.
10. Sala, G. and Baldratti, G., *Proc. Soc. Exp. Biol. Med.,* 95, 22, 1957.
11. Backle, R.M., *Br. Med. J.,* 1, 1378, 1959.

THE CRIMINALISTICS OF CONTROLLED SUBSTANCES

1.5 LEGITIMATE PHARMACEUTICAL PREPARATIONS

The Controlled Substances Act (CSA) of 1970 created a closed system for the production and distribution of legitimately manufactured controlled substances. The CSA includes contingencies to regulate the domestic commerce, importation, and exportation of these pharmaceutical preparations. Even with all of the controls that are in place, legitimate pharmaceuticals intended to help those in need are diverted onto the illegitimate market. Most of the diversion of these pharmaceuticals occurs at the retail rather than the wholesale level.

The analysis of pharmaceutical preparations in the forensic science laboratory is one of the most straightforward types of analysis. These samples are usually recognizable by their labels, which usually include the manufacturer's logo and name. There are some samples that even have the name of the product inscribed on the tablet or capsule. In those instances where the manufacturer's logo is not recognized, the *Physician's Desk Reference* (PDR) is a readily available source of information, which includes photographs and descriptions of the product along with information of the formulation. Another source of this information is the *Logo Index for Tablets and Capsules*.[1] This particular text lists data including inscriptions on most known products including generics. After the tablet or capsule has been tentatively identified in a reference text, it is the responsibility of the forensic chemist to conduct a series of analyses to verify the presence of a controlled substance. This verification process will usually consist of many of the same analytical processes utilized in the analysis and evaluation of any controlled substance.

1.5.1 Benzodiazepines

The benzodiazepines form one of the largest classes of abused pharmaceuticals. These products are sedative/hypnotics, tranquilizers, and anti-anxiety drugs; they produce a calming effect and are often prescribed as tranquilizers. The drugs in this class are numerous and are included under Schedule IV control because, while they do have a potential for abuse, there are recognized medical benefits that are both physiological and psychological. The most frequently diverted and abused benzodiazepines are alprazolam (Xanax) and diazepam (Valium). Other frequently abused benzodiazepines are lorazepam (Activan), triazolam (Halcion), chlordiazepoxide (Librium), flurazepam (Dalmane), and temazepam (Restoril). Another phenomenon that has been noted for several years is the abuse of legitimate pharmaceuticals in conjunction with illicit controlled substances. Clonazepam (Klonipin) is just such a product. It is an anxiety reducer that is used in combination with methadone and heroin.

There has been a recent influx of flunitrazepam (Rohypnol) into the Gulf Coast and other areas of the U.S. This product is a benzodiazepine manufactured principally in Colombia, Mexico, and Switzerland. It is also manufactured in lesser amounts in Argentina, Brazil, Peru, Uruguay, and Venezuela. It is neither manufactured nor marketed legally in the U.S. This is a powerful drug reported to be seven to ten times more potent than diazepam.

1.5.2 Other Central Nervous System Depressants

The oldest of the synthetic sleep-inducing drugs dates back to 1862. Chloral hydrate is marketed as a soft gelatinous capsule under the name Noctec, and controlled under Schedule V. Its popularity declined after the introduction of barbiturates. Barbiturates are the drugs prescribed most frequently to induce sedation. Roughly 15 derivatives of barbituric acid are currently in use to calm nervous conditions. In larger doses they are used to induce sleep.

The actions of barbiturates fall into four categories. Some of the ultrashort-acting barbiturates are hexobarbital (Sombulex), methohexital (Brevital), thiamylal (Surital), and thiopental (Pentothal). Short-acting and intermediate-acting barbiturates include pentobarbital (Nembutal), seco-

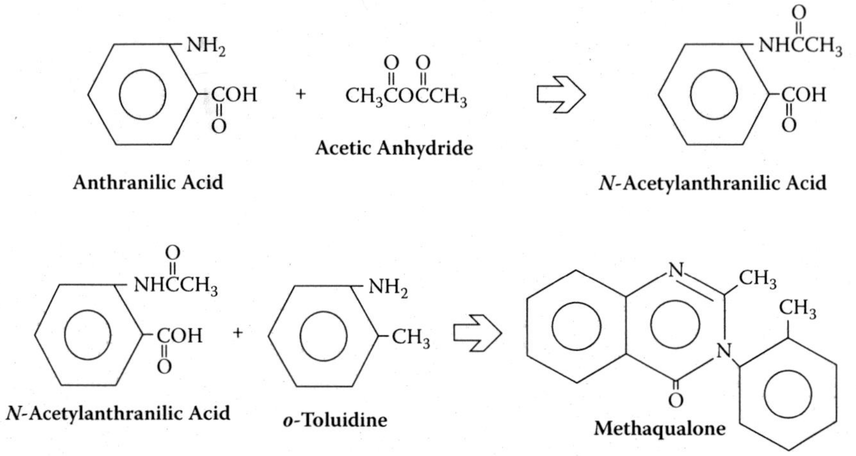

Figure 1.16 Clandestine laboratory synthesis of methaqualone.

barbital (Seconal), and amobarbital (Amytal). These three drugs have been among the most abused barbituric acid derivatives. Also included in these categories but not as abused are butabarbital (Butisol), talbutal (Lotusate), and aprobarbital (Alurate). The last category is the long-acting barbiturates. These drugs are used medicinally as sedatives, hypnotics, and anticonvulsants. The group includes phenobarbital (Luminal), mephobarbital or methylphenobarbital (Mebaral), and metharbital (Gemonil).

Three other CNS depressants that have been marketed as legitimate pharmaceutical preparations and have a history of abuse include glutethimide (Doriden), methaqualone (Quaalude, Parest, Mequin, Optimil, Somnafac, Sopor, and Mandrax), and meprobamate (Miltown, Equanil, and SK-Bamate). The route for the clandestine synthesis of methaqualone is shown in Figure 1.16.

1.5.3 Narcotic Analgesics

When one thinks of opium-like compounds, morphine and heroin immediately come to mind. However, there is another subset of this class of compounds that includes pharmaceutical preparations used to relieve pain, which are purchased legitimately or illegitimately from a pharmacy with a prescription. Frequently used pharmaceutical opiates include oxycodone (Percodan), hydromorphone (Dilaudid), hydrocodone (Tussionex and Vicodin), pentazocine (Talwin), and codeine combinations such as Tylenol with Codeine and Empirin with Codeine. All of these compounds are addictive.

Along with Tylenol with Codeine and Empirin with Codeine, which are Schedule III controlled substances, codeine is also available in combination with another controlled substance (butalbital) and sold under the trade name of Fiorinal with Codeine. It is available with acetaminophen in Phenaphen. Codeine is available in liquid preparations under the manufacturers' names Cosanyl, Robitussin A-C, Cheracol, Cerose, and Pediacof. Because of the amounts of codeine in these preparations, they are controlled under Schedule V. There are also pharmaceutical codeine tablets, which contain no drug other than codeine and are controlled under Schedule II.

While the compounds listed above are considered opiates, there is another class of compounds also classified as narcotic, but with synthetic origins. Meperidine (Demerol) is one of the most widely used analgesics for the relief of pain. Methadone (Amidone and Dolophine) is another of these synthetic narcotics. It was synthesized during World War II by German scientists because of a morphine shortage. Although it is chemically unlike morphine or heroin, it produces many of the same effects and is often used to treat narcotic addictions.

THE CRIMINALISTICS OF CONTROLLED SUBSTANCES

Dextropropoxyphene is one of those drugs that falls into one of two controlled substance schedules. When marketed in dosage form under the trade names Darvon, Darvocet, Dolene, or Propacet, dextropropoxyphene is a Schedule IV controlled substance. However, when marketed in bulk non-dosage forms, dextropropoxyphene is a Schedule II controlled substance. The significance here is that the penalties for possession of a Schedule II controlled substance are usually much greater than for possession of a Schedule IV controlled substance.

1.5.4 Central Nervous System Stimulants

Amphetamine (Benzedrine and Biphetamine), dextroamphetamine (Dexedrine), and methamphetamine (Desoxyn) are three of the best-known CNS stimulants and were prescribed for many years to treat narcolepsy. At one time, these drugs were sold over the counter without a prescription. For many years these drugs were sold as appetite suppressants. Their availability in the form of prescription drugs has all but been eliminated except under the close scrutiny of a physician. However, the clandestine laboratory production of methamphetamine in the form of a powder or granular material has been one of the major problems facing law enforcement personnel in the past 20 or so years in the U.S.

Phenmetrazine (Preludin) and methylphenidate (Ritalin) are two other CNS stimulants that have patterns of abuse similar to the amphetamine and methamphetamine products. In recent years, a number of pharmaceutical products have appeared on the market as appetite suppressants and as replacements for the amphetamines. These anorectic drugs include benzphetamine (Didrex), chlorphentermine (Pre-Sate), clortermine (Voranil), diethylpropion (Tenuate and Tepanil), fenfluramine (Pondimin), mazindol (Sanorex and Mazanor), phendimetrazine (Plegine, Bacarate, Melifat, Statobex, and Tanorex), and phentermine (Ionamin, Fastin, and Adipex-P).

1.5.5 Identifying Generic Products

There are a number of generic products on the market that are legitimate pharmaceutical preparations. These products will usually contain the active ingredient of the brand name product, but at the same time have a different formulation in the way of diluents and binders. These products are cataloged in various publications. When these products are encountered in the forensic science laboratory, the analyst will usually make a preliminary identification using one of the many publications listing the tablet or capsule's description and the code number that appears on the face of the product. This "preliminary" identification affords a starting point in the analytical process. The analyst will then proceed using the standard chemical techniques and instrumental methods to make an independent identification.

REFERENCE

1. Franzosa, E.S. and Harper W.W., The Logo Index for Tablets and Capsules, 3rd ed., U.S. Government Printing Office, Washington, D.C., 1995, 392–2401.

1.6 UNIQUE IDENTIFYING FACTORS

1.6.1 Packaging Logos

There are unique factors associated with controlled substance examinations that involve packaging. Heroin and cocaine are usually imported into the U.S. clandestinely packaged. Sometimes this packaging takes the form of legitimate household or commercial products that have been hollowed out or have natural crevices in which drugs can be stored for shipment. These kinds of packages will usually be transported via commercial carriers to distributors who will reclaim the drugs and repackage them for street distribution. Sometimes drugs are shipped via human beings who store packages in body cavities, or swallow small packages in order to clear customs checks at points of entry. In these cases, it is not unusual for the packaging to break while in the body of the person transporting the drug. This usually results in severe injury or death.

Another common way of transporting controlled substances is to package the controlled substance in brick-size, 1-kg packages for shipment to the U.S. This is often the case with shipments of heroin, cocaine, and marijuana, and the packages are usually wrapped in paper or tape. Sometimes a logo, serving as a type of trademark for the illicit distributor, will be affixed. Logos can take the form of any number of designs. They are applied using a stamping or printing device. Some commonly encountered designs include, but are not limited to, animals, symbols from Greek mythology, replications of brand name product logos, replications of the names of political figures, cartoon characters, and numbers.

When a number of these logos are encountered, examinations can be conducted to determine whether two logos have a common source. If the examiner determines that two logos are the same, and were produced using the same printing or stamping device, then the two packages must have originated from the same source. This kind of information is especially useful in tracking distribution networks.

Glassine envelopes measuring approximately 1×2 in. are commonly used to distribute heroin "on the street" directly to the primary user. More often than not, these glassine envelopes have rubber-stamped images affixed. These rubber stamped images take many forms. Cartoon characters or words with social implications are common. The examiner can determine whether these rubber-stamped images have a commonality of source and use this information to track distribution patterns of heroin within a geographical area.

1.6.2 Tablet Markings and Capsule Imprints

Counterfeit tablets and capsules, which closely resemble tablets and capsules of legitimate pharmaceutical companies, are readily available on the clandestine market. They generally contain controlled substances that have been formulated in such a way as to mimic legitimate pharmaceutical preparations.[1] They are designed to be sold either on the clandestine or the legitimate market. These counterfeits sometimes are expertly prepared and closely resemble the pharmaceutical products that they are designed to represent. At other times, they are poorly made, inadequate representations of the products they are purported to represent.

The examiner in these types of cases will evaluate the suspected tablets or capsules by examining both the class and individual characteristics of the products. Legitimate products are usually prepared with few significant flaws on tablet or capsule surfaces. The lettering or numbering will be symmetrical in every way. The tablet surfaces will have minimal chips or gouges and will usually be symmetrical. The homogeneity of the tablet will be of the highest quality. Counterfeits will usually have tabletting flaws. These flaws can take the forms of imperfect lettering or numbering, rough surfaces, or inconsistencies in the tablet formulation. This can result in different hardening characteristics of the tablet. Legitimate capsules will be highly symmetrical. The lettering or numbering will usually line up on both halves of the capsule.[2,3]

In recent years, methamphetamine and amphetamine tablets and capsules, crafted to mimic Dexedrine and Benzedrine, have been encountered with some frequency. These two products were distributed and used quite extensively on the legitimate market up until the 1970s. And while they are still available commercially with a prescription, they have been controlled under Schedule II since 1972 and their legal distribution and usage in the medical community have become fairly limited. Counterfeit barbiturate, methaqualone, and benzodiazepine tablets, sometimes from doc-

THE CRIMINALISTICS OF CONTROLLED SUBSTANCES

umented clandestine source laboratories from 20 years ago, have been encountered in recent seizures. Counterfeit Quaalude, Mandrax, and Valium tablets are examples of legitimate trademark products that have been the favorites of clandestine laboratory operators. The "look-alike" market was especially lucrative in the 1970s and 1980s and became a $50,000,000 a year industry.[4,5]

A unique problem, encountered with regularity up until 1975, involved the refilling of capsules. Legitimate capsules were diverted from legitimate manufacturing sources. The capsules were then emptied of their contents and refilled with some innocuous material, such as starch or baking soda, and sold. The original filling, usually containing a controlled substance, was then diverted for sale on the illicit market. These capsules can usually be identified by imperfections in their surface characteristics. There may be small indentations on the gelatinous surface of the capsule and fingerprints indicating excessive handling. The seal holding both halves of the capsule together will not be tight. And there will usually be traces of powder around the seal of the capsule. Refilling capsules by hand or by improvised mechanical devices is not easy and usually results in these visible powder residues. A more common problem today is the refilling of over-the-counter capsules with heroin for distribution at the retail level.

A similar problem that is encountered with some frequency in the forensic science laboratory is the pre-packaged syringe from a hospital, which is labeled and supposed to contain an analgesic such as meperidine. Patients complain they are receiving no relief from the injection they have been given. The syringes are then sent to the laboratory for analysis. Not infrequently, they are found to contain water, substituted for the active drug by an addicted doctor or nurse.

1.6.3 Blotter Paper LSD

LSD has been available for years in the forms of small tablets (microdots), small gelatinous squares, clear plastic-like squares (window panes), powders or crystals, liquid, or in capsules. The most commonly encountered form of LSD available today is impregnated blotter paper. This LSD medium is prepared by dissolving the clandestinely produced LSD powder in an alcohol solution, and then spraying or soaking the paper with the solution. The alcohol solution used most frequently is EverClear, a commercial ethyl alcohol product available in liquor stores. This LSD-impregnated paper is referred to as "blotter acid." It is usually distributed on sheets of paper perforated into 1/4 × 1/4 in. squares. These sheets of paper range in size to hold from 1 square up to 1000 squares. These sheets of blotter paper can be plain white or single colored with no design imprints. More often than not, there will be a brightly colored design on the paper. The design can be simple such as a black and white circle, or it can be extremely intricate. One such design was brightly colored and with a detailed depiction of the crucifixion of Jesus Christ. The design can cover each and every individual square of a 1000-perforated square sheet of paper, or one design can cover the entire sheet of blotter paper where each 1/4 × 1/4 in. perforation square makes up 1/1000 of the total design.

By examining the intricate designs on LSD blotter paper from different seizures, it is possible to determine whether there is a common source. Depending on the printing process and the quality of the image, the examiner may be able to characterize an exhibit as having originated from the image transfer process and a specific printing device. This ability to determine source commonality is most valuable in determining the origins of LSD exhibits seized from different parts of the world.

The processes described above are most valuable in linking seizures to a particular source. Investigators who are skillful and fortunate enough to seize printing or tabletting devices even without the actual controlled substances can have their efforts rewarded by terminating a controlled substance production operation. A qualified scientific examiner has the opportunity to use these devices as standards and to search reference collections of tablets, capsules, LSD blotter paper designs, or heroin or cocaine packaging logos to determine possible associations to past seizures. When this happens, the opportunity to eliminate another source of illicit drug distribution becomes a possibility.

REFERENCES

1. Franzosa, E.S., Solid dosage forms: 1975–1983, *J. Forensic Sci.*, 30, 1194–1205, 1985.
2. Eisenberg, W.V. and Tillson, A.H., Identification of counterfeit drugs, particularly barbiturates and amphetamines by microscopic, chemical, and instrumental techniques, *J. Forensic Sci.*, 11, 529–551, 1966.
3. Tillson, A.H. and Johnson, D.W., Identification of drug and capsule evidence as to source, *J. Forensic Sci.*, 19, 873–883, 1974.
4. Crockett, J. and Franzosa, E., Illicit solid dosage forms: drug trafficking in the United States, paper presented at the 6th Interpol Forensic Sciences Symposium in 1980.
5. Crockett, J. and Sapienza, F., Illicit solid dosage forms: drug trafficking in the United States, paper presented at the 10th Interpol Forensic Sciences Symposium in 1983.

1.7 ANALYZING DRUGS IN THE FORENSIC SCIENCE LABORATORY

1.7.1 Screening Tests

No other topic related to the identification of controlled substances causes as much controversy as testing specificity. Forensic science laboratories conduct two different categories of tests. Tests in the first category are called "screening tests." They include a series of tests used to make a preliminary determination of whether a particular drug or class of drugs is present. It must be emphasized that screening tests are not used to positively identify any drug. At best, screening tests can only be used to determine the possibility that members of a particular class of drug may be present. Some say that screening tests can result in "false positives," meaning either that the test indicates the possible presence of a controlled substance when none is present or that the test indicates the possible presence of one controlled substance when a different controlled substance is present. That should not be a problem, so long as it is understood that screening tests have very little if any specificity, and that a false positive test will only lead to more testing, not a false conclusion. The identification of any drug by a chemical analysis is a systematic process involving a progression from less specific methods to more specific methods. The most specific methods involve instrumental analyses. Properly trained scientists should know when a false positive is possible, and how to take steps to narrow the focus of the testing. The more tests used, the fewer the chances for error.

False negative screening tests also occur. Very weak or diluted samples containing controlled substances may yield a negative screening test. An example of this situation would be a 1% heroin sample cut with a brown powder. Testing this sample with Marquis reagent, which contains sulfuric acid and formaldehyde, may result in a charring of the brown powder and subsequent masking of the bleeding purple color characteristic of an opium alkaloid. Weak or old reagents may also yield false negatives. Examiner fallibility or inexperience in discerning colors may also result in false negatives. The possibility of a false negative leads many examiners to conduct a series of screening tests or, when warranted, to progress directly to more narrowly focused screening tests.

Specificity is the key to the forensic identification of controlled substances. There is no one method that will work as a specific test for any and all exhibits at any and all times. The choice of which specific method one utilizes must be determined by the type of controlled substance, the concentration of the controlled substance in the sample, the nature of the diluents and adulterants, the available instrumentation, and the experience of the examiner. There is an ongoing debate whether one can achieve this scientific certainty by combining a series of nonspecific tests. This is discussed later in this section.

1.7.1.1 Physical Characteristics

Occasionally an experienced forensic analyst can just look at an exhibit in a drug case and determine the probable nature of the substance. However, "probable natures" are not enough for

THE CRIMINALISTICS OF CONTROLLED SUBSTANCES

an identification, and most examiners will usually conduct more than one test before reporting the presence of a controlled substance. The morphology of botanical substances such as marijuana and the peyote cactus are familiar enough to many laboratory analysts. Marijuana is one of those controlled substances that is examined with such frequency in the laboratory that a preliminary identification is probable based on the morphology of the botanical substance, gross physical appearance, texture, and odor. However, even after a microscopic examination of the cystolithic hairs using a microscope, the modified Duquenois–Levine test is usually run to corroborate the identification. The peyote cactus with its button-like appearance is also unique. In a like manner, the identification of the opium poppy requires a confirmation of the morphine; and the identification of the psilocybin mushroom requires an identification of the psilocybin or the psilocin.

The physical characteristics of these four agronomic substances might enable an expert witness with a background in plant taxonomy and botany to make an identification based solely on these characteristics. The forensic analyst relies on the physical characteristics and corroborating chemical examinations to identify these materials as controlled substances.

1.7.1.2 Color Tests

The color test is usually the first chemical examination examiners conduct after a package suspected of containing controlled substances is opened and weighed. Small amounts of the unknown material are placed in depressions in a porcelain spot plate or a disposable plastic or glass spot plate. Chemical reagents are then added to the depressions and the results noted: color changes, the way in which the color changes take place (flashing or bleeding), the rate at which the color changes take place, and the intensity of the final colors. The most common color reagents are the Marquis reagent for opium alkaloids, amphetamines, and phenethylamines such as MDA or MDMA; cobalt thyocyanate reagent for cocaine and phencyclidine (PCP); Dille-Koppanyi reagent for barbiturates; Duquenois reagent for marijuana; and Ehrlich's reagent for LSD. A more complete listing of these tests is available in the literature.[1] Many of these tests are multistep and multicomponent.

These color tests are designed as a starting place for the examiner in deciding how to proceed as the pyramid of focus narrows in forming a conclusion. Adulterants and diluents can also cause color changes and are sometimes said to be responsible for "false positives." The resulting color changes are not really false. They simply reflect the presence of a substance that is not the primary focus of the analytical scheme. Problems of "false negatives" and "false positives" are usually recognized very early in the analytical scheme, and they are resolved logically and rationally.

1.7.1.3 Thin-Layer Chromatography

Thin-layer chromatography (TLC) is a separation technique. The method utilizes a glass plate that is usually coated evenly with a thin layer of adsorbant. The most commonly used adsorbant is silica gel. A small amount of the sample is put into solution with a chemical solvent. A capillary pipette is then used to place a small amount of the liquid onto the TLC plate approximately 2 cm from the bottom of the plate. A second capillary pipette containing a small amount of a known controlled substance in solution is used to place a second spot on the plate usually next to, but not overlapping, the first spot.

The plate is then placed into a tank containing a solvent system, which rises about 1 cm from the bottom of the tank. Through capillary action, the solvent will migrate up the plate, and the components of the unknown will usually separate as the solvent migrates. The separated components can usually be visualized using long-wave or shortwave ultraviolet light, a chemical spray, or some combination of both. The distance each sample migrates is then divided by the distance the solvent in the tank migrates up the plate (know as the Rf value). The result is then compared to published values that have been established for pure samples of the abused drugs. If one of the components of the unknown migrates the same distance up the plate as the known, the examiner has another piece of corroborating information. If the unknown does not contain a component that migrates the same distance as the known, there are many explanations. Perhaps the known and unknown are not the same. Perhaps there is a component in the unknown solution that is binding the chemical of interest to the silica gel. The explanations for matches are numerous. The explanations for non-matches are just as numerous.

The literature is replete with values for drug/solvent migration ratios. However, these values can be affected by many factors, including the storage conditions of the TLC plates and solvent temperature. It is not uncommon for the Rf values in the laboratory to differ from those in the literature. The importance of a TLC analysis lies in its ability to separate components in a mixture. A match is another piece of corroborating information. A non-match can usually be explained.

Using TLC to identify marijuana, hashish, or hash oil is a much more complicated process than using it to identify other controlled substances.[2] The TLC analysis of cannabis exhibits results in a series of bands on the thin-layer plate. Depending on the solvent system, the number of bands can range from at least three to at least six bands.[3] Each band will have a specific color and lie at a specified place on the plate corresponding to the known cannabinoids in a standard marijuana, hashish, or THC sample.[4] The key point here is that this type of identification involves a specific chromatographic pattern as opposed to one spot where a known is compared directly with an unknown. Even with the increased specificity of a TLC analysis in the examination of cannabis or a cannabis derivative, a modified Duquenois–Levine test is suggested.

1.7.2 Confirmatory Chemical Tests

1.7.2.1 Microcrystal Identifications

Microcrystal tests are conducted using a polarized light microscope and chemical reagents. These microscopic examinations are not screening tests. The analyst will usually place a small amount of the sample on a microscope slide, add a chemical reagent, and note the formation of a specific crystal formation. These crystals are formed from specified reagents. There should be very little subjectivity in evaluating a microcrystal test.[5] Either the crystal forms or it does not form. If the appropriate crystal forms in the presence of the reagent, the drug is present. If the crystal does not form and the drug is present, the problem is usually one in which the drug concentration is too dilute, or the reagent has outlived its shelf life.

One disadvantage of microcrystal tests is the absence of a hard copy of what the analyst sees. Unless a photograph is taken of the crystal formation, the examiner cannot present for review documentation of what he saw under the microscope. Microcrystal tests are an excellent way of evaluating the relative concentration of a drug in a sample to determine the kind of extraction technique for separation and further confirmation.

1.7.2.2 Gas Chromatography

Gas chromatography (GC) has been a standard operating procedure in forensic science laboratories for the past three decades. In this technique, a gaseous mobile phase is passed through a column containing a liquid-coated, stationary, solid, support phase. The most common form of GC uses a capillary column of a very fine diameter for separating the component of a mixture. The sample is usually put into solution using an organic solvent such as methanol. The liquid is then introduced into the injection port of the gas chromatograph using a fine needle syringe capable of delivering microliter quantities of the solution. The amount injected depends on the concentration of the sample: 1 µl (one one-hundredth of a milliliter) of 1 mg of solute per 1 ml of solvent is a typical injection amount. The sample is vaporized in the heated injection port, and with the aid of a carrier gas travels through the long capillary column where the different components are separated. There are many different kinds of capillary columns with different internal coatings, lengths (which

THE CRIMINALISTICS OF CONTROLLED SUBSTANCES 43

can vary from one foot up to tens of meters), and diameters (measured in micrometers). This separation is determined by the polarity and molecular size of each component. Each component exits the column onto a detector. A flame ionization detector (FID) is the most common detector used in most laboratories. Other types of less frequently encountered detectors include the nitrogen phosphorus detector and the electron capture detector.

As each component elutes from the column through the FID, a signal is generated, which results in a "peak" on a recording device. The recorder is used to document the resulting data. This recorder is usually a part of a data station that not only generates a representation of the chromatogram on a monitor, but also controls instrument parameters and ensures the consistency of the analysis. The peaks of interest are evaluated by their retention times (RTs) and by the areas under the peaks. The retention time data can be used either as confirmation of the probable identity of the substance generating the peak, or the data can be evaluated as screening information to determine the possible presence of a controlled substance. These RT data are compared to the retention time of a known standard injected onto the same column in the same instrument at the same temperature and rate flow conditions. The RTs of the known and the unknown should be almost the same within a very narrow window. The area under the peak can be used to quantitatively determine the relative concentration of the substance.

There are some disadvantages of GC. Retention times are not absolute and usually fall within a narrow window. Other compounds may fall within this same RT window. One way to overcome this problem is to analyze the same sample using a second capillary column with a different internal coating and to note its retention time as compared to the known standard. The values should be the same within a narrow RT window. A second disadvantage of GC is that some samples degrade in the injection liner at high temperatures and must be evaluated by using a derivatizing agent. This derivatizing agent is added to the drug and forms a molecular complex. The molecule complex remains intact as it passes from the injection port, through the column, and onto the detector.

GC by itself is a very powerful tool for the forensic analyst. Its most useful application today remains one in which it is interfaced with a mass spectrometer (mass selective detector), which serves as a detector and separate instrumental identification method unto itself. Gas chromatography/mass spectrometry (GS/MS) is discussed later in this section.

1.7.2.3 *High-Performance Liquid Chromatography*

This chromatographic technique is also a separation technique, but with a bit more selectivity than GC. In high-performance liquid chromatography (HPLC), the mobile phase is a liquid and the stationary phase is a solid support or a liquid-coated solid support. In GC, a carrier gas is used to carry the sample through the chromatography column. In HPLC, a high-pressure pump is used to carry the solvent containing the compound of interest through the column. Separation results from selective interactions between the stationary phase and the liquid mobile phase.[6] Unlike GC, the mobile phase plays a major role in the separation. HPLC can be used for the direct analysis of a wide spectrum of compounds and is not dependent on solute volatility or polarity. The operator need not worry about chemical changes in the molecule that can occur in GC due to thermal degradation.

HPLC chromatograms are evaluated based on retention time and area under the peak of interest. Retention time is not an absolute value, but a time within a narrowly defined window. The five basic parts of the liquid chromatograph include the solvent reservoir, the pump, the sample injection system, the column, and the detector. A recorder is used to document the resulting data. This recorder is usually a part of a data station that controls instrument parameters and ensures the consistency of the analysis. The most common detectors are the ultraviolet/visible detector (UV/VIS), the florescence detector, the electrochemical detector, the refractive index detector, and the mass spectrometer. The UV/VIS detector is the most widely used device, and it is dependent on the ability of the solute to absorb UV or visible light. The variable wavelength detector allows the analyst to select any wavelength in the UV or visible range. The diode array or rapid scan detector is also used, which allows a rapid scan of the entire UV spectrum to identify the components eluting from the column.

Because the components elute from the UV detector in solution, they do not undergo degradation or destruction. This one very useful characteristic of HPLC affords the analyst the option of collecting fractions of the eluent for further analysis. This is not possible in GC because the eluent is destroyed by the FID.

1.7.2.4 Capillary Electrophoresis

Capillary electrophoresis (CE) is a technique that separates components on the basis of charge-to-mass ratios under the influence of an electrical field. It uses high voltage for fast separations and high efficiencies. Osmotic flow is the main driving force in CE, especially at higher pH values, and results primarily from the interaction of positive ions in solution with the silanol groups on the capillary in the presence of an applied field. Narrow bore capillary columns of uncoated fused silica are used for heat dissipation during the separation process. The detector is normally a UV detector.

Micellar electrokinetic capillary chromatography (MECC) is a form of CE that allows for the separation of cations, neutral solutes, and anions.

CE has several advantages over HPLC and GC. The method can be used with ionic and neutral solutes, which present problems in GC. There is a higher efficiency, resolving power, and speed of analysis compared to HPLC. From a cost perspective, CE requires much less solvent than HPLC, and the CE capillary column is much less expensive than the HPLC or GC capillary columns. Two disadvantages of CE are the limited sensitivity for UV detection (30 to 100 times less than that of HPLC), and fraction collection is troublesome because of mechanical problems and small sample size. This technique uses a micelle as a run buffer additive to give separations that are both electrophoretic and chromatographic.

One of the advantages of MECC is the ability to separate racemic mixtures of compounds into the D- and L-isomers. This is an ability that is extremely valuable when identifying compounds where one isomer is controlled (dextropropoxyphene) and the other isomer is not controlled (levopropoxyphene). This is usually accomplished by adding cyclodextrins to the run buffer.

1.7.2.5 Infrared Spectrophotometry

Infrared (IR) spectrophotometry is one of the most specific instrumental methods for the identification of a controlled substance. A pure drug as a thin film on a KBr salt plate, or as crystals mounted in a KBr matrix, is placed into the sample compartment of the IR spectrophotometer. A source of electromagnetic radiation in the form of light from a Nernst glower passes light through the sample. The instrument, through a mechanical means, splits the beam into a reference beam and an incident beam. The reference beam passes unobstructed through a monochrometer to a photometer; the incident beam passes through the mounted sample through the same monochrometer to the photometer. The reference beam passes 100% unobstructed to the photometer. The incident beam passing through the sample has some of its energy absorbed by the sample. This energy is absorbed at different wavelengths across the infrared spectrum from 4000 cm^{-1} down to 250 cm^{-1}. The amount of relative absorption and where on this spectrum the absorption takes place are dependent on the molecular structure and, more specifically, the functional groups of the drug. Different functional groups and molecular interactions brought on by symmetrical and asymmetrical molecular stretching vibrations and in-plane and out-of-plane bending vibrations result in a number of peaks and valleys on the IR chart. The resultant spectrum is usually formed on an x/y coordinate axis. The wavelength (μ) or wave number (cm^{-1}) where the absorption occurs is depicted on the

THE CRIMINALISTICS OF CONTROLLED SUBSTANCES   45

x-axis, and a measure of the amount of light absorbed by the sample, but usually referenced by transmittance units from 0 to 100%, is depicted on the *y*-axis.

The IR spectrum of a suspected drug results in a specific pattern that can be used to positively determine the identity of the substance. For most controlled substances, the resulting spectrum consists of 20 to 70 peaks. These peaks form a pattern that is unique to the chemical structure of the drug. This pattern can then be compared with a reference IR spectrum of a primary drug standard. If the analyst determines that the two spectra match within the limits of scientific certainty, an identification is possible. It is rarely, if ever, possible to overlay the reference spectra with the spectra of the unknown and have a "perfect match." The analyst is looking for a match in the patterns. Any shifts in peak intensity or wave number must be evaluated in conjunction with the pattern. Small shifts of 1 or 2 cm^{-1} and minor intensity variations of individual peaks are expected. However, major variations must be evaluated on a case by case basis. Some authors refer to IR as a "fingerprint" identification method. This implies an ability to overlay two spectra and obtain a perfect match in every way. This degree of perfection is rarely, if ever, possible.

Another factor that must be considered is that when two spectra are being compared peak-by-peak as opposed to pattern-by-pattern, they ideally should be from the same instrument and collected at about the same time. Comparing a literature reference spectrum with an unknown for a pattern match is acceptable. Comparing the same literature reference spectrum wave number by wave number, absolute transmittance value by absolute transmittance value will probably result in minor differences.

IR does have limitations. To obtain an acceptable spectrum, the sample must be very clean and dry. For forensic exhibits, this usually means that most samples must go through extraction processes to remove impurities. In the past, sample size was a problem. However, because of advances in Fourier transform IR technology and the interfacing of an IR spectrophotometer with a microscope, evaluating microgram quantities of a sample results in excellent spectra that are conclusive for the identification of a controlled substance. IR has very definite limitations in its ability to quantitate controlled substances, and differentiating some isomers of controlled substances can pose problems.

1.7.2.6 *Gas Chromatography/Mass Spectrometry*

GC/MS is by far the most popular method of identifying controlled substances in the forensic science laboratory. In this method, a gas chromatograph is interfaced with a mass selective detector (MSD). The sample undergoing an examination is placed into solution with a solvent such as methanol. A very small injection volume of 1 or 2 µl is injected into the GC injection port. It then travels through the column where the different components of the sample are separated. The separated components can then be directed into the ionization chamber of the MSD where they are bombarded by an electron beam. In electron impact gas chromatography/mass spectrometry (EI MS), high-energy electrons impact the separated component molecules. The resulting spectrum of each component is typically complex with a large number of mass fragments. These fragments are represented as peaks of varying intensity that provide the basis for comparison with a primary reference standard. The components are then ionized and positively charged. This ionization also results in a fission or fragmentation process. The molecular fragments traverse into a magnetic field where they are separated according to their masses. In this magnetic field, larger mass fragments are less affected by the magnetic field, and smaller fragments are more affected and undergo a deflection. Upon exiting the magnetic field, these fragments impact a detector losing the charge generated by the beam of electrons impacting the sample. The result of this fragmentation process is a pattern unique for the substance that is being analyzed.

The resulting mass spectrum consists of an *x/y* coordinate axis. The numerical value on the *x*-axis represents the mass number determined by the number of neutrons and protons in the nucleus. It is usually the molecular weight of a specific fragment. The largest magnitude peak on the *x*-axis will often be the **molecular ion** and will represent the molecular weight of the unfragmented compound. There will usually be a very small peak to the right of the molecular ion which represents the molecular weight plus 1. The y-axis represents the relative abundance of each peak comprising the mass spectrum. The tallest peak on the y-axis is the **base peak** and represents that part of the molecule that is the most stable and undergoes the least amount of fragmentation. The base peak is assigned a relative abundance value of 100. The other peaks in the resulting spectrum are assigned relative values along the y-axis.

The numerical values on the x- and y-axis are calculated and assigned by the data station, which is interfaced with the mass spectrometer. The accuracy of these numbers is predicated on the fact that the instrument has been properly tuned. This tuning process can be compared to checking the channel tuning on a television set. This might be accomplished by opening a television guide to determine what programs are scheduled at a particular hour. The television is then turned on and the program for each channel checked. If the programs cited in the television magazine appear on corresponding channels at the proper times, the television has been proved to be properly tuned. The tuning of a mass analyzer presents an analogous situation.

The tuning process of a mass analyzer involves a procedure in which a chemical of a known molecular weight and fragmentation pattern is analyzed and the resulting data evaluated. This process includes verifying instrument parameters and the resulting spectrum. If the response of the tuning process falls within specified limits, the mass spectrometer is deemed operationally reliable, and the resulting data can be considered reliable. One such chemical used to tune mass spectrometers is perflurotributylamine (PFTBA).

Fragmentation patterns of controlled substances are typically unique. Once a fragmentation pattern has been obtained, the forensic analyst should be able to explain the major peaks of the spectrum and relate them to the molecular structure. If properly evaluated, mass spectral data can usually be used to form a conclusion as to the identity of a controlled substance.

GC/MS has many advantages in the analysis of controlled substances. The sample being analyzed need not be pure. Multicomponent samples are separated and each soluble organic component can be individually identified. The analyst must be aware of isomeric compounds that have very similar chemical structures and similar fragmentation patterns. These kinds of situations can usually be handled by noting the GC retention time data to discriminate between similar compounds. Possible coelution of compounds from the capillary GC column and thermal degradation as noted in the gas chromatography section of this chapter should also be recognized. GC/MS does not allow the forensic analyst to directly identify the salt form of the drug. This task can be accomplished by considering the solubility properties of the drug being analyzed. In using this knowledge and performing extractions prior to injection onto the GC column, the salt form can be determined indirectly.

When all methods of instrumental analysis of controlled substances are considered, GC/MS is recognized in most instances as one of the efficient analytical techniques. If the analyst is cognizant of maintaining instrument reliability standards and the guidelines of mass spectral interpretation, GC/MS affords one of the highest degrees of specificity in the identification of controlled substances.

1.7.2.7 Nuclear Magnetic Resonance Spectroscopy

Nuclear magnetic resonance (NMR) spectroscopy is one of the most powerful instrumental techniques available to the forensic chemist. In those laboratories fortunate enough to have NMR technology, extensive capabilities exist. Data interpretation of NMR spectra requires a high degree of expertise. This instrumental technique allows the analyst to detect paramagnetic atoms. (^{1}H, ^{2}H, ^{13}C, ^{15}N, ^{17}O, ^{31}P, ^{11}B, and ^{19}F are examples.) Most forensic applications of NMR focus on ^{1}H and ^{13}C. The resonant frequency of hydrogen (^{1}H) in the current high-field magnets ranges from 200 to 750 mHz. This instrument generates a high magnetic field more than capable of damaging encrypted data on the back of a credit card. The NMR is a very expensive instrument requiring a high degree of specialized expertise to maintain and interpret the resulting data. The NMR is the one instrument that affords the

THE CRIMINALISTICS OF CONTROLLED SUBSTANCES

analyst the ability to determine both the molecular structure and the three-dimensional orientation of some individual atoms of the molecule. This means that structural isomers can be determined directly. However, the extent of this kind of information is usually required only by research scientists in those instances where no other information is available from other instrumental methods, or where no primary analytical standard is available to confirm the presence of a controlled substance.

The major component of the NMR spectrometer is a high-field super-conducting magnet. The sample is dissolved in a deuterated solvent and then transferred to a long cylindrical glass tube usually measuring 5 mm in diameter. The tube is placed into the NMR probe located near the center of the magnetic field. In proton NMR, the magnetic field causes the hydrogen atoms on the molecule to orient in a particular direction. To obtain high-resolution spectra, the field produced by the magnet must be homogeneous over the entire area of the sample in the probe. The resonance frequencies for all protons in a molecule may be different. These frequencies are dependent on the molecular environment of the nucleus. This correlation between resonance frequencies and molecular environment enables the analyst to make judgments regarding the structure of the drug being analyzed.

The NMR spectrum is traced on a two-dimensional x/y coordinate axis. By evaluating an NMR proton spectrum, an analyst can determine an important factor that facilitates the identification of the compound — the area under each peak indicates the number of nuclei that are undergoing a transition and the number of protons that are present.

There are other types of examinations that are possible with high-field NMR. A carbon-13 (^{13}C) evaluation enables an analyst to determine the number of carbons and their relative positioning in the molecule. ^{13}C is an isotope of the more abundant ^{12}C. About 1% of naturally occurring carbon is ^{13}C. There are two additional NMR "2D experiments" that are very valuable to the forensic analyst. Correlation spectroscopy (COSY) measures proton to proton (^{1}H to ^{1}H) interactions; and nuclear overhauser effect spectroscopy (NOESY) measures the interaction of protons that are close to one another, but not necessarily on adjoining atoms. Carbon-13, COSY, and NOESY spectra are all much more difficult to interpret and require specialized knowledge.

In the forensic analysis of controlled substances, most molecules comprise carbon and hydrogen. Proton NMR provides a unique spectral pattern that can be used to identify a controlled substance. This pattern also enables the analyst to distinguish between the basic and a salt form of the drug. NMR cannot distinguish halogenated salt forms. For instance, it cannot distinguish between heroin hydrochloride and heroin hydrobromide. But it can distinguish between a heroin salt and heroin base.

REFERENCES

1. Johns, S.H., Wist, A.A., and Najam, A.R., Spot tests: a color chart reference for forensic chemists, *J. Forensic Sci.*, 24, 631–649, 1979.
2. Hughes, R.B. and Kessler, R.R., Increased safety and specificity in the thin-layer chromatographic identification of marijuana, *J. Forensic Sci.*, 24, 842–846, 1979.
3. Baggi, T.R., 3-Methylbenzthiazolinone-2-hydrazone (MBTH) as a new visualization reagent in the detection of cannabinoids on thin-layer chromatography, *J. Forensic Sci.*, 25, 691–694, 1980.
4. Parker, K.D., Wright, J.A., Halpern, A.F., and Hine, C.H., Preliminary report on the separation and quantitative determination of cannabis constituents present in plant material and when added to urine by thin-layer and gas chromatography, *Bull. Narc.*, 20, 9–14, 1968.
5. Fulton, C.C., *Modern Microcrystal Tests for Drugs*, John Wiley & Sons, New York, 1969.
6. Lurie, I.S. and Witmer, J.D., *High Performance Liquid Chromatography*, Marcel Dekker, New York, 1983.

1.7.3 Controlled Substances Examinations

Every examination made by a forensic chemist has a potential legal ramification or consequence. Forensic chemists must be prepared to depart from the familiar natural science setting of the laboratory and to enter the confrontational setting of the courtroom and be able to communicate with a prosecuting attorney, a defense attorney, a judge, 12 jurors, and on occasion, the press. The forensic chemist must be able to explain the significance of complicated analytical procedures to individuals with little or no scientific training. If the forensic analyst is to have any credibility on the witness stand, he must be able to describe what he has done in terminology understood by those individuals with whom he is communicating.

1.7.3.1 *Identifying and Quantitating Controlled Substances*

Whenever a controlled substance is identified, the possibility exists that an individual could be imprisoned or suffer some other legal consequence as a result. There is, therefore, an absolute, uncompromised requirement for certainty in the identification of controlled substances. Prior to 1960, the results of microscopic crystal tests, color screening tests, and TLC were considered definitive. From the 1960s through the mid-1970s, UV spectrophotometry and GC gained acceptance. It is interesting to look back 30 years and contemplate the absolute faith placed in a retention time on a gas chromatogram, or upon the UV absorption maxima in acidic or basic solutions. In some instances these numerical values were measured with a ruler!

From 1975 through 1985 there were major advances in IR and MS. During those years "specificity," as we understand the term today, was, for the first time, actually attainable in most cases. As the technology continually evolved, with increased Fourier transform peak resolution in IR and NMR, and multicomponent separations improved with capillary column GS, specificity also increased.

In the mid-1980s the advent of "designer drugs" (properly referred to as "controlled substance analogues") resurrected the problem of specificity. In attempts at circumventing existing controlled substance laws, clandestine laboratory chemists began to alter chemical structures of controlled drugs by increasingly sophisticated syntheses. By replacing a methyl group with an ethyl group, or by using a five-membered ring instead of a six-membered ring in a synthesis, these clandestine laboratory chemists developed what at the time were non-controlled analogues. The Controlled Substance Analogue and Enforcement Act of 1986 was passed by Congress, largely as a response to this problem. This particular piece of legislation also reinforced the responsibility of the chemist to accurately discriminate between controlled substances and endless lists of possible analogues.

A direct consequence of the new law's passage was the development of analytical procedures in Fourier transform infrared spectrophotometry (FTIR), Fourier transform nuclear magnetic resonance spectroscopy (FTNMR), gas chromatography/Fourier transform infrared spectroscopy (GC/FTIR), and CE. These instrumental methods have made their way into the forensic science laboratory and now provide the increased specificity required by the courts.

Controlled substances sold on the street are usually mixed with adulterants and diluents in a crude and mostly unspecified manner. In some laboratories, analysts are required to identify and quantitate both the controlled substance and the adulterant drugs and diluent materials. Color tests, TLC, and microcrystal tests of the pre-1960s vintage are still used for screening. These testing procedures were valid then and are still valid today, but today additional instrumental techniques are utilized to make the absolute identification and quantitation.

After the analysis has been completed, it must be documented. The final report must be clear, concise, and accurate, with all conclusions substantiated by analytical data. The data may be in the form of notations on paper in the analyst's writing, or on chromatograms, spectra, or other instrumental printouts. Dates must be checked, and the documented description of the exhibit(s) must be consistent with the actual exhibit. Each time a report is signed, the analyst places his or her reputation and credibility before the scrutiny of the court and his or her peers. Discovering a "mistake" after the report has been submitted to the courts is not good.

Cocaine can exist as either the hydrochloride (HCl) salt or as the base. Pursuant to federal law, there are sentencing guidelines based on the identification of cocaine as either the base or as the

THE CRIMINALISTICS OF CONTROLLED SUBSTANCES

salt form (usually HCl). Cocaine can be adulterated with benzocaine, procaine, lidocaine, or any combination of these non-controlled drugs, and further diluted with mannitol, lactose, or other processing sugars. A variety of instrumental techniques can be used to distinguish cocaine HCl from cocaine base. FTIR spectrophotometry is commonly available and used in many laboratories. The IR spectra of cocaine HCl and cocaine base are quite different and easily distinguished. The IR spectrum of a cocaine HCl sample mixed with an adulterant presents a problem. The same sample analyzed by GC/FTIR presents the chemist with a total response chromatogram showing all peaks in a mixture. The resulting IR spectrum and mass spectrum are identifiable. However, in this technique, cocaine HCl and cocaine base cannot be distinguished. At this point, NMR can provide a solution to distinguishing the two forms of cocaine and identifying the adulterants.

The solubility properties of controlled substances can be used to separate different forms of controlled substances. For instance, cocaine base is soluble in diethyl ether; cocaine HCl is insoluble. Therefore, if an analyst is analyzing a material that is believed to be cocaine in a questionable form, the analyst can try placing the material into solution with diethyl ether, separate the ether from the insolubles, evaporate the diethyl ether, and analyze the resulting powder by GC/MS. The resulting cocaine spectrum would indicate the presence of cocaine base because cocaine HCl would not have gone into solution.

Methamphetamine is produced in clandestine laboratories from the reaction of ephedrine with hydriodic acid and red phosphorus, or from the reaction of phenyl-2-propanone (P-2-P) with methylamine. Methamphetamine samples submitted to the forensic science laboratory usually contain precursors from the synthesis, by-products from side reactions, and adulterants such as nicotinamide that have been added by the clandestine laboratory operator. As is true of the mass spectrum of some other phenethylamines, the mass spectrum of methamphetamine may not provide enough specificity for positive identification. The most accurate way to identify many phenethylamines is with IR. However, NMR is at least as specific as FTIR, and it also allows for an identification in the presence of diluents. Unfortunately, NMR is not available in many laboratories. Nicotinamide is one of the more commonly encountered adulterants with methamphetamine and can easily be distinguished from isonicotinamide by NMR spectroscopy.

The IR spectrum of methamphetamine hydrochloride in a potassium chloride salt matrix is very specific, and GC/FTIR is excellent at separating the components of a methamphetamine sample. However, this method requires great care in selecting the optimized temperature and flow parameters, and column selection.

GC/MS is the method most often used for identifying heroin. The mass spectrum of heroin is very specific. Heroin is relatively simple to separate, and identification of the degradation products and the by-products of the heroin synthesis, from morphine and acetic anhydride, is relatively straightforward. Because morphine is derived from opium, many of the by-products from the opium processing are carried over to the final heroin product. Acetylcodeine and acetylmorphine are clearly identified from the corresponding mass spectra. The GC/FTIR also provides excellent spectra for making identifications of heroin, its by-products, degradation products, and precursors. The chloroform insoluble diluents from heroin samples can also be identified in a potassium bromide matrix by FTIR. These materials will usually consist of sugars such as mannitol and inositol. When the heroin has been isolated from diluents and adulterants, FTIR and NMR can be utilized to confirm the salt form of the heroin.

Phencyclidine, more properly identified as phenylcyclohexylpiperidine (PCP), is usually submitted to the laboratory as an exhibit of PCP base in diethyl ether, a powder, or sprayed or coated on marijuana. The analysis of PCP is relatively direct by GC/MS. The resulting mass spectrum is specific. The GC/FTIR spectrum of PCP is not as specific when one compares this spectrum with that of PCP analogues and precursors such as phenylcyclohexyl carbonitrile (PCC) and phenylcyclohexyl pyrrolidine (PCPy). FTIR spectrophotometry of the solid in a potassium bromide matrix is very specific. A word of caution is in order for anyone handling PCP. PCP is a substance that is believed to be easily absorbed through the skin of the analyst. Minimum handling is recommended.

1.7.3.2 Identifying Adulterants and Diluents

The terms *adulterants* and *diluents* are sometimes used in the context of illicitly distributed controlled substances. Adulterants are chemicals added to illicit drugs that, in and of themselves, can effect some sort of a physiological response. This response can range from very mild to quite severe. Diluents are chemicals added to controlled substances that are used more as fillers than to elicit a physiological response. They can be added to affect the color and composition for the sake of satisfying the user. Adulterants and diluents are usually added to the controlled substance mixture by those involved in illicit distribution. There is a third class of materials that is found in controlled substance mixtures. This class includes by-products. These by-products can be processing by-products, or they can exist as naturally occurring by-products found in botanical substances such as the coca leaf or the opium poppy.

Most "street" exhibits of heroin and cocaine contain adulterants and diluents. Samples taken from large-scale, brick-size, kilogram seizures will be relatively pure. Except for some by-products from the opium poppy and the coca leaf, there will be little in the way of foreign materials. Adulterants are encountered, in increasing proportions, as the heroin and cocaine progress down the distribution chain from the main supplier to the dealers to the users.

Adulterants commonly encountered in heroin include quinine, procaine, acetaminophen, caffeine, diphenhydramine, aspirin, phenobarbital, and lidocaine. Adulterants commonly encountered in cocaine include procaine, benzocaine, and lidocaine. Diluents found in heroin include different kinds of starches. It is not uncommon to find in heroin substances, such as calcium carbonate, that had been added during the morphine extraction processes. Diluents found in both cocaine and heroin include lactose, mannitol, sucrose, and dextrose.

The identification of adulterants and diluents may or may not be a requirement as a part of the identification scheme in the forensic science laboratory. In most instances, the requirements of the judicial system will be limited to the identification of the controlled substance. This will usually be accomplished by separating the sample into its component parts, and then identifying all or some of these components. In the case of a heroin exhibit, cut with quinine and mannitol, a capillary GC/MS examination might result in a chromatogram and corresponding spectra with an acetylcodeine peak, an acetylmorphine peak, a morphine peak, a quinine peak, and a heroin peak. The first two peaks are most probably processing by-products; the morphine is from the opium poppy; the heroin is the main peak of interest, and the quinine has probably been added as an adulterant. There is no need to separate the components by extractions to make the identifications. However, if the analyst is desirous of conducting an IR examination or an NMR examination to identify the heroin, an extraction of the heroin from a $3 N$ hydrochloric acid medium using chloroform is an option. Depending on whether the heroin exists as a salt (heroin hydrochloride) or as heroin base, a set of serial extractions can be conducted to isolate the heroin from the quinine and the other substances. The identification of cocaine in a mixture follows the same procedures. Depending on the type of analysis, the cocaine may or may not need to be chemically separated from the adulterants for an identification.

The simplest way to identify diluents in controlled substance mixtures is by microscopic identification. Common diluents along with the sugars/carbohydrates/starches described above include sodium chloride, calcium carbonate, and various types of amorphous materials. Because of their optical properties, these materials lend themselves well to a microscopic identification. Chemical separations are fairly easy because these materials are usually insoluble in solvents such as diethyl ether or hexane, and slightly soluble in solvents such as methanol. Most organic materials are soluble in methanol or some other polar solvent. The sugars/carbohydrates/starches can be further identified using IR following the separation if only one sugar is present. If not, HPLC can be used to identify the sugars.

THE CRIMINALISTICS OF CONTROLLED SUBSTANCES

Even if the identification of all adulterants, diluents, and by-products is not required in the final report generated by the analyst, such information can prove useful in evaluating trends and possible distribution patterns.

1.7.3.3 *Quantitating Controlled Substances*

A number of different methods can be used to quantitate controlled substances. Capillary column GC or HPLC are probably the two most utilized instrumental methods to accomplish this task. The choice of which instrumental method to use depends on the chemical properties of the substance in question. GC works well with those compounds that are not highly polar, are relatively stable at high temperatures, and are soluble in organic solvents such as methanol or chloroform. Even if these conditions exist, GC can still be used if a derivatizing agent is used.

If GC is used, the most common analytical method for quantitation involves the use of an internal standard, providing a consistent concentration of a known chemical in solution. To avoid the obvious problem of choosing an internal standard, which might be present in the sample as an adulterant or diluent, the internal standard can be a straight-chain hydrocarbon (tetracosane, eicosane, or dodecane) that is added in equal amounts to both the sample being analyzed and the calibration samples. The internal standard method is especially advantageous because the expected flame ionization detector response for the internal standard to the drug can be checked for each and every injection. The critical factor for each injection is the ratio of the detector response of the internal standard to the calibration solution of known concentration. This is especially critical if the sample size of the injection is off target by a minuscule amount. The absolute integration values for the known peak and the internal standard peaks may vary. However, the ratio will not be affected. If the detector is responding properly to the internal standard in solution, it is also responding properly for the substance being quantitated.

Controlled substances can also be quantitated using what is referred to as the external standard method. In this method, calibration standards of known concentrations are prepared. Injections are then made into the GC injection port, and a calibration table is established. The accuracy of this method is quite good, provided that the injection amounts used in establishing the calibration table are exactly the same from injection to injection. Even small variations of less than 10% volume, when dealing with a 1-μl injection, can lead to less than optimized results. This problem can be overcome by making multiple injections and checking the consistency of the detector response and the injection volume. The ability to be consistent can be developed by an analyst with a good eye. The ability to read the sample size on the microsyringe is, for some, as much an art as a scientific technique. Automatic injectors are now available on many gas chromatographs, which approach consistency from one injection to the next. However, this method will work only when there is a verifiable linear response of the detector within a specified concentration range.

In both the internal and external standard methods, there must be a linear response of the detector to the solutions of different concentrations. This is determined by injecting solutions of known concentrations and establishing a calibration table. With most instrument data stations, this is relatively simple. The instrument will then calculate the response ratio of internal standard to drug for the solution of unknown concentration and compare this to the response ratios of internal standard to drug for the solutions of known concentrations in the calibration table. This ratio can then be used to calculate the concentration of the drug that is being analyzed.

HPLC can be useful for quantitating controlled substances in solution. This instrumental method also measures the response of different compounds at different ultraviolet/visible absorption bands. These responses are then compared to calibration table values. Internal standards can be used in the same way they are used in GC quantitations. The limitations and comparisons of HPLC and GC are discussed elsewhere.

Ultraviolet/visible spectrophotometry (UV/VIS) is a technique that has been in use for many years. UV/VIS uses one of the basic tenets of physics — Beer's law. Absorption of monochromatic light is proportional to the concentration of a sample in solution. The concentration of an exhibit in solution can be determined by comparison with calibration tables. This type of analysis is dependent on the solubility properties of the substance being quantitated in acid, basic, and organic solutions. The UV/VIS method is accurate and reliable only when the compound of interest is pure with no interfering substances. GC and HPLC are used more often because of the added reliability check provided by the internal standard methodology.

NMR spectrometry can also be used for the quantitation of controlled substances. The quantitative analytical techniques in NMR are more complicated than those discussed above and require a specialized instrumental expertise.

All of the methods discussed are reliable and accurate when properly and conscientiously conducted. There is one very important difference that applies to any quantitative method when compared to an identification method. With proper methods, an analyst can make an identification of a controlled substance with scientific certainty. The quantitation of a controlled substance will usually result in values falling within a narrowly defined "window" of from one-tenth to one or two absolute percent. The reported value will usually be an average value.

1.7.3.4 Reference Standards

The first step in ensuring the accuracy of the identification of any controlled substance should be a collection of authenticated reference standards. Reference standards for the forensic science examinations should be 98+% pure. They can be purchased from a reputable manufacturer or distributor, synthesized by an organic chemist within the laboratory, or purified from a bulk secondary standard by using an appropriate methodology. "Reference Standards" that have been authenticated are available from the United States Pharmacopoeia (USP) and National Formulary (NF). Samples obtained from any other source should be authenticated using the appropriate methodology. This authentication process will involve a two-step process of first positively identifying the proposed reference standard and then determining the purity of this standard.

At a minimum, the identification of a reference standard should be conducted using IR and MS. The resulting spectra are then compared with reference spectra in the literature. The chemist should be able to evaluate data from both of these instruments and be able to explain the major peaks using, respectively, a functional group analysis or a molecular fragmentation analysis. If no literature spectra are available, a more sophisticated structural analysis such as NMR spectroscopy will be necessary to verify the chemical structure. Additional methods that can be used to supplement, but not replace, IR, MS, and NMR include optical crystallography, X-ray crystallography, and a melting point analysis.

The next step in the process is to quantitate the reference standard against a "primary standard." A primary standard is a sample that has been subjected to the authentication process and meets the criteria of a positive identification and 98+% purity. The quantitation methods of choice are GC or HPLC. With either method, the concentrations of the injections of both the primary standard and the authentication sample must be within the linear range of the detector. The method should utilize an internal standard. The results of all injections should have a relative standard deviation of less than 3%.[1]

If a primary standard is not available, a purity determination can be accomplished by a peak area percent determination using capillary GC with a flame ionization detector and HPLC using a photo-array ultraviolet detector. A third instrumental method using a differential scanning calorimeter (DSC) should also be considered. In a peak area percent analysis, the area percent of the standard compound is determined vs. any impurities that are present in the batch. A blank injection of the solvent is done prior to the standard injection to detect peaks common to both

THE CRIMINALISTICS OF CONTROLLED SUBSTANCES

the solvent and the authentication standard. The GC solution is checked for insolubles. If these insolubles are present, they can be isolated and identified by IR. Of course, if there are insolubles, the sample is no longer considered an authentication standard until it is purified and the foreign material is removed.

HPLC can also be used in a peak area percent analysis. For basic drugs, the analyst would use a gradient mobile phase using methanol and an acidic aqueous phosphate buffer. For neutral and acidic drugs, he would use a gradient with methanol and an acidic aqueous phosphate buffer containing sodium dodecyl sulfate. For anabolic steroids, he would use a methanol/water gradient mobile phase. As is the case with GC, with HPLC a blank injection of the solvent always precedes the injection of the authentication standard. Three wavelengths, 210 nm, 228 nm, and 240 nm, are monitored for most drugs. For anabolic steroids, the analyst should monitor 210 nm, 240 nm, and 280 nm. If the resulting UV spectra of all pertinent peaks are similar, the integration of the peaks with the most sensitive wavelengths is used for the calculation of purity.

DSC is a method of adding heat to a preweighed sample and monitoring temperature and heat flow as the sample goes through its melting point.[2] If decomposition does not occur during the melt, the peak shown on the thermogram can be used to determine the melting point and the molar concentration of any melt soluble impurities present. With these data, the analyst can determine the purity of the authentication standard. One drawback of DSC is that structurally dissimilar impurities such as sugars in a supposed heroin "standard" are not always detected by this method. This is because the impurity does not go into solution in the melting main component. With almost all authentication standards, most impurities will be structurally similar to the drug of interest. The dissimilar compounds should have been removed prior to the DSC analysis or detected by GC or HPLC.

REFERENCES

1. *CRC Handbook of Tables for Probability and Statistics*, 2nd ed., CRC Press, Boca Raton, FL, 1968, 5.
2. McNaughton, J.L. and Mortimer, C.T., Differential scanning calorimetry, *IRS; Phys. Chem. Ser. 2*, 10, 1975.

1.8 COMPARATIVE ANALYSIS

1.8.1 Determining Commonality of Source

Two different kinds of controlled substance analyses are routinely conducted in the forensic science laboratory. The first is the "identification." The goal is self-evident — to identify a controlled substance by name. The second, less common, type of analysis is the "comparative analysis." Its purpose is to determine a commonality of source. A comparative analysis will include a comprehensive examination of the sample's chemical and physical characteristics, with the goal of demonstrating, with a high degree of certainty, a common origin for two or more samples.[1]

Sometimes it is possible to determine when two items of evidence have a common origin just by physically fitting them together. This applies to exhibits such as a screwdriver and a broken blade, two large paint chips that have broken apart, or a piece of paper torn in two or more pieces. In the forensic examination of illicit drugs, it is possible to state with a high degree of certainty that two exhibits of a white powder share a common source. The wording in stating such a conclusion is critical. Words must be carefully selected to convey the conclusion clearly and concisely, without overstepping the scientific certainty that exists. The following quote, about two samples of cocaine, is from the transcript of a drug trial held in 1991. It illustrates the appropriate language to be used on such occasions.

After a review of all analytical data, it can be stated with a high level of scientific certainty and beyond a reasonable doubt that a close chemical relationship exists between [the two samples] strongly suggesting that they were derived from the same manufacturing process ... and that they were probably derived from the same batch.[2]

Before undertaking a detailed examination of two samples, a broad overview is desirable. The color and granularity of the exhibits should be examined, and then the components of the sample identified and quantitated. If all of the data from one exhibit compare favorably with all of the data from the second exhibit, the analyst can proceed to a second set of procedures to evaluate the processing by-products and trace materials in the exhibits. It is important to realize that to successfully evaluate two exhibits to determine commonality of source, each exhibit must be analyzed in the same way using the same methodology, instruments, and chemicals and solvents from the same containers.

Controlled substances such as cocaine and heroin are the simplest to compare because they are derived from botanical substances (the coca leaf and the opium poppy, respectively).[3,4] Many naturally occurring by-products from the plants are carried through the processing stages of the drugs, and these can be used to confirm the existence of a common source.

1.8.2 Comparing Heroin Exhibits

Capillary column gas chromatography (ccGC) and HPLC are the two methods most often utilized in comparing two or more heroin exhibits to determine whether they came from the same source. HPLC can be utilized in the first part of the analytical scheme because the components being evaluated usually are present in substantial amounts. The major components, including heroin, acetylmorphine, acetylcodeine, morphine, codeine, noscapine, papaverine, thebaine, and most diluents can be identified and quantitated. A high degree of resolving power is not required at this point in the analytical scheme. If the HPLC analysis demonstrates that the samples being compared are similar, the analyst proceeds to the second part of the analytical scheme.

In the second part of this scheme to evaluate the trace components of the exhibits, ccGC is usually the method of choice, both because of its resolving power and because of its ability to detect minute quantities of the component of interest. The second step of the isolation process involves multiple extractions and derivatizations to isolate the acidic and neutral compounds for analysis and evaluation. This process isolates the precursors, solvents, and respective contaminants, by-products, intermediates, and degradation products. It is desirable to remove the heroin from the sample during the extraction processes in order to keep most of the trace components at the same level of chromatographic attenuation. Once the heroin has been identified and quantitated, only then are the other elements analyzed. If after these two processes the analyst sees no chromatographic differences in the samples being evaluated, a conclusion can be formulated. The number of components from this second part of the process can number from 100 to 300. If all of these components are present in both exhibits at similar relative levels, a conclusion regarding commonality of source is warranted.

1.8.3 Comparing Cocaine Exhibits

The process is different for cocaine comparisons. For one thing, the cocaine need not be removed from the sample. Four different ccGC examinations can be conducted that evaluate and compare the by-products and impurities down to trace levels by:

1. Flame ionization gas chromatography (GC-FID) to evaluate cocaine hydrolysis products, manufacturing impurities, and naturally occurring alkaloids[5]

THE CRIMINALISTICS OF CONTROLLED SUBSTANCES

2. GC-FID to determine trimethoxy-substituted alkaloids as well as other minor naturally occurring tropanes[6]
3. Electron capture gas chromatography (GC-ECD) to determine the hydroxycocaines and N-nor related compounds[4]
4. GC-ECD to determine the ten intact truxillines[7]

These four gas chromatographic methods provide an in-depth evaluation of trace level components and allow the precise comparison of two different cocaine exhibits. The number of components evaluated ranges in the hundreds. These data provide the analyst with an abundance of analytical points to form a conclusion regarding commonality of source.

Extraction of the impurities and by-products can be accomplished using a derivatizing reagent.[8,9] Heptafluorobutyric anhydride (HFBA) is often used for this purpose. The GC-FID and GC-ECD analyses that follow will result in organic profiles of the many compounds from the cocaine and heroin samples being analyzed. A further MS analysis may serve to identify the chemical composition of many of the components of each exhibit. Many of the resulting peaks represent compounds formed during the manufacturing process; others will be oxidation or hydrolysis products of known compounds; and other peaks will have a degree of uncertainty regarding their exact chemical structure. However, what will be known is that these peaks are present in both exhibits being compared using the ccGC methods and represent cocaine and heroin manufacturing impurities or by-products.

REFERENCES

1. Perillo, B.A., Klein, R.F.X., and Franzosa, E.S., Recent advances by the U.S. drug enforcement administration in drug signature and comparative analysis, *Forensic Sci. Int.,* 69, 1–6, 1994.
2. Moore, J.M., Meyers, R.P., and Jiminez, M.D., The anatomy of a cocaine comparison case: a prosecutorial and chemistry perspective, *J. Forensic Sci.,* 38, 1305–1325, 1993.
3. Moore, J.M. and Cooper, D.A., The application of capillary gas chromatography-electron capture detection in the comparative analyses of illicit cocaine samples, *J. Forensic Sci.,* 38, 1286–1304, 1993.
4. Moore, J.M. and Casale, J.F., In-depth chromatographic analyses of illicit cocaine and its precursor, coca leaves, *J. Chromatogr.,* 674, 165–205, 1994.
5. Casale, J.F. and Waggoner, R.W., A chromatographic impurity signature profile analysis for cocaine using capillary gas chromatography, *J. Forensic Sci.,* 36, 1321–1330, 1991.
6. Casale, J.F. and Moore, J.M., 3´,4´,5´-Trimethoxy-substituted analogues of cocaine, *cis-/trans*-cinnamoylcocaine and tropacocaine: Characterization and quantitation of new alkaloids in coca leaf, coca paste and refined illicit cocaine, *J. Forensic Sci.,* 39, 462–472, 1994.
7. Moore, J.M., Cooper, D.A., Lurie, I.S., Kram, T.C., Carr, S., Harper, C., and Yeh, J., Capillary gas chromatographic-electron capture detection of coca leaf related impurities of illicit cocaine: 2,4-diphenylcyclobutane-1,3-dicarboxylic acids, 1,4-diphenylcyclobutane-2,3-dicarboxylic acids and their alkaloidal precursors, the truxillines, *J. Chromatogr.,* 410, 297–318, 1987.
8. Moore, J.M., Allen, A.C., and Cooper, D.A., Determination of manufacturing impurities in heroin by capillary gas chromatography with electron capture detection after derivatization with heptafluorobutyric acid, *Anal. Chem.,* 56, 642–646, 1984.
9. Moore, J.M., The application of chemical derivatization in forensic drug chemistry for gas and high performance liquid chromatographic methods of analysis, *Forensic Sci. Rev.,* 2, 79–124, 1990.

1.9 CLANDESTINE LABORATORIES

There are two kinds of clandestine laboratories. The first is the **operational** clandestine laboratory. This laboratory, usually operating in secrecy, is engaged in the production of controlled substances, precursors to controlled substances, or controlled substance homologues or analogues. The second is the **non-operational** clandestine laboratory. This usually is a storage facility that is under investigation because of information obtained from precursor and essential chemical monitoring.[1]

For the forensic scientist involved in the seizure of a clandestine laboratory, the task of evaluating the possibilities and probabilities begins prior to arrival at the laboratory site. The individual tasked with securing the laboratory for the purpose of collecting evidence must, for his own protection, be trained and certified competent in dealing with the safety and technical considerations of clandestine laboratory seizures. Forensic chemists may be asked to provide assistance in preparing search warrants based on available information, as when investigators know that certain chemicals and pieces of analytical equipment such as gas cylinders, and glassware such as large triple neck round bottom flasks have been purchased. This sort of information is critical in determining what kind of synthesis is taking place. The forensic scientist will also provide technical advice regarding the importance of specific safety considerations and offer suggestions on handling situations such as on-going reactions.

After the clandestine laboratory site has been secured by the appropriate law enforcement authorities, the forensic scientist may enter the site to evaluate the environment and decide on the most appropriate actions. The investigator's most important function is to minimize any health risk to enforcement personnel. This may involve ventilating the environment by opening doors, windows, and using a fan; securing open containers, turning off gases and water; and removing obstacles on the floor, which may prove hazardous to anyone entering the site. The investigator may also decide on whether chemical reactions in progress should be stopped or allowed to proceed. After all of these and other decisions are made and the site is secure, the forensic analyst will begin to sample, package, and mark evidence containers. This process will usually proceed slowly and methodically to ensure accuracy and completeness.

Once the clandestine laboratory has been seized and the evidence collected, the forensic analyst will proceed to the laboratory to complete the administrative processes of ensuring accountability and security. When the time approaches for the analytical procedures to commence, the person tasked with this process will attempt to identify as many of the samples as deemed necessary for the required judicial action. This may mean identifying any and all exhibits that were seized, or it may mean that only those exhibits required to form a conclusion regarding an identification of the final product are necessary. The extent of the analysis can be more of a legal question than a scientific question. The forensic scientist should be able to provide the basics of the reaction mechanisms. This information will be based on the chemicals at the site and those identified in the reaction mixtures. He should also be able to provide a theoretical yield of the final product based on the amounts of the chemical precursors.

After the work in the laboratory has been completed, the forensic scientist has the responsibility of assisting the legal authorities in understanding what was happening in the clandestine laboratory — what was being synthesized, how it was being synthesized, and what environmental ramifications existed due to the disposing of waste solvents and other chemicals found in the soil or plumbing. The forensic analyst must recognize his responsibilities as an expert witness and provide factual information in as much detail as necessary. However, this task carries with it the responsibility of avoiding unsubstantiated speculation.

Evaluating a clandestine laboratory, from the time of notification until the time of testimony in the courtroom, requires an open-minded and analytical approach. As information is gathered and data collection proceeds, the analyst may be involved in an ever-evolving decision-making process. This will probably require him to change his strategies as more information becomes available. Conclusions should be reserved until all the necessary exhibits have been collected and analyzed, the clandestine laboratory operator has been debriefed, the analytical data have been evaluated, and, if necessary, consultations with colleagues have been completed. In the courtroom, the forensic analyst will preserve his status as a credible expert witness by basing his testimony on factual data and possibilities that are within the realm of scientific probability.

1.9.1 Safety Concerns

A hazard evaluation is an absolute requirement prior to entering a clandestine laboratory. This should involve an evaluation of the physical and environmental hazards that may be present. This evaluation is usually the result of questioning other law enforcement personnel familiar with the laboratory, or the laboratory operator. Great care should be exercised in evaluating and acting on information from the laboratory operator. The forensic analyst should determine the minimum level of safety equipment required for entry into the laboratory. If there is knowledge regarding the type of drug being synthesized in the clandestine laboratory and the processing methodology, the forensic scientist will have some idea about the types of chemicals that may be encountered. If records are available regarding the purchasing activity of the clandestine laboratory operator, the quantities of the chemicals facing the investigators will be available.

All this information should be documented and used to decide the safest and most prudent manner in which to enter the clandestine laboratory. Other concerns that must be considered are the weather conditions, and entry and egress options. Extremes in either heat or cold can affect the way the safety and sampling equipment will function. These conditions will also affect how long the forensic chemist can be expected to work in the appropriate clothing. Egress options from a clandestine laboratory must be determined before entry. In the event of a fire or explosion, those individuals processing the clandestine laboratory must know how to exit the dangerous environment. As a part of the planning scenario for processing the clandestine laboratory, the appropriate authority should make the nearest medical facility aware of the fact that if an investigator is injured, medical attention will be sought. The medical facility may have some requirement for treating a chemical injury. This should be determined beforehand and a protocol to meet these requirements should be established.

The most important responsibility of the forensic analyst involved in a clandestine laboratory investigation and seizure is safety. Safety must be considered from a number of perspectives. The forensic scientist must be concerned with the safety and well-being of anyone entering the suspected clandestine laboratory. His training and experience will have prepared him to recognize many of the obvious dangers of the chemical hazards and physical hazards at the site. This awareness is not stagnant. There will usually be a condition that requires an immediate adjustment and reevaluation. He must be constantly aware of the possible hazards when the combination of two minimally unsafe conditions result in fatalities. This results from a failure to recognize that while each condition is dangerous in its own right, combining the dangers is a recipe for disaster if certain precautions are not followed.

For instance, if the odor of ether is detected in an enclosed dark room, a possible first step might be to turn on the lights. However, any short circuit in the light switch resulting in a spark could cause the ether vapors in combination with the oxygen in the air to explode. The correct action would be to obtain outside lighting equipment to determine the source of the ether vapors, rectify the conditions resulting in the ether vapors, ventilate the room, check the light switch and wiring, and then turn on the lights. This situation is one in which a chemical hazard and a physical hazard could combine and result in serious injury or death.

Before entering the clandestine laboratory, the forensic analyst must take precautions to ensure eye, lung, and skin protection. This will usually mean proper clothing including head gear, boots, outerwear, and gloves; safety glasses and/or a face shield; and the appropriate air purification and breathing apparatus. Consideration should also be given to use of air-monitoring devices, which can detect concentrations of combustible gases or vapors in the atmosphere, oxygen deficiencies, and gas concentrations to lower explosive limits. There are also devices available in the form of glass tubes filled with specific detection granules, which allow for the reasonable determination of airborne chemical hazards in the atmosphere. When these devices are used properly, the forensic scientist entering the clandestine laboratory maximizes his chances for protecting the safety of the seizure team, including himself.

Even after the atmosphere has been sampled and ventilation has progressed, once inside the clandestine laboratory, the forensic chemist should be aware of the many possibilities posing a threat. The potential chemical dangers include an explosion potential, flammable and combustible chemicals, corrosive chemicals, oxidizers, poisons, compressed gases, irritants, and booby traps. Physical hazards include but are certainly not limited to broken glass, bare electrical wiring, slippery floors, and loud noises. These chemical and physical hazards can be accentuated by a reduction in dexterity because of safety equipment and clothing, a narrow field of vision due to a breathing apparatus, diminished communications, physical and mental stress, heat or cold stress, a confined work space environment, and a prolonged period of time spent processing the clandestine laboratory.

After the laboratory processing has been completed, the forensic scientist should be a part of the team that reduces the level of environmental contamination to a controllable level. This will usually involve prior planning for the proper disposal of hazardous chemicals and protective clothing by a waste disposal authority. There should be a standard operating procedure for the decontamination of anyone who entered the clandestine laboratory. This should include provisions for an emergency shower and an eyewash station, first aid kits, and decontamination procedures for injured workers.

One of the most important factors anyone processing a clandestine laboratory must remember is the following: no matter how much protective clothing is available, no matter how much pre-planning is done, no matter how careful a person might be in collecting chemicals and assessing danger, if that person fails to recognize his or her limitations in knowledge or physical ability, a disaster is waiting to happen. The greatest danger facing anyone who processes a clandestine laboratory is a false sense of security.

1.9.2   Commonly Encountered Chemicals in the Clandestine Laboratory

The following tabulation of data is intended as an overview of those chemicals most frequently encountered as precursors in clandestine laboratory settings. A **precursor** is a chemical that becomes a part of the controlled substance either as the basis of the molecular skeleton or as a substituent of the molecular skeleton. This list is not all-inclusive. Modifications to typical synthetic routes on the parts of ingenious organic chemists are typical and cannot always be predicted.

Precursor	Controlled Substance
Acetic anhydride	Heroin
	Methaqualone
	Phenyl-2-Propanone (P-2-P)
Acetonitrile	Amphetamine
N-Acetylanthranilic acid	Methaqualone
	Mecloqualone
Acetylacetone	Methaqualone
4-Allyl-1,2-methylenedioxybenzene	3,4-Methylenedioxyamphetamine (MDA)
Ammonium formate	Amphetamine
	MDA
Amphetamine	alpha-Methyl fentanyl
Aniline	alpha-Methyl fentanyl
Anthranilic acid	Methaqualone
Benzaldehyde	Amphetamine
	P-2-P
Benzene	Amphetamine
	P-2-P
Benzyl cyanide	Methamphetamine
Bromobenzene	N-Ethyl-1-phenylcyclohexylamine (PCE)
	Phencyclidine (PCP)
	1-Phenylcyclohexylpyrrolidine (PCPy)
	P-2-P

THE CRIMINALISTICS OF CONTROLLED SUBSTANCES

Precursor	Controlled Substance
1-Bromo-2,5-dimethoxybenzene	4-Bromo-2,5-dimethoxyamphetamine (DOB)
Bromohydroquinone	DOB
5-Bromoisatin	Lysergic acid
ortho-Bromophenol	4-Bromo-2,5-dimethoxyphenethylamine (Nexus)
Bromosafrole	3,4-Methylenedioxyethylamphetamine (MDEA)
	3,4-Methylenedioxymethamphetamine (MDMA)
2-Bromothiophene	1-[1-(2-Thienyl)cyclohexyl]piperidine (TCP)
Chloroacetic acid	P-2-P
Chloroacetone	P-2-P
1-Chloro-2,5-dimethoxybenzene	Nexus
2-Chloro-*N*,*N*-dimethylpropylamine	Methadone
2-Chloroethylbenzene	Fentanyl
alpha-Chloroethylmethyl ether	P-2-P
Chlorohydroquinone	DOB
Chlorosafrole	MDEA
	MDMA
ortho-Cresol	4-Methyl-2,5-dimethoxyamphetamine (STP)
Diethylamine	Diethyltryptamine
	Lysergic acid diethylamide (LSD)
Ephedrine	Methamphetamine
	Methcathinone
Ergonovine	LSD
Ergotamine	LSD
Ethylamine	Ethylamphetamine
	3,4-Methylenedioxyethylamphetamine (MDEA)
N-Ethylephedrine	*N*-Ethyl-*N*-methylamphetamine
N-Ethylpseudoephedrine	*N*-Ethyl-*N*-methylamphetamine
ortho-Ethylphenol	4-Ethyl-2,5-dimethoxyamphetamine
Formamide	Amphetamine
	MDA
Hydroxycodeinone	Oxycotin
Isosafrole	4-Methylenedioxyamphetamine (MDA)
	3,4-Methylenedioxymethamphetamine (MDMA)
	MDEA
Lysergic acid	LSD
Methylamine	Methamphetamine
	MDMA
3,4-Methylenedioxyphenyl-2-propanon	MDA
	MDMA
	MDEA
N-Methyephedrine	*N*,*N*-Dimethylamphetamine
N-Methylpseudoephedrine	*N*,*N*-Dimethylamphetamine
Nitroethane	P-2-P
	Amphetamine
	MDA
1,2-Methylenedioxy-4-propenylbenzene	MDEA
N-Methylephedrine	P-2-P
N-Methylformamide	Methamphetamine
N-Methylformanilide	STP
2-Methyl-4-[3H]-quinazolinone	Methaqualone
Methyl-3,4,5-trimethoxybenzoate	Mescaline
Norpseudoephedrine	4-Methylaminorex
Phenethylamine	Fentanyl
	para-Fluoro fentanyl
	2-Methyl fentanyl
N-(1-Phenethyl)-piperidin-4-one	Fentanyl
	para-Fluoro fentanyl
N-(1-Phenethyl-4-piperidinyl)-aniline	Fentanyl
Phenylacetic acid	P-2-P

Precursor	Controlled Substance
Phenylacetonitrile	P-2-P
Phenylacetyl chloride	P-2-P
D-Phenylalanine	Amphetamine
	Methamphetamine
2-Phenyl-1-bromoethane	Fentanyl
1-Phenyl-2-bromopropane	alpha-Methyl fentanyl
Phenylmagnesium bromid	PCP
	PCPy
	P-2-P
Phenylpropanolamine	Amphetamine
	4-Methylaminorex
Phenyl-2-propanone (P-2-P)	Amphetamine
	Methamphetamine
Piperidin	Phencyclidine (PCP)
N-(4-Piperidinyl)aniline	Fentanyl
	alpha-Methyl fentanyl
Piperonal	MDA
	MDMA
	MDEA
Piperonylacetone	N-Hydroxy MDA
Propionic anhydride1	Fentanyl analogues
Propiophenone	Methamphetamine
Pyrrolidine	PCPy
Pseudoephedrine	Methamphetamine
Safrole	MDA
	MDMA
	3,4-Methylenedioxy P-2-P
3,4,5-Trimethoxybenzaldehyde	Mescaline
	3,4,5-Trimethoxyamphetamine

REFERENCE

1. Frank, R.S., The clandestine laboratory situation in the United States, *J. Forensic Sci.*, 28, 18–31, 1993.

1.9.3 Tables of Controlled Substances

1.9.3.1 Generalized List by Category of Physiological Effects and Medical Uses of Controlled Substances

Controlled Substances — Categorized Listing of the Most Commonly Encountered Controlled Substances

Drug	CSA Schedules	Trade or Other Names	Medical Uses
		Narcotics	
Heroin	I	Diacetylmorphine, Horse, Smack	None in U.S., analgesic, antitussive
Morphine	II	Duramorph, MS-Contin, Roxanol, Oramorph SR	Analgesic
Codeine	II, III, IV	Tylenol w/Codeine, Empirin w/Codeine, Robitussin A-C, Fiorinal w/Codeine, APAP w/Codeine	Analgesic, antitussive
Hydrocodone	II, III	Tussionex, Vicodin, Dycodan, Lorcet	Analgesic, antitussive

THE CRIMINALISTICS OF CONTROLLED SUBSTANCES

Controlled Substances — Categorized Listing of the Most Commonly Encountered Controlled Substances *(Continued)*

Drug	CSA Schedules	Trade or Other Names	Medical Uses
Hydromorphone	II	Dilaudid	Analgesic
Oxycodone	II	Percodan, Percocet, Tylox, Roxicet, Roxidone	Analgesic
Methadone and LAAM	I, II	Dolophine, Levo-alpha-acetylmethadol, Levomethadyl acetate	Analgesic, treatment of dependence
Fentanyl and analogues	I, II	Innovar, Sublimaze, Alfenta, Sufenta, Duragesic	Analgesic, adjunct to anesthesia, anesthetic
Other narcotics	II, III, IV, V	Percodan, Percocet, Tylox, Opium, Darvon, Talwin,[a] Buprenorphine, Meperidine (Pethidine)	Analgesic, antidiarrheal
Depressants			
Chloral hydrate	IV	Noctec, Somnos, Felsules	Hypnotic
Barbiturates	II, III, IV	Amytal, Fiorinal, Membutal, Seconal, Tuinal, Penobarbital, Pentobarbital	Sedative hypnotic, veterinary euthanasia agent
Benzodiazepines	IV	Ativan, Dalmane, Diazepam, Librium, Xanax, Serax, Valium, Tranxene, Verstran, Versed, Halcion, Paxipam, Restoril	Antianxiety, sedative, anticonvulsant, hypnotic
Glutethimide	II	Doriden	Sedative, hypnotic
Other depressants	I, II, III, IV	Equanil, Miltown, Noludar, Placidyl, Valmid, Methaqualone	Antianxiety, sedative, hypnotic
Stimulants			
Cocaine[b]	II	Coke, Flake, Snow, Crack	Local anesthetic
Amphetamine/methamphetamine	II	Biphetamine, Desoxyn, Dexedrine, Obetrol, Ice	Attention-deficit disorder, narcolepsy, weight control
Methylphenidate	II	Ritalin	Attention-deficit disorder
Other stimulants	I, II, III, IV	Adipex, Didrex, Ionamin, Melfiat, Plegine, Captagon, Sanorex, Tenuate, Tepanil, Prelu-2, Preludin	Weight control
Cannabis			
Marijuana	I	Pot, Acapulco Gold, Grass, Reefer, Sinsemilla, Thai Sticks	None
Tetrahydro-cannabinol	I, II	THC, Marinol	Antinauseant
Hashish and hashish oil	I	Hash, Hash Oil	None
Hallucinogens			
LSD	I	Acid, Blotter Acid, Microdots	None
Mescaline and peyote	I	Mescal, Buttons, Cactus	None
Phenethylamines	I	2,5-DMA, STP, MDA, MDMA, Ecstasy, DOM, DOB	None
Phencyclidine and analogues	I, II	PCP, PCE, PCPy, TCP, Hog, Loveboat, Angel Dust	None
Other hallucinogens	I	Bufotenine, Ibogaine, DMT, DET, Psilocybin, Psilocin	None

Controlled Substances — Categorized Listing of the Most Commonly Encountered Controlled Substances *(Continued)*

Drug	CSA Schedules	Trade or Other Names	Medical Uses
Anabolic Steroids			
Testosterone	III	Depo-testosterone, Delatestryl (Cypionate, Enanthate)	Hypogonadism
Nandrolone	III	Nandrolone, Durabolin, Deca-Durabolin, Deca	Anemia, breast cancer
Oxymetholone	III	Anadrol-50	Anemia

[a] Not designated a narcotic under the CSA.
[b] Designated a narcotic under the CSA.

1.9.3.2 Listing of Controlled Substances by Schedule Number

Listed below are those substances specifically controlled under the Controlled Substances Act as of June 26, 2006. This list does not include all controlled steroids or controlled substance analogues. These are classes of compounds that are controlled based on chemical and pharmacological criteria that were discussed earlier in this chapter.

Schedule I Controlled Substances

Controlled Substance	Synonym(s)
1-(1-Phenylcyclohexyl)pyrrolidine	PCPy, PHP, rolicyclidine
1-[1-(2-Thienyl)cyclohexyl]piperidine	TCP, tenocyclidine
1-[1-(2-Thienyl)cyclohexyl]pyrrolidine	TCPy
1-Methyl-4-phenyl-4-propionoxypiperdine	MPPP, synthetic heroin
1-(2-Phenylethyl)-4-phenyl-4-acetoxypiperidine	PEPAP, synthetic heroin
2,5-Dimethoxyamphetamine	DMA, 2,5-DMA
2,5-Dimethoxy-4-ethylamphetamine	DOET
2,5-Dimethoxy-4-(n)-propylthiophenethylamine	2C-T-7
3,4,5-Trimethoxyamphetamine	TMA
3,4-Methylenedioxyamphetamine	MDA, Love Drug
3,4-Methylenedioxymethamphetamine	MDMA, Ecstasy, XTC
3,4-Methylenedioxy-N-ethylamphetamine	N-ethyl MDA, MDE, MDEA
3-Methylfentanyl	China White, fentanyl
3-Methylthiofentanyl	China White, fentanyl
4-Bromo-2,5-dimethoxyamphetamine	DOB, 4-bromo-DMA
4-Bromo-2,5-dimethoxyphenethylamine	Nexus, 2-CB, has been sold as Ecstasy, i.e., MDMA
4-Methoxyamphetamine	PMA
4-Methyl-2,5-dimethoxyamphetamine	DOM, STP
4-Methylaminorex (*cis* isomer)	U4Euh, McN-422
5-Methoxy-3,4-methylenedioxyamphetamine	MMDA
5-Methoxy-N,N-diisopropyltryptamine	5-MeO-DIPT
Acetorphine	
Acetyldihydrocodeine	Acetylcodone
Acetylmethadol	Methadyl acetate
Acetyl-alpha-methylfentanyl	
Allylprodine	
Alphacetylmethadol except levo-alphacetylmethadol	
alpha-Ethyltryptamine	ET, Trip
Alphameprodine	
Alphamethadol	
alpha-Methylfentanyl	China White, fentanyl
alpha-Methylthiofentanyl	China White, fentanyl
alpha-Methyltryptamine	AMT

THE CRIMINALISTICS OF CONTROLLED SUBSTANCES

Schedule I Controlled Substances *(Continued)*

Controlled Substance	Synonym(s)
Aminorex	Has been sold as methamphetamine
Benzethidine	
Benzylmorphine	
Betacetylmethadol	
Betameprodine	
Betamethadol	
Betaprodine	
beta-Hydroxyfentanyl	China White, fentanyl
beta-Hydroxy-3-methylfentanyl	China White, fentanyl
Bufotenine	Mappine, N,N-dimethylserotonin
Cathinone	Constituent of "Khat" plant
Clonitazene	
Codeine methylbromide	
Codeine-N-oxide	
Cyprenorphine	
Desomorphine	
Dextromoramide	Palfium, Jetrium, Narcolo
Diampromide	
Diethylthiambutene	
Diethyltryptamine	DET
Difenoxin	Lyspafen
Dihydromorphine	
Dimenoxadol	
Dimepheptanol	
Dimethylthiambutene	
Dimethyltryptamine	DMT
Dioxaphetyl butyrate	
Dipipanone	Dipipan, phenylpiperone HCL, Diconal, Wellconal
Drotebanol	Metebanyl, oxymethebanol
Ethylmethylthiambutene	
Etonitazene	
Etorphine (except HCL)	
Etoxeridine	
Fenethylline	Captagon, amfetyline, ethyltheophylline amphetamine
Furethidine	
Gamma hydroxybutyric acid	GHB, gamma hydroxybutyrate, sodium oxybate
Heroin	Diacetylmorphine, diamorphine
Hydromorphinol	
Hydroxpethidine	
Ibogaine	Constituent of "Tabernanthe iboga" plant
Ketobemidone	Cliradon
Levomoramide	
Levophenacylmorphan	
Lysergic acid diethylamide	LSD, lysergide
Marihuana	Cannabis, marijuana
Mecloqualone	Nubarene
Mescaline	Constituent of "Peyote" cacti
Methaqualone	Quaalude, Parest, Somnafac, Opitimil, Mandrax
Methcathinone	N-Methylcathinone, "cat"
Methyldesorphine	
Methyldihydromorphine	
Morpheridine	
Morphine methylbromide	
Morphine methylsulfonate	
Morphine-N-oxide	
Myrophine	
N-Benzylpiperazine	BZP, 1-benzylpiperazine
N-Ethyl-1-phenylcyclohexylamine	PCE

Schedule I Controlled Substances *(Continued)*

Controlled Substance	Synonym(s)
N-Ethylamphetamine	NEA
N-Ethyl-3-piperidyl benzilate	JB 323
N-Hydroxy-3,4-methylenedioxyamphetamine	*N*-hydroxy MDA
N-Methyl-3-piperidyl benzilate	JB 336
N,N-Dimethylamphetamine	
Nicocodeine	
Nicomorphine	Vilan
Noracymethadol	
Norlevorphanol	
Normethadone	Phenyldimazone
Normorphine	
Norpipanone	
Parahexyl	Synhexyl
para-Fluorofentanyl	China White, fentanyl
Peyote	Cactus that contains mescaline
Phenadoxone	
Phenampromide	
Phenomorphan	
Phenoperidine	Operidine, Lealgin
Pholcodine	Copholco, Adaphol, Codisol, Lantuss, Pholcolin
Piritramide	Piridolan
Proheptazine	
Properidine	
Propiram	Algeril
Psilocybin	Constituent of "Magic Mushrooms"
Psilocyn	Psilocin, constituent of "Magic Mushrooms"
Racemoramide	
Tetrahydrocannabinols	THC, Delta-8 THC, Delta-9 THC, and others
Thebacon	Acetylhydrocodone, Acedicon, Thebacetyl
Thiofentanyl	China White, fentanyl
Tilidine	Tilidate, Valoron, Kitadol, Lak, Tilsa
Trimeperidine	Promedolum

Schedule II Controlled Substances

Controlled Substance	Synonym(s)
1-Phenyleyelohexylamine	Precursor of PCP
1-Piperidinoeyelohexanecarbonitrile	PCC, precursor of PCP
Alfentanil	Alfenta
Alphaprodine	Nisentil
Amobarbital	Amytal, Tuinal
Amphetamine	Dexedrine, Adderall, Obetrol
Anilerdine	Leritine
Benzoylecgonine	Cocaine metabolite
Bezitramide	Burgodin
Carfentanil	Wildnil
Coca leaves	
Cocaine	Methyl benzoylecgonine, Crack
Codeine	Morphine methyl ester, methyl morphine
Dextropropoxyphene, bulk (non-dosage forms)	Propoxyphene
Dihydrocodeine	Didrate, Parzone
Dihydroetorphine	DHE
Diphenoxylate	
Diprenorphine	M50-50
Ecgonine	Cocaine precursor, in coca leaves
Ethylmorphine	Dionin
Etorphine HCL	M 99

THE CRIMINALISTICS OF CONTROLLED SUBSTANCES | 65

Schedule II Controlled Substances *(Continued)*

Controlled Substance	Synonym(s)
Fentanyl	Duragesic, Oralet, Actiq, Sublimaze, Innovar
Glutethimide	Doriden, Dorimide
Hydrocodone	Dihydrocodeinone
Hydromorphone	Dilaudid, dihydromorphinone
Isomethadone	Isoamidone
Levo-alphacetylmethadol	LAAM, long-acting methadone, levomathadyl acetate
Levomethorphan	
Levorphanol	Levo-Dromoran
Meperidine	Demerol, Mepergan, pethidine
Meperidine intermediate-A	Meperidine precursor
Meperidine intermediate-B	Meperidine precursor
Meperidine intermediate-C	Meperidine precursor
Metazocine	
Methadone	Dolophine, Methadose, Amidone
Methadone intermediate	Methadone precursor
Methamphetamine	Desoxyn, D-desoxyephedrine, ICE, Crank, Speed
Methylphenidate	Concerta, Ritalin, Methylin
Metopon	
Moramide-intermediate	
Morphine	MS Contin, Roxanol, Oramorph, Duramorph, RMS, MSIR
Nabilone	Cesamet
Opium, granulated	Granulated opium
Opium, powdered	Powdered opium
Opium, raw	Raw opium, gum opium
Opium extracts	
Opium fluid extract	
Opium poppy	Papaver somniferum
Opium tincture	Laudanum
Oxycodone	OxyContin, Percocet, Endocet, Roxicodone, Roxicet
Oxymorphone	Numorphan
Pentabarbital	Nembutal
Phenazocine	Narphen, Prinadol
Phencyclidine	PCP, Sernylan
Phenmetrazine	Preludin
Phenylacetone	P2P, phenyl-2-propanone, benzyl methyl ketone
Piminodine	
Poppy straw	Opium poppy capsules, poppy heads
Poppy straw concentrate	Concentrate of poppy straw, CPS
Racemethorphan	
Racemorphan	Dromoran
Remifentanil	Ultiva
Secobarbital	Seconel, Tuinal
Sufentanil	Sufenta
Thebaine	Precursor of many narcotics

Schedule III Controlled Substances

Controlled Substance	Synonym(s)
1-Androstenediol	
1-Androstenedione	
$3\alpha,17\beta$-Dihydroxy-5α-androstane	
$3\beta,17\beta$-Dihydroxy-5α-androstane	
4-Androstenediol	4-AD
4-Androstenedione	
4-Dihydrotestosterone	Anabolex, Andractim, Pesomax, Stanolone
4-Hydrotestosterone	

Schedule III Controlled Substances *(Continued)*

Controlled Substance	Synonym(s)
4-Hydroxy-19-nortestosterone	
5-Androstenediol	
5-Androstenedione	
13β-Ethyl-7β-hydroxygon-4-en-3-one	
17α-Methyl-3β,17β-dihydroxy-5α-androstane	
17α-Methyl-3α,17β-dihydroxy-5α-androstane	
17α-Methyl-3α,17β-dihydroxyandrost-4-ene	
17α-Methyl-4-hydroxynandrolone	
17α-Methyl-Δ¹-dihydrotestosterone	17α-Methyl-1-testosterone
19-Nor-4-androstenediol	
19-Nor-5-androstenediol	
19-Nor-4-androstenedione	
19-Nor-5-androstenedione	
Amobarbital suppository dosage form	
Amobarbital and noncontrolled active ingredients	Amobarbital/ephedrine capsules
Anabolic steroids	"Body Building" drugs
Androstanedione	
Aprobarbital	Alurate
Barbituric acid derivative	Barbiturates not specifically listed
Benzphetamine	Didrex, Inapetyl
Boldenone	Equipoise, Parenebol, Vebonol, dehydrotestosterone
Bolasterone	
Buprenorphine	Buprenex, Temgesic, Subutex, Suboxone
Buprenorphine	Buprenex, Temgesic
Butabarbital (sec butabarbital)	Butisol, Butibel
Butalbital	Fiorinal, Butalbital with aspirin
Butobarbital (butethal)	Soneryl (UK)
Calusterone	Methosarb
Chlorhexadol	Mechloral, Mecoral, Medodorm, Chloralodol
Chlorotestosterone (same as clostebol)	If 4-chlorotestosterone then clostebol
Chlorphentermine	Pre-Sate, Lucofen, Apsedon, Desopimon
Clortermine	Voranil
Clostebol	alpha-Trofodermin, Clostene, 4-chlorotestosterone
Codeine combination product 90 mg/du	Emprin, Fiorinal, Tylenol, ASA or APAP w/codeine
Codeine and isoquinoline alkaloid 90 mg/du	Codeine with papaverine or noscapine
Dehydrochlormethyltestosterone	Oral-Turinabol
Dihydrocodeine combination product 90 mg/du	Synalgos-DC, Compal
Delta1-dihydrotestosterone	1-Testosterone
Dronabinol in sesame oil in soft gelatin capsule	Marinol, synthetic THC in sesame oil/soft gelatin
Dihydrotestosterone (same as stanolone)	See stanolone
Drostanolone	Drolban, Masterid, Permastril
Ethylestrenol	Maxibolin, Orabolin, Durabolin-O, Duraboral
Ethylmorphine combination product 15 mg/du	
Formebolone	Esiclene, Hubernol
Furazabol	Frazalon, Miotolon, Qu Zhi Shu
Gamma Hydroxybutyric Acid preparations	Zyrem
Fluoxymesterone	Anadroid-F, Halotestin, Ora-Testryl
Hydrocodone combination product <15 mg/du	Lorcet, Lortab, Vicodin, Vicoprofen, Tussionex, Norco
Hydrocodone and isoquinoline alkaloid <15 mg/du	Dihydrocodeinone + papaverine or noscapine
Ketamine	Ketaset, Ketalar, Special K, K
Lysergic acid	LSD precursor
Lysergic acid amide	LSD precursor
Mesterolone	Androviron, Proviron, Testiwop
Mestanolone	Assimil, Ermalone, Methylbol, Tanterone
Methandienone	Dianabol, Metabolina, Nerobol, Perbolin
Methandriol	Sinesex, Stenediol, Troformone

THE CRIMINALISTICS OF CONTROLLED SUBSTANCES

Schedule III Controlled Substances *(Continued)*

Controlled Substance	Synonym(s)
Methenolone	Primobolan, Primobolan Depot, Primobolan S
Methyldienolone	
Methyltestosterone	Android, Oreton, Testred, Virilon
Methyltrienolone	Metribolone
Methyprylon	Noludar
Mibolerone	Cheque, Matenon
Morphine combination product/ 50 mg/100 ml or g	
Nalorphine	Nalline
Nandrolone	Deca-Durabolin, Durabolin, Durabolin-50
Norbolethone	Genabol
Norclostebol	Anabol-4-19, Lentabol
Norethandrolone	Nilavar, Pronabol, Solevar
Opium combination product 25 mg/du	Paregoric, other combination products
Oxandrolone	Anavar, Lonavar, Provitar, Vasorome
Oxymesterone	Anamidol, Balnimax, Oranabol, Oranabol 10
Oxymetholone	Anadrol-50, Adroyd, Anapolon, Anasteron, Pardroyd
Pentobarbital suppository dosage form	WANS
Pentobarbital and noncontrolled active ingredients	FP-3
Phendimetrazine	Plegine, Prelu-2, Bontril, Melfiat, Statobex
Secobarbital suppository dosage form	Various
Secobarbital and noncontrolled active ingredients	Various
Stanozolol	Winstrol, Winstrol-V
Stenbolone	
Stimulant compounds previously excepted	Mediatric
Sulfondiethylmethane	
Sulfonethylmethane	
Sulfonmethane	
Talbutal	Lotusate
Tetrahydrogestrinone	THG
Testolactone	Teolit, Teslac
Testosterone	Android-T, Adrolan, Depotest, Dalatestryl
Thiamylal	Surital
Thiopental	Pentothal
Tiletamine and zolazepam combination product	Telazol
Trenbolone	Finaplix-S, Finajet, Parabolan
Vinbarbital	Delvinal, Vinbarbitone

Schedule IV Controlled Substances

Controlled Substance	Synonym(s)
Alprazolam	Xanax
Barbital	Veronal, Plexonal, barbitone
Bromazepam	Lexotan, Lexatin, Lexotanil
Camazepam	Albego, Limpidon, Paxor
Cathine	Constituent of "Khat" plant, (+)-norpseudoephedrine
Chloral betaine	Beta Chlor
Chloral hydrate	Noctac
Chlordiazepoxide	Librium, Libritabs, Lombitrol, SK-Lygen
Clobazam	Urbadan, Urbanyl
Clonazepam	Klonopin, Clonopin
Clorazepate	Tranxene
Clotiazepam	Trecalmo, Rize, Clozan, Veratran
Cloxazolam	Akton, Lubalix, Olcadil, Sepazon
Delorazepam	
Dexfenfluramine	Redux
Dextropropoxyphene dosage forms	Darvon, propoxyphene, Darvocet, Propacet

Schedule IV Controlled Substances *(Continued)*

Controlled Substance	Synonym(s)
Diazepam	Valium, Diastat
Dichloralphenazone	Midrin, dichloralantipyrine
Diethylpropion	Tenuate, Tepanil
Difenoxin 1 mg/25 µg AtSO4/du	Motofen
Estazolam	ProSom, Domnamid, Eurodin, Nuctalon
Ethchlorvynol	Placidyl
Ethinamate	Valmid, Valamin
Ethyl loflazepate	
Fencamfamin	Reactivan
Fenfluramine	Pondimin, Ponderal
Fenproporex	Gacilin, Solvolip
Fludiazepam	
Flunitrazepam	Rohypnol, Narcozep, Darkene, Roipnol
Flurazepam	Dalmane
Halazepam	Paxipam
Haloxazolam	
Ketazolam	Anxon, Loftran, Solatran, Contamex
Loprazolam	
Lorazepam	Ativan
Lormetazepam	Noctamid
Mazindol	Sanorex, Mazanor
Mebutamate	Capla
Medazepam	Nobrium
Mefenorex	Anorexic, Amexate, Doracil, Pondinil
Meprobamate	Miltown, Equanil, Deprol, Equagesic, Meprospan
Methohexital	Brevital
Methylphenobarbital (mephobarbital)	Mebaral, mephobarbital
Midazolam	Versed
Modafinil	Provigil
Nimetazepam	Erimin
Nitrazepam	Mogadon
Nordiazepam	Nordazepam, Demadar, Madar
Oxazepam	Serax, Serenid-D
Oxazolam	Serenal, Convertal
Paraldehyde	Paral
Pemoline	Cylert
Pentazocine	Talwin, Talwin NX, Talacen, Talwin Compound
Petrichloral	Pentaerythritol chloral, Periclor
Phenobarbital	Luminal, Donnatal, Bellergal-S
Phentermine	Ionamin, Fastin, Adipex-P, Obe-Nix, Zantryl
Pinazepam	Domar
Pipradrol	Detaril, Stimolag Fortis
Prazepam	Centrax
Quazepam	Doral
Sibutramine	Meridia
SPA	1-Dimethylamino-1,2-diphenylethane, Lefetamine
Temazepam	Restoril
Tetrazepam	Myolastan, Musaril
Triazolam	Halcion
Zaleplon	Sonata
Zopiclone	Lunesta
Zolpidem	Ambien, Ivadal, Stilnoct, Stilnox

THE CRIMINALISTICS OF CONTROLLED SUBSTANCES

Schedule V Controlled Substances

Controlled Substance	Synonym(s)
Codeine preparations — 200 mg/100 ml or 100 g	Cosanyl, Robitussin A-C, Cheracol, Cerose, Pediacof
Difenoxin preparations — 0.5 mg/25 µg AtSO4/du	Motofen
Dihydrocodeine preparations — 10 mg/200 ml or 100 g	Cophene-S, various others
Diphenoxylate preparations — 2.5 mg/25 µg AtSO4	Lomotil, Logen
Ethylmorphine preparations — 100 mg/100 ml or 100 g	
Opium preparations — 100 mg/100 ml or 100 g	Parepectolin, Kapectolin PG, Kaolin, Pectin P.G.
Pregabalin	Lyrica
Pyrovalerone	Centroton, Thymergix

The author gratefully acknowledges the assistance of Dr. Judy Lawrence, Pharmacologist, DEA Office of Diversion Control, for providing information utilized in compiling this listing of controlled substances.

CHAPTER **2**

Overview of Pathology of Drug Abuse: Scene of Death and the Autopsy

Charles V. Wetli, M.D.
Chief Medical Examiner, Office of the Suffolk County Medical Examiner, Hauppauge, New York

CONTENTS

Introduction 71
2.1   Excited Delirium 73
2.2   Body Packers 74
2.3   The Autopsy 74
References 77

INTRODUCTION

Paramount to any investigation, evaluation, or inquiry is the knowledge of terminal events, and pre-terminal characteristics of the victim. In most hospital deaths, the medical record readily provides this. In the world of forensic pathology, such history is often lacking, and reliance must be placed on an open mind with a conscious realization that drug abuse may have had a significant contribution to a person's death regardless of initial impressions: Infectious diseases such as hepatitis or endocarditis may be the result of intravenous drug abuse; cocaine may trigger convulsions or precipitate hypertensive crises and myocardial ischemia; central nervous system (CNS) depressants may lead to positional asphyxia, etc. And there must also be awareness that people with natural disease may, intentionally or not, abuse drugs, which may exacerbate their underlying disease process and significantly contribute to their death. Drugs create pathological states, with or without death, by their immediate pharmacologic effects, the way in which the drug is taken, by the cumulative effects of chronic abuse, and by interaction with pre-existing pathologic conditions.[1,2] Therefore, what once could have been discussed as a complication of hypertension (e.g., spontaneous aortic dissection) must now be evaluated as a possible effect of acute and chronic cocaine abuse.[3,4]

As noted in the prologue, every death scene must be approached with a conscious effort to evaluate the role of drugs and alcohol regardless of the apparent cause or manner of death. The scene investigator must therefore be ever cognizant of two possibilities: (1) Because a person has a disease it does not necessarily mean it is the cause of death, and (2) the scene of a drug overdose

Figure 2.1 Packets of drugs.

is frequently cleaned before investigators are even called. Consequently, it is important to evaluate all medication containers at the death scene, noting the identity of the drug and its purpose, the instructions for usage, and the number remaining. Such a preliminary inventory (followed later by a more complete inventory and drug confirmation) often leads to a suspicion of drug overdose. However, since others may well have previously tampered with the scene, a search should be made for containers that may be concealed: wastebaskets, beneath the bed, in a purse, etc. All medication and medication containers should be confiscated for a more complete inventory and possible toxicologic evaluation.[2] Likewise, all drug paraphernalia must be removed from the premises. Recognizing such paraphernalia requires that the investigator be aware of what illicit drugs prevail in a particular community and how they are used. Thus, a small spoon attached to the cap of a small vial, a gold-plated razor with a mirror, and a soda can with holes punched in the sides are all paraphernalia of cocaine abuse. Packets of drugs (often with a crude logo; Figure 2.1) and used syringes are particularly important because these items may be the only way to determine the type of drug being abused, its purity, and its excipients. This is especially true for "designer drugs," which may be many thousand times more potent than heroin and therefore difficult to detect on routine toxicologic analysis of biological specimens.

Besides actual drug containers and paraphernalia, observations should be made that might reflect orientation toward a drug subculture: certain tattoos, evidence of gang affiliation (clothes, hair style, etc.), magazines, posters of drug-oriented music groups, etc. Periodicals and books of right-to-die organizations such as the Hemlock Society and its members should suggest the possibility of suicide or assisted suicide. This literature provides specific instructions about using drugs and plastic bags to commit suicide, and gives suggestions about avoiding (or cooperating) with a medical examiner investigation.[5,6]

Following scrutiny of the environment, attention should turn to the victim. Of particular importance is to ascertain the exact position of the body when it was found[2] to establish the possibility of postural or positional asphyxia.[7] This is a situation where a person collapses in a position such that the airway (nose, mouth) is partially or completely obstructed. Because of the anesthetic effect of the drugs (with or without alcohol), the victim does not move to create an unobstructed airway, and death results from mechanical asphyxia. If the airway obstruction is partial, it may take some hours for death to actually occur from respiratory acidosis and carbon dioxide retention. During this time, the drugs and alcohol continue to be metabolized and eliminated in urine, sweat, or breath. Toxicologic analysis will then reveal a low level of drugs and, if the likelihood of positional asphyxia cannot be established, the cause of death may be a conundrum. At the scene of death it

OVERVIEW OF PATHOLOGY OF DRUG ABUSE: SCENE OF DEATH AND THE AUTOPSY

is important to interview the person who first discovered the body and ask specific questions to ascertain whether the airway could have been obstructed.

Examination of the victim at the scene should include a careful inspection of the hands and mouth for drug residue or pills, palpation for hyperthermia (or, better, a direct measurement with a plastic indicator strip or rectal thermometer), which could suggest death from a stimulant drug; tattoos, which could suggest a drug culture; and fine parallel scars of the wrists or neck suggestive of a prior suicide attempt. A nearby plastic bag, particularly in the death of an elderly person with a chronic disease, suggests a death from the combination of asphyxia and drug overdose to terminate prolonged suffering (a method advocated by right-to-die organizations).

A fairly common mistake of some scene investigators is failure to turn the body over (which may reveal previously hidden drugs or drug paraphernalia) and failure to adequately examine the clothing. Pockets must be turned out or cut open, and underwear searched since they may contain packets or residue of drugs. Two death scenes have sufficient characteristics to suggest specific syndromes of cocaine abuse: cocaine-induced excited delirium, and the cocaine body packer.

2.1 EXCITED DELIRIUM

Excited delirium is a medical emergency with a psychiatric presentation.[8] The etiology may be infectious or pharmacologic and today it is most often seen with the abuse of cocaine or amphetamines. A similar syndrome of acute exhaustive mania may be seen with psychiatric patients or schizophrenics who have been treated with neuroleptic medication and who have recently stopped taking their medication. Today, the term agitated or excited delirium is used for the same syndrome regardless of etiology (i.e., infectious, toxic, pharmacologic, or psychiatric). Clinical and neuropharmacologic studies have linked the neuroleptic malignant syndrome and drug-induced excited delirium to disturbances of dopamine release and transport in the striatum of the CNS.[9] The syndrome is characterized by bizarre and violent behavior, hyperthermia, and tremendous, unexpected, strength. It usually takes several people to restrain the victim who is otherwise likely to injure himself or herself or others. Shortly after being restrained, the victim suddenly collapses and dies, often in police custody. If cardiopulmonary resuscitation (CPR) is successful, there is still a potential for death in a few days from myoglobinuric nephrosis secondary to massive rhabdomyolysis.[10,11] The violence is often associated with extensive property damage, inappropriate disrobing, and varying injuries incurred from smashing glass or the struggle with law enforcement personnel. The injuries may, of themselves, be lethal and hence require careful evaluation and documentation. With cocaine-induced excited delirium, blood and brain concentrations of cocaine are typically quite low whereas concentrations of benzoylecgonine are relatively high.[12,13] The "typical" scenario is most often that of a male who has been in a violent struggle, who may be naked and with usually minor injuries sustained in a struggle with police. The most common injuries are those involving the ankles or wrists from fighting against handcuffs or hobble restraints. Scalp and neck injuries may also be seen, and require careful evaluation to exclude a traumatic death. Body temperatures of 104°F or more are common, and there is usually evidence of extensive property damage, especially smashed glass.

The exact mechanism of death in excited delirium has yet to be elucidated.[14,15] The sudden loss of vital signs with asystole or bradycardic pulse-less electrical activity strongly suggests a cardiac mechanism of death, which is also frequently accompanied by an underlying abnormality of the heart (e.g., hypertensive type cardiomegaly) and profound lactic acidosis with a pH of 7.0 or less. Since death often occurs shortly after a violent struggle with the police, there are often allegations that law enforcement tactics generally regarded as a sublethal use of force actually caused or contributed to the death. Most often such allegations allege death resulted from so-called restraint or positional asphyxia, the use of pepper spray or mace, the use of electric stun guns, or the misapplication of a law enforcement neck hold.[16]

2.2 BODY PACKERS

Body packers are individuals who swallow packets of drugs in one country and transport them to another, and subsequently retrieve the packets by the use of laxatives.[17] Occasionally, larger packets may be inserted in the vagina or rectum. The most popular drug smuggled by this method into the United States in the past two decades has been cocaine. More recently, a number of heroin body packers have been reported.[18] The amount smuggled may total nearly a kilogram of the drug. Death may occur from a pharmacologic overdose if a drug packet breaks or leaks, or if water should cross a semipermeable membrane (e.g., a condom used as a drug packet) and allow the drug to dialyze into the gastrointestinal lumen to be absorbed rapidly into the blood. Intestinal obstruction is another potentially fatal complication. Cocaine body packers may collapse or have fatal grand mal seizures aboard an airplane or in the airport, or may be found dead in a hotel room. Evidence in the hotel room death scene usually consists of passports, foreign currency, or airplane tickets indicating recent arrival from a drug-supplying country (e.g., Colombia), hyperthermia (high body temperature, wet towels, or other evidence suggesting attempts at cooling), seizure activity (usually bite marks of the lower lip or tongue), presence of laxatives or enemas and, sometimes, drug packets hidden in a closet or suitcase. Heroin body packers do not have evidence of hyperthermia or of seizure activity, but often have a massive amount of white frothy pulmonary edema fluid about the nose and mouth. Also, the bodies of heroin body packers are more likely to be dumped alongside a roadway, and accomplices may have attempted to remove the packets via a crude post-mortem laparotomy.[15]

Drug packets have been fashioned from balloons, condoms, and other materials. Most commonly, however, the drug is compressed into a cylinder about 1/2 in. in diameter and 1 in. long, wrapped in plastic and heat-sealed, and wrapped again in several layers of latex (e.g., fingers of latex gloves). The ends are tied and sometimes the packet is dipped in wax. The drug packets are visible radiographically, and they may be accentuated by a halo of radiolucency as gas seeps between the layers of wrapping material.[19]

2.3 THE AUTOPSY

External examination in cases of oral drug abuse (i.e., pills or liquid medications) is generally not rewarding unless actual medication or medication residue is observed in the mouth or on the hands. However, as noted earlier, multiple parallel scars on the wrists or neck suggest prior suicide attempts and a subsequent suicidal drug overdose. Bite marks (contusions and lacerations) of the tongue and lower lip should be specifically sought since these frequently accompany terminal convulsions, which may be the result of cocaine or tricyclic antidepressant toxicity.

The prevalence of cocaine requires careful inspection of the nasal septum (preferably with a nasal speculum) to detect inflammation, necrosis, or perforation (Figure 2.2) from the chronic nasal insufflation (snorting) of cocaine hydrochloride. Also, it should be noted that crystals of cocaine might occasionally be observed in the nasal hairs or attached to the bristles of a mustache.

Stigmata of intravenous drug abuse are, naturally, the identification of fresh, recent, and old injection sites (Figure 2.3). Sometimes these may not be evident if the user makes a conscious attempt to conceal such marks by using very small gauge needles, rotating injection sites, and by injecting in areas normally concealed even by warm weather clothing. This is especially likely to occur among those in the health professions or in occupations where inspections are frequent (e.g., police, military personnel). These abusers may inject into the ankle or foot, beneath a watchband,

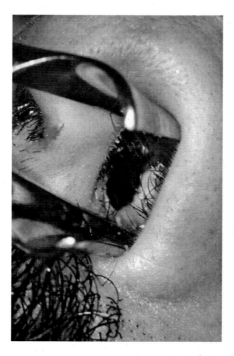

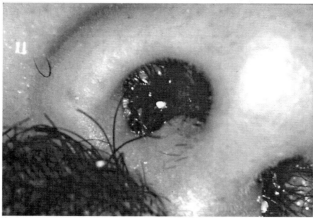

Figure 2.2 Inspection of the nasal septum.

in the auxiliary region, or even directly through the abdominal wall and into the peritoneal cavity. If the suspicion is high, "blind" incisions into these areas as well as more likely areas (e.g., antecubital fossae) may reveal extravasated blood in the subcutaneous tissue and around a vein, which is typical for a fresh or recent injection (Figure 2.4). Mostly, however, fresh and recent injection sites appear as small subcutaneous ecchymoses surrounding a cutaneous puncture. With cocaine, the needle puncture may be surrounded by a clear halo, which in turn is surrounded by an extensive ecchymoses; recent injection sites appear as poorly demarcated ecchymoses. Intravenous cocaine users may have little or no perivenous scarring even after years of intravenous injections.[4]

Repeated intravenous injections of narcotics generally leave characteristic hyperpigmented or hypopigmented zones of perivenous scarring commonly referred to as "tracks." These arise because narcotic addicts frequently mix heroin with oral medication containing starch or talc fillers.[1] These act like myriad microscopic splinters to elicit inflammatory (particularly granulomatous) reactions, which eventually form scar tissue. This process, plus venous thrombosis, may eventually occlude

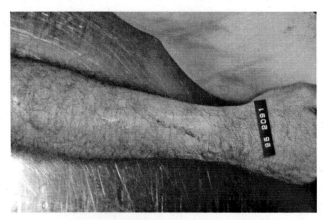

Figure 2.3 Stigmata of intravenous drug abuse are the identification of injection sites.

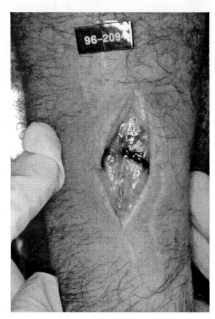

Figure 2.4 "Blind" incision reveals extravasated blood in the subcutaneous tissue and around a vein. This is typical for a fresh or recent injection.

the vein. Externally, these tracks appear as irregular subcutaneous "ropes" that follow the veins of the hands and forearms.

Round atrophic scars clustered predominantly on the arms and legs are frequently seen in intravenous drug abusers,[4] particularly cocaine abusers. These may represent healed abscesses or healed ischemic ulcers due to the vasoconstrictive effect of cocaine (which is also directly toxic to capillary endothelium). More rarely encountered are dramatic instances of necrotizing fasciitis (Figure 2.5), which may involve an entire extremity and be accompanied by a severe lymphedema, multiple surrounding ovoid scars, and cellulitis. In extreme cases, auto-amputation of the extremity may occur. The etiology of the fasciitis and the lymphedema is unknown.

Internally, some drugs (e.g., alcohol, ethchlorvynol) may impart a characteristic odor, and some medications contain dyes that may impart a red, green, or blue discoloration to the gastrointestinal tract. *In situ* changes typical of intravenous narcotic abuse include hepatosplenomegaly, enlargement of lymph nodes about the celiac axis and/or porta hepatis, and fecal impaction (from the pharmacologic property of opiates that inhibits intestinal motility).

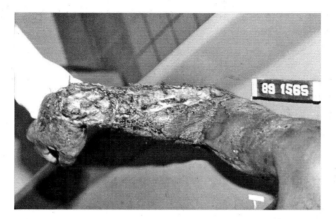

Figure 2.5 Necrotizing fasciitis.

Toxicologic analysis requires specimens be obtained for drug screening, confirmation, and quantitation as well as tissue distribution and evaluation of drug metabolites. Thus, samples for alcohol determination should be obtained from peripheral blood (e.g., femoral vein), vitreous fluid, and central blood (e.g., aorta or pulmonary trunk); brain alcohol determinations are often useful as well. Urine is ideal for qualitative drug screening. Drugs such as tricyclic antidepressants and propoxyphene are best evaluated by analyzing the liver for concentrations of the parent drug and its major metabolites. This is also important for drugs that give spuriously elevated levels in post-mortem blood because of leaching from tissue (tricyclic antidepressants and digitalis are particularly well known to leach from tissues and cause spurious increases in post-mortem blood samples). Other drugs, such as cocaine, not only readily hydrolyze in the post-mortem state but may leach from tissues as well, rendering interpretation of post-mortem drug concentrations in blood even more difficult. For cocaine, brain is the best substance for toxicologic analysis. For routine toxicologic evaluation, samples from the following sites are recommended: peripheral (femoral) blood, blood from aorta and pulmonary trunk, vitreous fluid, bile, liver, brain, and gastric content. In addition, one sample of blood should be centrifuged for post-mortem serum (preserved by freezing) and one preserved with sodium fluoride and refrigerated for long-term storage. Injection sites, the contents of the entire small intestine, hair, and other samples should be obtained as the case dictates.

In recent years, the concept of "post-mortem re-distribution of drugs" has emerged. This is based on the realization that many drugs may have slight or moderate elevations in the post-mortem state, and that the interpretation of post-mortem drug levels does not always correlate with ante-mortem levels. Consequently, popular references now include the post-mortem re-distribution ratio to allow for a more accurate interpretation of post-mortem drug levels.[18]

Finally, as a cautionary note, it should be realized that the gastric mucosa is an excretory organ. As such, water-soluble drugs will pass from the blood into gastric juices and therefore be detected in analysis of gastric contents, usually in very low or trace quantities. Therefore, trace amounts of drugs in the gastric content do not imply oral ingestion of the drug. Likewise, very low levels of alcohol in the gastric content do not imply recent ingestion. In evaluating drugs in gastric content, be sure to calculate the absolute amount of the drug present since most laboratories will report out the concentration of the drug, not the total amount present. Thus, 1 mg/L of drug in 50-mL total gastric content calculates to a total drug content of 0.05 mg.

REFERENCES

1. Wetli, C.V., in *Illicit Drug Abuse in Pathology of Environmental and Occupational Disease,* Craighead, J.D., Ed., Mosby-Year Book, St. Louis, chap. 15, 259–268, 1995.

2. Wetli, C.V., Investigation of drug-related deaths — An overview, *Am. J. Forensic Med. Pathol.*, 5, 111–120, 1984.
3. Mittleman, R.E. and Wetli, C.V., Cocaine and apparent "natural death," *J. Forensic Sci.*, 32, 11–19, 1987.
4. Mittleman, R.E. and Wetli, C.V., The pathology of cocaine abuse, *Adv. Pathol. Lab. Med.*, 4, 37–73, 1991.
5. Humphry, D., *Final Exit*, The Hemlock Society, Eugene, OR, 1991.
6. Haddix, T.L., Harruff, R.C., Reay, D.T., and Haglund, W.D., Asphyxial suicides, *Am. J. Forensic Pathol.*, 17, 308–311, 1996.
7. Bell, M.D., Rao, V.J., Wetli, C.V., and Rodriguez, R.N., Positional asphyxiation in adults — a series of 30 cases from the Dade and Broward County Florida Medical Examiner Offices from 1982 to 1990, *Am. J. Forensic Med. Pathol.*, 13(2), 101–107, 1992.
8. Wetli, C.V. and Fishbain, D.A., Cocaine-induced psychosis and sudden death in recreational cocaine users, *J. Forensic Sci.*, 30, 873–880, 1985.
9. Wetli, C.V., Mash, D., and Karch, S.B., Cocaine-associated agitated delirium and the neuroleptic malignant syndrome, *Am. J. Emerg. Med.*, 14, 425–428, 1996.
10. Mittleman, R.E., Rhabdomyolysis associated with cocaine and ethanol abuse, *Am. Soc. Clin. Pathol.*, 37, 95–104, 1995.
11. Roth, D., Alarcon, F.J., Fernandez, J.A., et al., Acute rhabdomyolysis associated with cocaine intoxication, *N. Engl. J. Med.*, 319, 673–677, 1988.
12. Raval, M.P. and Wetli, C.V., Sudden death from cocaine induced excited delirium: an analysis of 45 cases (abstract), *Am. J. Clin. Pathol.*, 104(3), 329, 1995.
13. Ruttenber, A.J., Lawler-Hernandez, J., Yin, M., et al., Fatal excited delirium following cocaine use: epidemiologic findings provide new evidence for mechanism of cocaine toxicity, *J. Forensic Sci.*, 42, 25–31, 1997.
14. Wetli, C.V., Excited delirium, in *Encyclopedia of Forensic and Legal Medicine*, Vol. 2, Payne-James, J. et al., Eds., Elsevier, Glasgow, 2005, 276–281.
15. Wetli, C.V., in *Excited Delirium in Death in Police Custody*, Ross, D. and Chan, T., Eds., Humana, Totowa, NJ, 2005.
16. Wetli, C.V., Death in custody, United States of America, in *Encyclopedia of Forensic and Legal Medicine*, Vol. 2, Payne-James, J. et al., Eds., Elsevier, Glasgow, 2005, 65–73.
17. Wetli, C.V. and Mittleman, R.E., The body packer syndrome — toxicity following ingestion of illicit drugs packaged for transportation, *J. Forensic Sci.*, 26, 492–500, 1981.
18. Wetli, C.V., Rao, A., and Rao, V.J., Fatal heroin body packing, *Am. J. Forensic Med. Pathol.*, 18(3), 312–318, 1997.
19. Beerman, R., Nunez, D., and Wetli, C.V., Radiographic evaluation of the cocaine smuggler, *Gastrointest. Radiol.*, 11, 3512–3540, 1986.

CHAPTER **3**

Heart Disease

Renu Virmani, M.D., F.A.C.C.,[1] Allen P. Burke, M.D.,[2] and Andrew Farb, M.D.[3]
[1] Medical Director, CVPath, International Registry of Pathology, Gaithersburg, Maryland
[2] Kernan Hospital Pathology Laboratory, University of Maryland Medical Center, Baltimore, Maryland
[3] U.S. Food and Drug Administration, Rockville, Maryland

CONTENTS

3.1 Techniques for Examination of the Heart 79
    3.1.1 Removal of the Heart 80
    3.1.2 Examination of Coronary Arteries 80
    3.1.3 Examination of Coronary Interventions 82
    3.1.4 Examination of the Myocardium in Ischemic Heart Disease 85
    3.1.5 Examination of the Heart in Cardiomyopathy 85
    3.1.6 Examination of the Heart Valves 86
    3.1.7 Prosthetic Heart Valves 90
    3.1.8 Examination of the Aorta 90
    3.1.9 Examination of the Heart in Apparent Cardiac Death without Morphologic
           Abnormality 90
    3.1.10 Evaluating Cardiac Hypertrophy 94
    3.1.11 Conclusions 95
References 95

3.1 TECHNIQUES FOR EXAMINATION OF THE HEART*

The forensic pathologist must examine the heart carefully and methodically in order to obtain maximal information to establish the cause of death. In establishing the manner of death, exclusion of non-cardiac causes is as important as establishing an arrhythmogenic cardiac substrate, because many natural deaths are due to chronic heart diseases that lower the threshold for ventricular fibrillation, without an acute finding. However, it is becoming more important to pinpoint the cause

---

* Reproduced in part and modified from Virmani, R., Ursell, P.C., and Fenoglio, J.J., Jr., Examination of the heart, *Human Pathology,* 18, 432, 1987, and Virmani, R., Ursell, P.C., and Fenoglio, J.J., Jr., Examination of the heart, in *Cardiovascular Pathology,* Virmani, R., Atkinson, J.B., and Fenoglio, J.J., Jr., Eds., W.B. Saunders, Philadelphia, 1991, pp. 1–20.

    The opinions or assertions contained herein are the private views of the authors and are not to be construed as official or as reflecting the views of the Department of the Army or Navy or the Department of Defense.

of natural deaths, for genetic counseling of surviving relatives, for instances of civil litigation, and in occasional deaths where the distinction between natural and accidental death may be difficult.

There is no one "correct" method of examining the heart. In cases of sudden unexpected death in adults, an approach should be utilized that evaluates a large portion of the ventricular myocardium, the site of the vast majority of lethal tachyarrhythmias, and that thoroughly inspects the coronary arteries, the most common site of the cause of ischemic ventricular lesions. In addition, preservation of basic anatomy, in case of further review when the heart can be retained, should be a goal in potentially difficult cases. Last, preservation of frozen tissue or blood in unexplained arrhythmic deaths in young people should be considered.

The preferred method of examination of the heart combines opening of each of the four chambers according to the direction of the flow of blood with bread loafing the myocardium.[1,2] After inspecting the heart *in situ* for pericardial disease, pericardial fluid, saddle emboli, intraventricular air, and relationships to surrounding structures, the heart is removed. The epicardial surfaces and origins of the great arteries are inspected. The coronary arteries are sectioned serially, and the valves inspected from above. The heart is bread-loafed from the apex to the papillary muscles, without cutting the atrioventricular valves, allowing measurements of ventricular free walls, assessment of ventricular dilatation, and characterization of scars and necrosis, facilitating diagnosis of ischemic heart disease and cardiomyopathies. Then, the base of the heart is opened by direction of flow of blood. Briefly, the right atrium is opened from the inferior vena cava to the tip of the atrial appendage; the right ventricle is opened along its lateral border through the tricuspid valve and annulus to the apex of the right ventricle with extension to the pulmonary outflow tract close to the ventricular septum. The left atrium is opened by cutting across the roof of the atrium between the left and right pulmonary veins, and the left ventricle is opened laterally between the anterior and posterior papillary muscles to the apex and then cut along the anterior wall adjacent to the ventricular septum through the aortic outflow tract.

3.1.1 Removal of the Heart

The examination of the adult heart begins after the anterior chest plate has been removed. A longitudinal cut through the anterior aspect of the pericardial sac is made. The amount of pericardial fluid is measured, and its character is noted. The surface of the visceral as well as parietal pericardium is also examined for exudates, adhesions, tumor nodules, or other lesions. A short longitudinal incision 2 cm above the pulmonary valve will enable a check for thromboemboli in the main pulmonary trunk *in situ*. The heart is removed by cutting the inferior vena cava just above the diaphragm and lifting the heart by the apex, reflecting it anteriorly and cephalad to facilitate exposure of the pulmonary veins at their pericardial reflection. After it is confirmed that the pulmonary veins enter normally into the left atrium, the pulmonary veins are cut. The aorta and the pulmonary trunk, the last remaining connections, are cut transversely 2 cm above the semilunar valves. Following removal of the heart from the pericardial cavity and before weighing the specimen, post-mortem blood clots should be removed manually and gently by flushing the heart with water from the left and right atria.

3.1.2 Examination of Coronary Arteries

For research in coronary atherosclerosis, the ideal method of examining the coronary arterial tree requires injecting the coronary arteries with a barium-gelatin mixture and studying the vessels in radiographs.[3,4] Alternatively, in cases of suspected coronary artery disease, the heart may be perfusion fixed with 10% buffered formaldehyde retrograde from the ascending aorta at 100 mm Hg pressure (Figure 3.1) for at least 1 h. In the absence of perfusion fixation, which is impractical for routine forensic evaluation, careful dissection of fresh or immersion-fixed coronary arteries is

HEART DISEASE

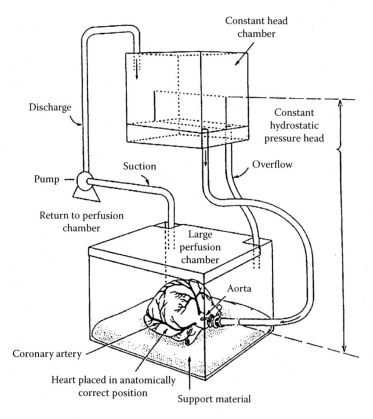

Figure 3.1 Diagram showing the method used for perfusion fixation of the heart. The constant head chamber is placed 135 cm above the perfusion chamber, and is connected via polyethylene tubing to the ascending aorta through the Lucite plug. The excess formaldehyde is suctioned back into the constant head chamber via a pump. Both chambers are covered in order to reduce formalin vapors. (Courtesy J. Frederick Cornhill, D. Phil.)

acceptable, provided that it is understood that precise assessment of percent stenosis is not possible, and that all segments are sectioned adequately in decalcified arteries if necessary.

For perfusion fixation, a specially constructed Lucite plug or a rubber stopper with central tubing is inserted into the aorta, taking care that the Lucite/rubber plug does not touch the aortic valve. The Lucite plug is attached to tubing that is connected to the perfusion chamber.[5] The latter is placed 135 cm above the specimen, and this provides gravity perfusion pressure that is equivalent to 100 mm Hg. As a result, the coronary arteries are fixed in a distended state that approximates the dimensions observed in living patients. Myocardial fixation is also affected, but cardiac chambers are not fixed in a distended state.

This method is fairly simple, does not require sophisticated equipment to achieve good fixation, and allows for immediate dissection after perfusion for approximately 30 min. If perfusion fixation is impractical, the heart should be fixed for 24 h in 10% formaldehyde (10 parts of formaldehyde to 1 part of specimen) before cutting. Radiography of the heart is recommended to determine the extent of coronary and valvular calcification but is not essential; if coronary arteries are heavily calcified, they need to be decalcified prior to cutting at 3- to 4-mm intervals.

The vessels that must be examined in all hearts include the four major epicardial coronary arteries: the left main, the left anterior descending, the left circumflex, and the right coronary arteries. However, it is not unusual to see severe luminal narrowing in smaller branches of the main coronary arteries; left diagonals, left obtuse marginal, ramus (intermediate) branch, and the posterior descending coronary arteries (Figure 3.2).

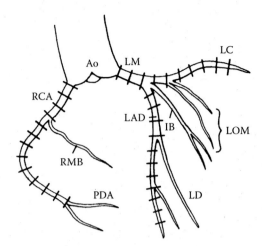

Figure 3.2 Diagram of the right and left epicardial coronary arteries as they arise from the aorta. The four major arteries that must be described in detail are right (RCA), left main (LM), left anterior descending coronary (LAD), and the left circumflex (LC) coronary arteries. Not uncommonly severe coronary (>75% cross-sectional area luminal narrowing) artery disease may affect the smaller branches (IB = intermediate or also called ramus branch, LD = left diagonal, LOM = left obtuse marginal, PDA = posterior descending artery, and RMB = right marginal branch).

Following fixation and/or decalcification, the coronary arteries are cut transversely at 3- to 4-mm intervals with a sharp scalpel blade by a gentle sawing motion (not by firm pressure) to confirm sites of narrowing and to evaluate the pathologic process (e.g., atherosclerotic plaques, thrombi, dissections) directly. If the coronary arteries are heavily calcified, it is desirable to remove the coronary arteries intact. Following dissection of the vessel from the epicardial surface, each coronary artery is carefully trimmed of excess fat and the intact arterial tree is placed in a container of formic acid for slow decalcification over 12 to 18 h.

Decalcification of isolated segments of vessel may be sufficient for cases in which the coronary arteries are only focally calcified. The areas of maximal narrowing are noted by specifying the degrees of reduction of the cross-sectional area of the lumen (e.g., 0 to 25%, 26 to 50%, 51 to 75%, 76 to 90%, 91 to 99%, and 100%). Most cardiologists agree that, in the absence of other cardiac disease, significant or severe coronary artery narrowing is that exceeding a 75% cross-sectional luminal narrowing. Particular attention should be paid to the left main coronary artery because disease in this vessel is very important clinically but frequently overlooked at autopsy.[6]

Cross sections from areas of maximal narrowing from each of the four major epicardial coronary arteries or their branches are selected for histological examination. Sections of all coronary arteries containing thrombi are taken to aid in determining the type of underlying plaque morphology, i.e., plaque rupture, or plaque erosion (ulceration). The site of maximal narrowing must be specified, i.e., proximal, middle, or distal coronary involvement. This is of great medicolegal importance in cases where the patient may have been inadequately examined in the physician's office or emergency room or in the hospital following chest pain. It is the location of the severe narrowing that determines if the patient is operable or not; presence of distal disease signifies non-operability.

3.1.3 Examination of Coronary Interventions

Coronary interventions consist primarily of open bypass surgery and percutaneous coronary interventions (PCI). The technique for evaluation of bypass grafts is tailored to the circumstances of death. In cases of perioperative death, or when there is a question of graft patency, careful dissection is necessary. In cases where it is not possible to perfusion fix the heart, the heart may be immersion fixed in 10% buffered formaldehyde overnight. Prior to cutting the arteries and the

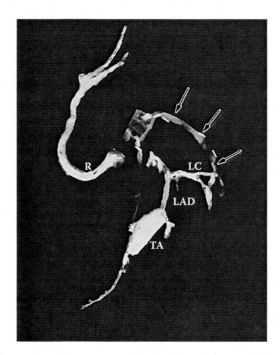

Figure 3.3 Radiograph of epicardial coronary arteries and saphenous vein bypass graft (arrows) to left circumflex (LC) removed at autopsy. Note focal calcification of the native arteries and absence of calcification of the vein graft. A portion of the left anterior coronary artery is surrounded by myocardium (bridged or tunneled coronary artery). Arteries are decalcified prior to sectioning and embedding in paraffin. (From Virmani, R., Ursell, P.C., and Fenoglio, J.J., Examination of the heart, in Virmani, R., Atkinson, J.B., and Fenoglio, J.J., Eds., *Cardiovascular Pathology*, W.B. Saunders, Philadelphia, 1991, pp. 1–20. With permission.)

grafts, it is useful to radiograph and decalcify them when necessary (Figure 3.3). The important features to document are the numbers of the grafts, patency of aortic anastomoses, sites of distal anastomoses, and patency of run-off arteries. It is helpful to remember that grafts that were never patent or closed soon after surgery have a cord-like appearance, without open lumen; that all types of anastomoses are possible, including Y-grafts, touch-down (end-to-end) anastomoses, and interpositions of radial arteries; and that characteristics of native artery at the distal anastomoses (presence of plaque, size of vessel) influence long-term patency.

After inspecting the aortic origin of vein grafts, the grafts themselves are inspected for lumen patency, fibrous intimal thickening, atherosclerotic plaques with or without calcification, and aneurysms. Twists, as well as excessive tautness between aorta and distal anastomosis, are noted.[7] Anastomotic sites are sectioned in different ways depending on whether the connection is end to end or end to side (Figure 3.4). When reporting the findings in the heart, it is important to mention each graft separately; including the location of the aortic orifice, whether it is involved by atherosclerotic ulcerated lesion or not, and if present mention if atheroemboli could have embolized and may be the source of the infarct noted in the heart. Describe the course of the graft and the native coronary vessel to which it is distally anastomosed. Give the size of the native vessel, i.e., less than or greater than 1 mm diameter; vessels less than 1 mm in diameter usually do not carry enough blood to meet the demands of the myocardium. Also, determine if there is severe distal disease present in the grafted vessel.

If the cause of death is related to surgery, the full extent of the saphenous vein grafts is best visualized by barium–gelatin mixture followed by radiography. It is best to inject all the vein grafts simultaneously and to obtain radiographs before injection of the coronary arteries. This enables more detailed study of the native coronary arteries distal to the graft as well as at the coronary

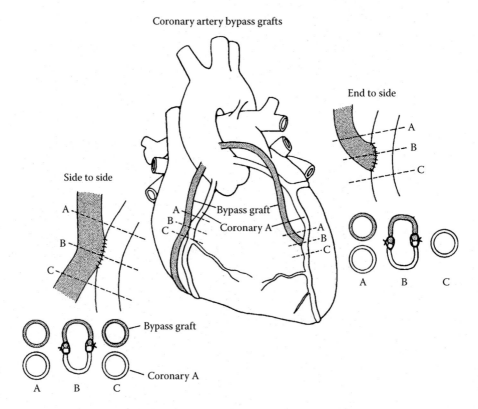

Figure 3.4 Diagram illustrating coronary artery bypass grafts that have end-to-side and side-to-side anastomoses in two separate grafts (shaded area) to left anterior descending and right coronary arteries, respectively. The figure illustrates the method used for sectioning of the anastomotic site with end-to-side and side-to-side anastomoses to demonstrate if any of the three mechanisms for obstruction in the anastomotic site are present (i.e., compression or loss of arterial lumen, which may occur if the majority of the arterial wall has been used for anastomosis; thrombosis at the site of anastomosis; and dissection of the native coronary artery at the site of anastomosis) and if the coronary artery has severe narrowing at the site of anastomosis due to severe atherosclerotic change. (Modified from Bulkley, B.H. and Hutchins, G.M., Pathology of coronary artery bypass graft surgery, *Arch. Pathol.*, 102:273, 1978. From Virmani, R., Ursell, P.C., and Fenoglio, J.J., Examination of the heart, in Virmani, R., Atkinson, J.B., and Fenoglio, J.J., Eds., *Cardiovascular Pathology*, W.B. Saunders, Philadelphia, 1991, pp. 1–20. With permission.)

graft anastomosis. Measurements of lumen diameters may be made from the radiographs. In those cases in which the internal mammary artery is anastomosed to the coronary system, the internal mammary artery is injected from where it has been severed during removal of the heart. The native coronary arteries are injected, fixed, and radiographed to evaluate the extent of disease in the remainder of the coronary arterial tree. If, as mentioned previously, it is not feasible to inject the heart with a barium–gelatin mixture, then the heart may be perfusion fixed with formaldehyde from the aortic stump, taking care that the graft orifices are below the Lucite plug, and the internal mammary artery should be ligated near the site of severance from the chest wall.

The grafts and native arteries may then be removed from the heart, radiographed, and cut at 3- to 4-mm intervals to determine the extent of luminal narrowing, the presence or absence of thrombi, and/or the extent of atherosclerosis in vein grafts and coronary arteries.[8–11]

The forensic pathologist is encountering intracoronary stents at an ever-increasing pace. As is the case with bypass grafts, the degree of evaluation depends on the circumstances of death. Incidentally found stents are commonly encountered in patients with a history of ischemic heart disease by post-mortem radiography. If a death occurs soon after PCI, the heart should be radiographed, site(s) of stenting established, and the stented segments fixed in formalin. The only method for

HEART DISEASE 85

determining in-stent thrombosis involves plastic embedding and sectioning or stent removal without damaging the lumen contents. Either of these procedures requires consultation with a laboratory specializing in such techniques. Immediate fixation of the stented segments and mailing them in adequate formalin to the consultant will provide for documentation of adequacy of stent placement, characterization of underlying plaque, therapeutic misadventures, and in-stent thrombosis.

3.1.4 Examination of the Myocardium in Ischemic Heart Disease

In the presence or absence of acute or healed myocardial infarction, the myocardium is best examined by slicing the ventricles in a manner similar to a loaf of bread. To evaluate the specimen, a series of short-axis cuts are made through the ventricles from apex to base (Figure 3.5A). This method is best accomplished using a long, sharp knife on the intact fixed specimen following examination of the coronary arteries. With the anterior aspect of the heart downward (against the cutting board), the cuts are made parallel to the posterior atrioventricular sulcus at 1- to 1.5-cm intervals from the apex of the heart to a point approximately 2 cm caudal to the sulcus or up to the mid-portion of the papillary muscles of the left ventricle.

The result is a series of cross sections through the ventricles, including papillary muscles with the atrioventricular valve apparatus left intact in the remainder of the specimen. The location and extent of the infarct is noted. Locations may be stated using terms relating to the standard anatomic terms of reference (e.g., anteroseptal, posterolateral). The extent of infarction may be described in terms of circumference of the ventricle involved[12–14] and longitudinal portion of the ventricle involved (e.g., basal third, middle third, apical third; Figure 3.5A and B).

The distribution within the wall is also described (e.g., transmural or subendocardial; transmural when the infarct extends from the endocardium to the epicardium, and subendocardial when <50% of the left ventricular wall is infarcted). The gross pathologic appearance of the myocardium serves as a relatively good index as to the age of the infarct but must be confirmed by histologic examination. Even if infarction cannot be identified grossly, it is important to section the myocardium in the distribution of the severely diseased coronary arteries more extensively.

3.1.5 Examination of the Heart in Cardiomyopathy

The short-axis sectioning (bread-loafing) method described above serves well for the examination of the cardiomyopathic heart. Cardiac hypertrophy and dilation may be demonstrated quite effectively by this method. If the left ventricular cavity measures >4 cm, excluding the papillary muscles, it is considered that the patient was in congestive heart failure prior to death even if there is no history to corroborate the autopsy findings. Left ventricular hypertrophy is said to be present if the left ventricular wall measures >1.5 cm. On the other hand, if the left ventricular wall measures <1.5 cm but the heart weight is increased and the left ventricular cavity is enlarged, then there will be microscopic appreciation of myocyte hypertrophy.

Histological examination of the myocardium is critical to determining the cause of the cardiomyopathy. Thus, in addition to sections of tissue with obvious gross pathology, samples of the walls of all four cardiac chambers, the septum, and papillary muscles should be taken. In the past, the right ventricle has been relatively ignored, but because of the greater awareness of right ventricular infarction and right ventricular dysplasia/cardiomyopathy, it should be a routine to examine the right ventricle carefully. For establishing the diagnosis of right ventricular cardiomyopathy, the most helpful single observation to make is one of fibrosis or scarring in the right ventricular wall with intermingling of fat; these lesions are most often seen in the inflow region of the right ventricle on the posterior wall or in the anterior wall of the right ventricular outflow tract. These lesions can be commonly appreciated grossly if a careful examination of the heart is carried out.

The heart also may be cut in four-chamber view by cutting the heart from the apex to base, along the acute margin of the right ventricle and the obtuse margin of the left ventricle and continuing the plane of section through the atria (Figure 3.6). This four-chamber view is best for

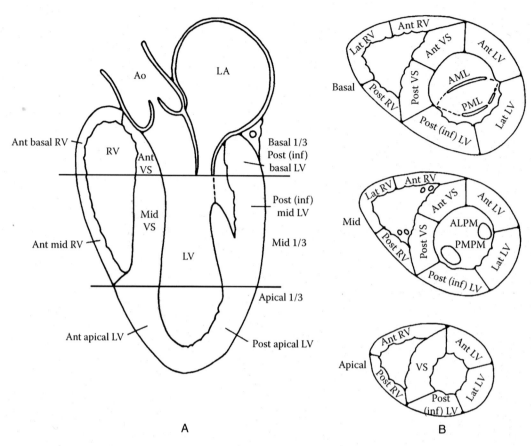

Figure 3.5 The location and extent of myocardial infarction must be indicated by the size, that is, how much of the base to apex is infarcted: basal one third, and/or middle one third, and/or apical one third or more than one third from base to apex. The diagram in (A) shows a long-axis view of the heart with regional nomenclature. (B) The location of the myocardial infarction in the left ventricle must also indicate the wall in which the infarction occurred: anterior, posterior, lateral, septal, or any combination of these. This diagram illustrates a short-axis view through the basal, middle, and apical portions of the right and left ventricles. (Ao = aorta; Ant = anterior; ALPM = anterolateral papillary muscle; AML = anterior mitral leaflet; Inf = inferior; LA = left atrium; LV = left ventricle; Mid = middle; PML = posterior mitral leaflet; PMPM = posteromedial papillary muscle; Post = posterior; RV = right ventricle; VS = ventricular septum) (Modified from Edwards, W.D., Tajik, A.J., and Seward, J.B., Standardized nomenclature and anatomic basis for regional tomographic analysis of the heart, *Mayo Clin. Proc.*, 56:479, 1981. From Virmani, R., Ursell, P.C., and Fenoglio, J.J., Examination of the heart, in Virmani, R., Atkinson, J.B., and Fenoglio, J.J., Eds., *Cardiovascular Pathology*, W.B. Saunders, Philadelphia, 1991, pp. 1–20. With permission.)

evaluating the atrial and ventricular chamber size. In cases of hypertrophic cardiomyopathy, the heart should be cut in the long-axis view of the left ventricular outflow tract. The plane of dissection of the aortic valve leaflet is through the right coronary and the posterior non-coronary leaflets, the anterior and the posterior mitral leaflets, the posterior and the anterior left atrial wall, ventricular septum, posterolateral wall of the left ventrical, and the anterior right ventricular wall (Figure 3.7). Sections to determine the presence of fibromuscular disarray are taken in the transverse plane, usually from the septal location with the largest dimension.

3.1.6 Examination of the Heart Valves

In the case of valvular heart disease, the valves are best studied intact. The atrial and ventricular aspect of the atrioventricular valves and the ventricular and arterial aspects of the semilunar valves

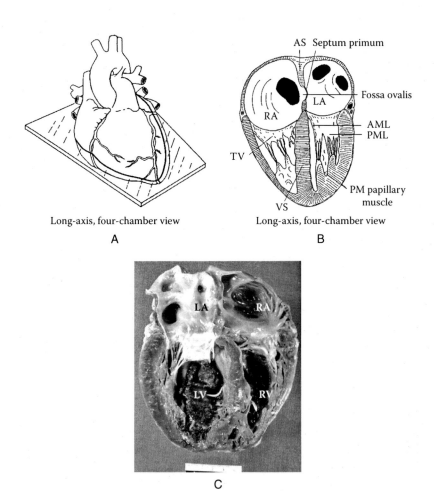

Figure 3.6 (A) Diagram of the heart demonstrating the ultrasonic tomographic plane used for obtaining the long-axis view of the heart. This four-chamber view is best used for evaluating the atrial and ventricular dimensions, intracavitary masses, ventricular and atrial septal defects, atrioventricular valve abnormalities, ventricular aneurysms, and the drainage of pulmonary veins. (B) Diagram demonstrating the four-chamber view of the heart. This method involves sectioning the heart from apex to base, along the acute margin of the right ventricle and the obtuse margin of the left ventricle and continuing the plane of sectioning through the atria. The bisected specimen that is photographed should match the ante-mortem cardiac image. (C) Tomographic analysis of a heart from a 17-year-old boy who developed progressive heart failure over the course of 8 months, showing four-chamber view with biventricular hypertrophy, four-chamber dilatation, and apical right and left ventricular thrombus. (RA = right atrium; LA = left atrium; VS = ventricular septum; TV = tricuspid valve; AML = anterior mitral leaflet; PML = posterior mitral leaflet) (Modified from Tajik, A.L., Seward, I., Hager, D.J., Muir, D.D., and Lie, J.T., Two-dimensional real-time ultrasonic imaging of the heart and great vessels: Technique, image orientation, structure identification and validation, *Mayo Clin. Proc.*, 53:271, 1978. From Virmani, R., Ursell, P.C., and Fenoglio, J.J., Examination of the heart, in Virmani, R., Atkinson, J.B., and Fenoglio, J.J., Eds., *Cardiovascular Pathology*, W.B. Saunders, Philadelphia, 1991, pp. 1–20. With permission.)

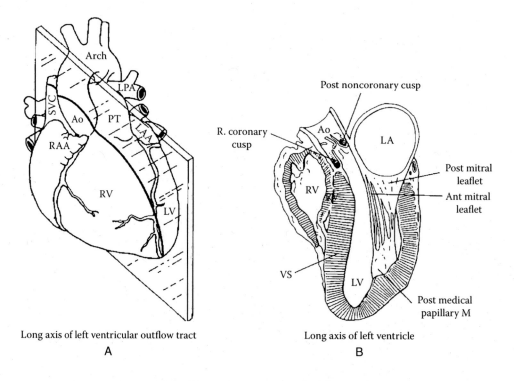

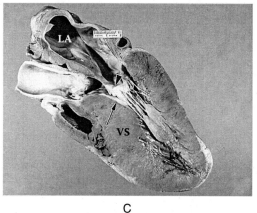

Figure 3.7 (A) Diagram of the heart demonstrating the ultrasonic plane of the long-axis view of the left ventricular outflow tract. The normal anatomic relationship of septal-aortic and mitral-aortic continuity is best shown by this plane of dissection. This method is used for aortic root pathology, including valvular, supravalvular, and intravalvular obstructions, left ventricular chamber size, posterior wall abnormalities, ventricular septal defects, mitral valve disease, and left atrial size. (B) Anatomic landmarks seen with a long-axis view of the left ventricle. The plane of dissection of aortic valve leaflets is through the right coronary and posterior non-coronary leaflets. (C) Left ventricular long-axis section in hypertrophic cardiomyopathy, showing asymmetric septal hypertrophy with a discrete left ventricular outflow tract plaque (arrow) and a thickened anterior mitral leaflet (arrow head). (Ao = aorta; LA = left atrium; LPA = left pulmonary artery; LV = left ventricle; RAA = right atrial appendage; RV = right ventricle; SVC = superior vena cava; VS = ventricular septum) (Modified from Tajik, A.J., Seward, J.B., Hager, D.J., Muir, D.D., and Lie, J.T., Two-dimensional real-time ultrasonic imaging of the heart and great vessels: Technique, image orientation, structure identification and validation, *Mayo Clin. Proc.*, 53:271, 1978. From Virmani, R., Ursell, P.C., and Fenoglio, J.J., Examination of the heart, in Virmani, R., Atkinson, J.B., and Fenoglio, J.J., Eds., *Cardiovascular Pathology*, W.B. Saunders, Philadelphia, 1991, pp. 1–20. With permission.)

are examined (Figure 3.8). Thus, the tricuspid valve is exposed by a lateral incision through the right atrium from the superior vena cava to 2 cm above the valve annulus. Similarly, the mitral valve may be studied following opening of the left atrium via an incision extending from one of the left pulmonary veins to one of the right pulmonary veins and another incision continuing through the atrium laterally to a point 2 cm above the annulus. If a valve abnormality requires closer inspection, the atria, including the interatrial septum, may be removed 1 to 2 cm above the atrioventricular valves (Figure 3.8A). The ventricular aspects of the atrioventricular valves may be viewed following removal of the serial slices of ventricle as described previously.

The semilunar valves are best studied after removal of the aorta (Figure 3.8C) and the main pulmonary artery at a point just above the coronary ostia or valve annulus. In selected cases, the valvular pathology may be best visualized using a four-chamber cut[15–17] in the plane including both the acute and obtuse margins of the heart (Figure 3.6). The aortic valve may be demonstrated by a left ventricular long-axis cut passing from the apex through the outflow tract, ventricular septum, anterior mitral valve leaflet, and aortic valve (Figure 3.7). Measurement of the circumference of annuli, especially in valvular stenosis, is on the whole not very useful. In ectasia of the aorta, it is

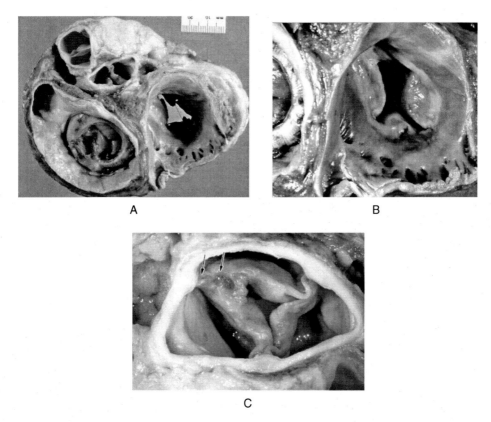

Figure 3.8 (A) The appearance of the atrioventricular valves after removal of both the atria. The mitral valve has been replaced with a bioprosthetic porcine valve, which shows a tear in the muscular leaflet close to the ring. (B) The right atrium has been removed close to the tricuspid valve. Note the valve margins are thickened and the commissure between the posterior and the septal leaflet is fused secondary to chronic rheumatic valvulitis. (C) The aortic valve is examined on removal of the aorta close to the sinotubular junction. There is diffuse thickening of the valve, which is more marked at the free margins with one of the three commissures fused (arrow). These changes are consistent with chronic rheumatic valvulitis. (From Virmani, R., Ursell, P.C., and Fenoglio, J.J., Examination of the heart, in Virmani, R., Atkinson, J.B., and Fenoglio, J.J., Eds., *Cardiovascular Pathology*, W.B. Saunders, Philadelphia, 1991, pp. 1–20. With permission.)

indeed a must to measure the aortic annulus as the valve will be normal in appearance but the annulus will be dilated. Examination of the heart valves should document the type and severity of the valvular disease and its effect on the cardiac chambers and this includes microscopic evaluation.

In cases in which histology of a valve may be helpful, the leaflets are sectioned together with a portion of the adjacent chambers and/or vessel walls. For example, the posterior leaflet of the mitral valve is sectioned including a portion of the left atrium and left ventricular free wall, while the anterior leaflet includes the ventricular septum and non-coronary cusp of the aortic valve. In cases of rheumatic heart disease, sections of the atrial appendages are submitted for histological examination because the incidence of Aschoff's nodules is highest in these structures.

3.1.7 Prosthetic Heart Valves

The objectives for examinations of valve implants include determination of (1) the type of implant (bioprosthesis or mechanical valve) and its size and position regarding annulus and chamber; (2) adequacy of movement of the valve apparatus; (3) presence of thrombi, vegetations, and paravalvular abscesses or leaks; and (4) evidence of valve degeneration.[15] In particular, paravalvular abscesses may not be visible without careful inspection of the native annulus following removal of the implant. Demonstration of any pathology may be enhanced using short-axis cuts through the atrioventricular junction.

3.1.8 Examination of the Aorta

Because atherosclerosis is the most common lesion affecting the aorta, the aorta should be opened longitudinally along its posterior or dorsal aspect from the ascending aorta through the bifurcation and into both common iliac arteries. The extent of disease and the types of lesions may then be described. While this method enables inspection of the complete intimal surface, it may not be optimal for certain types of pathology, such as aortic aneurysms, which may best be demonstrated by cross-sectional slices 1 to 1.5 cm apart in the perfusion-fixed, distended specimen (Figure 3.9). Aortic dissections may be examined by a longitudinal cut (long-axis cut) with the aorta cut into anterior and posterior halves (Figure 3.10) or by transverse cut at 1- to 1.5-cm intervals after the aorta has been allowed to fix for 24 h in a distended state or free floating in anatomic position in formaldehyde.

3.1.9 Examination of the Heart in Apparent Cardiac Death without Morphologic Abnormality

In a significant proportion of apparent arrhythmic deaths, in which toxicologic and scene investigation do not result in a non-natural cause, the gross and histological examination of the heart is normal. In the past, it was assumed that histological examination of the specialized conduction system held the key to finding a possible abnormality to explain death. In the last decades, however, it has become clearer that a large proportion of sudden deaths with normal hearts are due to genetic defects in the cardiac ion channels. It must always be kept in mind that the origin of arrhythmias is generally in the working myocardium. Nevertheless, examination of the conduction system is still worthwhile, in that it allows evaluation of areas at the base of the heart, including small vessels, which may be prone to arterial dysplasia, or small vessel disease, which has been implicated in sudden death.

With practice and careful attention to anatomic landmarks, the conduction system is relatively easily sampled histologically.[18,19] In most humans, the sinus node is a spindle-shaped structure located in the sulcus terminalis on the lateral aspect of the superior vena cava and the right atrium (Figure 3.11). In some patients, it is a horseshoe-shaped structure wrapped across the superior aspect of this cavoatrial junction. Histologically, the sinus node consists of relatively small

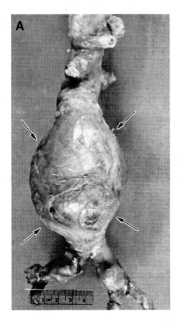
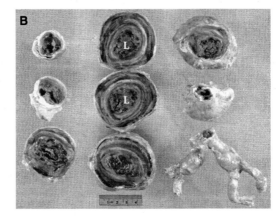

Figure 3.9 (A) External view of the abdominal aorta with an infrarenal aneurysm (arrows). Note the size, which is best expressed as the largest diameter. In this case, it is 7 cm. (B) Same aneurysm cut transversely at 1.0 to 1.5 cm apart. Note the extent of luminal (L) narrowing secondary to an organizing thrombus. (From Virmani, R., Ursell, P.C., and Fenoglio, J.J., Examination of the heart, in Virmani, R., Atkinson, J.B., and Fenoglio, J.J., Eds., *Cardiovascular Pathology*, W.B. Saunders, Philadelphia, 1991, pp. 1–20. With permission.)

diameter, haphazardly oriented atrial muscle cells admixed with connective tissue, collagen, and elastic fibers (Figure 3.12). Often, the artery to the sinus node can be identified in or around the nodal tissue. Because the sinus node is not visible grossly, the entire block of tissue from the suspected area should be taken and serially sectioned, either in the plane perpendicular to the sulcus terminalis (parallel to the long axis of the superior vena cava) or in the plane containing the sulcus (perpendicular to the vessel). In small infants, serial sectioning of the entire cavoatrial junction is preferred.

There are no anatomically distinct muscle tracts for conduction through the atria. The impulse is collected in the atrioventricular node, which is located within the triangle of Koch in the floor of the right atrium. In the heart dissected in the traditional manner along the lines of blood flow, this region is delineated by the following landmarks: the tricuspid valve annulus inferiorly, the coronary sinus posteriorly, and the continuation of the valve guarding the coronary sinus (tendon of Todaro) superiorly (Figure 3.11). The atrioventricular node lies within Koch's triangle (Figure 3.11), and the apex of the triangle anteriorly denotes the point at which the common bundle of His penetrates the fibrous annulus to reach the left ventricle. After penetrating the fibrous annulus at the crest of the ventricular septum, the bundle of His divides into left and right bundle branches.

Thus, the tissue excised for study of the conduction system must include this area completely. From the opened right atrioventricular aspect (with the aortic outflow tract adjacent to the cutting surface) the block to be excised reaches from the anterior margin of the coronary sinus to the medial papillary muscle of the right ventricle, including 1 cm of atrium and ventricle on both sides of the valve. Alternatively, from the left ventricle outflow tract, the block can be cut perpendicular to the aortic valve from the margin of attachment of the anterior leaflet of the mitral valve to the left edge of the membranous septum.

The block should include the non-coronary cusp of the aortic valve and the crest of the ventricular septum (Figure 3.13). In either case, the block of tissue removed should be divided in the plane perpendicular to the annulus, from posterior to anterior; the block to be sectioned should

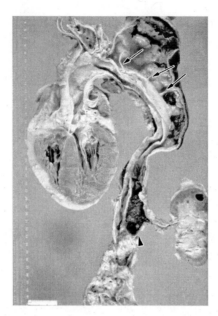

Figure 3.10 The heart has been cut in the long-axis plane, exposing the right and left ventricles and the aortic root and valve. In this plane, the anterior wall of the aorta has been removed. Note the dissecting aneurysm that starts just distal to the subclavian artery and extends along the greater curvature of the aorta to just below the left renal artery (arrowhead). Within the false lumen there are fibrous strands (arrows) connecting the outer media and adventitia to the inner media and intima. Note also the organizing thrombus within a fusiform aneurysm distal to the subclavian and within the abdominal aorta of the false lumen. (From Virmani, R., Ursell, P.C., and Fenoglio, J.J., Examination of the heart, in Virmani, R., Atkinson, J.B., and Fenoglio, J.J., Eds., *Cardiovascular Pathology*, W.B. Saunders, Philadelphia, 1991, pp. 1–20. With permission.)

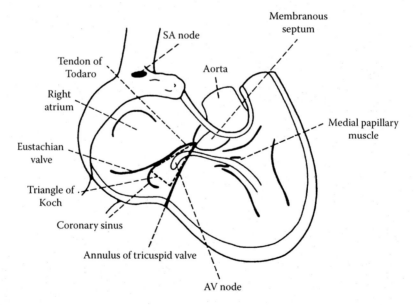

Figure 3.11 Diagram of location of the atrioventricular (AV) and sinoatrial (SA) nodes along with the landmarks that help in locating their positions during sectioning of the heart. (Modified from Davies, M.J., Anderson, R.H., and Becker, A.E., *The Conduction System of the Heart*, Butterworth & Co., London, 1983. From Virmani, R., Ursell, P.C., and Fenoglio, J.J., Examination of the heart, in Virmani, R., Atkinson, J.B., and Fenoglio, J.J., Eds., *Cardiovascular Pathology*, W.B. Saunders, Philadelphia, 1991, pp. 1–20. With permission.)

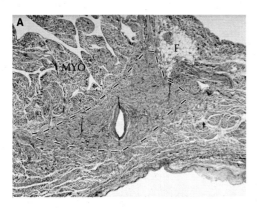 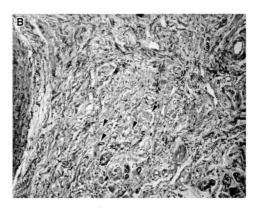

Figure 3.12 (A) The sinus node (outlined) lies in the subepicardium. The superficial layer is surrounded by epicardial fat (F), and the deeper layers anastomose with the surrounding atrial myocardium (MYO). (Movat stain, × 25.) (From Virmani, R., Ursell, P.C., and Fenoglio, J.J., Examination of the heart, in Virmani, R., Atkinson, J.B., and Fenoglio, J.J., Eds., *Cardiovascular Pathology*, W.B. Saunders, Philadelphia, 1991, pp. 1–20. With permission.) (B) High-power view of the SA node showing fibrous tissue, elastin fibers, and small SA node haphazardly arranged fibers.

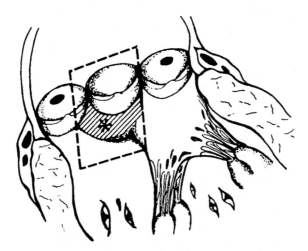

Figure 3.13 Diagram of landmarks for excising the major conduction from the left outflow tract. The membranous septum is marked by an asterisk. (From Virmani, R., Ursell, P.C., and Fenoglio, J.J., Examination of the heart, in Virmani, R., Atkinson, J.B., and Fenoglio, J.J., Eds., *Cardiovascular Pathology*, W.B. Saunders, Philadelphia, 1991, pp. 1–20. With permission.)

be marked with India ink so its orientation can be maintained throughout the embedding process. The atrioventricular node, bundle, and bundle branches are histologically easily identifiable. The atrioventricular node consists of a network of muscle fibers that are smaller than the atrial and ventricular fibers. The cytoplasm is pale in comparison with the ventricular myocardium, but striations and intercalated disk are present. The nuclei are oval in longitudinal sections. The conduction tissue is markedly cellular due to the presence of a large number of endothelial cells and there is a greater amount of elastic tissue than in the surrounding myocardium. As the node extends to penetrate the fibrous body and become the bundle of His, the fibers are less plexiform and more longitudinally oriented (Figure 3.14).

Genetic analysis of mutations that may be the cause of sudden cardiac death in morphologically normal hearts is a complex undertaking. The numerous syndromes associated with sudden death without structural heart disease were originally described by clinical features (e.g., long QT syndrome, Brugada syndrome, polymorphous ventricular tachycardia). As the

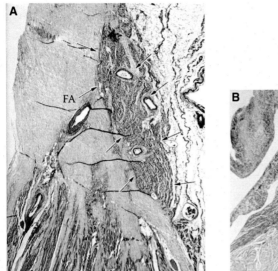
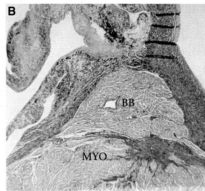

Figure 3.14 (A) The atrioventricular node (arrows) is shown nested against the fibrous annulus (FA). (From Virmani, R., Ursell, P.C., and Fenoglio, J.J., Examination of the heart, in Virmani, R., Atkinson, J.B., and Fenoglio, J.J., Eds., *Cardiovascular Pathology*, W.B. Saunders, Philadelphia, 1991, pp. 1–20. With permission.) (B) The bundle of His branching portion. Note the location underneath the fibrous body (FB) and above the septal myocardium (MYO). (Movat stain, × 25.)

genetic bases for these lesions have been discovered, terminology has slowly shifted to the genes or proteins involved, including sodium and potassium channels (LQT genes/Brugada syndrome), calcium channel-related genes (ryanodine receptor/RyR2), ankyrin-B, etc. From a diagnostic standpoint, some of these mutations are more likely to cause sudden death during exertion, some more specifically with drowning, and others at rest. From this starting point, the hundreds of possible mutations may potentially be screened, in the dozens of exons in each target gene. Archiving frozen tissue is critical in maintaining the possibility of a genetic diagnosis, as enhanced techniques allowing for simultaneous screening of multiple genes become possible. At the time of this writing, the genetic diagnosis of sudden death due to cardiac ion channel disease, in the absence of a family history, is difficult and time consuming, and nearly impossible with archived paraffin-embedded tissue, which greatly limits the size of DNA segments that can be sequenced.

3.1.10 Evaluating Cardiac Hypertrophy

One of the most important decisions while examining the heart is to determine if the heart is normal or abnormal. The heart may not show any anatomic structural abnormality except that it is hypertrophied. Because cardiac hypertrophy may be a cause of death if severe, and physiologic in cases of chronic conditioning, the criteria for increased heart weight are important. We usually utilize the tables published by the Mayo Clinic giving the 95% confidence intervals for the height and weight of male and female individuals from birth to 99 years.[20,21] We recommend that at least four sections of the left ventricle be examined from the four walls of the heart and one section of the posterior wall of the right ventricle; sections should be taken from the mid-ventricular slice. In elderly individuals we also like to take one section each from both the atria, as amyloidosis and drug reactions may be limited to the atria.

3.1.11 Conclusions

This brief description of the examination of the heart is no substitute for the practice of examination and cutting open the heart oneself. In practice, not all methods may be applicable in each laboratory, for each individual, or in all situations. The description is geared more to the forensic pathologist and the examination of the adult heart with the intent of making the method easy yet thorough; a careful examination of the heart is worth the time and effort.

REFERENCES

1. Layman, T.E. and Edwards, J.E., A method for dissection of the heart and major pulmonary vessels, *Arch. Pathol.*, 82, 314, 1966.
2. Ludwig, J. and Titus, J.L., Heart and vascular system, in Ludwig, J., Ed., *Current Method of Autopsy Practice*, W.B. Saunders, Philadelphia, 1979.
3. Hales, M.R. and Carrington, C.B., A pigment gelatin mass for vascular injection, *Yale J. Biol. Med.*, 43, 257, 1971.
4. Hutchins, G.M., Buckley, B.H., Ridolfi, R.L. et al., Correlation of coronary arteriograms and left ventriculograms with postmortem studies, *Circulation,* 56, 32, 1977.
5. Glagov, S., Eckner, F.A.O., and Ler, M., Controlled pressure fixation approaches for hearts, *Arch. Pathol.*, 76, 640, 1963.
6. Isner, J.M., Kishel, J., Kent, K.M., et al., Accuracy of angiographic determination of the left main coronary arterial narrowing: angiographic-histologic correlative analysis in 28 patients, *Circulation,* 63, 1056, 1981.
7. Roberts, W.C., Lachman, A.S., and Virmani, R., Twisting of an aortic-coronary bypass conduit: a complication of coronary surgery, *J. Thorac. Cardiovasc. Surg.,* 75, 722, 1978.
8. Atkinson, J.B., Forman, M.B., Perry, J.M., and Virmani, R., Correlation of saphenous vein bypass graft angiography with histologic changes at autopsy, *Am. J. Cardiol.,* 55, 952, 1985.
9. Atkinson, J.B., Forman, M.B., Vaughn, W.K., et al., Morphologic changes in long-term saphenous bypass grafts, *Chest,* 88, 341, 1985.
10. Buckley, B.H. and Hutchins, C.M., Accelerated "atherosclerosis": A morphologic study of 97 saphenous vein coronary artery bypass grafts, *Circulation,* 55, 163, 1977.
11. Buckley, B.H. and Hutchins, G.M., Pathology of coronary artery bypass graft surgery, *Arch. Pathol.,* 102, 273, 1978.
12. Virmani, R. and Roberts, W.C., Quantification of coronary arterial narrowing and of left ventricular myocardial scarring in healed myocardial infarction with chronic, eventually fatal, congestive heart failure, *Am. J. Med.,* 68, 831, 1980.
13. Hackel, B.D. and Ratliff, N.J., Jr., A technique to estimate the quantity of infarcted myocardium post mortem, *Am. J. Pathol.,* 61, 242, 1974.
14. Lichtig, C., Glagov, S., Feldman, S., and Wissler, R.W., Myocardial ischemia coronary artery atherosclerosis: A comprehensive approach to postmortem studies, *Med. Clin. North Am.,* 57, 79, 1973.
15. Roberts, W.C., Technique of opening the heart at autopsy, in *The Heart,* 5th ed., Hurst, J.W., Logue, R.B., Schlant, R.C., and Wenger, N.K., Eds., McGraw-Hill, New York, 1982.
16. Edwards, W.D., Anatomic basis for tomographic analysis of the heart at autopsy, in *Cardiology Clinics: Cardiac Morphology,* Vol. 2, No. 4, Weller, B.F., Ed., W.B. Saunders, Philadelphia, 1984.
17. Tajik, A.J., Seward, J.B., Hagler, D.J., et al., Two dimensional real-time ultrasonic imaging of the heart and great vessels: Techniques, image orientation, structure identification and validation, *Mayo Clin. Proc.,* 53, 271, 1978.
18. Davies, M.J., Anderson, R.H., and Becker, A.E., *The Conduction System of the Heart,* Butterworth, London, 1983.
19. Anderson, R.H., Ho, S.Y., Smith, A., et al., Studies of the cardiac conduction tissue in the pediatric age group, *Diagn. Histopathol.,* 4, 3 1981.

20. Scholz, D.G., Kitzman, D.W., Hagen, P.T., Ilstrup, D.M., and Edwards, W.D., Age-related changes in normal human hearts during the first 10 decades of life. Part I (Growth): a quantitative anatomic study of 200 specimens from subjects from birth to 19 years old, *Mayo Clin. Proc.,* 63, 126, 1988.
21. Kitzman, D.W., Scholz, D.G., Hagen, P.T., Ilstrup, D.M., and Edwards, W.D., Age-related changes in normal human hearts during the first 10 decades of life. Part II (Maturity): a quantitative anatomic study of 765 specimens from subjects 20–99 years old, *Mayo Clin. Proc.,* 63, 137, 1988.
22. Virmani, R., Ursell, P.C., and Fenoglio, J.J., Examination of the heart, in *Cardiovascular Pathology,* Virmani, R., Atkinson, J.B., and Fenoglio, J.J., Eds., W.B. Saunders, Philadelphia, 1991, 1–20.

CHAPTER **4**

Vascular Effects of Substance Abuse*

Frank D. Kolodgie, Ph.D.,[1] Allen P. Burke, M.D.,[2] Jagat Narula, M.D., Ph.D.,[3] Florabel G. Mullick, M.D.,[1] and Renu Virmani, M.D., F.A.C.C.[4]

[1] Armed Forces Institute of Pathology, Washington, D.C.
[2] Kernan Hospital Pathology Laboratory, University of Maryland Medical Center, Baltimore, Maryland
[3] University of California, Irvine, School of Medicine and Medical Center, Irvine, California
[4] CVPath, International Registry of Pathology, Gaithersburg, Maryland

CONTENTS

4.1 Cocaine 98
    4.1.1 Vasospasticity and Microvascular Resistance.......................................101
    4.1.2 Thrombosis 101
    4.1.3 Accelerated Atherosclerosis 102
    4.1.4 Endothelial Dysfunction..102
    4.1.5 Hemodynamic Alterations 103
    4.1.6 Vasculitis..103
    4.1.7 Synergy with Other Drugs 104
4.2 Methamphetamine 105
    4.2.1 Heroin 105
    4.2.2 Nicotine...106
    4.2.3 Solvents ("Glue Sniffing") 106
    4.2.4 Vasculopathies Associated with Legitimate Medications.....................106
        4.2.4.1 Ergot Alkaloids...106
    4.2.5 Ephedrine and Pseudoephedrine 107
    4.2.6 Phenylpropanolamine 108
    4.2.7 L-Tryptophan 108
References 108

Statistics provided by the Drug Abuse Warning Network (DAWN) over the past two decades have documented an increasing prevalence in substance abuse as manifested by emergency room and Medical Examiner data (i.e., drug mentions). For example, the Office of the Chief Medical Examiner (OCME) has reported a marked increase in the number of drug abuse deaths in Maryland

---

* The opinions or assertions contained herein are the private views of the authors and are not to be construed as official or as reflecting the views of the Department of the Army or Navy or the Department of Defense.

from 1986 to 1993, with drug deaths increasing sharply from 119 cases in 1986 to 356 in 1993, a 199% increase over seven years.[1] Narcotic drugs, specifically heroin, have played a major role in the rising number of drug abuse deaths.[1] Not surprisingly, cardiovascular complications have accompanied this increase. However, characterizing the effects of drugs of abuse on the vasculature is difficult because not all abused drugs result in anatomic changes. Direct human studies are scarcely available, and the studies that exist are performed under limited, controlled conditions which do not replicate the usage picture or conditions of the drug abuser. The drugs may have multiple effects depending on the dose, route of administration, impurities, underlying risk factors for cardiovascular disease, and concomitant use of other drugs such as ethanol and caffeine. In this section, the underlying pathogenic mechanisms associated with substance abuse leading to vascular complications (Table 4.1) are discussed.

Vasoconstriction at the epicardial or microvascular level may result in ischemia of almost any organ, but the vessel often fails to show any morphologic change. Drugs may also lead to formation of intravascular thrombi resulting in organ infarcts. A common complication of drug abuse may be cutaneous or cerebral manifestations of vasculitis. In some instances, acute hemodynamic worsening of hypertension may also lead to dissection of the aorta and rupture of arterial aneurysms resulting in intracranial hemorrhage.

There are several morphologic manifestations of drug-induced vascular disease. Vasoconstriction in itself is rarely identifiable by histologic methods, although contraction band necrosis of smooth muscle cells has rarely been reported in cases of clinically documented vasoconstriction. Chronic vasoconstriction may result in medial hypertrophy. Luminal thrombosis may be secondary to endothelial damage, underlying atherosclerosis, or effects of drugs on the clotting cascade. Atherosclerosis, which is a complex process involving lipid metabolism, endothelial dysfunction, immune activation, and thrombosis may be accelerated in persons exposed to drugs (Figure 4.1). Fibrointimal proliferation (increased numbers of intimal smooth muscle cells either via migration from the media or intimal proliferation) may be secondary to toxic endothelial damage. Inflammatory vascular diseases (vasculitis) have been described as a drug-related effect. The two major types of drug-induced vasculitis occur either via antigen-antibody complex deposition, usually in arterioles and venules (small vessel or hypersensitivity vasculitis, Figure 4.2), or via direct toxic damage (toxic vasculitis, Figure 4.3), generally involving muscular arteries. Both types of vasculitis are characterized by fibrinoid necrosis of vascular walls, especially toxic vasculitis with occlusion by luminal thrombosis and/or fibrointimal proliferation and vessel rupture.

4.1 COCAINE

Of all the known drugs of abuse associated with vascular toxicity, cocaine is the most common. The recent increase in cocaine abuse has predominantly occurred due to the availability of cocaine base, known on the street as crack, which produces an instant euphoria when smoked. The mechanisms of cocaine-induced vascular toxicity are complex. Acute administration of cocaine (whether in the base or hydrochloride form) causes an increase in heart rate and blood pressure. Myocardial oxygen consumption increases from systemic catecholamine release and increased alpha-adrenergic effects due to a blockade of norepinephrine reuptake.[2–4] Cocaine also acts as a local anesthetic by inhibiting sodium influx into cells, and this is most likely responsible for the vasodilatory action of the drug. The anesthetic effects of cocaine are expected at higher doses while the sympathomimetic actions are more likely to be prevalent at lower concentrations. Cocaine is detected in the circulation immediately after its consumption with a plasma half-life of approximately 1 h. However, the half-life for euphoria is less than 1 h which may lead to the repetitive use of cocaine.

The blood cocaine level required to produce the euphoric effects is approximately 10^{-7} to 10^{-5} mol/L; median plasma levels following intravenous cocaine use in cocaine-related deaths are reported to be approximately 6×10^{-7} mol/L to 3×10^{-4} mol/L.[5–7] "Binge users" of cocaine are

Table 4.1 Pathologic Vascular Manifestations of Substance Abuse

Drugs	Vasospasm	Thrombosis	Hypersensitivity Vasculitis	Necrotozing (Toxic) Arteritis	Fibrointimal Proliferation	Accelerated Atherosclerosis	Veno-Occlusive Disease
Recreational							
Cocaine	X	X	X	X	X	X	—
Heroin	—	—	X	—	—	—	X
Amphetamine and methamphetamine	X	X	—	X	X	—	—
Nicotine	X	X	X	—	—	X	—
Glue sniffing/solvents	X	—	—	—	—	—	—
Prescription							
Tricyclic antidepressants and phenothiazines	X	—	—	—	—	—	—
Ergot alkaloids	X	X	—	—	X	—	—
Ephedrine/pseudoephedrine	X	—	X	X	—	—	—
Non-Prescription							
Phenylpropanolamine and anorexiants	X	—	—	X	—	—	—
L-Tryptophan	X	—	—	X	X	—	—

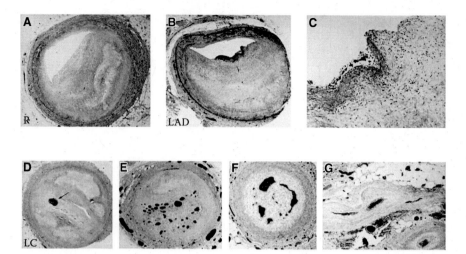

Figure 4.1 Cocaine-induced coronary atherosclerosis. The right (A) and the left anterior descending (LAD, B) coronary arteries are severely narrowed by atherosclerotic plaque. The LAD (B) shows a superficial luminal thrombus (plaque erosion) consisting of fibrin and few inflammatory cells. The left circumflex (D,E,F) shows organized thrombus totally occluding the lumen. In (D), the recanalized channel is occluded by a thrombus (arrow). (G) Epicardial small branches of coronary arteries show severe intimal proliferation probably secondary to an organizing thrombus. The patient, a 30-year-old male, was a known cocaine abuser.

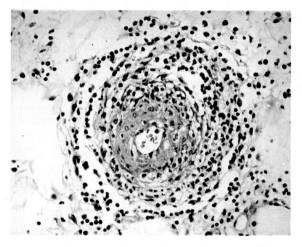

Figure 4.2 Small cell (hypersensitivity) vasculitis. There is a predominantly lymphoid infiltrate surrounding an arteriole, with focal neutrophilic karyorrhexis within the arterial wall. The patient had a cutaneous rash (palpable purpura) following exposure to diazepam, to which she was sensitized.

known to use high doses for extended periods, oftentimes up to 200 h.[8] Plasma concentrations during a "binge" have not been documented, although it is thought that the effects of cocaine on the cardiovascular system are especially significant during bingeing. Following absorption, cocaine is cleared from the circulation, primarily hydrolyzed to benzoylecgonine and metabolized to ecgonine methyl ester (by plasma cholinesterases). At least in cerebral vessels, cocaine metabolites appear to be biologically active and may partially contribute to cocaine's toxic effects.[9] Furthermore, because of individual variability in plasma cholinesterase activity, cocaine abusers with low enzyme levels may be predisposed to the cardiotoxic effects of the drug. In humans, cocaine is rapidly metabolized, and less than 1% is excreted in urine; the major fraction of an administered dose of cocaine is recovered in urine predominantly as ecgonine methyl ester and benzoylecgonine.[10,11]

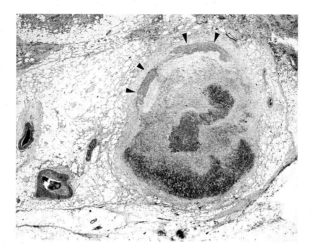

Figure 4.3 Toxic arteritis (polyarteritis). There is segmental destruction of the media with aneurysm formation. Residual intact media is present (arrowheads). The patient was a 24-year-old amphetamine addict who expired from mesenteric arteritis and peritoneal hemorrhage.

4.1.1 Vasospasticity and Microvascular Resistance

Coronary spasm has been repeatedly proposed as a mechanism of the unexplained sudden cardiac death in young cocaine abusers.[12] Clinical studies with intranasal cocaine administration in patients undergoing coronary arteriography for the evaluation of chest pain have demonstrated a moderate reduction in luminal caliber and microvascular resistance.[13] Although cocaine-induced vasospasm has not been demonstrated clinically, ergonovine-induced coronary spasm has been reported to occur at the site of severe coronary lesions in young cocaine abusers.[14] Animal experiments have confirmed that cocaine results in only a minimal diffuse diminution in coronary artery caliber.[15] Such non-critical reduction in luminal diameter is presumably clinically insignificant. It therefore seems likely that acceleration of atherosclerotic lesions must form a substrate for the hypersensitive vasoconstrictive response of a vessel to cocaine consumption. In support of this, cocaine-induced vasoconstriction has been shown to be enhanced at sites of significant fixed stenosis.[16]

Alternatively, coronary vasospasm in cocaine abusers may be associated with an increase in adventitial mast cells. A significantly higher prevalence of adventitial mast cells in victims of cocaine-associated sudden cardiac death has been reported when compared to individuals without a history of substance abuse.[17] Similarly, increased adventitial mast cells have been demonstrated at autopsy in patients who had clinically documented vasospastic angina in the absence of severe atherosclerotic coronary disease.[18] Mast cells are a rich source of histamine, which is often used as a provocative test to induce spasm in patients with suspected variant angina.[19,20] Furthermore, other mast cell products such as prostaglandin D2 and leukotrienes C4 and D4 are also modulators of vascular smooth muscle tone; prostaglandin D2-induced vasoconstriction is 5- to 10-fold more potent than norepinephrine.[21]

4.1.2 Thrombosis

Multiple studies have reported angiographic evidence of coronary thrombosis in young cocaine abusers, predominantly associated with minor atherosclerotic irregularities of coronary arteries. On the other hand, the autopsy data from the young patients with cocaine abuse-associated acute coronary thrombosis leading to sudden cardiac death have demonstrated that approximately 40% of patients suffer from severe atherosclerotic lesions of one or more major coronary arteries.[22,23] The average age of the cocaine abusers in these reports was approximately 30 years. However, the

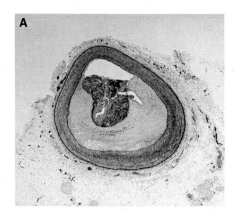 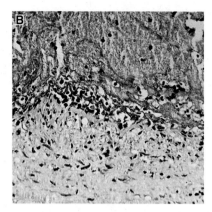

Figure 4.4 Cocaine-induced coronary thrombosis. (A) There is moderate (50%) luminal narrowing by atherosclerotic plaque composed of fibrointimal thickening consisting of smooth muscle cells in a proteoglycan-collagen matrix. (B) A higher magnification demonstrating a platelet thrombus overlying a plaque rich in smooth muscle cells and proteoglycans (plaque erosion).

decreased prevalence of angiographically determined atherosclerotic disease in cocaine abusers may result from angiographic underestimation of the atherosclerotic lesions due to the relatively diffuse nature of the disease.[24–26] The thrombi isolated from these autopsy examinations have been demonstrated to be rich in platelets[17,22,23] and are characteristically not associated with rupture of the underlying plaques (Figure 4.4).

The mechanism of cocaine-induced thrombosis is not clear. Reports of the direct effects of cocaine on platelet function *in vitro* have been inconclusive and contradictory: cocaine either stimulates or inhibits aggregation.[27–31] However, it is thought that cocaine-induced platelet activation may occur *in vivo* due to indirect effects of the drug. Evidence in support of this hypothesis comes from studies in which platelet activation assessed *ex vivo* by P-selectin expression was increased in long-term habitual cocaine abusers and in dogs treated with cocaine.[32,33] Alternatively, coronary spasm may also explain the increased prevalence of thrombosis associated with cocaine abuse.

4.1.3 Accelerated Atherosclerosis

Recent post-mortem studies in patients have emphasized that accelerated atherosclerosis may be an important etiologic factor in cocaine-induced acute coronary syndromes.[17,22–24] Kolodgie et al.[35] conducted a retrospective analysis of aortic sudanophilic lesions in asymptomatic young (median age, 25 years) cocaine abusers. After controlling for known risk factors of atherosclerosis, cocaine abuse was the only significant predictor of the extent of sudanophilia, suggesting that cocaine abuse was an independent risk factor for lipid infiltration in the vessel wall.[35] Accelerated atherosclerosis attributed to cocaine has been demonstrated experimentally in hypercholesterolemia-induced atherosclerosis in rabbits.[36] Also, cocaine abusers with coronary thrombosis have an increase in inflammatory cell infiltrate in severely narrowed atherosclerotic coronary arteries (Figure 4.1). Various mechanisms such as cocaine-related increase in plasma lipids, direct and indirect increase in endothelial permeability, higher prevalence of mast cells and other inflammatory cells in plaques may contribute to the lesions as discussed below.

4.1.4 Endothelial Dysfunction

As described above, atherosclerotic lesions occur prematurely and are likely to be more severe in cocaine abusers. Furthermore, these lesions develop regardless of the presence of conventional risk factors. Cocaine-induced endothelial cell dysfunction may be one of the predisposing factors,

VASCULAR EFFECTS OF SUBSTANCE ABUSE 103

but whether this involves a direct and/or indirect action of the drug is unknown. Cocaine has been shown to disrupt the balance of endothelial prostacyclin and thromboxane production, which may be related to the increased tendency toward thrombosis and vasospasm observed in some cocaine abusers.[37,38] *In vitro* cell culture studies have demonstrated that cocaine increases the permeability function of endothelial cell monolayers as a possible mechanism of accelerated atherosclerosis.[36] Cocaine-treated endothelial cell monolayers demonstrated an increased permeability to horseradish peroxidase without affecting cell viability. Furthermore, cocaine-induced release of intracellular calcium stores may result in dysregulation of cytoskeletal integrity.[39] It has also been suggested that cocaine may suppress endothelial cell growth,[39] cause focal loss of endothelial cell integrity, or produce areas of extensive endothelial cell sloughing.[40,41]

As discussed earlier, the sympathomimetic effects of cocaine are associated with a transient but marked increase in blood pressure and some degree of vasoconstriction. These transient hemodynamic aberrations may cause endothelial injury. Indeed, cholesterol-fed rabbits typically develop atherosclerotic lesions in the thoracic aorta at sites of increased endothelial cell turnover.

Cocaine-related endothelial dysfunction may be associated with impairment of endothelium-dependent vasorelaxation. Forearm blood flow during acetylcholine infusion in long-term cocaine abusers was significantly lower when compared with subjects without a prior history of drug abuse.[42] Whether attenuation of endothelial-dependent vasodilatory mechanisms by cocaine results from lethal injury to the endothelium, insensitivity of smooth muscle cells to nitric oxide, or inhibition of enzymatic pathways responsible for nitric oxide synthesis remains to be determined.

4.1.5 Hemodynamic Alterations

Hypertension-related vascular complications have been commonly reported with sympathomimetic drugs such as cocaine. Sympathomimetic actions secondary to acute or chronic cocaine abuse are well documented and may result from peripheral inhibition of neuronal reuptake of monoamines and increased epinephrine release from the adrenal medulla as well as central activation of the sympathetic nervous system. The transient increase in blood pressure, at least after acute cocaine abuse, has been associated with aortic dissection (Figure 4.5), rupture of aortic aneurysms, and hemorrhagic strokes in patients with preexisting hypertension.[43-45] Recently, intracranial hemorrhage has also been shown to be associated with cocaine abuse.[46-49] Of the 17 non-traumatic cases of intracranial hemorrhage analyzed at autopsy, 10 were associated with cocaine: 7 cases had intracerebral hemorrhage while 3 had ruptured berry aneurysms.[49] No pathologic evidence of vasculopathy was present in these patients.

4.1.6 Vasculitis

Cocaine vasculitis has rarely been observed. Occasional cases of hypersensitivity vasculitis, similar to development of an Arthus reaction in experimental animals,[50-56] have been observed. Vasculitis characteristically results in fibrinoid necrosis of arteriolar and venular walls associated with disintegrating polymorphonuclear cells and histochemical localization of immunoglobulins and complement.[57,58] The lesions may eventually evolve into loose granulomas consisting of pallisading lymphocytes admixed with eosinophils and macrophages and, seldom, giant cells.[57,58] The most common site of vascular involvement in humans is skin; kidneys are involved in one-half and liver in a third.[58]

Cocaine is also reported to induce systemic necrotizing arteritis of predominantly medium- and small-sized cerebral arterial vessels frequently at branch points.[54,59] Affected areas characteristically have marked necrotic lesions with neutrophilic infiltration and various stages of healing. No giant cells or granulomas are seen, and the vascular adventitia is not involved. The mechanism of drug-induced necrotizing vasculitis has not been established and could be either immunological or directly toxic.

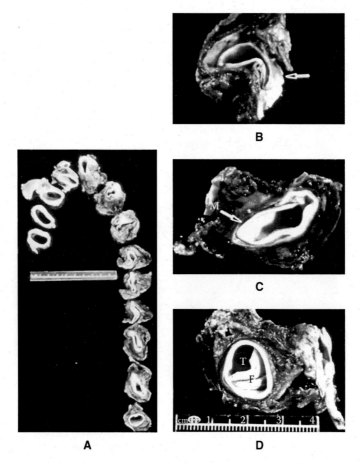

Figure 4.5 Cocaine-induced aortic dissection. (A) Multiple cross-sections through the aorta from the ascending aorta to the descending thoracic segment demonstrate dissection beginning at the aortic arch. (B) A cross-section through the descending thoracic aorta demonstrates the rupture site (arrow) of the false lumen. This rupture resulted in hemothorax and the death of the patient, who was a 24-year-old habitual cocaine abuser. (C) The dissection plane within the media (M) is clearly evident in this cross-section that demonstrates the intimal tear. (D) The true (T) and false (F) lumens can be distinguished readily in this cross-section demonstrating the medial flap.

4.1.7 Synergy with Other Drugs

It is estimated that half the individuals consume alcohol during cocaine bingeing, and this promotes hepatic transformation of cocaine to cocaethylene.[60–67] Cocaethylene has a substantially longer half-life and therefore its persistent systemic presence may increase the likelihood of cocaine cardiotoxicity.[68] Cocaethylene has more potent sodium channel blocking activity compared to cocaine and its proarrhythmic effects may also be related to sudden death in the setting of ischemic myocardium.[69]

Another common drug that may be abused with cocaine is morphine. Morphine is a known secretogogue of mast cells that have been shown to be present in strikingly higher numbers in cocaine-associated atherosclerotic lesions. Mast cells are believed to play an important role in cocaine-related vasospastic manifestations.[70]

Similarly, synergistic interactions have been demonstrated for cocaine and cigarette smoking. Both agents are known to increase the metabolic demands on the heart but may also reduce oxygen supply. Moliteno et al.[71] have reported the influence of intranasal cocaine and cigarette smoking, alone and together, on myocardial oxygen demand and coronary artery dimensions in 42 subjects with and without atherosclerosis. Although none of the patients developed chest pain

VASCULAR EFFECTS OF SUBSTANCE ABUSE 105

or ischemic electrocardiographic changes after cocaine use or cigarette smoking, oxygen demand increased by approximately 10% after either cigarette smoking or cocaine use, and by 50% after their simultaneous consumption. While the diameter of the normal coronary artery decreased by 6 to 7% with the use of either or both substances, reduction in the luminal diameter of the diseased artery segments for cigarette smoking, cocaine use, and both substances was 5%, 10%, and 20%, respectively.

4.2 METHAMPHETAMINE

The vascular effects of amphetamines have considerable similarity with sympathomimetic amines (ephedrine, phenylpropanolamine) and cocaine, which is alike structurally. Methamphetamine is abused orally, intravenously, or smoked in a crystal form ("ice"). Methamphetamine is metabolized to amphetamine, independent of the route of administration. Acute toxicity to amphetamine may manifest as rhabdomyolysis, disseminated intravascular coagulation, pulmonary edema, vascular spasm, and acute myocardial infarction. The ring-substituted amphetamines 3,4-methylenedioxymethyl-amphetamine (MDMA, "ecstasy") and 3,4-methylenedioxyethylamphetamine (MDEA, "eve") have emerged as popular recreational drugs of abuse over the last decade.[72] Pharmacological studies indicate that these substances produce a mixture of central stimulant and psychedelic effects, many of which appear to be mediated by brain monoamines, particularly serotonin and dopamine.[73]

Chronic use of amphetamines may result in systemic and coronary artery vasospasm that results in an increased cardiac workload, impaired myocardial blood supply, and congestive failure, similar to end-stage hypertension. Sudden cardiac death may also occur. A few reports describe acute myocardial infarction associated with amphetamine abuse.[74] Potential explanations include coronary vasospasm, excessive catecholamine discharge resulting in ischemic myocardial necrosis, and catecholamine-mediated platelet aggregation with subsequent thrombus formation. The syndrome closely resembles acute myocardial infarction by cocaine abuse. As with cocaine toxicity, a deleterious effect of associated treatment with beta-blockers in the setting of myocardial infarction has also been observed.[71,75] Acute renal failure due to accelerated hypertension following the ingestion of 3,4-methylenedioxymethamphetamine ("ecstasy") has been reported.[76]

A necrotizing vasculitis resembling polyarteritis nodosa (Figure 4.3) has been reported in young abusers of methamphetamine, which may affect cerebral or visceral arteries. Histologically, there is fibrinoid necrosis of the media and intima of muscular arteries, with a neutrophilic, eosinophilic, lymphocytic, and histiocytic infiltrate. Lesions at various stages may be seen with fresh thrombi in early lesions, florid intimal proliferation with marked luminal narrowing in subacute lesions, and destruction of the elastic lamina with replacement by collagen and luminal obliteration in later lesions. The cerebral effects of amphetamines are similar to those of other sympathomimetic amines (ephedrine and phenylpropranolamine).

4.2.1 Heroin

Heroin (diacetylmorphine) is a synthetic morphine derivative which, after administration, is hydrolytically deacetylated to 6-acetyl-morphine and excreted in the urine. Heroin has been associated with cerebral arteritis[77] and visceral polyarteritis.[78] Heroin may also have a direct toxic effect on the terminal hepatic veins,[79] the acute lesion being described as an inflammatory infiltrate of neutrophils and mononuclear cells in sinusoidal lumina and terminal veins, which progresses to fibrosis of the central veins. Heroin is also associated with glomerular injury which may result in malignant hypertension. This heroin-associated nephropathy seen in African American intravenous drug addicts has given way in the 1990s to HIV-associated nephropathy as a result of shared needles.[80]

4.2.2 Nicotine

Nicotine is well known to stimulate the release of catecholamines, resulting in vasoconstriction and other vascular effects of catecholamine release.[81,82] In addition, there may be direct toxicity of nicotine to vascular endothelial cells *in vitro*,[83] and an inhibition of apoptosis, which may contribute to an increase in smooth muscle cells within atherosclerotic plaques, possibly by monoclonal proliferation.[84] Nicotine has been found to be chemotactic for human neutrophils but not monocytes,[85] and in contrast to most other chemoattractants for neutrophils, does affect degranulation or superoxide production. Thus, nicotine may promote inflammation which may indirectly contribute to some of the associated vasculopathies. Nicotine transdermal patches used to help nicotine addiction have been associated with a leucocytoclastic vasculitis.[86,87]

4.2.3 Solvents ("Glue Sniffing")

Inhalation abuse of volatile solvents, previously known generically as "glue sniffing," is typically pursued by adolescents.[88] Glue sniffing has been associated with myocardial infarction, presumably secondary to coronary spasm as no fixed coronary lesions were identified by angiography.[89] The mechanism of sudden death in solvent sniffers is believed to be related to enhanced cardiac sensitivity to endogenous catecholamines.[90]

4.2.4 Vasculopathies Associated with Legitimate Medications

The sympathomimetic effects of tricyclic antidepressants are well documented, and overdose with these tricyclic amines is a major source of morbidity and mortality.[91] The most common cardiovascular effect of tricyclic amines is orthostatic hypotension, which is particularly serious in the elderly because it may lead to falls resulting in serious physical injuries. Severe orthostatic hypotension is more likely to develop in depressed patients with left ventricular impairment and/or in patients taking other drugs such as diuretics or vasodilators.[92] With chronic therapeutic administration, tricyclic antidepressants and phenothiazines have been associated with myocardial ischemia and infarction in the absence of fixed coronary lesions.[93]

4.2.4.1 Ergot Alkaloids

The ergot alkaloids are characterized by a nucleus of lysergic acid with the addition of side chains which divide the group into amino acids and amine alkaloids. Ergotamine, an example of an amino acid alkaloid, and methysergide, an example of an amine alkaloid, are both currently used in the prophylaxis and treatment of migraine headaches. The scleroticum of the fungus *Claviceps purpurea* is especially rich in ergot alkaloid, and was responsible for outbreaks of epidemic ergotism (St. Anthony's fire) following the mass ingestion of improperly stored rye in wet seasons. Ergot alkaloids have been used in large doses as an abortafacient.[94]

The toxic effects of ergot alkaloids include acute poisoning resulting in vasospasm and gangrene (usually as a complication of the induction of abortion), and acute idiosyncratic vasospasm secondary to a small dose of the drug. In this country, by far the most common form of ergot alkaloid toxicity is secondary to chronic ingestion of ergotamine, although outbreaks of St. Anthony's fire are still occasionally documented in developing countries.[94,95] Of recent incidence, bromocriptine mesylate, when used for the suppression of lactation in the puerperium, has been reported to cause generalized or focal vasospasm affecting the cardiac and/or cerebral blood vessels.[95]

The most common clinical manifestations of ergot alkaloid vasospasm are upper and lower extremity ischemia, which may result in claudication and ischemic ulcers of gangrene.[96] Other vasospastic sequelae of methylsergide or ergotamine toxicity include transient ischemic attacks, stroke (Figure 4.6), cardiac angina, and intestinal angina. Angiographic studies reveal narrowed

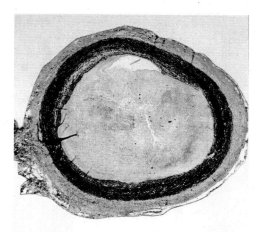

Figure 4.6 Ergotamine-induced fibrointimal proliferation. The carotid artery demonstrates marked narrowing by minimally cellular fibrointimal proliferation. The patient was a 45-year-old woman with chronic ergotamine toxicity who expired from a cerebrovascular accident. Elastic van Gieson stain.

vessels, which may show gradual smooth narrowing or irregular outlines with focal stenosis.[96,97] Laboratory studies are generally normal. A history will reveal chronic ingestion of ergotamine or methysergide, usually for migraine headaches, often by self-medication or doses exceeding the therapeutic recommendations. Symptoms often remit following cessation or lowering of medication dosage.

Pathologically, there are few vascular changes in acute cases of ergot poisoning, although contraction bands and medial necrosis may be noted within arterial walls. Chronic forms of ergotamine toxicity may have normal histologic findings[98] or changes consistent with chronic vasoconstriction, including medial hypertrophy, intimal proliferation, intimal hyalinization, and luminal thrombosis.

The mechanism(s) of ergot alkaloid toxicity are not yet completely clear. Physiologic doses result in vasoconstriction of painfully dilated cranial arteries, generally by the interaction of ergot with alpha-adrenergic receptors (alpha-adrenergic blockade) and serotonin antagonism.[99] Toxic vasoconstriction may occur secondarily to a direct effect of ergot on the arterial media, exacerbated by a direct toxic effect on the capillary endothelium. High levels of platelet-derived growth factor have been detected in an individual with chronic ergotism, suggesting that growth factors are released as a result of chronic endothelial damage.[98]

4.2.5 Ephedrine and Pseudoephedrine

Ephedrine and pseudoephedrine are sympathomimetic amines that may cause hypertension and tachyarrhythmias due to beta-adrenergic stimulation. Toxic effects may result from overdose, drug interactions (e.g., serotonin reuptake inhibitors), or diseases that increase sensitivity to sympathomimetic agents.[100] Reported adverse events range in severity from tremor and headache to death and include reports of stroke, myocardial infarction, chest pain, seizures, insomnia, nausea and vomiting, fatigue, and dizziness.[101,102] Ephedrine is the preferred vasoconstrictor for the treatment of hypotension after epidural and spinal anesthesia in obstetrics because it preserves uterine perfusion better than pure alpha-adrenergic agonists. Although during pregnancy the vasoconstrictor response to ephedrine is diminished, its stimulatory effect on nitric oxide synthase may release nitric oxide.[103]

The incidence of patients developing cerebral hemorrhage, presumably by the development of toxic vasculitis, is rare.[104] Reported cases of cerebral hemorrhage secondary to ephedrine are fewer than those complicating the use of phenylpropanolamine and amphetamines.[104-107] Clinical man-

108 PATHOLOGY, TOXICOGENETICS, AND CRIMINALISTICS OF DRUG ABUSE

agement of ephedrine overdose is mostly supportive and requires establishing respiration, initiating emesis, administering activated charcoal and a cathartic, and monitoring the patient's blood pressure, ECG, fluid intake, and urinary output.[108]

4.2.6 Phenylpropanolamine

Phenylpropanolamine is a synthetic sympathomimetic amine that is found in cold medications and diet pills. Although the vascular effects of phenylpropanolamine were previously considered minor, relative to ephedrine and amphetamine, increasing reports of toxicity in patients taking larger doses of this drug, especially in diet pills, have led to a reappraisal of the potential toxicity of the drug.

Cerebral hemorrhage has been reported in phenylpropanolamine toxicity after a dose of 50 mg or more.[106] In some commonly used anorexiants, including methamphetamine and phenylpropanolamine, an association with stroke has been reported.[108,109] Angiography in individuals with phenylpropanolamine toxicity has demonstrated vascular beading that has been ascribed to both vasospasm and to vasculitis.[106,110] In occasional instances in which histologic examination was performed, a necrotizing vasculitis has been identified.[105,106] It is unknown what proportions of phenylpropanolamine-, amphetamine-, and ephedrine-induced cerebral hemorrhages are due to vasculitis, and what proportions are due to vasospam related to catecholamine release.[106]

4.2.7 L-Tryptophan

The eosinophilia-myalgia syndrome associated with the ingestion of L-tryptophan was first recognized in late 1989.[111] Similar pathologic manifestations of eosinophilic myalgia syndrome share many features with the toxic oil syndrome caused by ingestion of adulterated rapeseed oil in Spain.[112] Although available over the counter in the U.S., L-tryptophan is dispensed only by prescription in Germany. Epidemiologic studies strongly suggest that the offending toxin is a contaminant used in the preparation of tryptophan, and not tryptophan itself.[113] Putative offending agents from suspected lots of L-tryptophan include 1,1'-ethylidenebis(tryptophan) and 3-phenylamino-1,2-propanediol, an aniline derivative. Most symptomatic patients are those that chronically ingest large doses of tryptophan (500 mg to several grams a day), although a dose-related toxic effect was not observed in an epidemiological study of German patients.[111] Vascular effects include pulmonary hypertension resulting from obstruction of pulmonary vessels.[112] Intermittent coronary spasm resulting in episodes of myocardial damage has also been reported.[115] Fibrointimal proliferation of small coronary arteries has also been described in patients with eosinophilia-myalgia syndrome associated with L-tryptophan.[116]

Because L-tryptophan is metabolized to a number of compounds, including kynurenine, quinolate, serotonin, 5-hydroxyindoacetic acid, and homovanillic acid, a potential vasospastic role of one or more of these compounds has been investigated. A recent study did not find a link between any of these compounds and coronary vasospasm, but implicated increased levels of eosinophil granule major basic protein.[115]

REFERENCES

1. Li L, Smialek JE. Observations on drug abuse deaths in the state of Maryland. *J Forensic Sci* 1996;41:106–9.
2. Muscholl E. Effect of cocaine and related drugs on the uptake of noradrenaline by heart and spleen. *Br J Pharmacol* 1961;62:352.
3. Fuder H, Bath F, Wiebelt H, Muscholl E. Autoinhibition of noradrenaline release from the rat heart as a function of the biophase concentration. Effects of exogenous alpha-adrenoceptor agonists, cocaine, and perfusion rate. *Naunyn Schmiedebergs Arch Pharmacol* 1984;325:25–33.

VASCULAR EFFECTS OF SUBSTANCE ABUSE

4. Perper JA, Van Thiel DH. Cardiovascular complications of cocaine abuse. *Recent Dev Alcohol* 1992;10:343–61.

5. Van Dyke C, Barash PG, Jatlow P, Byck R. Cocaine: plasma concentrations after intranasal application in man. *Science* 1976;191:859–61.

6. Poklis A, Maginn D, Barr JL. Tissue disposition of cocaine in man: a report of five fatal poisonings. *Forensic Sci Int* 1987;33:83–8.

7. Poklis A, Mackell MA, Graham M. Disposition of cocaine in fatal poisoning in man. *J Anal Toxicol* 1985;9:227–9.

8. Gawin FH. Cocaine addiction: psychology and neurophysiology [published erratum appears in *Science* 1991 Aug 2;253(5019):494]. *Science* 1991;251:1580–6.

9. Madden JA, Powers RH. Effect of cocaine and cocaine metabolites on cerebral arteries *in vitro*. *Life Sci* 1990;47:1109–14.

10. Ambre J. The urinary excretion of cocaine and metabolites in humans: a kinetic analysis of published data. *J Anal Toxicol* 1985;9:241–5.

11. Jeffcoat AR, Perez-Reyes M, Hill JM, Sadler BM, Cook CE. Cocaine disposition in humans after intravenous injection, nasal insufflation (snorting), or smoking. *Drug Metab Dispos* 1989;17:153–9.

12. Minor RL, Jr., Scott BD, Brown DD, Winniford MD. Cocaine-induced myocardial infarction in patients with normal coronary arteries [see comments]. *Ann Intern Med* 1991;115:797–806.

13. Lange RA, Cigarroa RG, Yancy CW, Jr., Willard JE, Popma JJ, Sills MN, McBride W, Kim AS, Hillis LD. Cocaine-induced coronary-artery vasoconstriction [see comments]. *N Engl J Med* 1989;321:1557–62.

14. Smith HW, Liberman HA, Brody SL, Battey LL, Donohue BC, Morris DC. Acute myocardial infarction temporally related to cocaine use. Clinical, angiographic, and pathophysiologic observations. *Ann Intern Med* 1987;107:13–8.

15. Hale SL, Alker KJ, Rezkalla S, Figures G, Kloner RA. Adverse effects of cocaine on cardiovascular dynamics, myocardial blood flow, and coronary artery diameter in an experimental model. *Am Heart J* 1989;118:927–33.

16. Flores ED, Lange RA, Cigarroa RG, Hillis LD. Effect of cocaine on coronary artery dimensions in atherosclerotic coronary artery disease: enhanced vasoconstriction at sites of significant stenoses. *J Am Coll Cardiol* 1990;16:74–9.

17. Kolodgie FD, Virmani R, Cornhill JF, Herderick EE, Smialek J. Increase in atherosclerosis and adventitial mast cells in cocaine abusers: an alternative mechanism of cocaine-associated coronary vasospasm and thrombosis. *J Am Coll Cardiol* 1991;17:1553–60.

18. Forman MB, Oates JA, Robertson D, Robertson RM, Roberts LJ, Virmani R. Increased adventitial mast cells in a patient with coronary spasm. *N Engl J Med* 1985;313:1138–41.

19. Kaski JC, Crea F, Meran D, Rodriguez L, Araujo L, Chierchia S, Davies G, Maseri A. Local coronary supersensitivity to diverse vasoconstrictive stimuli in patients with variant angina. *Circulation* 1986;74:1255–65.

20. Ginsburg R, Bristow MR, Kantrowitz N, Baim DS, Harrison DC. Histamine provocation of clinical coronary artery spasm: implications concerning pathogenesis of variant angina pectoris. *Am Heart J* 1981;102:819–22.

21. Burke JA, Levi R, Guo ZG, Corey EJ. Leukotrienes C4, D4 and E4: effects on human and guinea-pig cardiac preparations *in vitro*. *J Pharmacol Exp Ther* 1982;221:235–41.

22. Mittleman RE, Wetli CV. Cocaine and sudden "natural" death. *J Forensic Sci* 1987;32:11–9.

23. Dressler FA, Malekzadeh S, Roberts WC. Quantitative analysis of amounts of coronary arterial narrowing in cocaine addicts. *Am J Cardiol* 1990;65:303–8.

24. Sheikh KH, Harrison JK, Harding MB, Himmelstein SI, Kisslo KB, Davidson CJ, Bashore TM. Detection of angiographically silent coronary atherosclerosis by intracoronary ultrasonography. *Am Heart J* 1991;121:1803–7.

25. Tobis JM, Mallery J, Mahon D, Lehmann K, Zalesky P, Griffith J, Gessert J, Moriuchi M, McRae M, Dwyer ML, et al. Intravascular ultrasound imaging of human coronary arteries *in vivo*. Analysis of tissue characterizations with comparison to *in vitro* histological specimens. *Circulation* 1991;83:913–26.

26. McPherson DD, Hiratzka LF, Lamberth WC, Brandt B, Hunt M, Kieso RA, Marcus ML, Kerber RE. Delineation of the extent of coronary atherosclerosis by high-frequency epicardial echocardiography. *N Engl J Med* 1987;316:304–9.

27. Heesch CM, Negus BH, Steiner M, Snyder RW, II, McIntire DD, Grayburn PA, Ashcraft J, Hernandez JA, Eichhorn EJ. Effects of *in vivo* cocaine administration on human platelet aggregation. *Am J Cardiol* 1996;78:237–9.
28. Kugelmass AD, Oda A, Monahan K, Cabral C, Ware JA. Activation of human platelets by cocaine. *Circulation* 1993;88:876–83.
29. Jennings LK, White MM, Sauer CM, Mauer AM, Robertson JT. Cocaine-induced platelet defects. *Stroke* 1993;24:1352–9.
30. Rezkalla SH, Mazza JJ, Kloner RA, Tillema V, Chang SH. Effects of cocaine on human platelets in healthy subjects. *Am J Cardiol* 1993;72:243–6.
31. Togna G, Tempesta E, Togna AR, Dolci N, Cebo B, Caprino L. Platelet responsiveness and biosynthesis of thromboxane and prostacyclin in response to *in vitro* cocaine treatment. *Haemostasis* 1985;15:100–7.
32. Kugelmass AD, Shannon RP, Yeo EL, Ware JA. Intravenous cocaine induces platelet activation in the conscious dog. *Circulation* 1995;91:1336–40.
33. Rinder HM, Ault KA, Jatlow PI, Kosten TR, Smith BR. Platelet alpha-granule release in cocaine users. *Circulation* 1994;90:1162–7.
34. Fogo A, Superdock KR, Atkinson JB. Severe arteriosclerosis in the kidney of a cocaine addict. *Am J Kidney Dis* 1992;20:513–5.
35. Kolodgie FD, Virmani R, Cornhill JF, Herderick EE, Malcom GT, Mergner WJ. Cocaine: an independent risk factor for aortic sudanophilia. A preliminary report. *Atherosclerosis* 1992;97:53–62.
36. Kolodgie FD, Wilson PS, Cornhill JF, Herderick EE, Mergner WJ, Virmani R. Increased prevalence of aortic fatty streaks in cholesterol-fed rabbits administered intravenous cocaine: the role of vascular endothelium. *Toxicol Pathol* 1993;21:425–35.
37. Eichhorn EJ, Demian SE, Alvarez LG, Willard JE, Molina S, Bartula LL, Prince MD, Inman LR, Grayburn PA, Myers SI. Cocaine-induced alterations in prostaglandin production in rabbit aorta. *J Am Coll Cardiol* 1992;19:696–703.
38. Cejtin HE, Parsons MT, Wilson L, Jr. Cocaine use and its effect on umbilical artery prostacyclin production. *Prostaglandins* 1990;40:249–57.
39. Welder AA, Grammas P, Fugate RD, Rohrer P, Melchert RB. A primary culture system of rat heart-derived endothelial cells for evaluating cocaine-induced vascular injury. *Toxicol Methods* 1993;3:109–18.
40. Gilloteaux J, Dalbec JP. Transplacental cardiotoxicity of cocaine: atrial damage following treatment in early pregnancy. *Scanning Microsc* 1991;5:519–29; discussion 29–31.
41. Jones LF, Tackett RL. Chronic cocaine treatment enhances the responsiveness of the left anterior descending coronary artery and the femoral artery to vasoactive substances. *J Pharmacol Exp Ther* 1990;255:1366–70.
42. Havranek EP, Nademanee K, Grayburn PA, Eichhorn EJ. Endothelium-dependent vasorelaxation is impaired in cocaine arteriopathy. *J Am Coll Cardiol* 1996;28:1168–74.
43. Gadaleta D, Hall MH, Nelson RL. Cocaine-induced acute aortic dissection. *Chest* 1989;96:1203–5.
44. Cohle SD, Lie JT. Dissection of the aorta and coronary arteries associated with acute cocaine intoxication. *Arch Pathol Lab Med* 1992;116:1239–41.
45. McDermott JC, Schuster MR, Crummy AB, Acher CW. Crack and aortic dissection. *Wis Med J* 1993;92:453–5.
46. Aggarwal SK, Williams V, Levine SR, Cassin BJ, Garcia JH. Cocaine-associated intracranial hemorrhage: absence of vasculitis in 14 cases. *Neurology* 1996;46:1741–3.
47. Nalls G, Disher A, Daryabagi J, Zant Z, Eisenman J. Subcortical cerebral hemorrhages associated with cocaine abuse: CT and MR findings. *J Comput Assist Tomogr* 1989;13:1–5.
48. Green RM, Kelly KM, Gabrielsen T, Levine SR, Vanderzant C. Multiple intracerebral hemorrhages after smoking "crack" cocaine. *Stroke* 1990;21:957–62.
49. Nolte KB, Brass LM, Fletterick CF. Intracranial hemorrhage associated with cocaine abuse: a prospective autopsy study. *Neurology* 1996;46:1291–6.
50. Merkel PA, Koroshetz WJ, Irizarry MC, Cudkowicz ME. Cocaine-associated cerebral vasculitis. *Semin Arthritis Rheum* 1995;25:172–83.
51. Gradon JD, Wityk R. Diagnosis of probable cocaine-induced cerebral vasculitis by magnetic resonance angiography. *South Med J* 1995;88:1264–6.

52. Giang DW. Central nervous system vasculitis secondary to infections, toxins, and neoplasms. *Semin Neurol* 1994;14:313–9.
53. Morrow PL, McQuillen JB. Cerebral vasculitis associated with cocaine abuse. *J Forensic Sci* 1993;38:732–8.
54. Fredericks RK, Lefkowitz DS, Challa VR, Troost BT. Cerebral vasculitis associated with cocaine abuse. *Stroke* 1991;22:1437–9.
55. Kaye BR, Fainstat M. Cerebral vasculitis associated with cocaine abuse. *JAMA* 1987;258:2104–6.
56. Cerebral vasculitis associated with cocaine abuse or subarachnoid hemorrhage? [letter]. *JAMA* 1988;259:1648–9.
57. Krendel DA, Ditter SM, Frankel MR, Ross WK. Biopsy-proven cerebral vasculitis associated with cocaine abuse. *Neurology* 1990;40:1092–4.
58. Enriquez R, Palacios FO, Gonzalez CM, Amoros FA, Cabezuelo JB, Hernandez F. Skin vasculitis, hypokalemia and acute renal failure in rhabdomyolysis associated with cocaine [letter]. *Nephron* 1991;59:336–7.
59. Daras M, Tuchman AJ, Koppel BS, Samkoff LM, Weitzner I, Marc J. Neurovascular complications of cocaine. *Acta Neurol Scand* 1994;90:124–9.
60. Barinaga M. Miami vice metabolite [news]. *Science* 1990;250:758.
61. Hearn WL, Flynn DD, Hime GW, Rose S, Cofino JC, Mantero-Atienza E, Wetli CV, Mash DC. Cocaethylene: a unique cocaine metabolite displays high affinity for the dopamine transporter. *J Neurochem* 1991;56:698–701.
62. Jatlow P, Hearn WL, Elsworth JD, Roth RH, Bradberry CW, Taylor JR. Cocaethylene inhibits uptake of dopamine and can reach high plasma concentrations following combined cocaine and ethanol use. *NIDA Res Monogr* 1991;105:572–3.
63. Hearn WL, Rose S, Wagner J, Ciarleglio A, Mash DC. Cocaethylene is more potent than cocaine in mediating lethality. *Pharmacol Biochem Behav* 1991;39:531–3.
64. Perez-Reyes M, Jeffcoat AR. Ethanol/cocaine interaction: cocaine and cocaethylene plasma concentrations and their relationship to subjective and cardiovascular effects. *Life Sci* 1992;51:553–63.
65. Perez-Reyes M. Subjective and cardiovascular effects of cocaethylene in humans. *Psychopharmacology (Berl)* 1993;113:144–7.
66. Covert RF, Schreiber MD, Tebbett IR, Torgerson LJ. Hemodynamic and cerebral blood flow effects of cocaine, cocaethylene and benzoylecgonine in conscious and anesthetized fetal lambs. *J Pharmacol Exp Ther* 1994;270:118–26.
67. Wilson LD, Henning RJ, Suttheimer C, Lavins E, Balraj E, Earl S. Cocaethylene causes dose-dependent reductions in cardiac function in anesthetized dogs. *J Cardiovasc Pharmacol* 1995;26:965–73.
68. Randall T. Cocaine, alcohol mix in body to form even longer lasting, more lethal drug [news]. *JAMA* 1992;267:1043–4.
69. Xu YQ, Crumb WJ, Jr., Clarkson CW. Cocaethylene, a metabolite of cocaine and ethanol, is a potent blocker of cardiac sodium channels. *J Pharmacol Exp Ther* 1994;271:319–25.
70. Klein LM, Lavker RM, Matis WL, Murphy GF. Degranulation of human mast cells induces an endothelial antigen central to leukocyte adhesion. *Proc Natl Acad Sci USA* 1989;86:8972–6.
71. Moliterno DJ, Willard JE, Lange RA, Negus BH, Boehrer JD, Glamann DB, Landau C, Rossen JD, Winniford MD, Hillis LD. Coronary-artery vasoconstriction induced by cocaine, cigarette smoking, or both. *N Engl J Med* 1994;330:454–9.
72. Milroy CM, Clark JC, Forrest AR. Pathology of deaths associated with "ecstasy" and "eve" misuse. *J Clin Pathol* 1996;49:149–53.
73. Steele TD, McCann UD, Ricaurte GA. 3,4-Methylenedioxymethamphetamine (MDMA, "Ecstasy"): pharmacology and toxicology in animals and humans. *Addiction* 1994;89:539–51.
74. Bashour TT. Acute myocardial infarction resulting from amphetamine abuse: a spasm-thrombus interplay? *Am Heart J* 1994;128:1237–9.
75. Ragland AS, Ismail Y, Arsura EL. Myocardial infarction after amphetamine use. *Am Heart J* 1993;125:247–9.
76. Woodrow G, Harnden P, Turney JH. Acute renal failure due to accelerated hypertension following ingestion of 3,4-methylenedioxymethamphetamine ('ecstasy'). *Nephrol Dial Transplant* 1995;10:399–400.
77. King J, Richards M, Tress B. Cerebral arteritis associated with heroin abuse. *Med J Aust* 1978;2:444–5.

78. Citron BP, Halpern M, McCarron M, Lundberg GD, McCormick R, Pincus IJ, Tatter D, Haverback BJ. Necrotizing angiitis associated with drug abuse. *N Engl J Med* 1970;283:1003–11.

79. de Araujo MS, Gerard F, Chossegros P, Porto LC, Barlet P, Grimaud JA. Vascular hepatotoxicity related to heroin addiction. *Virchows Arch A Pathol Anat Histopathol* 1990;417:497–503.

80. Bakir AA, Dunea G. Drugs of abuse and renal disease. *Curr Opin Nephrol Hypertens* 1996;5:122–6.

81. Murphy DA, O'Blenes S, Nassar BA, Armour JA. Effects of acutely raising intracranial pressure on cardiac sympathetic efferent neuron function. *Cardiovasc Res* 1995;30:716–24.

82. Grassi G, Seravalle G, Calhoun DA, Bolla GB, Giannattasio C, Marabini M, Del Bo A, Mancia G. Mechanisms responsible for sympathetic activation by cigarette smoking in humans. *Circulation* 1994;90:248–53.

83. Pitillo R, Cigarette smoking and endothelial injuy: A review. *Tobacco Smoking and Atherosclerosis.* 1989, New York: Plenum Press.

84. Wright SC, Zhong J, Zheng H, Larrick JW. Nicotine inhibition of apoptosis suggests a role in tumor promotion. *FASEB J* 1993;7:1045–51.

85. Totti ND, McCusker KT, Campbell EJ, Griffin GL, Senior RM. Nicotine is chemotactic for neutrophils and enhances neutrophil responsiveness to chemotactic peptides. *Science* 1984;223:169–71.

86. Lagrue G, Verra F, Lebargy F. Nicotine patches and vascular risks [letter; comment]. *Lancet* 1993;342:564.

87. Van der Klauw MM, Van Hillo B, Van den Berg WH, Bolsius EP, Sutorius FF, Stricker BH. Vasculitis attributed to the nicotine patch (Nicotinell). *Br J Dermatol* 1996;134:361–4.

88. Steffee CH, Davis GJ, Nicol KK. A whiff of death: fatal volatile solvent inhalation abuse. *South Med J* 1996;89:879–84.

89. Cunningham SR, Dalzell GW, McGirr P, Khan MM. Myocardial infarction and primary ventricular fibrillation after glue sniffing. *Br Med J (Clin Res Ed)* 1987;294:739–40.

90. McLeod AA, Marjot R, Monaghan MJ, Hugh-Jones P, Jackson G, Timmis AD, Smyth P, Monaghan M, Walker L, Daly K, McLeod AA, Jewitt DE. Chronic cardiac toxicity after inhalation of 1,1,1-trichloroethane Milrinone in heart failure. Acute effects on left ventricular systolic function and myocardial metabolism. *Br Med J (Clin Res Ed)* 1987;294:727–9.

91. Warrington SJ, Padgham C, Lader M. The cardiovascular effects of antidepressants. *Psychol Med Monogr Suppl* 1989;16:i–iii, 1–40.

92. Glassman AH, Preud'homme XA. Review of the cardiovascular effects of heterocyclic antidepressants. *J Clin Psychiatry* 1993;54 Suppl:16–22.

93. Chamsi-Pasha H, Barnes PC. Myocardial infarction: a complication of amitriptyline overdose. *Postgrad Med J* 1988;64:968–70.

94. Magee R. Saint Anthony's fire revisited. Vascular problems associated with migraine medication. *Med J Aust* 1991;154:145–9.

95. Weaver R, Phillips M, Vacek JL. St. Anthony's fire: a medieval disease in modern times: case history. *Angiology* 1989;40:929–32.

96. Iffy L, McArdle JJ, Ganesh V, Hopp L. Bromocriptine related atypical vascular accidents postpartum identified through medicolegal reviews. *Med Law* 1996;15:127–34.

97. McKiernan TL, Bock K, Leya F, Grassman E, Lewis B, Johnson SA, Scanlon PJ. Ergot induced peripheral vascular insufficiency, non-interventional treatment. *Cathet Cardiovasc Diagn* 1994;31:211–4.

98. Raroque HG, Jr., Tesfa G, Purdy P. Postpartum cerebral angiopathy. Is there a role for sympathomimetic drugs? *Stroke* 1993;24:2108–10.

99. Pietrogrande F, Caenazzo A, Dazzi F, Polato G, Girolami A. A role for platelet-derived growth factor in drug-induced chronic ergotism? A case report. *Angiology* 1995;46:633–6.

100. Oliver JW, Abney LK, Strickland JR, Linnabary RD. Vasoconstriction in bovine vasculature induced by the tall fescue alkaloid lysergamide. *J Anim Sci* 1993;71:2708–13.

101. Skop BP, Finkelstein JA, Mareth TR, Magoon MR, Brown TM. The serotonin syndrome associated with paroxetine, an over-the-counter cold remedy, and vascular disease [see comments]. *Am J Emerg Med* 1994;12:642–4.

102. Wiener I, Tilkian AG, Palazzolo M. Coronary artery spasm and myocardial infarction in a patient with normal coronary arteries: temporal relationship to pseudoephedrine ingestion. *Cathet Cardiovasc Diagn* 1990;20:51–3.

103. Adverse events associated with ephedrine-containing products — Texas, December 1993–September 1995. *MMWR Morb Mortal Wkly Rep* 1996;45:689–93.
104. Li P, Tong C, Eisenach JC. Pregnancy and ephedrine increase the release of nitric oxide in ovine uterine arteries. *Anesth Analg* 1996;82:288–93.
105. Wooten MR, Khangure MS, Murphy MJ. Intracerebral hemorrhage and vasculitis related to ephedrine abuse. *Ann Neurol* 1983;13:337–40.
106. Glick R, Hoying J, Cerullo L, Perlman S. Phenylpropanolamine: an over-the-counter drug causing central nervous system vasculitis and intracerebral hemorrhage. Case report and review. *Neurosurgery* 1987;20:969–74.
107. Forman HP, Levin S, Stewart B, Patel M, Feinstein S. Cerebral vasculitis and hemorrhage in an adolescent taking diet pills containing phenylpropanolamine: case report and review of literature. *Pediatrics* 1989;83:737–41.
108. Nadeau SE. Intracerebral hemorrhage and vasculitis related to ephedrine abuse [letter]. *Ann Neurol* 1984;15:114–5.
109. Sawyer DR, Conner CS, Rumack BH. Managing acute toxicity from nonprescription stimulants. *Clin Pharm* 1982;1:529–33.
110. Kokkinos J, Levine SR. Possible association of ischemic stroke with phentermine. *Stroke* 1993;24:310–3.
111. Fallis RJ, Fisher M. Cerebral vasculitis and hemorrhage associated with phenylpropanolamine. *Neurology* 1985;35:405–7.
112. Mayeno AN, Gleich GJ. The eosinophilia-myalgia syndrome: lessons from Germany [editorial; comment]. *Mayo Clin Proc* 1994;69:702–4.
113. Tabuenca JM. Toxic-allergic syndrome caused by ingestion of rapeseed oil denatured with aniline. *Lancet* 1981;2:567–8.
114. Carr L, Ruther E, Berg PA, Lehnert H. Eosinophilia-myalgia syndrome in Germany: an epidemiologic review [see comments]. *Mayo Clin Proc* 1994;69:620–5.
115. Campagna AC, Blanc PD, Criswell LA, Clarke D, Sack KE, Gold WM, Golden JA. Pulmonary manifestations of the eosinophilia-myalgia syndrome associated with tryptophan ingestion. *Chest* 1992;101:1274–81.
116. Hertzman PA, Maddoux GL, Sternberg EM, Heyes MP, Mefford IN, Kephart GM, Gleich GJ. Repeated coronary artery spasm in a young woman with the eosinophilia-myalgia syndrome. *JAMA* 1992;267:2932–4.
117. Hayashi T, James TN. Immunohistochemical analysis of lymphocytes in postmortem study of the heart from fatal cases of the eosinophilia myalgia syndrome and of the toxic oil syndrome. *Am Heart J* 1994;127:1298–308.

CHAPTER **5**

Myocardial Alterations in Drug Abusers

Steven B. Karch, M.D., FFFLM
Consultant Pathologist and Toxicologist, Berkeley, California

CONTENTS

5.1   Epidemiology 116
5.2   Mechanism of Myocardial Hypertrophy 116
5.3   Consequences of Myocardial Hypertrophy 117
5.4   Other Stimulant-Related Disorders 117
5.5   Myocardial Disease in Opiate Abusers 119
References 119

Specific diseases of the myocardium of drug abusers are rarely reported, and the true incidence of myocardial disease in this group remains unknown. The absence of myocardial disease among drug abusers is probably more apparent than real. Many pathologists still do not recognize modest degrees of hypertrophy as representing disease. Another confounder preventing accurate estimation of myocardial disease in drug abusers is that observed frequency of any particular myocardial lesion depends upon the population being studied, and the drugs that they use. Patterns of drug abuse have changed a great deal over the last decade. It is likely that the type of lesions encountered has changed as well.

Prior to the advent of the cocaine and HIV pandemics, when heroin was the main drug of abuse, the incidence of myocardial disease among drug users was apparently the same as in controls. In Siegel and Helpern's classic paper on the "Diagnosis of Death from Intravenous Narcotism," heart disease was never even mentioned,[1] nor were any significant cardiac abnormalities recorded in Wetli's study of 100 consecutively autopsied drug abusers.[2] When Louria analyzed the discharge diagnosis of addicts admitted to Bellevue Hospital's general medical service, 40 years ago, he found that the incidence of endocarditis was less than 10%; no other types of heart disease were mentioned.[3]

The advent of HIV, coupled with the rise in cocaine and methamphetamine abuse, has drastically changed the landscape. So has the unarguable fact that we now live (or soon will live) in the age of the molecular autopsy; hearts that look normal at autopsy, and which even appear normal under the microscope may, in fact, be diseased (channelopathies and other heritable disorders). At the same time, it has also become very clear that the extracellular matrix, the tissue surrounding myocytes, is not just inert scaffolding but, rather, an active, hormone-secreting tissue, exerting potent effects on myocardial structure (the process of myocardial remodeling).

5.1 EPIDEMIOLOGY

Whether or not damage occurs to the myocardium depends both on the drug and the way it is administered. In areas where the injection of pills meant for oral use is common practice, granulomatous lung disease and pulmonary hypertension will be encountered.[4-6] Both abnormalities are induced by the expients found in the pills, rather than the drug itself. Even though granulomatous disease involving the pulmonary vasculature and interstitium is relatively common among injection drug users, the clinical consequences of these lesions are difficult to estimate, and the finding may often be overlooked.[7] The practice of injecting crushed pills is much more common in some places than others, so the presence of granulomas, while diagnostically useful, cannot always be assumed. Most adult drug abusers practice polypharmacy; attempts at correlating specific drugs with certain types of lesions is a difficult, if not impossible exercise.

Earlier studies of heart disease in drug users must be interpreted with very great caution, particularly those studies where the diagnosis was not confirmed by toxicological testing. One study of 168 drug-related deaths found a 100% incidence of heart disease,[8] but since toxicological findings were not known for all the patients, and since the limits of detection for drugs were far higher in the early 1980s than today, and since all of the patients were referred because they were suspected of having heart disease in the first place, not a great deal can be concluded about the real incidence of the problem.

Sudden unexpected death in young adults, aged 18 to 35 years, accounts for an important subset of drug-related deaths. A study of cases occurring over a 10-year period in Galway, Ireland, found that a large proportion, over one-third, of sudden deaths in young adults were secondary to epilepsy, and/or chemical/drug poisoning. In total, these deaths amounted to 9% of the deaths occurring in the study population.[9] In Australia, where the lifetime use of cocaine is rising, only 3% of the population over age 14 was using cocaine in 1991, but that number had increased to 4.5% in 1998, and cocaine accounted for 10% of all illicit drug-related deaths in that country. Most of these deaths appear to have been the result of acute myocardial infarction.[10] Reliable statistics for the incidence of cocaine-related and/or heroin-related heart disease in the United States are not available.

5.2 MECHANISM OF MYOCARDIAL HYPERTROPHY

Even in the absence of solid epidemiological data, certain generalizations are possible. The hearts of chronic stimulant abusers, whether of cocaine or methamphetamine, or even MDMA, are enlarged, and often manifest changes consistent with the known effects of prolonged catecholamine excess. Myocardial hypertrophy in cocaine abusers has been confirmed by comparisons of cocaine abusers' electrocardiograms to those of age-sex-matched controls, to those of asymptomatic cocaine users in rehabilitation, and to cocaine users seeking treatment for chest pain.[11-13] Myocardial hypertrophy has been reported in separate, controlled, autopsy studies of cocaine, methamphetamine, MDMA, and ephedrine users.[14-17] The increases are generally quite modest, averaging 10 to 11% over that predicted by standard nomograms.[18]

Molecular biologists have shown that stimulant-type drugs cause increases in the myocardial expression and activation of cAMP response binding protein, otherwise known as CREB. CREB is one of the transcriptional factors that regulate gene expression, mainly through the action of a large group of different kinases. These include protein kinase A, calcium calmodulin kinase II, and mitogen-activated protein kinase. All three can induce CREB phosphorylation at serine position 133.[19] The result is increased myosin production and myocardial hypertrophy,[20] primarily because more calmodulin is produced. Calmodulin is a small, acidic protein. It binds to Ca^{2+}-binding proteins and, in conjunction with calcium and other molecules, it acts as a second messenger, controlling diverse biochemical processes in many different cell types, not just myocytes. Calmodulin kinase II activity is required for normal atrioventricular nodal conduction,[21] and calmodulin itself protects against structural heart disease.[22] It appears that cocaine users develop myocardial hypertrophy because cocaine directly activates calmodulin kinase II.[23] Whether the same process occurs in methamphetamine, ephedrine, or MDMA abusers is not yet known.

The hearts of heroin abusers generally do not show evidence of myocardial hypertrophy unless, of course, the abusers are simultaneously abusing stimulants, an increasingly common practice. It appears that heroin does not lead to CREB phosphorylation, at least not in the myocardium, although there is evidence for CREB activation in the brain.[24] Heroin abusers may not be uniquely subject to myocardial hypertrophy, but HIV-related disease is common among heroin users, as are a multitude of other "lifestyle" disorders such as hepatitis (types A, B, and C)[25,26] and tuberculosis.[27] If one of these associated disorders leads to restriction of the pulmonary bed, and pulmonary hypertension, at least some degree of right ventricular hypertrophy is to be anticipated.

5.3 CONSEQUENCES OF MYOCARDIAL HYPERTROPHY

Left ventricular hypertrophy is the normal cardiac adaptation to a prolonged increase in arterial blood pressure or, at least, to the activation of the genes responding to a pressure increase. One of the earliest results of the pioneering Framingham Study was the clear demonstration that patients with electrocardiographic evidence of left ventricular hypertrophy are at increased risk both for sudden cardiac death and for acute myocardial infarction.[28] Hypertensive patients with left ventricular hypertrophy have substantially more premature ventricular beats than normotensives,[29] and even more than hypertensives who still have normal size hearts. Recent studies have shown that calmodulin-dependent mechanisms are responsible for both the increase in ectopy and for the occurrence of sudden death in cocaine users (and non-drug-using hypertensives), even in the absence of clinically apparent myocyte hypertrophy. Enlarged hearts are prone to QT dispersion (defined as the difference between the longest and shortest QT interval measured in each of the 12 leads of the cardiogram). Dispersion equates to electrical inhomogeneity; the greater the degree of dispersion, the higher the probability a reentrant type arrhythmia will occur.[30,31]

The problem for death investigators is that changes in heart weight, amounting to less than 10% of predicted weight, are likely to go unrecognized at autopsy. The result is that a possible cause of death may be missed. Even if wall thickness is fastidiously measured, which is not always the case, a 10% increase is likely go undetected. Small changes go unnoticed mainly because several different systems are used for determining normality. Some pathologists still believe that arbitrary cutoffs can be used: 380 or 400 g for men and 350 g for women. Others determine normality by using a formula; heart weights less than 0.4% of the body weight (0.45% for women) are considered normal.[32] The most accurate approach is to use a nomogram based on a large series of autopsies. Several have been published, including the Mayo Clinic nomogram relating heart weight both to height and to weight.[18] Any value more than 2 standard deviations above the predicted mean is considered abnormal. Unfortunately, the range is so wide that some hearts may wrongly be classified as normal.

5.4 OTHER STIMULANT-RELATED DISORDERS

Reports of cardiomyopathy in cases where neither biopsy nor arteriogram was performed[33–37] are difficult to interpret, and the diagnosis of cardiomyopathy in such cases should be considered unconfirmed; the underlying disease is as likely to be ischemic as to be drug mediated. The few reported cases of ephedrine-related cardiomyopathy fall into this category, although when cases have occurred, it has only been in abusers consuming massive amounts of ephedrine for prolonged periods.[38–40] However, dilated cardiomyopathy, in the proven absence of ischemia, has been documented in methamphetamine abusers,[41] and it seems likely that the reported number of new cases will increase.

When direct examination of the hearts of stimulant users has been performed, most of the observed changes appear to be related to catecholamine.[42,43] Chronic catecholamine toxicity is a well-recognized entity in humans and animals. In fact, norepinephrine "myocarditis" was first described nearly 50 years ago,[44,45] and its histological features are indistinguishable from those seen in patients with pheochromocytoma. Contraction band necrosis is the earliest recognizable lesion in both humans and animals.[46]

Several distinct features can be used to distinguish catecholamine-induced necrosis from ischemic necrosis. The most obvious is the distribution of the lesions. In ischemic injury, all cells supplied by a given vessel are affected, leading to a homogeneous zone of necrosis. In catecholamine injury, individual necrotic myocytes are to be found interspersed between normal cells, and the pattern of injury cannot be related to the pattern of blood supply.[47] Ischemic and catecholamine necrosis can also be distinguished by the arrangement of the myofilaments. In ischemia the myofilaments remain in register. In cases of catecholamine toxicity, the arrangement of the filaments is disrupted. In addition, a mononuclear, predominantly lymphocytic, infiltrate may be seen after 12 h (as opposed to the neutrophilic infiltrate seen during the initial phases of ischemic infarction). Necrotic myocytes are eventually reabsorbed and replaced by non-conducting fibrous tissues. After repeated bouts of necrosis, the myocardium becomes increasingly fibrotic, leading to systolic dysfunction and, more importantly, abnormal impulse propagation.[47]

Biopsy findings in a group of cocaine users with recent onset of chest pain and congestive heart failure demonstrated changes very similar to those described above, with microfocal interstitial fibrosis evident in all cases.[43] Lymphocytic infiltrates were seen in only two of the cases, and there were no eosinophils present. Contraction band necrosis (CBN) is a prominent artifact of endomyocardial biopsies, so the presence of these lesions in biopsied drug users is impossible to assess, even though CBN may well be associated with cocaine use. In fact the first reports of CBN in cocaine users were published in the European literature in the 1920s. They were promptly forgotten for another 50 years, until they were rediscovered in a report that appeared in the *New England Journal of Medicine* in 1986.[48]

A biopsy of one of the patients in the *New England Journal of Medicine* report did show eosinophilic myocarditis, but such cases are extremely rare and still reportable. In fact, there has only been one additional reported instance of cocaine-associated eosinophilic myocarditis in the last decade.[49] Even if a known cocaine user were found to have an eosinophilic infiltrate in his or her heart, it would more likely be the result of allergy to expients mixed with the drug, than from the cocaine itself. The variety of expients used to dilute cocaine and heroin is not tracked by any official agency (although it very likely is by some government agencies), and it clearly varies by location and drug origin. An Italian report, now more than a decade old, found that lidocaine and caffeine were the two agents most frequently used to adulterate cocaine. More recently, an assortment of medications has been detected in cocaine specimens, including multiple samples containing diltiazem.

Amphetamines seem to be associated with the same changes in the heart that are associated with cocaine abuse.[50,51] The Japanese literature contains one report describing a long-term methamphetamine abuser who collapsed while being arrested. His heart was hypertrophied, but there was no evidence of myocardial disarray. Endocardial thickening, with increased numbers of elastic fibers, was apparent in all the ventricles and in the atria. There was also narrowing of the lumen of the AV nodal artery secondary to interstitial fibrosis and scar formation. The authors believed that compression of the nodal artery by scarring accounted for the individual's sudden death.[52]

5.5 MYOCARDIAL DISEASE IN OPIATE ABUSERS

Distinctions between the hearts of opiate and stimulant abusers have become increasingly blurred. In the uncommon situation where an individual is a pure opiate abuser, morphologic changes are uncommon. Autopsy studies of heroin abusers done during the 1960s and early 1970s did not even mention the occurrence of heart disease.[1,53] Clinical studies from that period are equally unrevealing. Among addicts admitted to Bellevue Hospital's general medicine service, the incidence of endocarditis was under 10% and no other cardiac disorders were even mentioned.[3] Whether or not opiates visibly damage the myocardium, undetectable interactions may be occurring at the molecular level. Randomized clinical trials published in 2005 showed convincingly that the mortality of patients with myocardial infarction increases when they are treated with morphine.[54] Why that should be is impossible to say.

Myocardial fibrosis is not uncommon in opiate abusers, but it probably just signifies concomitant stimulant abuse. Larger areas of fibrosis may represent zones of healed infarction, even if they were not diagnosed during life. Although a handful of case reports have appeared in the literature,[55,56] there is no evidence that coronary artery disease is more common among heroin abusers than in the general population. Nonetheless, intravenous drug injectors, no matter what the drug, are prone to pulmonary hypertension as a consequence of granuloma formation in the pulmonary bed.[57] Rarely a talc granuloma may be seen in the myocardium.[58]

Infectious disease now accounts for most of the changes seen in the hearts of drug abusers. HIV may involve the heart. The most common manifestations of HIV are dilated cardiomyopathy, myocarditis, pulmonary hypertension, pericardial effusion, endocarditis, and HIV-associated malignant neoplasm. Although highly active antiretroviral therapy (HAART) does prolong many patients' lives, it has no effect on the cardiac sequelae of HIV, which will continue to evolve without specific treatment.[59]

There are also reports of myocardial infarction in young patients infected with HIV receiving protease inhibitors, raising concerns about premature arteriosclerosis and coronary artery disease in this patient group. It appears that metabolic alterations produced by antiretroviral therapy worsen the cardiovascular risk profile of patients infected with HIV.[60] When coronary artery disease occurs in an HIV-infected drug abuser, it is impossible to say whether it is a consequence of disease or addiction. Unfortunately, drug users continue to use drugs even after they are infected with HIV. As with coronary artery disease, in many cases it will also be impossible to tell whether sudden death in a drug user is related to the drug or to the virus. Some cardiotropic viruses can cause myocardial infarction and even myocarditis, but are detectable only by advanced DNA polymerase technology, a methodology beyond the reach of most medical examiners' offices.[61]

REFERENCES

1. Siegel, H., M. Helpern, and T. Ehrenreich, The diagnosis of death from intravenous narcotism. With emphasis on the pathologic aspects, *J. Forensic Sci.,* 11(1), 1–16.
2. Wetli, C.V., J.H. Davis, and B.D. Blackbourne, Narcotic addiction in Dade County, Florida. An analysis of 100 consecutive autopsies, *Arch. Pathol.,* 93(4), 330–343, 1972.
3. Louria, D.B., T. Hensle, and J. Rose, The major medical complications of heroin addiction, *Ann. Intern. Med.,* 67(1), 1–22, 1967.
4. Bainborough, A.R. and K.W. Jericho, Cor pulmonale secondary to talc granulomata in the lungs of a drug addict, *Can. Med. Assoc. J.,* 103(12), 1297–1298, 1970.
5. Arnett, E.N., W.E. Battle, J.V. Russo, and W.C. Roberts, Intravenous injection of talc-containing drugs intended for oral use. A cause of pulmonary granulomatosis and pulmonary hypertension, *Am. J. Med.,* 60(5), 711–718, 1976.

6. Conen, D., D. Schilter, L. Bubendorf, M.H. Brutsche, et al., Interstitial lung disease in an intravenous drug user, *Respiration*, 70(1), 101–103, 2003.
7. Wolff, A.J. and A.E. O'Donnell, Pulmonary effects of illicit drug use, *Clin. Chest Med.*, 25(1), 203–216, 2004.
8. Dressler, F.A. and W.C. Roberts, Modes of death and types of cardiac diseases in opiate addicts: analysis of 168 necropsy cases, *Am. J. Cardiol.*, 64(14), 909–920, 1989.
9. Bennani, F.K. and C.E. Connolly, Sudden unexpected death in young adults including four cases of SADS: a 10-year review from the west of Ireland (1985–1994), *Med. Sci. Law*, 37(3), 242–247, 1997.
10. Vasica, G. and C.C. Tennant, Cocaine use and cardiovascular complications, *Med. J. Aust.*, 177(5), 260–262, 2002.
11. Brickner, M.E., J.E. Willard, E.J. Eichhorn, J. Black, et al., Left ventricular hypertrophy associated with chronic cocaine abuse, *Circulation*, 84(3), 1130–5, 1991.
12. Om, A., S. Ellahham, G.W. Vetrovec, C. Guard, et al., Left ventricular hypertrophy in normotensive cocaine users, *Am. Heart. J.*, 125(5 Pt. 1), 1441–1443, 1993.
13. Chakko, S., S. Sepulveda, K.M. Kessler, M.C. Sotomayor, et al., Frequency and type of electrocardiographic abnormalities in cocaine abusers (electrocardiogram in cocaine abuse), *Am. J. Cardiol.*, 74(7), 710–713, 1994.
14. Karch, S.B., G.S. Green, and S. Young, Myocardial hypertrophy and coronary artery disease in male cocaine users, *J. Forensic Sci.*, 40(4), 591–595, 1995.
15. Karch, S.B., B.G. Stephens, and C.H. Ho, Methamphetamine-related deaths in San Francisco: demographic, pathologic, and toxicologic profiles, *J. Forensic Sci.*, 44(2), 359–368, 1999.
16. Blechman, K., S.B. Karch, and B. Stephens, Demographic, pathologic, and toxicological profiles of 127 decedents testing positive for ephedrine alkaloids, *Forensic Sci. Int.*, 139(2–3), 271, 2004.
17. Patel, M.M., M.G. Belson, A.B. Longwater, K.R. Olson, and M. Miller, Methylenedioxymethamphetamine (ecstasy)-related myocardial hyperthermia, *J. Emerg. Med.*, 29(4), 451–454, 2005.
18. Kitzman, D.W., D.G. Scholz, P.T. Hagen, D.M. Ilstrup, et al., Age-related changes in normal human hearts during the first 10 decades of life. Part II (Maturity): A quantitative anatomic study of 765 specimens from subjects 20 to 99 years old, *Mayo Clin. Proc.*, 63(2), 137–146, 1988.
19. Bilecki, W. and R. Przewlocki, Effect of opioids on Ca^{2+}/cAMP responsive element binding protein, *Acta Neurobiol. Exp.* (Warsaw), 60(4), 557–567, 2000.
20. Sun, L.S. and A. Quamina, Extracellular receptor kinase and cAMP response element binding protein activation in the neonatal rat heart after perinatal cocaine exposure, *Pediatr. Res.*, 56(6), 947–952, 2004.
21. Khoo, M.S., P.J. Kannankeril, J. Li, R. Zhang, et al., Calmodulin kinase II activity is required for normal atrioventricular nodal conduction, *Heart Rhythm*, 2(6), 634–640, 2005.
22. Zhang, R., M.S. Khoo, Y. Wu, Y. Yang, et al., Calmodulin kinase II inhibition protects against structural heart disease, *Nat. Med.*, 11(4), 409–417, 2005.
23. Henning, R., D. Ivancsits, J. Haley, et al., Cocaine activates calmodulin kinase II and causes cardiac ventricular hypertrophy and arrhythmias, *Circulation*, III, iii–603, 2004.
24. Laviolette, S.R., R.A. Gallegos, S.J. Henriksen, and D. van der Kooy, Opiate state controls bi-directional reward signaling via GABAA receptors in the ventral tegmental area, *Nat. Neurosci.*, 7(2), 160–169, 2004.
25. Schaefer, M., A. Heinz, and M. Backmund, Treatment of chronic hepatitis C in patients with drug dependence: time to change the rules? *Addiction*, 99(9), 1167–1175, 2004.
26. Piccolo, P., L. Borg, A. Lin, D. Melia, et al., Hepatitis C virus and human immunodeficiency virus-1 co-infection in former heroin addicts in methadone maintenance treatment, *J. Addict Dis.*, 21(4), 55–66, 2002.
27. Muga, R., H. Guardiola, and C. Rey-Joly, Evaluation of drug addicts with associated pathology. Clinical and therapeutic aspects of the integral attention, *Med. Clin.* (Barcelona), 122(16), 624–635, 2004.
28. Gordon, T. and W.B. Kannel, Premature mortality from coronary heart disease. The Framingham study. *J. Am. Med. Assoc.*, 215(10), 1617–1625, 1971.
29. Messerli, F.H., H.O. Ventura, D.J. Elizardi, F.G. Dunn, et al., Hypertension and sudden death. Increased ventricular ectopic activity in left ventricular hypertrophy, *Am. J. Med.*, 77(1), 18–22, 1984.

30. Hnatkova, K., M. Malik, J. Kautzner, Y. Gang, et al., Adjustment of QT dispersion assessed from 12 lead electrocardiograms for different numbers of analysed electrocardiographic leads: comparison of stability of different methods, *Br. Heart J.*, 72(4), 390–396, 1994.

31. Anderson, K.P., Sympathetic nervous system activity and ventricular tachyarrhythmias: recent advances, *Ann. Noninvasive Electrocardiol.*, 8(1), 75–89, 2003.

32. Ludwig, J., *Current Methods of Autopsy Practice*, 2nd ed., W.B. Saunders, Philadelphia, 1979.

33. Wiener, R.S., J.T. Lockhart, and R.G. Schwartz, Dilated cardiomyopathy and cocaine abuse. Report of two cases, *Am. J. Med.*, 81(4), 699–701, 1986.

34. Chokshi, S.K., R. Moore, N.G. Pandian, and J.M. Isner, Reversible cardiomyopathy associated with cocaine intoxication, *Ann. Intern. Med.*, 111(12), 1039–1040, 1989.

35. Duell, P.B., Chronic cocaine abuse and dilated cardiomyopathy, *Am. J. Med.*, 83(3), 601, 1987.

36. Hogya, P.T. and A.B. Wolfson, Chronic cocaine abuse associated with dilated cardiomyopathy, *Am. J. Emerg. Med.*, 8(3), 203–204, 1990.

37. Mendelson, M.A. and J. Chandler, Postpartum cardiomyopathy associated with maternal cocaine abuse, *Am. J. Cardiol.*, 70(11), 1092–1094, 1992.

38. Naik, S.D. and R.S. Freudenberger, Ephedra-associated cardiomyopathy, *Ann. Pharmacother.*, 38(3), 400–403, 2004.

39. To, L.B., J.F. Sangster, D. Rampling, and I. Cammens, Ephedrine-induced cardiomyopathy, *Med. J. Aust.*, 2(1), 35–36, 1980.

40. Schafers, M., D. Dutka, C.G. Rhodes, A.A. Lammertsma, et al., Myocardial presynaptic and postsynaptic autonomic dysfunction in hypertrophic cardiomyopathy, *Circ. Res.*, 82(1), 57–62, 1998.

41. Wijetunga, M., T. Seto, J. Lindsay, and I. Schatz, Crystal methamphetamine-associated cardiomyopathy: tip of the iceberg? *J. Toxicol. Clin. Toxicol.*, 41(7), 981–986, 2003.

42. Karch, S.B. and M.E. Billingham, The pathology and etiology of cocaine-induced heart disease, *Arch. Pathol. Lab. Med.*, 112(3), 225–230, 1988.

43. Peng, S.K., W.J. French, and P.C. Pelikan, Direct cocaine cardiotoxicity demonstrated by endomyocardial biopsy, *Arch. Pathol. Lab. Med.*, 113(8), 842–845, 1989.

44. Szakacs, J.E., R.M. Dimmette, and E.C. Cowart, Jr., Pathologic implication of the catecholamines, epinephrine and norepinephrine, *U.S. Armed Forces Med. J.*, 10, 908–925, 1959.

45. Szakacs, J.E. and A. Cannon, L-Norepinephrine myocarditis, *Am. J. Clin. Pathol.*, 30(5), 425–434, 1958.

46. Rosenbaum, J.S., M.E. Billingham, R. Ginsburg, G. Tsujimoto, et al., Cardiomyopathy in a rat model of pheochromocytoma. Morphological and functional alterations, *Am. J. Cardiovasc. Pathol.*, 1(3), 389–399, 1988.

47. Karch, S.B. and M.E. Billingham, Myocardial contraction bands revisited, *Hum. Pathol.*, 17(1), 9–13, 1986.

48. Isner, J.M., N.A. Estes III, P.D. Thompson, M.R. Costanzo-Nordin, et al., Acute cardiac events temporally related to cocaine abuse, *N. Engl. J. Med.*, 315(23), 1438–1443, 1986.

49. Talebzadeh, V.C., J.C. Chevrolet, P. Chatelain, C. Helfer, et al., Eosinophilic myocarditis and pulmonary hypertension in a drug-addict. Anatomo-clinical study and brief review of the literature, *Ann. Pathol.*, 10(1), 40–46, 1990.

50. Smith, H.J., A.H. Roche, M.F. Jausch, and P.B. Herdson, Cardiomyopathy associated with amphetamine administration, *Am. Heart J.*, 91(6), 792–797, 1976.

51. Rajs, J. and B. Falconer, Cardiac lesions in intravenous drug addicts, *Forensic Sci. Int.*, 13(3), 193–209, 1979.

52. Nishida, N., N. Ikeda, K. Kudo, and R. Esaki, Sudden unexpected death of a methamphetamine abuser with cardiopulmonary abnormalities: a case report, *Med. Sci. Law*, 43(3), 267–271, 2003.

53. Kringsholm, B. and P. Christoffersen, Lung and heart pathology in fatal drug addiction. A consecutive autopsy study, *Forensic Sci. Int.*, 34(1–2), 39–51, 1987.

54. Meine, T.J., M.T. Roe, A.Y. Chen, M.R. Patel, et al., Association of intravenous morphine use and outcomes in acute coronary syndromes: results from the CRUSADE Quality Improvement Initiative, *Am. Heart J.*, 149(6), 1043–1049, 2005.

55. Yu, S.L., C.P. Liu, Y.K. Lo, and S.L. Lin, Acute myocardial infarction after heroin injections, *Jpn. Heart J.*, 45(6), 1021–1028, 2004.

56. Sztajzel, J., H. Karpuz, and W. Rutishauser, Heroin abuse and myocardial infarction, *Int. J. Cardiol.*, 47(2), 180–182, 1994.
57. Robertson, C.H., Jr., R.C. Reynolds, and J.E. Wilson III, Pulmonary hypertension and foreign body granulomas in intravenous drug abusers. Documentation by cardiac catheterization and lung biopsy, *Am. J. Med.*, 61(5), 657–664, 1976.
58. Riddick, L., Disseminated granulomatosis through a patent foramen ovale in an intravenous drug user with pulmonary hypertension, *Am. J. Forensic Med. Pathol.*, 8(4), 326–333, 1987.
59. Barbaro, G. and E.C. Klatt, HIV infection and the cardiovascular system, *AIDS Rev.*, 4(2), 93–103, 2002.
60. Neumann, T., M. Miller, S. Esser, G. Gerken, et al., Atherosclerosis in HIV-positive patients, *Z. Kardiol.*, 91(11), 879–888, 2002.
61. Kuhl, U., M. Pauschinger, T. Bock, K. Klingel, et al., Parvovirus B19 infection mimicking acute myocardial infarction, *Circulation*, 108(8), 945–950, 2003.

CHAPTER **6**

Valvular Heart Disease

Michael D. Bell, M.D.
District Medical Examiner, Palm Beach Medical Examiner Office, West Palm Beach, Florida

CONTENTS

6.1 Infective Endocarditis...123
6.2 Fenfluramine-Associated Regurgitant Valve Disease 126
References 127

6.1 INFECTIVE ENDOCARDITIS

Although intravenous (IV) drug abuse is a recognized risk factor for infectious endocarditis, this complication is not a frequent complication among IV drug users. The incidence of infective endocarditis in IV drug abusers is estimated at 1.5 to 2.0 cases per 1000 IV drug abusers admitted to the hospital[1] or 1 to 20 cases per 10,000 IV drug users per year. IV drug abusers with infective endocarditis are more likely to be young men (average age = 29 years, M:F = 3:1) compared with non-addicts with endocarditis (average age = 50, M:F = 2:1).[2] The frequency of underlying heart disease in IV drug abusers with endocarditis is 26% compared with 60% of non-addicts with endocarditis. In a cohort of 85 IV drug abusers, echocardiography failed to detect any valvular vegetation consistent with endocarditis.[3] Eight IV drug abusers had thickened or redundant leaflets (with or without prolapse) of the mitral, aortic, or tricuspid valve. Focally thickened leaflets of the mitral and tricuspid valves have been reported in other series of asymptomatic IV drug abusers who were examined by echocardiography.[4] These subtle morphologic abnormalities may be the stratum upon which endocarditis builds. Most researchers agree that endothelial injury or damage initiates fibrin, platelet, and bacterial depositions that produce endocarditis.

In Dressler and Robert's series of 80 autopsied IV drug abusers with infective endocarditis, the tricuspid valve was involved in half of the victims compared with 15% of victims dying of acute endocarditis who did not use IV drugs.[5] Why IV drug users are more likely to develop right-sided endocarditis than non-IV drug users is not known. Postulated factors include physical damage by injected particulate debris, especially if pills are crushed and then injected. Drug-induced pulmonary hypertension in IV drug abusers may cause increased right ventricular pressure and more turbulence flow, resulting in tricuspid valve injury. However, IV drug abusers can, and often do, have left-sided valve involvement. The aortic and mitral valves are involved in 25% and 20% respectively of IV drug abusers with infective endocarditis. Most cases of acute endocarditis in

123

Table 6.1 Uncommon Pathogens in Endocarditis of Intravenous Drug Abusers[11]

Group B *Streptococcus* (*Streptococcus agalactiae*)[12]
Coagulase-negative *Staphylococcus*
Gram-negative bacteria (*Pseudomonas, Serratia, Kingella*, etc.)
Corynebacterium spp., *Neisseria sicca, Rothia denticariosua*
Haemophilus spp.
Erysipelothrix
Anaerobic bacteria (*Bacteroides, Veillonella, Eikenella,*
   Fusobacterium spp., *Clostridium* spp., etc.)
Fungi (*Candida* spp.)

IV drug abusers are caused by *Staphylococcus aureus* as compared with other streptococcal species commonly responsible for endocarditis in those not injecting IV drugs.[6] Outbreaks of methacillin-resistant *S. aureus* endocarditis in IV drug users have been reported in Detroit, Boston, and Zurich. Polymicrobial infection is seen in 8 to 9% of cases of infective endocarditis that involve IV drug abusers, while *Streptococcus viridans* causes right-sided endocarditis in 11% of IV drug abusers. Fungal, usually non-albicans *Candida* species endocarditis is usually superimposed on valves previously damaged by an earlier episode of bacterial endocarditis and usually has a more indolent clinical course. Other unusual pathogens causing endocarditis in IV drug abusers are summarized in Table 6.1.

Grossly, infective endocarditis is characterized by friable, white or tan vegetations found on the valve leaflets along the closure lines. Vegetations may be single or, more often, multiple. In one clinical series the mean vegetation size in IV drug abusers with acute right-sided bacterial endocarditis was 1.5 0.7 cm.[6] The size, color, and appearance of the vegetations can vary, however. Streptococcal vegetations grow more slowly than staphylococcal vegetations, but may become larger. Fungal vegetations are usually larger than bacterial vegetations. Vegetations occur more often on the atrial side of the atrioventricular valves and on the ventricular side of the aortic or pulmonic valves. Suppurative bacteria such as *Staphylococcus* may cause valve perforation, resulting in acute valvular insufficiency. Infection may extend into the adjacent myocardium producing necrotic fistulas, aneurysms, or ring abscess (usually of the aortic valve). Further extension results in pericarditis, found in 4 to 27% of cases of left-sided infective endocarditis.[7] Involvement of the chordae tendinae may lead to rupture and valvular insufficiency. Tricuspid and pulmonic vegetations may embolize to the lungs, resulting in the formation of suppurative abscesses (Figure 6.1 and Figure 6.2). Perforation, indentation, or aneurysm of the valve cusp or chordae tendinae is presumptive evidence of healed endocarditis.

Microscopically, acute bacterial endocarditis is characterized by masses of fibrin, platelets, and polymorphonuclear leukocytes with bacterial colonies on the valve surface. Bacteria are less frequent after antibiotic treatment, and may not be demonstrable by Gram stain, even if present.[8] Later, the microscopic appearance is characterized by organization with capillary proliferation, a mixed cellular infiltrate, and the formation of granulation tissue. If the individual survives, the lesions eventually heal by fibrosis and re-endothelialization. Calcification may be present in the healed lesions.

The clinical diagnosis of acute infectious endocarditis includes the acute onset of fever, chills, and heart murmur. Right-sided valve murmurs (as in IV drug abusers) may be less audible than left-sided valve murmurs because the reduced chamber pressures of the right heart produce less turbulence and less noise. Signs of early tricuspid insufficiency may be minimal with only an atrial or ventricular gallop and no murmur. Later, a systolic regurgitant murmur, louder with inspiration, appears. Large "v" waves in the neck veins and a pulsating liver are signs of severe tricuspid regurgitation.[9] Confirmation of the diagnosis includes isolation of the causative organism from two or more blood cultures and identification of valvular vegetation by echocardiography. The criteria for the clinical diagnosis of infective endocarditis have recently been revised. Bacteremia is char-

VALVULAR HEART DISEASE

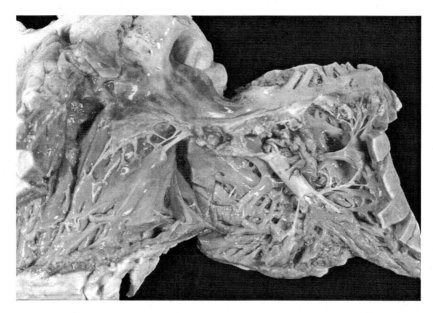

Figure 6.1 Large necrotizing vegetations on the tricuspid valve of this 31-year-old addict who commonly injected drug subcutaneously ("skin popping"). Blood cultures were positive for *Streptococcus hominus*.

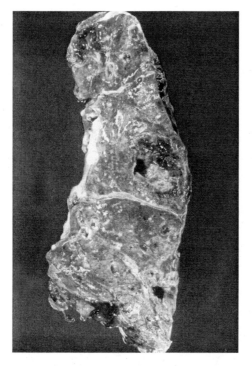

Figure 6.2 The lung from the victim in Figure 6.1 has multiple suppurative abscesses and extensive dark red consolidation.

Table 6.2   Comparison of Right-Sided and Left-Sided Endocarditis

Right-Sided	Left-Sided
IV drug abusers most common	Congenital heart disease most common
Staphylococcus aureus most common	*Streptococcus viridans* most common
Occasional polymicrobial involvement	Polymicrobial involvement rare
Presents with pleuropneumonic symptoms	Symptoms from distal systemic embolization more common
10% of all infective endocarditis	90% of all infective endocarditis
Heart failure is unusual	Heart failure is common
Good prognosis with frequent cure after medical therapy	Poor prognosis with poor success rate using medical therapy
Usually does not require immediate valve replacement	Usually requires immediate valve replacement

acteristic of endocarditis, and most IV drug abusers with endocarditis have positive blood cultures even after a few days of antibiotic treatment. True culture-negative endocarditis is rare in IV drug abusers, and negative blood cultures suggest another cause for their illness.

The occurrence of chest pain with dyspnea, along with characteristic abnormalities of the chest radiograph (multiple segmental infiltrates with lower lobe predilection), suggests septic pulmonary emboli from a right-sided valvular vegetation. Systemic embolization can occur in right-sided endocarditis from septic pulmonary vein thrombi, left-sided valvular involvement, or paradoxical embolization through a patent foramen ovale. Table 6.2 compares the clinical features of right-sided and left-sided endocarditis.[10] Mortality in IV drug abusers with acute right-sided endocarditis varies from 4 to 14%.[6]

The source of the infecting organisms is usually from the addict's own body (skin or mouth flora), or soft tissue infection at the injection site, not contaminants in the drugs or the drug paraphernalia.[13] Cultures of heroin samples and drug paraphernalia have failed to demonstrate the presence of common pathogens.

6.2 FENFLURAMINE-ASSOCIATED REGURGITANT VALVE DISEASE

Fenfluramine is a sympathomimetic amine chemically similar to amphetamine, but with less stimulant activity. Fenfluramine was a popular anorectic agent in the 1990s, prescribed alone or in combination with another sympathomimetic amine, phentermine. Prescriptions for these appetite suppressants exceeded 18 million in 1996. Fenfluramine's anorectic effect is thought to result from its ability to promote serotonin release and decrease brain re-uptake.

Connolly et al.[14] described 24 women with regurgitant valve disease that had its onset after they took fenfluramine-phentermine ("fen-phen") for 1 to 28 months. One-fifth of these women required valve surgery and one-third developed pulmonary hypertension. Macroscopic features in the removed valves from these women included irregular nodular leaflet thickening, thickened and tethered glistening white leaflets, leaflets with "stuck on" or "onlay" plaques, and chordal fusion. Valve vegetations, commissural fusion, and annular dilatation were not seen. Microscopically, fibromyxoid plaques and nodules were seen to lie on top of the affected leaflet or encase the chordae tendinae. Myofibroblasts proliferated in the extracellular matrix. The onlay plaques are usually found to be superficial to the elastic fiber layer in the mitral valve. Ultimately these pathologic changes result in a thickened immobile regurgitant valve. Other pathologists have confirmed these findings.[15,16] Later case control and meta-analysis studies,[17,18] however, did not demonstrate as much clinically significant mitral valve disease as the original Connolly study, but by then, fenfluramine was already removed from the U.S. market.

REFERENCES

1. Weinstein, L. and Brusch, J.L., Endocarditis in intravenous drug abusers, in *Infective Endocarditis*, Weinstein, L. and Brusch, J.L., Eds., Oxford University Press, New York, 1996, 194–209.
2. Reisberg, B.E., Infective endocarditis in the narcotic addict, *Prog. Cardiovasc. Dis.*, 22, 193–204, 1979.
3. Willoughby, S.B., Vlahov, D., and Herskowitz, A., Frequency of left ventricular dysfunction and other echocardiographic abnormalities in human immunodeficiency virus seronegative intravenous drug abusers, *Am. J. Cardiol.*, 71, 446–447, 1993.
4. Pons-Llado, G., Carreras, F., Borras, X. et al., Findings on Doppler echocardiography in asymptomatic intravenous heroin users, *Am. J. Cardiol.*, 69, 238–241, 1992.
5. Dressler, F. and Roberts, W., Infective endocarditis in opiate addicts: analysis of 80 cases studied at autopsy, *Am. J. Cardiol.*, 63, 1240–1257, 1989.
6. Hecht, S.R. and Berger, M., Right-sided endocarditis in intravenous drug users: prognostic features in 102 episodes, *Ann. Int. Med.*, 117, 560–566, 1992.
7. Buchbinder, N.A. and Roberts, W.C., Left-sided valvular active infective endocarditis: a study of forty-five patients, *Am. J. Med.*, 53, 20–35, 1972.
8. McFarland, M.M., Pathology of infective endocarditis, in *Infective Endocarditis*, 2nd ed., Kaye, D., Ed., Raven Press, New York, 1992, 57–83.
9. Cannon, N.J. and Cobbs, C.G., Infective endocarditis in drug addicts, in *Infective Endocarditis*, Kaye, D., Ed., University Park Press, Baltimore, 1976, 111–127.
10. Chan, P., Ogilby, J.D., and Segal, B., Tricuspid valve endocarditis, *Am. Heart J.*, 117, 1140–1146, 1989.
11. Sande, M.A., Lee, B.L., Mills, J., Chambers, H.F., III, Endocarditis in intravenous drug users, in *Infective Endocarditis*, 2nd ed., Kaye, D., Ed., Raven Press, New York, 1992, 345–359.
12. Watanakunakorn, C. and Habte-Gabr, E., Group B streptococcal endocarditis of tricuspid valve, *Chest*, 100, 569–571, 1991.
13. Wetli, C.V., in *Illicit Drug Abuse in Pathology of Environmental and Occupational Disease,* Craighead, J.D., Ed., Mosby-Year Book, St. Louis, 1995, 259–268.
14. Connolly, H.M., Crary, J.L., McGoon, M.D., Hensrud, D.D., Edwards, B.S., Edwards, W.D., and Schaff, H.V., Valvular heart disease associated with fenfluramine-phentermine, *N. Engl. J. Med.*, 337, 581–588, 1997.
15. Volmar, K.E. and Hutchins, G.M., Aortic and mitral fenfluramine-phentermine valvulopathy in 64 patients treated with anorectic agents, *Arch. Pathol. Lab. Med.*, 125, 1555–1561, 2001.
16. Steffee, C.H., Singh, H.K., and Chitwood, W.R., Histologic changes in three explanted native cardiac valves following use of fenfluramines, *Cardiovasc. Pathol.*, 8, 245–253, 1999.
17. Gardin, J.M., Schumacher, D., Constantine, G. et al., Valvular abnormalities and cardiovascular status following exposure to dexfenfluramine or phentermine/fenfluramine, *J. Am. Med. Assoc.*, 283, 1738–1740, 2000.
18. Sachdev, M., Miller, W.C., Ryan, T., and Jollis, J.G., Effect of fenfluramine-derivative diet pills on cardiac valves: a meta-analysis of observational studies, *Am. Heart J.*, 144, 1065–1073, 2002.

CHAPTER **7**

Lung Disease

Michael D. Bell, M.D.
District Medical Examiner, Palm Beach Medical Examiner Office, West Palm Beach, Florida

CONTENTS

7.1 Pulmonary Effects and Pathology of Smoked Illicit Drugs 129
7.2 Complications of Intravenous Drug Abuse: Granulomatous
    Pneumonitis/Arteriopathy 132
7.3 Aspiration Pneumonia 133
References 135

7.1 PULMONARY EFFECTS AND PATHOLOGY OF SMOKED ILLICIT DRUGS

Heroin is usually smoked by heating a mixture of heroin and caffeine on foil, then inhaling the resultant vapor through a straw. Cocaine freebase or "crack" cocaine is also heated and the vapors inhaled, as is crystallized methamphetamine. Finally, dried *Cannabis sativa* is smoked as a cigarette, or in a pipe. Ascribing a specific pulmonary dysfunction or pathology to a specific drug is difficult, because drug users consistently smoke more than one drug. In one study of 100 heroin users, 88% smoked heroin, 79% inhaled cocaine, 71% smoked marijuana, and 98% smoked cigarettes[1] and had been doing so, on average, for 26 years. These confounding factors must be considered before assigning causation of a specific pathology to a specific drug. Several review articles summarizing the pulmonary changes in drug users have been published.

Bailey et al.[2] performed an autopsy study of cocaine abusers' lungs and found the most common changes were pulmonary congestion (88%), edema (77%), and acute/chronic alveolar hemorrhage (71%). Similar findings were reported by Murray et al.[3,4] who found hemosiderin-laden macrophages in 35% (7 of 20) of the victims of cocaine intoxication and concluded that occult alveolar hemorrhage occurs more frequently in cocaine users than is clinically recognized. Murray also noted pulmonary artery medial hypertrophy in 20% (4 of 20) of cocaine abusers who had no histological evidence of foreign material embolization. The cause of the alveolar hemorrhage was thought to be ischemic damage to the capillary endothelium secondary to constriction of the pulmonary vascular bed after cocaine inhalation, or possibly a result of some direct toxic effect of cocaine on the capillary endothelium. Neither hypothesis is proved.

Hemosiderin-laden macrophages may be seen in bronchoalveolar lavage fluid or in bronchoscopy biopsy specimens. One cocaine abuser who presented with diffuse alveolar hemorrhage had

129

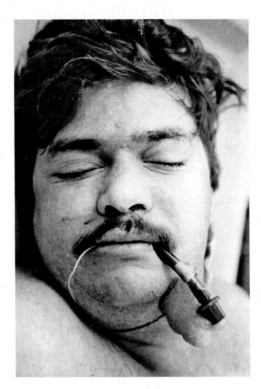

Figure 7.1 Abundant blood-tinged foam escapes from the end of the endotrachial tube in this drug abuser with pulmonary edema.

no vasculitis, and electron microscopy did not demonstrate any disruption in the alveolar or capillary basement membranes.[4] Pulmonary hemorrhage has not only been associated with alkaloidal "crack" cocaine smoking, but also with intravenous and nasal routes of administration.[5] Pulmonary congestion in fatal cocaine intoxication is usually ascribed to the slow cessation of cardiac function associated with brain stem hypoxia during terminal seizures, or else to direct cocaine toxicity.

Fatal and nonfatal pulmonary edema (Figure 7.1) has been reported in cocaine smokers who have no obvious cardiac or central nervous system disease.[5-8] In some of these individuals the pulmonary edema resolved without specific treatment, and chest radiographs have shown normal cardiac silhouettes. The homodynamic status of patients with cocaine-associated pulmonary edema has never been studied. One patient underwent bronchoalveolar lavage and the lavage fluid was found to have an elevated protein level (four times normal), suggesting that the edema was due to altered alveolar capillary permeability.[7] Bronchial biopsy usually has shown no histological abnormalities[7] or only "mild interstitial inflammatory changes."[8]

Pneumonitis, as defined by widening of the alveolar septae in the presence of a polymorphous infiltrate (lymphocytes, neutrophils, macrophages, eosinophils) or fibrosis, was seen in one-fourth of the victims studied by Bailey et al.,[2] while Patel et al.[9] have described a patient with broncholitis obliterans and organizing pneumonia (BOOP) associated with regular use of freebase cocaine during the weeks prior to the onset of his clinical symptoms (nonproductive cough, fever, dyspnea). An open lung biopsy revealed patchy bronchocentric interstitial and intra-alveolar chronic inflammation, with lymphocytes, macrophages, and few polymorphonuclear leukocytes and eosinophils; granulation tissue and collagen occupied bronchioles and adjacent alveolar ducts, but the blood vessels were normal. A hypersensitivity reaction to cocaine, or a cocaine adulterant, was the presumed cause. A similar mechanism also presumably explains the occurrence of "crack lung," a clinical syndrome characterized by chest pain, hemoptysis, and diffuse alveolar infiltrates, a constellation of symptoms and signs see only with smoking "crack"

LUNG DISEASE

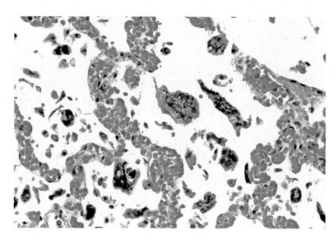

Figure 7.2 Intra-alveolar macrophages contain coarse black pigment in a crack cocaine abuser.

cocaine (Figure 7.2). Finally, 11% of the cocaine fatalities have polarizable birefringent material, usually talc, within the lungs. Most of these victims were, not unexpectedly, intravenous drug abusers.[10,11] Other diluents, such as starch and cellulose fibers, may be recognized by their typical pattern of birefringence.

Sometimes users of cocaine freebase, or "crack" cocaine, forcefully blow smoke into another user's mouth in order to augment the drug's effect (more absorption). Smokers also prolong the Valsalva maneuver in order to avoid expiring the precious cocaine smoke. The resulting increased intra-alveolar pressure ruptures the alveolar walls, allowing air to dissect along the perivascular tissues, into the mediastinum and surrounding cavities. This basic mechanism has been responsible for all types of barotrauma including pneumothorax, pneumo-mediastinum,[12–14] pneumo-pericardium,[15] pneumoperitoneum,[16] and subcutaneous emphysema. In the few cases to be reported,[17] where the duration of cocaine use prior to clinical symptoms was accurately known, patients freebased cocaine for 8 to 12 h and snorted cocaine for 1 h. Thus, it seems unlikely to occur on the first puff, but the possibility cannot be dismissed either. The clinical course of cocaine-associated barotrauma is generally nonfatal. This barotrauma is a nonspecific finding; it has been described in marijuana smokers,[18] and presumably occurs in smokers of methamphetamine as well.

Individuals with asthma who smoke heroin and cocaine are subject to acute severe exacerbation of their asthma.[19–22] There is nothing to distinguish nondrug-related asthma from asthma occurring secondary to drug usage, although bronchial mucus plugs and pulmonary hyperinflation were observed at autopsy in 64.7% of those with asthma who also had a history of drug or alcohol abuse.[23] Sudden death in this population may be the result of status asthmaticus, although it could also be the result of cocaine's arrhythmic effects, direct or indirect in the setting of an acute asthmatic attack. Insufflation of cocaine hydrochloride has also been associated with near-fatal status asthmaticus.[24] Blackened sputum and pulmonary cytologic specimens with excessive carbonaceous material are highly suggestive of crack cocaine use.[25] As crack is smoked, a dark, tarry residue forms on the inside of the pipe's bowl and barrel. Many smokers consider this residue to be concentrated cocaine and they scrape it free, reheat it, and vigorously inhale it. As a result, coarse, intracellular black particles, and intra-alveolar macrophages filled with black pigment, may be seen in crack cocaine abusers at autopsy (Figure 7.2).

The long-term pulmonary effects and pathology of smoking cocaine are unknown. Pulmonary function studies are confounded by the fact that cocaine smokers also smoke tobacco and marijuana in addition to cocaine. Cocaine smokers have a reduced diffusing capacity of carbon monoxide, but no spirometric abnormalities have been demonstrated.[26] Marijuana and tobacco smoking both produce similar changes in the bronchial mucosa; the histopathological changes include basal and goblet cell hyperplasia, squamous cell metaplasia, basement membrane thickening, inflammation, and increased nuclear variation and N/C ratio. Cocaine smoking does not produce these changes to the degree seen in the former groups.

7.2 COMPLICATIONS OF INTRAVENOUS DRUG ABUSE: GRANULOMATOUS PNEUMONITIS/ARTERIOPATHY

Intravenous drug abusers may crush oral medications and suspend them in water for intravenous injection. Methadone[27] and propoxyphene[28] are examples of oral drugs abused in this fashion. Pill filler material contains insoluble particles. Once these insoluble particles reach the lung, they cause thrombosis, granulomatous inflammation, and fibrosis. The granulomas have numerous multinucleated giant cells and contain birefringent foreign material (Figure 7.3; Table 7.1). When abundant, the granulomas and foreign material impart a granular texture to the lung. In addition to their morphology, the foreign particles can be identified by selected-area electron diffraction and energy dispersive x-ray analysis. The functional consequence of these lesions is often pulmonary hypertension with its accompanying complications, including cor pulmonale and sudden death. In nonfatal cases, patients may present with dyspnea, mild hypoxemia, and diffuse micronodules apparent on their chest radiographs. Gallium scanning can be used to demonstrate reduced diffusion across the parenchyma capacity; serum angiotensin-converting enzyme concentration in the lung is also elevated. The granulomatous and fibrotic reaction may be in the interstitium, presumably because the particles migrate through the arterial walls[29] and vascular remodeling occurs. Thromboembolic vascular remodeling produces recanalized arteries and intimal fibrosis. Plexiform and angiomatoid vascular lesions may also be seen. Large fibrotic pulmonary masses have been described with huge particle counts and occasional giant cells. The fibrotic masses are usually bilateral, asymmetric, and confined to the middle and upper lung fields. These are similar to the progressive massive fibrosis seen in complicated pneumoconiosis.[30–32]

Pulmonary hypertension due to pulmonary artery thromboses has been reported to result from the repeated intravenous injection of "blue velvet," a mixture of paregoric and tripelennamine (Pyribenzamine) tablets,[33,34] although this practice no longer seems very popular. Methylphenidate (Ritalin) tablets contain talc (magnesium silicate) and cornstarch, which can cause pulmonary hypertension and sudden death, often within 6 to 7 months of abusing the drugs. It is a practice in some areas to use Ritalin tablets as stimulants to counteract the sedative effects of methadone maintenance in addicts.

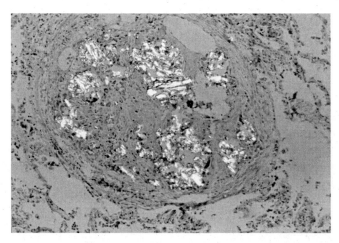

Figure 7.3 Abundant birefringent material lies within this pulmonary artery thrombus from an intravenous drug abuser (hematoxylin and eosin, polarized light, original magnification 80×).

LUNG DISEASE

Table 7.1 Common Foreign Material Found in the Lungs of IV Drug Abusers

Foreign Material	Drugs	Appearance	Notes
Talc	Methylphenidale (Ritalin) Methadone Tripelennamine HCl (Pyribenzamine) Propoxyphene (Darvon) Meperidine (Demerol) Benzedrine Dilaudid	Birefringent refractile crystalline needles 5–23 µm long or plates, colorless or pale yellow on H & E	Most common type of foreign material
Cornstarch	Barbiturates Paragoric Tripelennamine HCl (Pyribenzamine) Pentazocine (Talwin)	Birefringent refractile 8–12 µm round particles of varying size, colorless on H & E, form "Maltese cross" with polarized light, PAS+, diastase resistant	Often seen with talc particles
Microcrystalline cellulose	Pentazocine (Talwin) Methaqualone (Quaalude), Percodan Acetaminophen/aspirin with codeine Phenobarbital	Large (10–250 µm), irregular birefringent crystals, pale gray on H & E, PAS+, diastase resistant, Congo red+, methenamine silver+	
Cotton fibers	Heroin and other IV drugs	Refractile, birefringent small filaments, ring-shape or curvilinear on cross-section, very pale blue on H & E	
Crospovidone	Hydromorphone, propoxyphene	100 µm basophilic globular or coral-shaped mass; does not polarize; seen with H & E, mucicarmine, Congo red, and Movat stains	

While cornstarch can cause foreign body granulomas to form, the reaction is generally milder and less frequent than the granulomatous inflammation caused by talc,[35] which is irritating to tissues and may cause thrombosis with occlusion of pulmonary arterioles and capillaries, and a granulomatous inflammation with parenchyma fibrosis.[29] The end result is a restrictive lung disease with impaired oxygen transfer across the alveolar-capillary membrane and pulmonary hypertension. The pulmonary arteries may have multiple intravascular and perivascular foreign body granulomas filled with birefringent talc. The pulmonary arteries may also have medial hypertrophy, fibrointimal hyperplasia, and angiomatoid lesions (Figure 7.4).[36,37]

Pulmonary emphysema has been described in a subgroup of intravenous drug abusers who inject methylphenidate (Ritalin-SA). These patients present, complaining of dyspnea, at an average age of 36 years. All have moderate to severe airflow obstruction with hyperinflation on chest radiography. The bullae are often seen in the lower lobes and the disease may mimic the emphysema seen in alpha-1-antitrypsin deficiency. Morphologically, there is panacinar emphysema with no interstitial fibrosis and variable degrees of pulmonary talc granulomatosis.[38]

7.3 ASPIRATION PNEUMONIA

Alcoholism is a common predisposing condition for aspiration pneumonia. Aspiration of orogastric material (bacteria, acid, food. including milk, and charcoal-lavage material) can also occur in victims rendered unconscious by drugs directly (narcotics) or indirectly by drug-induced seizures (cocaine). The posterior segments of the upper lobes or superior segments of the left lower lobe are involved when the victim is recumbent during aspiration. The basal lung segments are affected when the victim is upright and the anterior segment of the middle lobe is involved when the victim is prone or inclined forward. Gastric acid can produce bronchiolitis, hemorrhagic edema, and diffuse alveolar damage if the agonal period is prolonged or delayed.

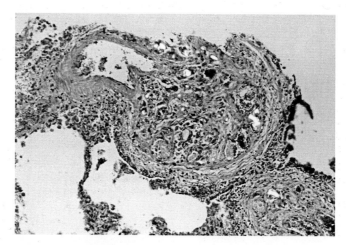

Figure 7.4 Angiomatoid lesion with birefringent talc in an intravenous drug abuser (hematoxylin and eosin, polarized light, original magnification 80×).

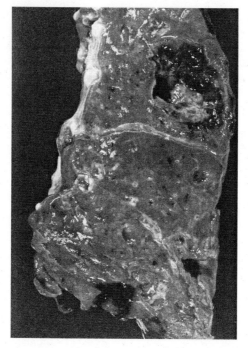

Figure 7.5 This sectioned lung has multiple abscess cavities. The victim was a 31-year-old cocaine "skin popper."

Microscopically, gastric acid aspiration produces a distinctive bronchocentric pallor of the pulmonary tissues. Fluid contaminated with *Streptococcus pneumoniae* or *Klebsiella pneumoniae* characteristically produces subpleural pneumonia with hemorrhagic edema.[39] Aspiration pneumonia often is found to consist of a mixture of both aerobic and anaerobic bacteria. Striated muscle and vegetable fibers can be seen within the bronchioles and alveoli microscopically. Necrotizing bacteria may produce lung abscesses. Septic thromboemboli from tricuspid valve endocarditis can also produce multiple lung abscesses and pneumonia in the intravenous drug abuser (Figure 7.5 and Figure 7.6).

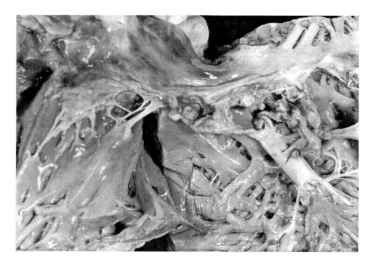

Figure 7.6 The victim in Figure 7.5 had acute bacterial endocarditis of the tricuspid valve with septic thromboemboli.

REFERENCES

1. Buster, M.C.A., Rook, L., van Brussel, G.H., et al., Chasing the dragon, related to the impaired lung function among heroin users, *Drug Alcohol Depend.*, 68, 221–228, 2002.
2. Bailey, M.E., Fraire, A.E., Greenberg, S.D., Barnard, J., and Cagle, P.T., Pulmonary histopathology in cocaine abusers, *Hum. Pathol.*, 25, 203–207, 1994.
3. Murray, R.J., Smialek, J.E., Golle, M., and Albin, R.J., Pulmonary artery medial hypertrophy in cocaine users without foreign particle microembolization, *Chest*, 96, 1050–1053, 1989.
4. Murray, R.J., Albin, R.J., Mergner, W., and Criner, G.J., Diffuse alveolar hemorrhage temporally related to cocaine smoking, *Chest*, 93, 427–429, 1988.
5. Allred, R.J. and Ewer, S., Fatal pulmonary edema following intravenous "freebase" cocaine use, *Ann. Emerg. Med.*, 10, 441–442, 1981.
6. Efferen, L., Palat, D., and Meisner, J., Nonfatal pulmonary edema following cocaine smoking, *NY State J. Med.*, 89, 415–416, 1989.
7. Cucco, R.A., Yoo, O.H., Cregler, L., and Chang, J.C., Nonfatal pulmonary edema after "freebase" cocaine smoking, *Am. Rev. Respir. Dis.*, 136, 179–181, 1987.
8. Hoffman, C.K. and Goodman, P.C., Pulmonary edema in cocaine smokers, *Radiology*, 172, 463–465, 1989.
9. Patel, R.C., Dutta, D., and Schonfeld, S.A., Freebase cocaine use associated with bronchiolitis obliterans organizing pneumonia, *Ann. Intern. Med.*, 107, 186–187, 1987.
10. Forrester, J.M., Steele, A.W., Waldron, J.A., and Parsons, P.E., Crack lung: an acute pulmonary syndrome with a spectrum of clinical and histopathologic findings, *Am. Rev. Respir. Dis.*, 142, 462–467, 1990.
11. Kissner, D.G., Lawrence, W.D., Selis, J.E., and Flint, A., Crack lung: pulmonary disease caused by cocaine abuse, *Am. Rev. Respir. Dis.*, 136, 1250–1252, 1987.
12. Shesser, R., Davis, C., and Edelstein, S., Pneumomediastinum and pneumothorax after inhaling alkaloidal cocaine, *Ann. Emerg. Med.*, 10, 213–215, 1981.
13. Aroesty, D.J., Stanley, R.B., and Crockett, D.M., Pneumomediastinum and cervical emphysema from the inhalation of "freebase" cocaine: report of three cases, *Otolaryngol. Head Neck Surg.*, 94, 372–374, 1986.
14. Bush, M.N., Rubenstein, R., Hoffman, I., and Bruno, M.S., Spontaneous pneumomediastinum as a consequence of cocaine use, *NY State J. Med.*, 84, 618–619, 1984.
15. Adrouny, A. and Magnusson, P., Pneumopericardium from cocaine inhalation [letter], *N. Engl. J. Med.*, 313, 48–49, 1985.

16. Andreone, P., L'Heureux, P., and Strate, R.G., An unusual case of massive nonsurgical pneumoperitoneum: case report, *J. Trauma*, 29, 1286–1288, 1989.
17. Shesser, R., Davis, C., and Edelstein, S., Pneumomediastinum and pneumothorax after inhaling alkaloidal cocaine, *Ann. Emerg. Med.*, 10, 213–215, 1981.
18. Birrer, R.B. and Calderon, J., Pneumothorax, pneumomediastinum, and pneumopericardium following Valsalva maneuver during marijuana smoking, *NY State J. Med.*, 84, 619–620, 1984.
19. Rubin, R.B. and Neugarten, J., Cocaine-associated asthma, *Am. J. Med.*, 88, 438–439, 1990.
20. Rebhun, J., Association of asthma and freebase smoking, *Ann. Allergy*, 60, 339–342, 1988.
21. Rao, A.N., Polos, P.G., and Walther, F.A., Crack abuse and asthma: a fatal combination, *NY State J. Med.*, 511–512, 1990.
22. Hughes, S. and Calvery, P.M.A., Heroin inhalation and asthma, *Br. Med. J.*, 297, 1511–1512, 1988.
23. Levenson, T., Greenberger, P.A., Donoghue, E.R., and Lifschultz, B.D., Asthma deaths confounded by substance abuse: an assessment of fatal asthma, *Chest*, 110, 604–610, 1996.
24. Averbach, M., Casey, K.K., and Frank, E., Near fatal status asthmaticus induced by nasal insufflation of cocaine, *South. Med. J.*, 89, 340–341, 1996.
25. Greenebaum, E., Copeland, A., and Grewal, R., Blackened bronchoalveolar lavage fluid in crack smokers: a preliminary study, *Am. J. Clin. Pathol.*, 100, 481–487, 1993.
26. Itkonen, J., Schnoll, S., and Glassroth, J., Pulmonary dysfunction in "freebase" cocaine users, *Arch. Intern. Med.*, 144, 2195–2197, 1984.
27. Lamb, D. and Roberts, G., Starch and talc emboli in drug addicts' lungs, *J. Clin. Pathol.*, 25, 876–881, 1972.
28. Butz, W.C., Pulmonary arteriole foreign body granulomata associated with angiomatoids resulting from the intravenous injection of oral medications, e.g. Propoxyphene hydrochloride (Darvon), *J. Forensic Sci.*, 14, 317–326, 1969.
29. Puro, H.E., Wolf, P.J., Skirgaudas, J., and Vazquez, J., Experimental production of human "Blue Velvet" and "Red Devil" lesions, *J. Am. Med. Assoc.*, 197, 1100–1102, 1966.
30. Crouch, E. and Churg, A., Progressive massive fibrosis of the lung secondary to intravenous injection of talc. A pathologic and mineralogic analysis, *Am. J. Clin. Pathol.*, 80, 520–526, 1983.
31. Pare, J.A.P., Fraser, R.G., Hogg, J.C., Howlett, J.G., and Murphy, S.B., Pulmonary "mainline" granulomatosis: talcosis of intravenous methadone abuse, *Medicine*, 58, 229–239, 1979.
32. Sieniewicz, D.J. and Nidecker, A.C., Conglomerate pulmonary disease: a form of talcosis in intravenous methadone abusers, *Am. J. Roent.*, 135, 697–702, 1980.
33. Wendt, V.E., Puro, H.E., Shapiro, J., Mathews, W., and Wolf, P.L., Angiothrombotic pulmonary hypertension in addicts, *J. Am. Med. Assoc.*, 188, 755–757, 1964.
34. Szwed, J.J., Pulmonary angiothrombosis caused by "blue velvet" addiction, *Ann. Intern. Med.*, 73, 771–774, 1970.
35. Hahn, H.H., Schweid, A.I., and Beaty, H.N., Complications of injecting dissolved methylphenidate tablets, *Arch. Int. Med.*, 123, 656–659, 1969.
36. Lewman, L.V., Fatal pulmonary hypertension from intravenous injection of methylphenidate (Ritalin) tablets, *Hum. Pathol.*, 3, 67–70, 1972.
37. Hopkins, G.B. and Taylor, D.G., Pulmonary talc granulomatosis, *Am. Rev. Resp. Dis.*, 101, 101–104, 1970.
38. Sherman, C.B., Hudson, L.D., and Pierson, D.J., Severe precocious emphysema in intravenous methylphenidate (Ritalin) abusers, *Chest*, 92, 1085–1087, 1987.
39. Wright, J.L., Consequences of aspiration and bronchial obstruction, in Thurlbeck, W.M. and Churg, A.M., *Pathology of the Lung*, 2nd ed., Thieme Medical, New York, 1995, chap. 31.

CHAPTER **8**

Disorders of the Central Nervous System

Michael D. Bell, M.D.
District Medical Examiner, Palm Beach Medical Examiner Office, West Palm Beach, Florida

CONTENTS

8.1	Alcohol Related	137
8.2	Drug Related: Excited Delirium	139
8.3	Drug-Induced Cerebrovascular Disease	140
8.4	Drug-Associated Cerebral Vasculitis	143
8.5	Drug-Induced Seizure Disorder	145
8.6	Drug-Induced Movement Disorders	146
8.7	Drug-Induced Anoxic Ischemic Encephalopathy	146
8.8	Drug-Associated Central Nervous System Infections	146
8.9	Heroin Smokers' Encephalopathy	148
References		148

8.1 ALCOHOL RELATED

Marchiafava-Bignami[1-3] disease is a demyelinating disorder affecting the corpus callosum. It was first described in malnourished Italian men who drank cheap red wine. It has since been described in other countries and as occurring with other alcoholic beverages. Grossly, there is a discolored or partially cystic demyelinated region in the genu and body of the corpus callosum with sparing of the thin fibers along the dorsal[4] and ventral surfaces of the corpus callosum. The optic chiasm and anterior commissures may also be involved. The lesion is bilateral and symmetric with sparing of the gray matter. Microscopically, there is demyelination sparing of the axon cylinders. The number of oligodendrocytes is reduced. Lipid-laden macrophages are often abundant.

Central pontine myelinolysis (CPM) is a demyelinating disorder of the central basis pons that was first described in malnourished alcoholics by Adams.[4] Patients with CPM experience a sudden change in mental status, flaccid quadriparesis with hyperreflexia, pseudobulbar palsy, and an extensor plantar response unless coma obscures these signs. CPM is associated with the rapid correction or overcorrection of hyponatremia[5] and the symptoms appear a few days (average 6 days) after overcorrection with intravenous sodium leads to a rise of at least 20 mmol/L. Grossly, victims will be found to have a discolored, finely granular demyelinated zone in the central basis pontis, with

137

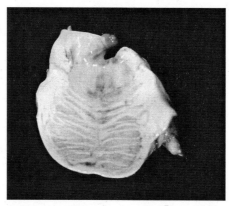

Figure 8.1 Discolored granular zone of myelinolysis in the central pons of this 28-year-old alcoholic who was treating aggressively for hyponatremia.

sparing of the tegmentum, ventral pons, and corticospinal tracts (Figure 8.1).[6] Extrapontine myelinolysis has become more recognized.[7] The demyelinated area varies from a few millimeters to the entire basis pontis and may be triangular, diamond, or butterfly shaped. Microscopically, there is demyelination with relative preservation of axon cylinders and neurons. Axonal spheroids are commonly observed. Acute lesions contain lipid-laden macrophages, but no other inflammatory cells. Oligodendrocytes are reduced or absent and reactive astrocytes are present.

Cerebellar degeneration of alcoholics is clinically manifested by truncal instability, lower extremity ataxia, and wide-based gait, symptoms appearing gradually over months or years.[3] The pathogenesis is still unknown and may be due to the direct toxic effect of alcohol or to thiamine deficiency, or from rapid correction or overcorrection of hyponatremia similar to central pontine myelinolysis. Grossly, the folia of the rostral vermis and anterosuperior cerebellar hemispheres are atrophic and shrunken with widened interfolial sulci. A sagittal section through the vermis rather than the usual coronal sectioning best demonstrates this. Microscopically, the folial crests are more severely affected than the depths of the interfolial sulci, which help to distinguish the changes from those seen in anoxic-ischemic injury. There is Purkinje cell loss, patchy granular cell loss, molecular layer atrophy, and gliosis with Bregmann glial proliferation.

Acute alcohol intoxication can cause death due to central cardiopulmonary paralysis.[3] While blood ethanol concentrations over 450 to 500 mg/dl are usually considered lethal, there is considerable variability due to tolerance. Children are considered more susceptible to the lethal effects than are adults. Cerebral edema may be present or the neuropathologic examination may be normal. Delirium tremens or withdrawal seizures are not associated with any specific neuropathologic abnormalities.[8]

Chronic alcohol use may be associated with cerebral atrophy, although this is a disputed effect of alcoholism.[3] The cerebral atrophy thought to be a result of chronic alcoholism involves the upper dorsolateral frontal lobes, but may extend inferiorly to the inferior frontal gyri and posteriorly to the superior parietal lobule.[1] There is mild ventricular enlargement. Microscopic changes are not specific. This type of cerebral atrophy may be associated with a dementia that is potentially reversible at its early stages.[9]

Fetal alcohol syndrome is a constellation of birth defects found in children of alcohol-abusing mothers. It is the most common cause of birth defects associated with mental retardation. Other clinical manifestations include irritability, seizures, hypotonia, and cerebellar dysfunction. The neuropathology findings are nonspecific and include microcephaly, compensatory hydrocephalus, neuroglial heterotopia of the ventricles or leptomeninges, and atrophy or hypoplasia of the cerebellum or centrum semiovale.[3,10]

The autopsy manifestations of Wernicke encepholopathy (gaze paralysis, ataxia, nystagmus, and mental confusion) and Korsakoff psychosis (retrograde amnesia, impaired short-term memory)

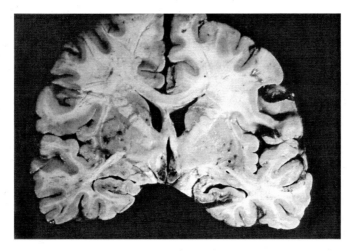

Figure 8.2   Coronal section of cerebrum demonstrates the mammillary body hemorrhage in Wernicke–Korsakoff syndrome.

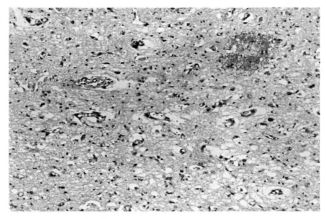

Figure 8.3   Ball hemorrhage, capillary proliferation, and gliosis are present in this alcoholic with Wernicke encephalopathy (hematoxylin and eosin, original magnification 20×).

seen in alcoholics[11] include petechiae and pink discoloration of the mammillary bodies (Figure 8.2).[3] The morphologic features (seen in 1.7 to 2.7% of consecutive autopsies) include petechiae and pink discoloration of the mammillary bodies (Figure 8.2), hypothalamus, periventricular region of the thalamus, periaqueductal gray matter, and beneath the floor of the fourth ventricle.[1] The lesions are bilateral and symmetric when present. These gross features are seen in only 50% of acute cases;[12] therefore, microscopic examination is essential. The lesions vary with the stage and severity of the deficiency. Acute lesions consist of dilated, congested capillaries with perivascular ball and ring hemorrhages and ischemic neuronal changes (Figure 8.3). Chronic lesions have vascular endothelial cell swelling and proliferation and gliosis. Affected blood vessels may have irregular or bead-like swellings.

8.2 DRUG RELATED: EXCITED DELIRIUM

Excited delirium is a drug-induced delirium or psychosis accompanied by agitation, and hyperthermia, and often ending with respiratory arrest and sudden death. Cocaine is the drug most often implicated in this syndrome,[13] but amphetamines have also been implicated in some cases. The syndrome is not due to any contaminants ingested along with the drug.

Table 8.1 Comparison between Neuroleptic Malignant Syndrome and Cocaine-Induced Agitated Delirium

Symptom	NMS	Cocaine Delirium
Hyperthermia	++	++
Delirium	++	++
Agitation	+	++
Akinesia/rigidity	++	−

Note: ++ = present in almost all cases; + = present in many cases; − = may occur late during syndrome.[16]

Chronic cocaine users have increased synaptic dopamine uptake in the ventral striatum. Victims of fatal cocaine-associated excited delirium, however, do not show this increase. Cocaine abusers also have increased serotonin transporter upregulation in dopaminergic areas of the brain. Serotonin is thought to modulate dopamine transmission. Some researchers believe that victims of fatal cocaine-associated excited delirium have a distinctive receptor phenotype differing from that of chronic cocaine users without excited delirium. The pathogenesis of cocaine-induced excited delirium is unknown. One hypothesis is that cocaine initially elevates brain dopamine levels causing the delirium. This cocaine-induced brain dopamine elevation has been demonstrated in animals.[14] Chronic cocaine use reduces brain dopamine metabolism[15] potentiating the effect of cocaine on brain dopamine levels. As the cocaine concentration falls, brain dopamine falls triggering the syndrome, which is similar to the neuroleptic malignant syndrome (NMS) in Parkinson's disease or in patients withdrawn from levodopa, a dopaminergic drug. Some authors consider cocaine-induced psychosis as a variant of NMS in which patients also have hyperthermia, autonomic instability, and delirium (Table 8.1). NMS is characterized by diffuse muscular rigidity, but this is not seen in cocaine-induced excited delirium. One author has suggested that akinesia of the respiratory muscles may be the fatal mechanism of sudden death in these victims.[16]

There are no specific gross or microscopic findings in victims dying of cocaine-induced agitated delirium. A post-mortem core body temperature, if taken soon after death, will be elevated. A thorough post-mortem examination is essential to rule out other causes of sudden death. Cocaine and its metabolites must be present in toxicology specimens. Victims dying of agitated delirium have post-mortem blood cocaine concentrations (average = 0.6 mg/L with range of 0.14 to 0.92 mg/L) that are ten times lower than those concentrations in victims of cocaine overdose.[17]

Agitated delirium may occur following cocaine ingestion by all routes of administration (snorting, smoking, injection), but never after just chewing coca leaves. The majority of victims are men. Soon after cocaine ingestion, the person becomes paranoid, delirious, and aggressive. The victim is often seen running, yelling, breaking glass and overturning furniture, disrobing, and hiding. Witnesses report that the person has unexpected strength. The victim often becomes calm and quiet before having a cardiopulmonary arrest, often during police custody or medical transport. This disorder is frequently accompanied by sudden death. Restraint procedures that could compromise respiration should be avoided. The restrained person should be closely observed, especially after the agitation subsides.[18]

8.3 DRUG-INDUCED CEREBROVASCULAR DISEASE

Drug-induced cerebrovascular disease or stroke is any nontraumatic intracerebral hemorrhage (including subarachnoid hemorrhage) or cerebral infarction that results directly or indirectly from drug ingestion. An accurate clinical history and/or positive toxicologic testing are needed to corroborate the recent drug ingestion. In all, 47% of patients less than 35 years old who present with an acute stroke have drug use as a predisposing condition.[19] Clinically, a patient with cere-

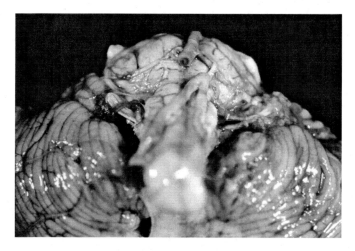

Figure 8.4 There is an occlusive thrombus in the basilar artery of this 28-year-old cocaine addict.

brovascular disease presents with sudden loss of function, neurologic deficit, and involvement of the corresponding vascular supply that occurs within minutes or rarely hours after drug ingestion. If the blood vessel is occluded through pharmacological vasoconstriction or vasospasm, ischemia and infarction occurs. If the vessel is damaged, hemorrhage results.

Cocaine is frequently associated with intracerebral hemorrhage.[20–24] Other stimulant drugs including amphetamine,[19,25] phenylpropanolamine,[26] phencyclidine,[26] pseudoephedrine,[26] and methylphenidate,[19,26] have all been associated with intracranial hemorrhage.

Cocaine blocks the uptake of catecholamines at adrenergic nerve endings, potentiating sympathetic responses, leading to a dose-dependent elevation of arterial pressure and heart rate in humans[27] and dogs.[28] Amphetamine and methamphetamine can also produce transient hypertension and tachycardia. Researchers postulated that intracerebral hemorrhage occurs because of sudden marked elevation in systemic blood pressure in susceptible persons with preexisting vascular malformations. This would include such disorders as arterio-venous malformations, berry aneurysms,[29] or Charcot–Bouchard microaneurysms in hypertensive individuals.

In half of patients with cocaine-associated intracerebral or subarachnoid hemorrhage, no demonstrable structural lesion is identified.[30–32] Another postulated mechanism of intraparenchymal hemorrhage in cocaine users is acute increased cerebral blood flow into an area of ischemia produced by prior cocaine-induced vasoconstriction.[33] Interestingly, intrauterine exposure to cocaine does not influence the prevalence or severity of intraventricular hemorrhage in the preterm infant.[34]

Cocaine can cause cerebral infarction by arterial thrombosis, arterial embolism, arterial spasm, and circulatory compromise with secondary cerebral hypoperfusion. In the latter case, cocaine can cause acute myocardial infarction or ventricular arrhythmia resulting in hypotension and secondary cerebral hypoperfusion. The middle cerebral artery is most commonly affected with resulting sudden paraplegia.[35] The anterior cerebral, posterior cerebral, and basilar/vertebral arteries can also be affected resulting in a variety of clinical signs and symptoms (Figure 8.4 and Figure 8.5). Most victims develop symptoms suddenly, within 3 h of cocaine ingestion. Other victims wake up with the neurologic deficit after heavy drug use the previous evening. Cannabis has recently been implicated in causing multiple nonfatal ischemic strokes in a 36-year-old man with no other risk factors. The mechanism for cannabis-induced stroke is unknown. No matter how convincing the case report, causation is established only by randomized clinical trials or, as in this case, with a nested case control study. Such studies are lacking.

The most common sites of cocaine-induced intracerebral hemorrhage are the cerebral hemispheres (57%) followed by the putamen (18%), and subarachnoid and intraventricular sites (Figure 8.6 and Figure 8.7). Cocaine-induced subarachnoid hemorrhage is usually due to rupture of a

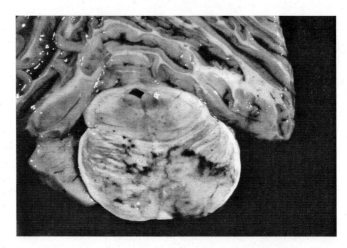

Figure 8.5 There is an irregular zone of infarction in the basis pontis of the victim in Figure 8.4. He was found comatose at home.

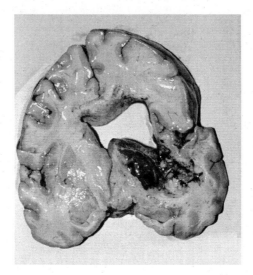

Figure 8.6 This 35-year-old woman developed an acute intracerebral hematoma after cocaine use.

preexisting arterio-venous malformation or berry aneurysm of the cerebral arteries[35] (Figure 8.8). In a recent retrospective study from San Diego, 21% of victims dying from ruptured berry aneurysms had cocaine or methamphetamine (or both) in their post-mortem blood.[36] This was higher than the 5% incidence of cocaine or methamphetamine intoxication in all adult autopsies from the same jurisdiction.

If no vascular malformation is found to explain the subarachnoid hemorrhage in a drug addict, one must consider a traumatic cause for the subarachnoid hemorrhage (such as extracranial vertebral artery laceration[37]) before blithely ascribing it to cocaine or another stimulant. Intraparenchymal hemorrhage due to cocaine use can occur in sites typical of patients with hypertension-related intracerebral hemorrhage. The blood vessels, when examined, are usually normal both on gross and microscopic exam.[38] Charcot–Bouchard microaneurysms, or lipohyalinosis, are typically seen in hypertensive cerebral hemorrhage[39] and are not seen in drug-induced intracerebral hemorrhage. Patients are usually in their third to fifth decades of life with both men and women affected equally. Intracerebral hemorrhage occurs after snorting, smoking, or injecting cocaine. The time between drug use and symptom onset is usually within 3 h, but can range from immediate to 12 h. Most

DISORDERS OF THE CENTRAL NERVOUS SYSTEM

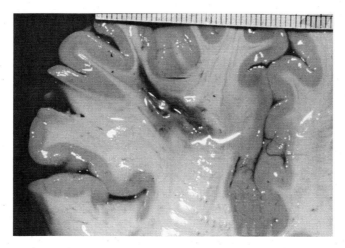

Figure 8.7 This brown slit-like cavity in the frontal white matter is all that remains of a previous cocaine-induced intracerebral hemorrhage.

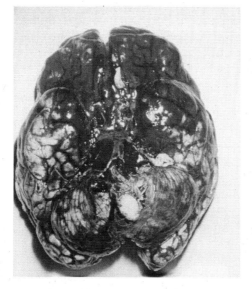

Figure 8.8 Subarachnoid hemorrhage in cocaine abusers is often due to a berry aneurysm that ruptures from the sudden blood pressure elevation caused by cocaine.

patients present with acute headache or in coma. Confusion is a less frequent presenting symptom. There is 36% mortality in patients who present to the emergency room with acute stroke strongly linked to recent drug use.[19]

8.4 DRUG-ASSOCIATED CEREBRAL VASCULITIS

Cerebral vasculitis has been associated with cocaine, ephedrine, and amphetamine use. The association between cerebral vasculitis and cocaine use is tenuous and supported by only a few (eight) case reports, some of which have only angiographic evidence ("beading" or segmental arterial narrowing) of vasculitis with no histological confirmation (Table 8.2).[40,41] Since "beading" is considered by many to be a sign of vasospasm, the causation argument becomes circular. The remaining case reports do show histological evidence of vasculitis, but no angiographic narrowing

Table 8.2   Reported Cases of Cocaine-Associated Vasculitis

Report	Age/Sex	Route	Clinical syndrome	Angiogram	Time interval	Pathology	Outcome
Kaye, 1987	22 M	Nasal	Cerebral infarct	Beading, occlusion, narrowing	Unknown	None	Improvement with steroids
Klonoff, 1989	29 F	Smoke	ICH	Beading, narrowing	Unknown	None	Stabilized after hematoma removed
Krendel, 1990	36 M	Smoke	Weakness, dysarthria, confusion	Occlusion, narrowing	3.5 weeks	Acute vasculitis, small cortical vessels, cortical infarct with multinucleated giant cells	Improvement with steroids
Krendell, 1990	31 F	Smoke, IV	Coma, cerebral edema	Normal	42 days	Lymphocytic infiltration, small vessels and larger vessel normal, no granulomas, multiple cystic, necrotic, and gliotic areas in white matter with multinucleated giant cells	Death
Fredericks, 1991	32 M	Nasal, IV	Confusion, ataxia	Normal	13 days	Lymphocytic infiltration, small vessels and endothelial swelling	Improvement with steroids
Morrow, 1993	25 F	Nasal	Seizure, coma	Not done	5 days	Lymphocytic infiltration in small vessels of cortex and brainstem, small infarcts, cerebral edema with diffuse encephalomalacia	Death
Merkel, 1995	32 M	Nasal	ICH	Normal	2 days	Non-necrotizing leukocytoclastic vasculitis, neutrophils and mononuclear cells in venules	Improvement without steroids
Merkel, 1995	20 M	Nasal	ICH	Narrowing	<6 months	Neutrophil infiltration and fibrinoid degeneration in small arterioles and veins	Partial recovery

or other abnormalities.[42–45] Half of the victims presented with encephalopathy and coma without intracranial hemorrhage or infarction. The other half presented with intracerebral hemorrhage or cerebral infarction. Transient ischemic attacks (TIA) with multimodal segmental arterial stenosis on angiography have been reported in chronic cocaine users.[46] All these patients were young (mean age = 28 years with age range = 22 to 36) with multiple routes of drug administration used (nasal insufflation, smoking, intravenous injection). Histological examination demonstrated acute and chronic small vessel inflammation. Four cases had lymphocytic infiltration in the cerebral blood vessels. Two cases had polymorphonuclear leukocyte infiltration in the small arteries and venules of the brain. No giant cells or granulomas were seen in any case. The pathogenesis of cocaine-associated cerebral vasculitis remains unknown. Methamphetamine and structurally related drugs have reportedly caused necrotizing cerebral vasculitis.

8.5 DRUG-INDUCED SEIZURE DISORDER

Drug-induced seizures are, by definition, seizures that occur after the ingestion of a drug, that are not caused by other pathologic processes (intracranial hemorrhage or blunt head trauma). An accurate clinical history or positive toxicology testing should corroborate actual ingestion of the drug.

Cocaine has been reported to lower the threshold for seizures and commonly does cause seizures.[47] In one series of patients with seizure activity as the primary admitting diagnosis, cocaine was the most common drug of abuse detected.[48] At least in this series, cocaine-induced seizure was found to be more likely brief and self-limiting, compared to seizures caused by the other drugs of abuse (amphetamine, methamphetamine, phencyclidine, and sedative-hypnotic withdrawal). Seizures may also initiate a terminal cardiac arrhythmia, a theory that has gained more acceptance, but the suggestion has yet to be proved.[49,50]

Fatal seizures associated with cocaine use have been reported.[51] There are no specific gross or microscopic neuropathologic findings in fatal cocaine-induced seizure victims. Tongue contusions are nonspecific findings in patients who die of terminal seizures (Figure 8.9).

Cocaine-induced seizure is a common neurologic complication (2.3 to 8.4%) of cocaine users who present with seizures to the emergency room[52] that affects both men and women.[53] The average age is 27 years with a range of 17 to 42 years. Seizures occur after snorting, smoking, or injecting cocaine. The seizures are usually generalized, tonic–clonic, isolated, and self-limiting. They usually last less

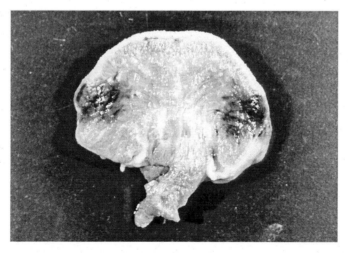

Figure 8.9 This cross section of tongue demonstrates the contusions that may be seen in drug-induced seizures.

than 5 min and can occur with first-time and chronic cocaine users. The interval between cocaine ingestion and seizure onset varies from minutes to 12 h. In one emergency room study, 11 of 137 patients (8%) with cocaine intoxication presented with seizures as their chief problem and none died.[52]

8.6 DRUG-INDUCED MOVEMENT DISORDERS

Parkinson's syndrome has been reported in addicts who receive the synthetic meperidine analog contaminated with MPTP (1-methyl-4-phenyl-1,2,3,6-tetrahydropyridine). MPTP is produced during the careless synthesis of MPPP (1-methyl-4-phenyl-4-propionoxypiperidene) in clandestine laboratories. Neurotoxic symptoms include resting tremor, rigidity, bradykinesia, and other signs and symptoms of parkinsonism. Neuropathologic examination has demonstrated substantia nigra degeneration confined to the zona compacta. There is astrocytosis, focal gliosis, and deposition of extraneuronal melanin pigment.[54] It has been reported that MPPP contaminated with MPTP causes a Parkinson's syndrome within days of injection.[55] MPTP-induced Parkinson's syndrome can also result from snorting the drug.[56] The severe rigidity observed in MPTP-induced parkinonism has been implicated in the asphyxiation death of one victim who was unable to move his head from a suffocating posture.[57] Post-mortem neuropathological examination of this individual also revealed severe neuronal loss in his substantia nigra. Cocaine use also has been associated with movement disorders. This may be related to the fact that concentrations of alpha-synmuclein, a pre-synaptic protein found in Lewy bodies in Parkinson's disease, are increased in the midbrain dopamine neurons of chronic cocaine abusers.

8.7 DRUG-INDUCED ANOXIC ISCHEMIC ENCEPHALOPATHY

Abused drugs commonly produce anoxic-ischemic encephalopathy.[58–60] This can occur from insufficient oxygen reaching the blood from the lungs, insufficient oxygen carriage, or inadequate cerebral blood perfusion. This is a common mechanism in drug abusers who have a delayed death after drug intoxication. In the older literature on fatal heroin overdose, cerebral edema with increased brain weight was observed in nearly 90%. This finding conflicts with the author's own experience, where most cases of fatal heroin intoxication manifested neither cerebral edema nor increased brain weight.

The morphology of anoxic-ischemic encephalopathy is variable in its affect on different parts of the brain. In the gray matter, the watershed zones are commonly affected with laminar necrosis involving lamina zones III, V, VI. The h1 segment (Sommer's sector) and end plate in the hippocampus, are commonly involved. Other vulnerable sites include the Purkinje cells of the cerebellum, the caudate, and the putamen. The brain is often swollen and soft with a pale or dusky gray matter. Laminar necrosis may be apparent if sufficient time has elapsed between the time of anoxia and death. Microscopic changes are not recognizable until 6 to 8 h after the anoxic-ischemic insult. The affected neurons become shrunken with eosinophilic cytoplasm and nuclear pyknosis, and gradually disappear. There is also nonspecific capillary proliferation, with endothelial swelling, spongiform change, and gliosis in the affected neuropil. Hypoxic injury to the cerebral white matter with glossy softening and loss of myelin (hypoxic leukoencephlaopathy) is less commonly seen in drug overdoses where death is delayed.

8.8 DRUG-ASSOCIATED CENTRAL NERVOUS SYSTEM INFECTIONS

Primary fungal cerebritis due to *Rhizopus* has been reported in cocaine,[61] heroin,[62–66] and amphetamine[67] users with no other systemic foci identified at autopsy. Victims are usually men in

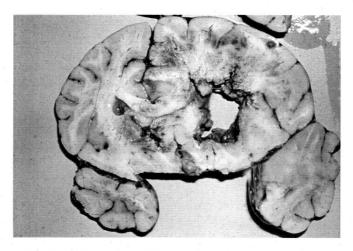

Figure 8.10 Coronal section of brain with multiple necrotic abscesses in an intravenous drug abuser.

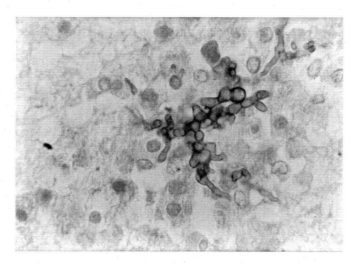

Figure 8.11 Within the necrotic cerebral cavities of the patient in this figure are branching, septated fungi (Gomori methanamine silver, original magnification 80×).

their third or fourth decades of life. They present with hemiplegia, facial weakness, and headache. The brain lesions are usually multiple with frequent bilateral involvement of the basal ganglia. The phycomycoses are angiotrophic fungi that commonly occlude and invade the cerebral blood vessels causing hemorrhagic infarcts. Fungal cerebritis or meningitis has been reported in intravenous drug abusers (Figure 8.10 and Figure 8.11) with human immunodeficiency virus (HIV) infection. In addition to fungal cerebritis, HIV-infected intravenous drug abusers can develop a large variety of central nervous infections and neoplasms (Table 8.3), thereby fulfilling the criterion for acquired immunodeficiency syndrome (AIDS). Intravenous drug abusers with valvular endocarditis may develop central nervous system complications from emboli, both septic and bland infarction, which may affect a single or multiple vessels. The resultant lesions may be ischemic or suppurative, resulting in septic or aseptic meningitis, brain abscess, or encephalopathy.[68] This is more likely to occur with left-sided valvular endocarditis than right-sided endocarditis alone. *Staphylococcus aureus* is a more common etiologic microorganism in intravenous drug abusers than non-intravenous drug abusers and it is more likely to produce neurologic complications. Intravenous drug abusers can develop significant and life-threatening neurologic sequelae from toxins produced by *Clostridium tetani and botulinum* wound infections. Tetanus is commonly associated with subcutaneous

Table 8.3   Central Nervous System Infections in Intravenous Drug Abusers with AIDS

HIV encephalitis
Progressive multifocal leukoencephalopathy
Cytomegalovirus ventriculitis and *cerebritis*
Toxoplasma cerebritis
Cryptococcal meningitis and *cerebritis*
Histoplasma cerebritis
Nocardia cerebritis
Mycobacterium infections (including tuberculosis, avian-intracellulare)
Fungal meningitis and cerebritis (*Candida, Aspergillus, Rhizopus*)
Cysticercosis
Entameba histolytica
Acanthameba castellani

injection or "skin popping." Mexican "Black tar" heroin use was a risk factor in cases of botulism occurring in intravenous drug abusers during the mid-1990s. Nasal insufflation of drugs can also cause frontal sinusitis and overlying frontal lobe abscess.[69] Clostridia outbreaks reported from the United Kingdom involved mainly Iranian heroin.[70]

8.9 HEROIN SMOKERS' ENCEPHALOPATHY

Spongiform encephalopathy of obscure origin occurs in users of smoked drugs, but most cases have been in heroin abusers. An epidemic outbreak of spongiform leukoencephalopathy occurred in the Netherlands in 1982. It involved nearly 50 patients, many of whom died, none of whom fully recovered.[71] The only factor common to all the individuals was that they all smoked heroin. All of the reported cases have had thorough toxicological investigation, but no agents have been identified. Sporadic cases have occurred over the last quarter century, mainly in Europe. A few of the victims have been cocaine users and several have been drug injectors. More recent magnetic resonance imaging (MRI) studies have shown diffuse white matter changes in all cases. Histologically there is widespread confluent vacuolar degeneration of the deep white matter, with evidence of severe, extensive, axonal injury.[72] Various etiologies have been proposed including some uncharacterized defect in mitochondrial function or a direct toxic effect upon lipid-rich myelin. It may be that the disease has a latent period after the putative toxin is absorbed, but before symptoms appear. If so, that would explain the consistently negative toxicology testing results.

REFERENCES

1. Courville, C.B., *Effects of Alcohol on the Nervous System of Man*, San Lucas Press, Los Angeles, 1966.
2. Bohrod, M.G., Primary degeneration of the corpus callosum (Marchiafava's disease), *Arch. Neurol. Psychiatry,* 47, 465–473, 1942.
3. Schocet, S.S., Jr., Exogenous toxic-metabolic diseases including vitamin deficiency, in Davis, R.L. and Robertson, D.M., Eds., *Textbook of Neuropathology*, Williams & Wilkins, Baltimore, 1985, 372–402.
4. Adams, R.D., Victor, M., and Mancall, E.L., Central pontine myelinolysis: a hitherto undescribed disease occurring in alcoholics and malnourished patients, *Arch. Neurol. Psychiatry,* 81, 154–172, 1959.
5. Norenberg, M.D., Leslie, K.O., and Robertson, A.S.. Association between rise in serum sodium and central pontine myelinolysis, *Ann. Neurol.,* 11, 128–135, 1982.
6. Norenberg, M.D. and Gregorios, J.B., Central nervous system manifestations of systemic disease, in Davis, R.L. and Robertson, D.M., Eds., *Textbook of Neuropathology*, Williams & Wilkins, Baltimore, 1985, 422–423.

DISORDERS OF THE CENTRAL NERVOUS SYSTEM

7. Laureno, R. and Karp, B.I., Myelinolysis after correction of hyponatremia, *Ann. Intern. Med.,* 126, 57–62, 1997.

8. Powers, J.M. and Haroupian, D.S., Central nervous system, in Damjanov, I. and Linder, J., Eds., *Anderson's Pathology,* 10th ed., Mosby-Year Book, St. Louis, 1996, 2791.

9. Tomlinson, B.E., Aging and the dementias, in Adams, J.H. and Duchen, L.W., Eds., *Greenfield's Neuropathology,* 5th ed., Oxford University Press, New York, 1992.

10. Claren, S.K., Recognition of fetal alcohol syndrome, *J. Am. Med. Assoc.,* 245, 2436–2439, 1981.

11. Cravioto, H., Korein, J., and Silberman, J., Wernicke's encephalopathy: a clinical and pathological study of 28 autopsied cases, *Arch. Neurol.,* 4, 510–519,1961.

12. Harper, C., Wernicke's encephalopathy: a more common disease than realized. A neuropathological study of 51 cases, *J. Neurol. Neurosurg. Psychiatry,* 42, 226–231, 1979.

13. Campbell, B.G., Cocaine abuse with hyperthermia, seizures and fatal complications, *Med. J. Aust.,* 149, 387–389, 1988.

14. Pettit, H.O., Pan, H., Parsons, L.H., Justice, J.B., Jr., Extracellular concentrations of cocaine and dopamine are enhanced during chronic cocaine administration, *J. Neurochem.,* 55, 798–804, 1990.

15. Karoum, F., Suddath, R.L., and Wyatt, R.J., Chronic cocaine and rat brain catecholamines: long term reduction in hypothalamic and frontal cortex dopamine metabolism, *Eur. J. Pharm.,* 186, 1–8, 1990.

16. Kosten, T.R. and Kleber, H.D., Rapid death during cocaine abuse: a variant of the neuroleptic malignant syndrome? *Am. J. Drug Alcohol Abuse,* 14, 335–346, 1988.

17. Wetli, C.V. and Fishbain, D.A., Cocaine-induced psychosis and sudden death in recreational cocaine users, *J. Forensic Sci.,* 30, 873–880, 1985.

18. Davis, G.D., Cocaine-induced excited delirium. *Forensic Pathology Check Sample,* No. FP 96-9, American Society of Clinical Pathologists, Chicago, 1996.

19. Kaku, D.A. and Lowenstein, D.H., Emergence of recreational drug abuse as a major risk factor for stroke in young adults, *Ann. Intern. Med.,* 113, 821–827, 1990.

20. Levine, S.R., Brust, J.C.M., Futrell, N., Ho, K.L., Blake, D., Millikan, C.H. et al., Cerebrovascular complications of the use of the "crack" form of alkaloidal cocaine, *N. Engl. J. Med.,* 323, 699–704, 1990.

21. Mody, C.K., Miller, B.L., McIntyre, H.B., Cobb, S.K., and Goldberg, M.A., Neurologic complications of cocaine abuse, *Neurology,* 38, 1189–1193, 1988.

22. Mangiardi, J.R., Daras, M., Geller, M.E., Weitzner, I., and Tuchman, A.J., Cocaine-related intracranial hemorrhage. Report of nine cases and review, *Acta Neurol. Scand.,* 77, 177–180, 1988.

23. Aggarwal, S.K., Cocaine-associated intracranial hemorrhage: absence of vasculitis in 14 cases, *Neurology,* 46, 1741–1743, 1996.

24. Buttner, A., Mall, G., Penning, R. et al., The neuropathology of cocaine abuse, *Leg. Med.,* 5, S240–S242, 2003.

25. Harrington, H., Heller, H.A., Dawson, D., Caplan, L., and Rumbaugh, C., Intracerebral hemorrhage and oral amphetamine, *Arch. Neurol.,* 40, 503–507, 1983.

26. Sloan, M.A., Kittner, S.J., Rigamonti, D., and Price, T.R., Occurrence of stroke associated with use/abuse of drugs, *Neurology,* 41, 1358–1364, 1991.

27. Fischman, M.W., Schuster, C.R., Resnekov, L., Shick, J.F.E., Krasnegar, N.A., Fennell, W., and Freedman, D.X., Cardiovascular and subjective effects of intravenous cocaine administration in humans, *Arch. Gen. Psych.,* 33, 983–989, 1976.

28. Wilkerson, R.D., Cardiovascular effects of cocaine in conscious dogs: Importance of fully functional autonomic and central nervous systems, *J. Pharmacol. Exp. Ther.,* 246, 466–471, 1988.

29. Davis, G.D. and Swalwell, C.I., The incidence of acute cocaine or methamphetamine intoxication in deaths due to ruptured cerebral (berry) aneurysms, *J. Forensic Sci.,* 41, 626–628, 1996.

30. Nolte, K.B., Brass, L.M., and Fletterick, C.F., Intracranial hemorrhage associated with cocaine abuse: a prospective autopsy study, *Neurology,* 46, 1291–1296, 1996.

31. Levine, S.R., Brust, J.C.M., Futrell, N., Brass, L.M., Blake, D., Fayad, P., Schultz, L.R., Millikan, C.H., Ho, K.-L., and Welch, K.M.A., A comparative study of the cerebrovascular complications of cocaine: alkaloidal versus hydrochloride: a review, *Neurology,* 41, 1173–1177, 1991.

32. Fessler, R.D., Esshaki, C.M., Stankewitz, R.C., Johnson, R.R., and Diaz, F.G., The neurovascular complications of cocaine, *Surg. Neurol.,* 47, 339–345, 1997.

33. Caplan, L., Intracerebral hemorrhage revisited, *Neurology,* 38, 624–627, 1988.

34. McLenan, D.A., Ajayi, O.A., Rydman, R.J., and Pildes, R.S., Evaluation of the relationship between cocaine and intraventricular hemorrhage, *J. Nat. Med. Assoc.*, 86, 281–287, 1994.

35. Daras, M., Tuchman, A.J., Koppel, B.S., Samkoff, L.M., Weitzner, I., and Marc, J., Neurovascular complications of cocaine, *Acta Neurol. Scand.*, 90, 124–129, 1994.

36. Davis, G.G. and Swalwell, C.I., The incidence of acute cocaine or methamphetamine intoxication in deaths due to ruptured cerebral (berry) aneurysms, *J. Forensic Sci.*, 41, 626–628, 1996.

37. Contostavlos, D.L., Massive subarachnoid hemorrhage due to laceration of the vertebral artery associated with fracture of the transverse process of the atlas, *J. Forensic Sci.*, 16, 40–56, 1971.

38. Nolte, K.B. and Gelman, B.B., Intracerebral hemorrhage associated with cocaine abuse, *Arch. Pathol. Lab. Med.*, 113, 812–813, 1989.

39. Fisher, C.M., Pathological observations in hypertensive cerebral hemorrhage, *J. Neuropathol. Exp. Neurol.*, 30, 536–550, 1971.

40. Kaye, B.R. and Fainstat, M., Cerebral vasculitis associated with cocaine abuse, *J. Am. Med. Assoc.*, 258, 2104–2106, 1987.

41. Klonoff, D.C., Andrews, B.T., and Obana, W.G., Stroke associated with cocaine use, *Arch. Neurol.*, 46, 989–993, 1989.

42. Krendel, D.A., Ditter, S.M., Frankel, M.R., and Ross, W.K., Biopsy-proven cerebral vasculitis associated with cocaine abuse, *Neurology*, 40, 1092–1094, 1990.

43. Morrow, P.L. and McQuillen, J.B., Cerebral vasculitis associated with cocaine abuse, *J. Forensic Sci.*, 38, 732–738, 1993.

44. Fredericks, R.K., Lefkowitz, D.S., Challa, V.R. et al., Cerebral vasculitis associated with cocaine abuse, *Stroke*, 22, 1437–1439, 1991.

45. Merkel, P.A., Koroshetz, W.J., Irizarry, M.C., and Cudkowicz, M.E., Cocaine-associated cerebral vasculitis, *Sem. Arthritis Rheum.*, 25, 172–183, 1995.

46. Moore, P.M. and Peterson, P.L., Nonhemorrhagic cerebrovascular complications of cocaine abuse, *Neurology*, 39, 302, 1989 (Suppl. 1; abstr.).

47. Pascual-Leone, A., Dhuna, A., Altafullah, I., and Anderson, D.C., Cocaine-induced seizures, *Neurology*, 40, 404–407, 1990.

48. Olson, K.R., Kearney, T.E., Dyer, J.E., Benowitz, N.L., and Blanc, P.D., Seizures associated with poisoning and drug overdose, *Am. J. Emerg. Med.*, 12, 392–395, 1994.

49. Rugg-Gunn, F.J., Simister, R.J., Squirrell, M., Holdright, D.R., and Duncan, J.S., Cardiac arrhythmias in focal epilepsy: a prospective long-term study, *Lancet*, 364, 2212–2219, 2004.

50. P-Codrea Tigaran, S., Dalager-Pedersen, S., Baandrup, U., Dam, M., and Vesterby-Charles, A., Sudden unexpected death in epilepsy: is death by seizures a cardiac disease? *Am. J. Forensic Med. Pathol.*, 26(2), 99–105, 2005.

51. Lathers, C.M., Tyau, L.S.Y., Spino, M.M., and Agarwal, I., Cocaine induced seizures, arrhythmias and sudden death, *J. Clin. Pharmacol.*, 28, 584–593, 1988.

52. Derlet, R.W. and Albertson, T.E., Emergency department presentation of cocaine intoxication, *Ann. Emerg. Med.*, 18, 182–186, 1989.

53. Lowenstein, D.H., Massa, S.M., Rowbotham, M.C., Collins, S.D., McKinney, H.E., and Simon, R.P., Acute neurologic and psychiatric complications associated with cocaine abuse, *Am. J. Med.*, 83, 841–846, 1987.

54. Davis, G., Williams, A., Markey, S., et al., Chronic parkinsonism secondary to intravenous injection of meperedine analogs, *Psych. Res.*, 1, 249–254, 1979.

55. Langston, J., Ballard, P., Tetrud, J., and Irwin, I., Chronic parkinsonism in humans due to a product of meperidine-analog synthesis, *Science*, 219, 979–980, 1983.

56. Wright, J.M., Wall, R.A., Perry, T.L., and Paty, D.W., Chronic parkinsonism secondary to intranasal administration of a product of meperidine-analog synthesis [letter], *N. Engl. J. Med.*, 310, 325, 1984.

57. Kaplan, J. and Karluk, D., Suffocation due to drug-induced parkinsonism [abstr.], paper presented at National Association of Medical Examiner Meeting, Traverse City, MI, Sept. 1996.

58. Brierley, J., The neuropathology of brain hypoxia, in *Scientific Foundations of Neurology*, M. Critchley, Ed., F.A. Davis, Philadelphia, 1972.

59. Adams, J., Brierley, J., Connor, R., and Treip, C.S., The effects of systemic hypotension upon the human brain: clinical and neuropathological observations in 11 cases, *Brain*, 89, 235–268, 1966.

DISORDERS OF THE CENTRAL NERVOUS SYSTEM

60. Norenberg, M.D. and Gregorios, J.B., Central nervous system manifestations of systemic disease, in Davis, R.L. and Robertson, D.M., Eds., *Textbook of Neuropathology,* Williams & Wilkins, Baltimore, MD, 1985, 403–414.
61. Wetli, C.V., Weiss, S.D., Cleary, T.J., and Gyori, E.L., Fungal cerebritis from intravenous drug abuse, *J. Forensic Sci.,* 29, 260–268, 1984.
62. Hameroff, S., Eckholdt, J., and Linderburg, R., Cerebral phycomycosis in a heroin addict, *Neurology,* 20, 261–265, 1970.
63. Kasantikul, V., Shuangshoti, S., and Taecholarn, C., Primary phycomycosis of the brain in heroin addicts, *Surg. Neurol.,* 28, 468–472, 1987.
64. Masucci, E.F., Fabara, J.A., Saini, N., and Kurtzke, J.F., Cerebral mucomycosis (phycomycosis) in a heroin addict, *Arch. Neurol.,* 39, 304–306, 1982.
65. Adelman, L. and Aronson, S., The neuropathologic complications of narcotics addiction, *Bull. N.Y. Acad. Med.,* 45, 225–234, 1969.
66. Pierce, P.F., Jr., Solomon, S.L., Kaufman, L., Garagusi, V.F., Parker, R.H., and Ajello, L., Zygomycetes brain abscesses in narcotic addicts with serological diagnosis, *J. Am. Med. Assoc.,* 248, 2881–2882, 1982.
67. Micozzi, M.S. and Wetli, C.V., Intravenous amphetamine abuse, primary mucomycosis, and acquired immunodeficiency, *J. Forensic Sci.,* 30, 504–510, 1985.
68. Ziment, I., Nervous system complications in bacterial endocarditis, *Am. J. Med.,* 47, 593–607, 1969.
69. Rao, A.N., Brain abscess: a complication of cocaine inhalation, *N.Y. State J. Med.,* 10, 548–550, 1988.
70. Severe illness and death among injecting drug users in Scotland: a case-control study, *Epidemiol. Infect.,* 133(2), 193–204, 2005.
71. Wolters, E.C., van Wijngaarden, G.K., Stam, F.C. et al., Leucoencephalopathy after inhaling "heroin" pyrolysate, *Lancet,* 4;2(8310), 1233–1237, 1982.

CHAPTER **9**

Toxicogenetics in Drug Abuse: Pharmacogenomics for Toxicology*

Robert M. White, Sr., Ph.D.[1] and Steven H.Y. Wong, Ph.D.[2]
[1] Technical Director, DSI Laboratories, Fort Myers, Florida
[2] Professor of Pathology, Director, Clinical Chemistry/Toxicology, TDM, Pharmacogenomics, and Proteomics, Medical College of Wisconsin, and Scientific Director, Toxicology Department, Milwaukee County Medical Examiner's Office, Milwaukee, Wisconsin

CONTENTS

9.1 Clinical Applications 158
      9.1.1 Depression 158
      9.1.2 Opiate Toxicity 158
      9.1.3 Forensic Toxicology 159
9.2 Conclusions 161
Glossary..161
References 161

The Great Paracelsus (Phillipus Aureolus Theophrastus Bombastus von Hohenheim-Paracelsus, 1493–1541) is remembered by toxicologists for his famous quote: "All substances are poisons; there is none which is not a poison. The right dose differentiates a poison from a remedy."[2] Indeed, the basic principle from the quote still applies today. The right dose of morphine that will produce a blood level of approximately 0.07 to 0.083 mg/L is essential for the relief of pain. An overdose that results in a markedly increased blood level (0.2 to 2.3 mg/L) can cause death due to central nervous system depression.[3] In general, the same applies to all chemical substances. However, as an important exception to Paracelsus's statement, there are instances in which a drug should be avoided completely. An example is found in the administration of succinylcholine as a skeletal muscle relaxant in surgery patients. Most patients can convert succinylcholine into inert metabolites through an enzyme called pseudocholinesterase because most patients possess two alleles for the common gene that can produce active enzyme. However, a certain small percentage of patients carries the genes that are aberrant or silent and, thus, either produce protein (enzyme) that is defective in its function or cannot produce the protein that is capable of inactivating administered

* This chapter was partially rewritten with modifications and updates from Reference 1, with permission from the publisher, Medical Laboratory Observer.

153

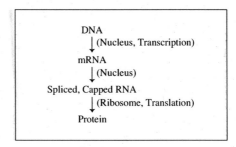

Figure 9.1   Central dogma.

succinylcholine at all; these patients expire or suffer severe sequelae from administration of the drug.[4] Along the same line of thinking, the dose of a given drug for certain individuals may differ from that used for the majority of the population due to genetic differences between the individual and the general population (e.g., a reduced dose of 6-merecaptopurine in the presence of reduced thiopurine methyl transferase or TPMT activity due to a genetic deficiency in synthesis of the active enzyme).[5] Therefore, in the third millennium, an expansion of Paracelsus's statement might be that the "right dose" for one individual may not be the "right dose" or even the right drug for another due to differences in each individual's genetic makeup. The determination of what is the "right dose" and, in some cases, what is even the right drug for a given individual constitutes the reason for the development of the sciences of pharmacogenetics and pharmacogenomics.

Although often used interchangeably, there are subtle differences between pharmacogenetics and pharmacogenomics. Pharmacogenomics is concerned with the systematic assessment of how chemical compounds (e.g., drugs) modify the overall expression pattern in certain tissues. Pharmacogenomics is not focused on the differences between individuals. Rather, pharmacogenomics focuses on differences among several drugs or compounds with regard to a generic set of expressed or non-expressed genes. The focus in pharmacogenomics is on compound variability. In contrast, pharmacogenetics focuses on individual traits with respect to one compound or drug. Thus, pharmacogenetics, which historically actually preceded pharmacogenomics, looks at the responses of different individuals to one drug while pharmacogenomics studies the differences among several compounds with regard to a single genome.[6–11] For the purposes of this brief introduction, the two terms will be used interchangeably unless stated otherwise.

Before embarking upon a cursory journey through pharmacogenomics, a very brief discussion of DNA (deoxyribonucleic acid) and its products is in order. DNA is the genetic code that determines all of an individual's characteristics including the synthesis of the proper proteins essential for life. The so-called "central dogma" of molecular biology is outlined in Figure 9.1.[10] DNA is a long chain of chemically linked (phosphate bond), single nucleotides. Although there is a great deal more detail to the system due to phenomena such as splice variants,[8] etc., basically DNA is transcribed in the cell nucleus by an enzyme called RNA polymerase to yield messenger RNA or mRNA. DNA sequences called promoters and enhancers also are required to initiate RNA synthesis. Silencers balance the effects of promoters and enhancers when synthesis is not required. A stop codon (a series of the nucleotides that tells the polymerase to stop transcription) also is required so that only the required RNA and not an almost infinitely long RNA is produced. Regions of the mRNA from DNA that do not code for amino acids are called introns. The introns are spliced out before the completed mRNA is capped (*vide infra*) and exported from the nucleus for translation. The regions of the mRNA that do code for protein are called exons. RNA that has had the introns removed is capped on the 5′ end with a special nucleotide called 7-methylguanosine and has a poly-A (poly-adenosine) "tail" added to the 3′ end. The capped mRNA with its poly-A "tail" is then translated into protein in a cellular apparatus called a ribosome.[6]

Also required before pharmacogenomics can be discussed is a basic knowledge of proteins that are the end product of the transcription of DNA and the translation of RNA. Essentially, a protein is a long chain of chemically linked (amide or peptide bond) amino acids. The sequence in the chain of amino acids is called the primary structure. The chain may form loops and/or helices (secondary structure) and the loops and helices may fold to form the tertiary structure. Further, the protein may exist by itself, associate with other protein chains like itself (e.g., dimerize to form an aggregate of two like chains), or associate with dissimilar protein chains to form the final, active structure, which is known as the quaternary structure. Further, a protein may be chemically and functionally changed ("post-translational modification") by the addition of phosphate groups (phosphorylation), glucuronic acid groups (glucuronidation), or other groups or by the addition or removal of amino acids or short stretches of amino acids called polypeptides. The study of proteins, which is closely related, but separate from molecular biology, is called proteomics.[12]

Proteins can act as hormones (e.g., insulin, glucagons, chorionic gonadotrophin, etc.), enzymes, which are biological catalysts (e.g., lactate dehydrogenase, alkaline phosphatase, creatine kinase, etc.), structural components (e.g., troponin, collagens, etc.), receptors (e.g., opiate receptors, cholesterol receptors, etc.), and a plethora of other functions essential for life itself. When a protein is formed from DNA that was in the correct sequence, the DNA is correctly transcribed, and the RNA is correctly translated; a fully functional protein usually results. However, if the DNA code is incorrect (although exceptions exist here, also) or there is a defect in the machinery that creates the protein from the original DNA code, a partially functional protein, a non-functional protein, or even a protein that is deleterious to cell function may be produced. Gene duplication, where the gene is functional and codes for the correct protein, can result in the overproduction of protein.[13]

Also before pharmacogenomics can be discussed, it is helpful to review a few pharmacologic fundamentals. First, although it sounds obvious, before a drug can have any effect on an individual, the drug must somehow enter the individual's body. Entry can be accomplished through inhalation (e.g., a bronchodilator used for the treatment of asthma), absorption through the skin (e.g., a topical anesthetic such as cocaine or lidocaine) or mucous membranes (e.g., pilocarpine eye drops), parenterally (any number of drugs that may be delivered intravenously, intramuscularly, or subcutaneously), or, most commonly, orally (a large number of drugs including such common substances as aspirin and acetaminophen) where the drug is absorbed from the gastrointestinal tract. Once inside an individual, a drug needs to be transported to the site where it will have its effect. A drug may have no action whatsoever (e.g., inulin), may act directly on a receptor to produce the desired effect (e.g., morphine for analgesia), or may require activation (e.g., the production of morphine from codeine for analgesia). Both before and after the desired effect has been produced, drugs may be excreted (multiple routes such as urine and bile) unchanged (e.g., free morphine) or excreted as metabolites (e.g., the excretion of morphine glucuronide, which is an inactive metabolite of morphine) or a combination.[14] Proteins are essential to carry out all of the aforementioned steps in drug metabolism.

Proteins play an active role in the disposition of drugs and their metabolites (*vide infra*). Proteins in the intestinal enterocytes such as BCRP (breast cancer resistance protein), MRP2 (multidrug resistance-associated protein), and MDR1 (multidrug resistance protein) are involved in the transport of xenobiotics into the intestinal lumen. A member of the peptide transporter family such as PepT1 facilitates absorption from the gut lumen and tubular reabsorption in the kidney. Drugs such as valaciclovir, valganciclovir, and captopril are known to be transported by PepT1. OCTN2, which is part of the organic cation transporter family, is involved in both the efflux and influx of drugs such as quinidine and verapamil. Although numerous polymorphisms exist among the transporter proteins, their influence on pharmacogenomics is unclear and still in its infancy.[15] However, a clear example of how a protein and a mutation of that protein can affect a drug's absorption is found with the cardiac glycoside digoxin. *P*-Glycoprotein, which is a membrane protein that functions as an exporter of xenobiotics from cells, is a product of the MDR1 (multidrug resistance) gene. Although several models have been proposed for *P*-glycoprotein's action, basically *P*-glycoprotein acts to move xenobiotics from epithelial cells into the adjacent lumen. *P*-Glycoprotein is found in numerous cells associated with excretory function. In the case of digoxin (and certain other drugs), reduced intestinal absorption of the drug can be associated with induction (increased amounts) of the enzyme or the C3435T (cytosine replaces thymidine at position 3435 in the DNA sequence that codes *P*-glycoprotein) mutation of *P*-glycoprotein. Thus, the mutant form of the protein causes a lowered overall intestinal absorption of digoxin by excreting more back into the intestinal lumen than the wild-type protein.[16]

Once a drug has entered the bloodstream it is transported to various parts of the body where the drug may be activated or inactivated by certain enzymes (*vide infra*) by a process commonly referred to as biotransformation or metabolism, be excreted unchanged, interact with a receptor or other location where the desired (and, sometimes, undesired or side effect) action(s) may take place, or be stored (e.g., the retention of 9-tetrahydrocannabinol or THC in body fat or lead in bone) for future uses such as those previously described. Many drugs and other xenobiotics express their pharmacodynamic action by interacting with a specific protein receptor. As an example, morphine acts at what are called μ receptors. Indeed, polymorphism is exhibited by the various opiate receptors.[17]

Perhaps the best-characterized and most extensively studied area in pharmacogenomics is biotransformation, which is commonly referred to as metabolism. Fundamentally, biotransformation or metabolism can be divided into two areas — Phase I and Phase II. Both Phase I and Phase II are designed to make xenobiotics more polar and, thus, more water soluble. By being more polar and more water soluble, metabolites are more easily excreted into excretory fluids such as urine. Phase I reactions include hydrolysis, reduction, and oxidation. Phase I metabolism may activate a drug (known in this case as a prodrug) into a biologically active form, or Phase I may inactivate an active drug. An example of activation is seen with the conversion of Tegafur into the active anticancer agent 5-fluorouracil (5-FU). An example of deactivation is seen with the oxidation of ethanol into acetaldehyde by alcohol dehydrogenase and the further oxidation of acetaldehyde into acetate by aldehyde dehydrogenase. Phase II biotransformation may or may not be preceded by Phase I biotransformation. Phase II biotransformation reactions involve glucuronidation, sulfation, acetylation, methylation, conjugation with glutathione, and conjugation with amino acids such as glycine, taurine, and glutamic acid.[18]

Hydolysis as a Phase I chemical breakdown pathway has been mentioned above in the case of pseudocholinesterase and its variants. Reduction of the drug 5-fluorouracil, which was discussed above under activation of Tegafur, shows polymorphism in the 5-FU reduction when 5-FU is metabolized (deactivated) to its reduction product, 5-fluorodihydrouracil, in rare individuals who are deficient in the enzyme dihydropyrimidine dehydrogenase (DPD). Individuals who are deficient in DPD show toxicity, which may be fatal, to bone marrow and intestines due to increased levels of 5-FU.[15]

Since a more polar (and, thus, more water soluble) product usually results, oxidation is one of the commonest metabolic pathways in mammals. Due to genetic polymorphism, the metabolism of the most routinely observed analyte in toxicology, ethanol or ethyl alcohol, actually is more complex than usually visualized by the simple pathway depicted in Figure 9.2.

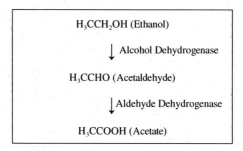

Figure 9.2 Metabolic pathway for oxidation of ethanol.

TOXICOGENETICS IN DRUG ABUSE: PHARMACOGENOMICS FOR TOXICOLOGY

The first enzyme in the oxidation of ethanol, alcohol dehydrogenase, is a zinc-containing dimer, which means that the functional enzyme consists of two protein chains and the element zinc. The subunits are encoded on chromosome 4 by six different genetic loci (ADH1A, ADH1B*1, ADH1C*1, and ADH4 to ADH7; formerly ADH1 through ADH7, respectively). The subunits are designated α, β, γ, π, χ, or σ. ADH1A (formerly ADH1) codes the protein for α subunits. ADH1B (formerly ADH2) codes for β subunits. ADH1C (formerly ADH3) codes for γ subunits. To further add to the complexity of the system, there are three allelic variants of the beta subunit designated β_1, β_2, and β_3 and two allelic variants of the gamma chain designated γ_1 and γ_2 arising from, respectively, ADH1B*1, ADH1B*2, ADH1B*3, ADH1C*1, and ADH1C*2. The nine subunits of ADH can combine to form homodimers (i.e., both chains are identical) and the α, β, and γ chains and their allelic variants heterodimers (i.e., the two chains are different) with each other, but not with the other types of chains. The different molecular forms of ADH are divided into four classes. Class I contains ADH1A, ADH1B*1, and ADH1C*1, which can be considered isozymes. ADH1B enzymes that differ in the type of β subunit are known as allelozymes as are ADH1C enzymes that differ in the type of γ subunit. Accordingly, the protein product of ADH1B*1 is an allelozyme composed of β_1 subunits, the protein product of ADH1B*2 is an allelozyme composed of β_2 subunits, and the protein product of ADH1B*3 is an allelozyme composed of β_3 subunits. Class II contains ADH4, which is made up of two π subunits. Class III contains ADH5, which is made up of two χ subunits. Class IV contains ADH7, which is made up of two σ subunits. It is the Class I and Class II ADH isozymes that are of the most interest to the practicing toxicologist as it is these isozymes that are involved in the oxidation of ethanol and methanol. The protein product of ADH1B*2 is an atypical isozyme that is responsible for an unusually rapid conversion of ethanol into acetaldehyde in 85% of Asians, but is expressed to a lesser degree in Caucasians, Native Americans, and Asian Indians. Conversely, in about 25% of African Americans there is an abundance of the $\beta_3\beta_3$ form. European Caucasians have a predominance of the homodimer from the ADH1B*1 gene.[20] Aldehyde dehydrogenase (ALDH) oxidizes aldehydes (like acetaldehyde) to the corresponding carboxylic acid. In all, 12 ALDH genes (ALDH1 through ALDH10, SSDH, and MMSDH) have been identified in humans. ALDH2 is primarily responsible for oxidizing simple aldehydes like acetaldehyde. A genetic polymorphism for ALDH2 has been identified in humans. A high percentage of Japanese, Chinese, Koreans, Taiwanese, and Vietnamese populations are deficient in ALDH2 due to a point mutation ($Glu_{487} \rightarrow Lys_{487}$). This inactive allelic variant of ALDH2 known as ALDH2*2 is found in the same population that has a high incidence of the atypical form of ADH, ADH2*2, which means that these individuals rapidly convert ethanol to acetaldehyde, but only slowly convert acetaldehyde to acetic acid. As a result, many Asians experience a flushing syndrome after consuming alcohol. Thus, what is considered to be very simple by most toxicologists, especially those who deal with driving under the influence (DUI) forensic cases, actually can be quite rich in detail for certain individuals within a diverse array of ethnic groups.[19–22]

In addition to the example of the oxidation of ethanol given above, numerous other oxidative pathways for xenobiotics exist in humans and other animals. Many of the oxidations of drugs are the result of a group of enzymes known as CYPs (from *CY*tochrome *P*450, the 450 being derived from the cytochrome's maximal absorbance of light at 450 nm). The cytochrome P450s or CYPs are categorized according to amino acid sequence homology. CYPs that have less than 40% homology are placed in the same family (e.g., 1, 2, 3, etc.). CYPs that are 40 to 55% identical are assigned to different subfamilies (e.g., 1A, 1B, 1C, etc.). P450 enzymes that are more than 55% identical are classified as members of the same subfamily (e.g., 2B1, 2B2, 2B3, etc.). The P450 enzymes are expressed in numerous tissues, but are especially prevalent in liver. CYPs so numerous that their complete description is beyond the scope of this basic introduction exist in mammalian physiology.[18] However, the CYPs that are important to human drug metabolism are within its scope.[23]

The final step in drug metabolism is elimination. As stated above, elimination can occur with the unchanged drug, a drug that has been subjected to Phase I metabolism, a drug that has been

158 PATHOLOGY, TOXICOGENETICS, AND CRIMINALISTICS OF DRUG ABUSE

subjected to Phase II metabolism, or a combination. Also, as briefly discussed above, the proteins involved in elimination can be subject to polymorphism and, thus, are involved in pharmacogenomics.

A few brief examples of the applications of pharmacogenomics are given in the sections below.

9.1 CLINICAL APPLICATIONS

Three applications of pharmacogenomics are demonstrated in depression, opiate toxicity, and forensic toxicology.

9.1.1 Depression

To provide therapeutic efficacy, the tricyclic antidepressant nortriptyline must achieve serum levels of 5 to 150 ng/ml.[24] Usually, a therapeutic level is achieved by adjustment of a standard dose. Nortriptyline is metabolized to its hydroxy metabolite, 10-hydroxynortriptyline, by CYP2D6. Individuals with different genotypes and multiple copies of CYP2D6 metabolize nortriptyline at markedly different rates. When poor metabolizers of debrisoquin (a drug used to determine an individual's CYP2D6 status) with no functional CYP2D6 gene, extensive metabolizers with one functional CYP2D6 gene, extensive metabolizers with two functional CYP2D6 genes, ultra-rapid metabolizers with duplicated CYP2D6*2 genes, and one ultra-rapid metabolizer with 13 copies of the CYP2D6*2 gene are compared, the results are quite striking. On one end of the spectrum, the individuals with no functional copy of CYP2D6 have maximal levels of serum nortriptyline of 51 to 71 ng/ml. On the other end of the spectrum, an individual with 13 copies of the CYP2D6*2 gene had a maximal serum level of only 13 ng/ml. Needless to say, this represents an outstanding example where a "standard dose" will not necessarily achieve the required serum level of the active drug and, thus, the desired results.[13]

Selective serotonin-reuptake inhibitors such as fluvoxetine, paroxetine, and fluoxetine exert their action probably through the serotonin transporter protein. The serotonin transporter gene (5-HTT) shows several polymorphisms. One polymorphism is in the transcriptional control region upstream of the 5-HTT coding sequence. It is either a 44-base-pair insertion (long variant) or deletion (short sequence). One group has reported that individuals homozygous for the long variant and heterozygous individuals respond better to fluvoxamine than do individuals who are homozygous for the short variant.[25] Interestingly, another group reported just the opposite.[26] The disparity between the studies is a reminder that other factors that may never be separated out affect genomic expression and phenotypic response.

9.1.2 Opiate Toxicity

A 62-year-old male, who had previously received chemotherapy but currently was prescribed only valproate for post-traumatic generalized seizure, is admitted for bilateral pneumonia limited to the lower lobes.[27] Although there is no evidence of *Pneumocystis carinii*, yeast is found in the bronchoalveolar lavage. The patient is treated with ceftriaxone, clarithromycin, and voriconazole for yeast and codeine for cough. The patient's level of consciousness deteriorates. Serum BUN and creatinine levels that increase are normalized with hydration. Administration of naloxone results in a dramatic improvement in the patient's level of consciousness.

The patient's blood levels of codeine, morphine, and their metabolites were determined by liquid chromatography/mass spectrometry. The patient's level of codeine was above therapeutic as were the levels of morphine, morphine-3-glucuronide (active metabolite), and morphine-6-glucuronide (inactive metabolite). Duplication or multiduplication of the CYP2D6 gene was determined using restriction-fragment-length polymorphism analysis of the patient's genomic DNA. The CYP2D6 and CYP3A4 phenotypes also were determined.

TOXICOGENETICS IN DRUG ABUSE: PHARMACOGENOMICS FOR TOXICOLOGY

Dextromethorphan was administered to the patient as a probe after he was stabilized. Because dextromethorphan is metabolized by CYP2D6 into dextrorphan and 3-hydroxymorphinan by CYP3A4, the ratio of dextromethorphan to dextrorphan was less than 0.0005, which was compatible with an ultra-rapid CYP2D6 metabolizer.

Normally, about 80% of codeine is converted into norcodeine by CYP3A4 or converted into codeine glucuronide. The conversion of codeine into morphine by CYP2D6 represents only about 10% of normal clearance of codeine. In the patient described, there was ultra-rapid conversion of codeine into morphine by his three or more CYP2D6 alleles. To exacerbate the situation, the patient's CYP3A4 was inhibited by administration of clarithromycin and voriconazole and the accumulation of glucuronides (acute renal failure).

Thus, in contrast to the clinical scenario in which 7 to 10% of the white population receive no analgesic benefit from codeine due to homozygosity for nonfunctional CYP2D6 alleles, the patient described above had a toxic amount of morphine and one of its active metabolites due to ultra-rapid metabolism. The patient's ultra-rapid metabolism due to multiple copies of the CYP2D6 gene was intensified by inhibition of CYP3A4 that normally metabolizes the majority of the codeine to norcodeine.

9.1.3 Forensic Toxicology

This section outlines the application of pharmacogenomics as molecular autopsy, as proposed by Figure 9.3.[28] Several upcoming chapters by Holmgren and Ahlner,[29] Sajantila et al.,[30] and Wong et al.[31] summarize the current practice of using pharmacogenomics as molecular autopsy — an adjunct for forensic pathology/toxicology, by considering long QT syndrome, and effect on driving. Several cases are included to illustrate the applications.

A 9-year-old born with probable fetal alcohol syndrome is treated with a combination of methylphenidate, clonidine, and fluoxetine for multiple behavioral problems. Over a period of time, the individual is hospitalized in status epilepticus followed by cardiac arrest and expires. Based on the levels of fluoxetine and its metabolite, norfluoxetine, in the deceased's post-mortem blood, the adoptive parents are suspected of homicide, and the remainder of the adopted children are removed from the household. Due to the vociferous claims of the adoptive parents that there was no foul play involved, the deceased individual is tested for genetic polymorphism. Indeed, a polymorphism in the CYP2D6, which resulted in the poor metabolism of fluoxetine, was discovered. Based on the results of the post-mortem genetic testing, the adoptive parents of the deceased were exonerated and reunited with the remainder of the children.[32]

One of the cases of a recently published study of assessing pharmacogenomic methadone death certification involved a 41-year-old woman who was 6 months pregnant and recently diagnosed with heart murmur and rheumatoid arthritis.[33] She was treated with methadone and tricyclic antidepressants for her depression. After celebrating New Year's Eve with her husband, she was found unresponsive in her living room the following morning. Toxicology analysis showed methadone, 0.7 mg/L, amitriptyline, 1.5 mg/L, and nortriptyline, 2.2 mg/L. Pharmacogenomics tests showed CYP2D6*4 homozygous, corresponding to a poor metabolizer as a result of deficient CYP2D6 enzyme. The lack of enzyme predisposed her to the inability to hydroxylate methadone, amitriptyline, and nortriptyline, resulting in an overall accumulation and drug toxicity. Death certification showed the cause of death to be mixed drug overdose, and manner of death, accident.

In the study of 25 fentanyl cases, one decedent, a 44-year-old white woman, had a history of drug abuse including cocaine, marijuana, and pain medications and psychiatric problems.[34] Complaining to her boyfriend about her knee pain during a rummage sale, she obtained some narcotic patches and put them on. Later in the evening, her boyfriend noticed she seemed disoriented, and after about 24 h, she was found not breathing. One Duragesic fentanyl patch was found on her left upper arm, and another adhered to a blanket. Toxicology analysis showed: fentanyl 19 µg/L and

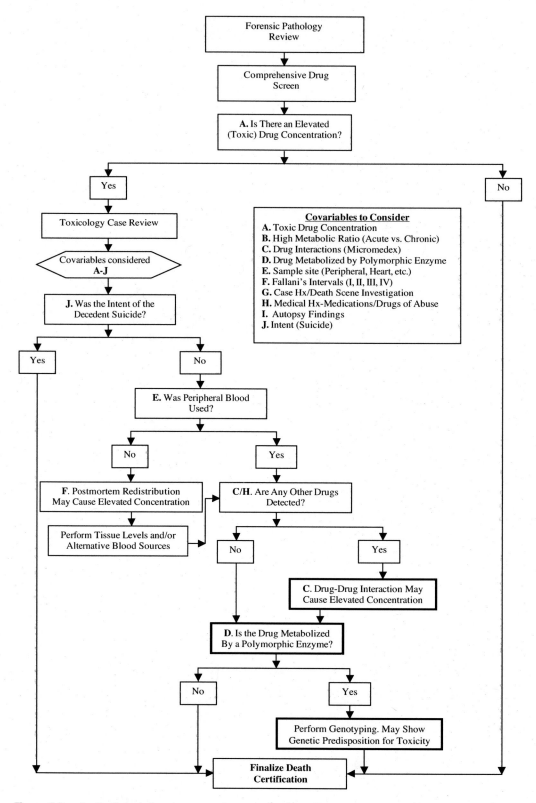

Figure 9.3 Application of pharmacogenomics as molecular autopsy.

norfentanyl 7.6 µg/L with a metabolic ratio of 2.5, cyclobenzaprine 0.16 mg/L, tramadol 0.06 mg/L, diphenhydramine 0.08 mg/L, and citalopram, 0.22 mg/L. Pharmacogenomics testing showed that she was compound heterozygous for CYP3A4*1B and CYP3A5*3, resulting in decreased enzyme activities. Death was certified to be mixed drug overdose for cause of death, and accident for manner of death. Together with findings from the other cases, the higher fentanyl concentration and high metabolic ratios in the individuals with CYP3A5*3 homozygous variant suggested that CYP3A5 mediates fentanyl metabolism. Thus, homozygous CYP3A5*3 variant would result in decreased CYP3A5 enzyme activity.

9.2 CONCLUSIONS

Pharmacogenomics as molecular autopsy may serve as a useful adjunct for drug death certification for forensic pathology/toxicology. Since most drug deaths involved multiple drug ingestion, drug–drug interactions will likely contribute to the toxicity and will complicate the interpretation. However, the knowledge derived from post-mortem pharmacogenomics studies would enhance the understanding of pharmacogenomics in "ante-mortem" drug metabolism/therapy, and hence, the emergence of personalized medicine.

GLOSSARY[35]

Allele: One or several forms of a gene of a single individual compared with other individuals. An allele is present on a specific site (genetic locus) of a chromosome controlling a particular characteristic and giving rise to noticeable hereditary difference. A single allele is inherited separately from maternal and paternal origin. Thus, with the exception of unmatched sex chromosomes, every individual has two alleles for each gene.

Genotype: The precise genetic constitution (i.e., genomes, genes, or alleles at one locus or place) that determines the phenotype (observable characteristics) of an organism.

Heterozygote: An individual who carries a pair of different alleles of a particular gene (inherited from two parents) on each member of a pair of chromosomes.

Homozygote: An individual whose genotype has two identical alleles (each derived from one parent) at a given locus or place on a pair of homologous chromosomes.

Phenotype: The observable characteristics or physical appearance of an organism resulting from and determined by its expressed genes.

Polymorphism: "Many faces." The difference in genetic sequences among individuals, groups, or populations.

Wild-type: The allele, genotype, or phenotype that naturally occurs in the normal population or, in the case of microbes, the standard laboratory strain of a given organism.

Xenobiotic: A foreign chemical including drugs, industrial chemicals, pollutants, pyrolysis products in food, and toxins produced by plants and animals.

REFERENCES

1. White, R.M. and Wong, S.H.Y., Pharmacogenomics and its applications, *MLO*, 20–27, 2005.
2. Gallo, M.A., History and scope of toxicology, in *Casarett & Doull's Toxicology. The Basic Science of Poisons,* 6th ed., McGraw-Hill Medical, New York, 2001.
3. Baselt, R.C., Ed., *Disposition of Toxic Drugs and Chemicals in Man*, 7th ed., Biomedical Publications, Foster City, CA, 2004.
4. Moss, D.W. and Henderson, A.R., Clinical enzymology, in *Tietz Textbook of Clinical Chemistry*, 3rd ed., E.A. Ashwood and C.A. Burtis, Eds., W.B. Saunders, Philadelphia, 1999.

5. Innocenti, F., Iyer, L., and Ratain, M.J., Pharmacogenomics of chemotherapeutic agents in cancer treatment, in *Pharmacogenomics. The Search for Individualized Therapies*, J. Licinio and M.-L. Wong, Eds., Wiley-VCH, Weinheim, Germany, 2002.

6. Lindpainter, K., The role of pharmacogenomics in drug discovery and therapeutics, in *Pharmacogenomics. The Search for Individualized Therapies*, J. Licinio and M.-L. Wong, Eds., Wiley-VCH, Weinheim, Germany, 2002.

7. Ito, R.K. and Demers, L.M., Pharmacogenomics and pharmacogenetics: future role of molecular diagnostics in the clinical diagnostic laboratory, *Clin. Chem.,* 50(9), 1526–1527, 2004.

8. Wong, S.H.Y., Linder, M., and Valdes, R., Jr., *Principles of Pharmacogenomics and Introduction to PharmacoProteomics*, AACC Press, Washington, D.C., in press.

9. Moridani, M., Pharmacogenomics, *CAP Today*, 2004.

10. Strachan, T. and Read, A.P., DNA structure and gene expression, in *Human Molecular Genetics 3*, Garland Science/Taylor & Francis, London, 2004.

11. Strachan, T. and Read, A.P., Human gene expression, in *Human Molecular Genetics 3*, Garland Science/Taylor & Francis, London, 2004.

12. Proteins, in *Molecular Biology of the Cell*, B. Alberts, A. Johnson, J. Lewis, M. Raff, K. Roberts, and P. Walker, Eds., Garland Science/Taylor & Francis, London, 2002.

13. Dahlél, P., Dahl, M.-L., Ruiz, M.L.B., and Bertilsson, L., 10-Hydroxylation of nortriptyline in white persons with 0, 1, 2, 3, and 13 functional CYP2D6 genes, *Clin. Pharmacol. Ther.,* 63(4), 444–452, 1998.

14. Rozman, K.K. and Klaassen, C.D., Absorption, distribution, and excretion of toxicants, in *Casarett & Doull's Toxicology. The Basic Science of Poisons*, 6th ed., McGraw-Hill Medical, New York, 2001.

15. Tirona, R.G. and Kim, R.B., Pharmacogenomics of drug transporters, in *Pharmacogenomics. The Search for Individualized Therapies*, J. Licinio and M.-L. Wong, Eds., Wiley-VCH, Weinheim, Germany, 2002.

16. Fromm, M.F. and Eichelbaum, M., The pharmacogenomics of human P-glycoprotein, in *Pharmacogenomics. The Search for Individualized Therapies*, J. Licinio and M.-L. Wong, Eds., Wiley-VCH, Weinheim, Germany, 2002.

17. Resine, T., Pharmacogenomics of opioid systems, in *Pharmacogenomics. The Search for Individualized Therapies*, J. Licinio and M.-L. Wong, Eds., Wiley-VCH, Weinheim, Germany, 2002.

18. Parkinson, A., Biotransformation of xenobiotics, absorption, distribution, and excretion of toxicants, in *Casarett & Doull's Toxicology. The Basic Science of Poisons*, 6th ed., McGraw-Hill Medical, New York, 2001.

19. Jones, A.W., Disposition and fate of ethanol in the body, in *Medical-Legal Aspects of Alcohol*, 4th ed., J.C. Garriott, Ed., Lawyers & Judges, Tucson, 2003.

20. Jones, A.W., The biochemistry and physiology of alcohol: applications to forensic science and toxicology, in *Medical-Legal Aspects of Alcohol*, 4th ed., J.C. Garriott, Ed., Lawyers & Judges, Tucson, 2003.

21. Hurley, T.D., Edenberg, H.J., and Li, T.-K., Pharmacogenomics of alcoholism, in *Pharmacogenomics. The Search for Individualized Therapies*, J. Licinio and M.-L. Wong, Eds., Wiley-VCH, Weinheim, Germany, 2002.

22. Whitfield, J.B., Alcohol and gene interactions, *Clin. Chem. Lab. Med.,* 43(5), 480–487, 2005.

23. Wong, S.H.Y., Society of Forensic Toxicologists' Meeting, Washington, D.C., September, 2004.

24. Ashwood, E.A. and Burtis, C.A., Eds., *Tietz Textbook of Clinical Chemistry*, 3rd ed., W.B. Saunders, Philadelphia, 1999.

25. Smeraldi, E., Zanardi, R., Benedetti, F., Di Bella, D., Perez, J., and Catalona, M., Polymorphism with the promoter of the serotonin transporter gene and antidepressant efficacy of fluvoxamine, *Mol. Psychiatry*, 3, 508–511, 1998.

26. Kim, D.K., Lim, S.-W., Lee, S., Sohn, S.E., Kim, S., Hahn, C.G., and Carroll, B.J., Serotonin transporter gene polymorphism and antidepressant response, *NeuroReport,* 11(1), 215–219, 2000.

27. Gasche, Y., Daali, Y., Fathi, M., Chiappe, A., Cottini, S., Dayer, P., and Desmules, J., Codeine intoxication associated with ultrarapid CYP2D6 metabolism, *N. Engl. J. Med.,* 351, 2827–2831, 2004.

28. Jannetto, P.J., Wong, S.H.Y., Gock, S., Sahin, E., and Jentzen, J.M., Pharmacogenomics as an adjunct to forensic toxicology: genotyping oxycodone cases for cytochrome P450 (CYP) 2D6, *J. Anal. Toxicol.,* 26, 438–477, 2002.

29. Holmgren, P. and Ahlner, J., Pharmacogenomics for forensic toxicology — Swedish experience, in Wong, S.H.Y., Linder, M., and Valdes, R., Jr., Eds., *Principles of Pharmacogenomics and Introduction to PharmacoProteomics*. AACC Press, Washington, D.C., in press.
30. Sajantila, A., Lunetta, P., and Ojanper, I., Postmortem pharmacogenetics — towards molecular autopsies, in Wong, S.H.Y., Linder, M., and Valdes, R., Jr., Eds., *Principles of Pharmacogenomics and Introduction to PharmacoProteomics*. AACC Press, Washington, D.C., in press.
31. Wong, S.H., Gock, S.B., Shi, R., Jin, M., Wagner, M.A., Schur, C., Jannetto, P.J., Sahin, E., Bjerke, J., Nuwayhid, N., and Jentzen, J.M., Pharmacogenomics as molecular autopsy for forensic pathology and toxicology, in Wong, S.H.Y., Linder, M., and Valdes, R., Jr., Eds., *Principles of Pharmacogenomics and Introduction to PharmacoProteomics*. AACC Press, Washington, D.C., in press.
32. Wong, S.H.Y., Wagner, M.A., Jentzen, J.M., Schur, C., Bjerke, J., Gock, S.B., and Chang, C.J., Pharmacogenomics as an adjunct of molecular autopsy for forensic pathology/toxicology: does genotyping CYP 2D6 serve as an adjunct for certifying methadone toxicology, *J. Forensic Sci.*, 48, 1406–1415, 2003.
33. Salee, F.R., DeVane, C.L., and Ferrell, R.E., Fluoxetine-related death in a child with cytochrome P450 2D6 genetic deficiency, *J. Child Adolesc. Psychopharmacol.*, 27, 27–34, 2000.
34. Jin, M., Gock, S.B., Jannetto, P.J., Jentzen, J.M., and Wong, S.H.Y., Pharmacogenomics as molecular autopsy for forensic toxicology: genotyping cytochrome P450 *3A4*1B* and *3A5*3* for 25 fentanyl cases, *J. Anal. Toxicol.*, in press.
35. Zhang, Y.-H. and Zhang, M., *A Dictionary of Gene Technology Terms*, Parthenon, New York, 2001.

CHAPTER **10**

Toxicogenetics in Drug Abuse: Heritable Channelopathies and Myopathies

Kathryn A. Glatter, M.D., Jonica Calkins, M.D., and Sanjay J. Ayirookuzhi, M.D.
Department of Cardiology and Internal Medicine, University of California, Davis, California

CONTENTS

10.1 Disorders of the Ion Channel 167
    10.1.1 Long QT Syndromes 167
        10.1.1.1 Epidemiology 167
        10.1.1.2 Clinical Features..167
        10.1.1.3 Pathophysiology 168
        10.1.1.4 Genetics 168
        10.1.1.5 Treatment 168
    10.1.2 Brugada Syndrome..169
        10.1.2.1 Epidemiology 169
        10.1.2.2 Clinical Features..169
        10.1.2.3 Pathophysiology 169
        10.1.2.4 Genetics 170
        10.1.2.5 Treatment 170
    10.1.3 Catecholaminergic Polymorphic Ventricular Tachycardia 170
        10.1.3.1 Epidemiology 170
        10.1.3.2 Clinical Features..170
        10.1.3.3 Pathophysiology 171
        10.1.3.4 Genetics 171
        10.1.3.5 Treatment 171
10.2 Disorders of the Heart Muscle..171
    10.2.1 Arrhythmogenic Right Ventricular Dysplasia...171
        10.2.1.1 Epidemiology 171
        10.2.1.2 Clinical Features..171
        10.2.1.3 Pathophysiology 172
        10.2.1.4 Genetics 172
        10.2.1.5 Treatment 173
    10.2.2 Hypertrophic Cardiomyopathy 173
        10.2.2.1 Epidemiology 173

	10.2.2.2	Clinical Features	173
	10.2.2.3	Pathophysiology	173
	10.2.2.4	Genetics	174
	10.2.2.5	Treatment	174
10.3	Drug Causes of Sudden Death		174
	10.3.1	Ephedra	174
	10.3.2	Methamphetamine	175
	10.3.3	Cocaine	175
10.4	Molecular Diagnosis of Cardiovascular Disease		176
	10.4.1	Collection of DNA from Blood Samples	176
	10.4.2	Collection of DNA from Tissue Samples	176
Acknowledgments			176
References			177

Sudden cardiac arrest remains the major cause of death in the U.S. and the developed Western world.[1-3] Most cases are a consequence of cardiac ischemia, coronary artery disease, and acute myocardial infarction-induced ventricular fibrillation (arrhythmias). Autopsy findings generally reveal atherosclerosis and occluded cardiac vessels in these patients, leading to a clear diagnosis.

However, genetic causes of cardiac arrhythmias are not rare, and the first indication of their presence is often an unexplained sudden death. Some of these disorders may demonstrate gross morphologic alterations at autopsy; hypertrophic cardiomyopathy is the most obvious, but other disorders represent a diagnostic challenge for the forensic pathologist, because at autopsy the heart is structurally normal.

It is important to be familiar with these genetic causes of sudden cardiac death, and the diagnostic difficulties they present, so that they can at least be considered as possible causes of death when the autopsy is otherwise normal. Sudden death in cases of drug overdose may also be due to an ion channel disease and not a simple function of direct drug toxicity. Pathologists need to consider these disorders and other etiologies of cardiac death, as described below.

This chapter contains a brief discussion of the clinical presentation of genetic, molecular, and cellular abnormalities and the appropriate diagnostic measures for the evaluation of channelopathies, cardiomyopathies, and chemical causes of sudden cardiac death (see list below). Finally, we provide an overview for forensic pathologists on the appropriate methods for the collection of tissue samples used for molecular testing of these entities.

Disorders of the Ion Channel

1. Long QT syndromes (LQTS)
2. Brugada syndrome (BS)
3. Catecholaminergic polymorphic ventricular tachycardia (Ryanodine receptor defect) (CPMVT)

Disorders of the Heart Muscle

1. Arrhythmogenic right ventricular dysplasia (ARVD)
2. Hypertrophic cardiomyopathy (HCM)

Chemical Causes of Sudden Cardiac Death

1. Ephedra ("ma huang")
2. Methamphetamine
3. Cocaine

TOXICOGENETICS IN DRUG ABUSE: HERITABLE CHANNELOPATHIES AND MYOPATHIES

10.1 DISORDERS OF THE ION CHANNEL

10.1.1 Long QT Syndromes

LQTS is one of the more common and best known of the ion channelopathies.[4,5] It can be inherited as a dominant gene or can be seen in cases of acquired LQTS after taking common drugs including antipsychotics, anti-arrhythmic drugs, or allergy medications.[6,7]

10.1.1.1 Epidemiology

Currently it is estimated that 1 in 5000 people carry a LQTS genetic mutation.[4,5] With the inclusion of drug-induced or acquired LQTS cases, many of which have the same genetic ion channel defects as seen with congenital LQTS, some experts believe that the true incidence of LQTS is actually 1 in 1000.[8,9] Certainly it is one of the more common genetic causes of sudden death, and it is being diagnosed with increasing frequency as more pathologists become aware of its existence.

10.1.1.2 Clinical Features

Most patients with an LQTS mutation will never experience any symptoms. LQTS families are usually discovered when a young person tragically dies suddenly, has no findings at autopsy, and other family members are found to have a prolonged QT interval on electrocardiogram (ECG). At least 10% of affected patients may present with sudden death as their first (and last) symptom.[10-13]

Each genetic subtype (described below) has its own trigger for events (Table 10.1).[10-14] LQT1 patients usually experience symptoms (syncope, cardiac arrest, or sudden death) during catecholamine-driven types of activities such as running, exercise, or with strong emotion (e.g., during an argument). An unexplained drowning in a person able to swim could be due to an LQT1 mutation.[10,13,15,16] LQT2 (*HERG*) mutations may cause sudden death due to auditory triggers, as with an alarm clock or the telephone ringing.[15-17] Episodes in the rare LQT3 (sodium channel) subtype may occur during sleep or during periods of slow heart rates.[10,13]

Although LQTS is an autosomal disease, females are far more likely to experience symptoms than males.[10-14] In some cases LQTS can be diagnosed by noting a prolonged QT_C interval (>450 ms) on the ECG. However, up to 30% of gene-positive patients may have a normal or only borderline prolonged QT_C interval, making diagnosis impossible in some cases.[10-14,18] Exercise testing may reveal an otherwise concealed form of LQTS.[19,20]

There is a weak association in the literature between SIDS (sudden infant death syndrome) and LQTS, although probably fewer than 5% of all SIDS cases are due to ion channel mutations.[21,22] Other, more common causes of SIDS include placing the infant prone, co-sleeping with overlaying by adults, and inborn errors of metabolism.

As with many ion channelopathies causing unexplained sudden death, autopsy findings are unremarkable. Venous blood saved in an EDTA-containing tube (or perhaps snap-frozen myocardial tissue) can be tested at a research laboratory for the presence of LQTS ion channel mutations.

Table 10.1   Long QT Syndrome Genes

Disease	Chromosome Locus	Gene	Gene Product
LQT1	11p15.5	KVLQT1	I_{Ks}, subunit
LQT2	7q35-36	HERG	I_{Kr}, subunit
LQT3	3p21-23	SCN5A	Na channel
LQT4	4q25-27	ankyrin 2	ankyrin-B
LQT5	21p22.1	*minK* (*KCNE1*)	I_{Ks}, subunit
LQT6	21p22.1	*MiRP1* (*KCNE2*)	I_{Kr}, subunit
LQT7	17q23	KCNJ2	I_{Kr}, subunit

10.1.1.3 Pathophysiology

The fundamental defect in LQTS is prolonged ventricular repolarization and a tendency toward the occurrence of torsades de pointes (polymorphic ventricular tachycardia) and ventricular fibrillation.[4,5] The LQTS ion channel mutation leads to this abnormality in repolarization, and evidence of it can be seen on the ECG as a prolonged QT interval. Beta-blocker medications (described below) do not shorten the QT interval; they are believed to act, in part, by blocking EADs (early after-depolarizations), which initiate the ventricular arrhythmias.

10.1.1.4 Genetics

To date, a total of seven genes have been identified as causing long QT syndrome.[23–26] The mutant ion channel that causes clinical LQTS is inherited in an autosomal dominant fashion with incomplete penetrance and was originally known as the "Romano-Ward Syndrome." With the advent of genetic testing, it has become clear that each LQTS genetic subtype represents a unique disease, with different triggers to arrhythmias. The genes that encode the potassium channels *KVLQT1* (on chromosome 11) and *minK* (on chromosome 21) interact to form the cardiac I_{Ks} (inward slow potassium) current; mutations in each cause LQT1 and LQT5, respectively.[5,23,24] The potassium channels *HERG* (on chromosome 7) and *MiRP1* (on chromosome 21) interact to form the I_{Kr} (inward rapid potassium) current, and defects in each cause LQT2 and LQT6, respectively.[25] Mutations in the sodium cardiac channel SCN5A cause LQT3 (on chromosome 3).[26] The gene responsible for LQT4 was recently identified as a mutation in the ankyrin-B protein.[27] The potassium channel mutations cause a "loss of function" in the channel (or a "dominant-negative effect," in the case of the *HERG* mutation), whereas defects in the sodium channel cause a "gain of function."[4,5] LQT7 is due to a defect in the α-subunit of the I_{Kr} channel (gene product *KCNJ2*).

In the unlikely event that a mutant copy of the I_{Ks} channel is inherited from each parent (mutations in the *KVLQT1* and *minK* genes), the child will suffer from a clinically severe form of autosomal dominant LQTS, and from autosomal recessive congenital deafness. This condition is known as the "Jervell and Lange-Nielsen syndrome" (JLNS).[28,29] JLNS was first described in 1957 in a Norwegian family in which three congenitally deaf children died suddenly before the age of 10.[30] It is actually quite rare, with an estimated incidence of 1.6 to 6 cases per million.[29]

In a somewhat more likely event, it is possible that an individual carrying a *KCNH2* mutation on a mutant allele might also carry a different *KCNH2* polymorphism on the nonmutant allele. Relatives who inherit the one without the other would be asymptomatic, but when both mutations are simultaneously present, reduction of Ik would be substantial and result in a clinically significant form of LQTS. This situation has actually been demonstrated to occur in humans, raising the possibility that compound mutations may be more common than had previously been suspected.[31]

10.1.1.5 Treatment

There is no consensus on how to treat patients with LQTS.[4,13,32] Most physicians would advocate an implantable defibrillator (ICD) for those patients who have survived a cardiac arrest, or possibly even in those with syncopal events.[33] Dual chamber pacemakers, even with beta-blocker therapy, have been shown to be ineffective in symptomatic patients.[34]

It is generally recommended that beta-blocker therapy should be initiated in asymptomatic LQTS patients.[11–14] The exact dose or type of beta-blocker medication to be used is unclear. In patients unable (or unwilling) to take medications, an ICD may then be recommended. Restriction from heavy physical activity is also suggested in affected patients. Data from the International LQTS Registry have shown that symptomatic LQT1 patients have a low recurrence rate after starting beta-blocker medication (19% recurrence), LQT2 patients have an intermediate rate (41% recur-

TOXICOGENETICS IN DRUG ABUSE: HERITABLE CHANNELOPATHIES AND MYOPATHIES 169

rence), and LQT3 patients a higher rate (50%).[10] Sympathectomy to modify the effect of adrenaline upon the heart has been shown to be ineffective at preventing events.[34]

10.1.2 Brugada Syndrome

The Brugada syndrome (BS) is another inherited ion channelopathy that causes unexplained sudden death, particularly in middle-aged males.[35–37] It is relatively common in southeast Asia and should particularly be considered in the autopsy of subjects with this ethnicity.[38]

10.1.2.1 Epidemiology

A Brugada syndrome consensus report published in 2002 estimated the incidence of the disease worldwide at up to 66 cases per 10,000 people.[39] Although it is an autosomal dominant disease, it affects males more commonly than females, in an 8:1 male:female ratio. The reason for this gender difference is unknown. The gene is much more prevalent in Southeast Asia than in the U.S., and Brugada syndrome is thought to cause the entity known as *Lai Tai* ("death during sleep") in Thailand, a relatively common cause of sudden unexplained death among young healthy men.[38]

10.1.2.2 Clinical Features

The Brugada brothers reported eight cases of cardiac arrest in 1992, in young healthy patients with right bundle branch block patterns on ECG.[40] Since then, more has been learned about BS, although much about the disease remains a mystery.[41,42] It is not known why some patients with Brugada become symptomatic and others remain clinically silent. However, once BS subjects experience a symptom (syncope or aborted cardiac arrest), it becomes a very lethal disease with a high clinical penetrance.[43–45] Several studies have found that the 5-year recurrence rate following a resuscitated cardiac arrest was 62%.[39,41,43–45] Most arrhythmic events occur for the first time when patients are in their early 40s, but episodes have been described over a wide age range (2 to 77 years). Symptomatic patients with Brugada experience polymorphic ventricular tachycardia degenerating into ventricular fibrillation, leading to syncope or even death. The episodes occur most commonly during sleep but may also happen with exercise or at rest.

The ECG in a patient with Brugada is frequently abnormal and provides the best way to diagnose BS. A right bundle branch block-type pattern is often noted in right precordial leads V1–V3 with concomitant ST segment elevation.[35–37,46] In many patients with BS, the ECG abnormalities can normalize or be unmasked by pharmacologic challenge with a sodium channel blocking drug such as procainamide, flecainide, or ajmaline.[47,48]

Many patients with Brugada will have abnormal test results during invasive electrophysiology (EP) studies.[49,50] Inducibility of malignant ventricular arrhythmias in this group of patients is not rare, and it may portend a worse clinical prognosis than for those patients who have normal EP studies.[35–37,49,50] The usual cardiac tests in BS are normal including echocardiogram, cardiac magnetic resonance imaging (MRI), and biopsy. Autopsy findings of the heart in patients with BS are also unremarkable.

10.1.2.3 Pathophysiology

The mutation in the *SCN5A* gene results in either a reduced sodium channel current or failure of the sodium channel to express. The disease is caused by a defect in the α-subunit of the cardiac sodium channel gene (*SCN5A*).[37,41,51,52] Numerous *SCN5A* mutations have been described that produce BS, but most lead to a "loss of function" in the cardiac sodium channel. Interestingly, LQT3 (a completely different disease) is also due to mutations in the *SCN5A* gene but leads to a "gain of function" in the sodium channel.[51–55]

The mutant sodium channel demonstrates more abnormal function at higher temperatures. There are numerous reports in the literature of patients with BS experiencing symptoms during febrile illnesses.[35–37]

Recently it has been shown that the Y1102 polymorphism of the *SCN5A* gene is present in 13% of African Americans, and that its presence has been linked to the occurrence of lethal arrhythmias in African American families with ventricular tachycardia. The prevalence of the Y1102 polymorphism in a series of sudden deaths in this population has been established; it is present in 28% of African Americans who die of unexplained arrhythmias. Adjusted for age and sex, the relative risk of an unexplained arrhythmic death in individuals with this polymorphism was 8.4 (95% CI 2.1 to 28.6, $P = 0.001$) when compared with noncardiac deaths in this subgroup. The presence of the Y1102 allele appears to be a risk factor in African Americans for sudden cardiac death even in the absence of obvious morphological findings.[56]

10.1.2.4 Genetics

BS is an ion channelopathy inherited in an autosomal dominant fashion. To date, only 20% of Brugada cases have been linked to the *SCN5A* gene; the precise ion channel mutations causing the remaining 80% of cases are unknown.[40–42] The *SCN5A* gene is one of the largest ion channel genes known, with at least 28 exons identified thus far.[51,52]

10.1.2.5 Treatment

Medications are largely ineffective at treating BS.[39] Amiodarone, beta-blocker, and calcium channel blocking agents have all been tried and do not prevent sudden death in high-risk patients, although sotalol may be useful.[57] The recommended treatment for symptomatic patients with BS is ICD implantation, particularly as the recurrence rate for such subjects is high. Patients who have not yet experienced an arrhythmic event but spontaneously exhibit the abnormal ECG findings are at intermediate risk for an episode and may benefit from prophylactic implantation of a defibrillator.[49,50,58]

10.1.3 Catecholaminergic Polymorphic Ventricular Tachycardia

CPMVT is a newly described inherited disorder of cardiac calcium channels. It is another arrhythmogenic disorder characterized by sudden unexplained death associated with exercise.

10.1.3.1 Epidemiology

The disease has thus far been described in several Finnish and Italian families.[59–62] The epidemiology of this disorder has not yet been fully characterized and is so far limited to small case series. Its true incidence is likely much higher than is currently appreciated since most cases are undiagnosed.

10.1.3.2 Clinical Features

CPMVT was first described by Leenhardt et al. in 1995 in 21 children.[63] This disorder is characterized by syncopal spells in childhood and adolescence, which are often triggered by exercise or stress (catecholamines). Cardiac arrest and sudden death also occur. The disease has a mortality of 30 to 50% by the age of 30 in affected individuals.[62] Due to its autosomal dominant nature, there is often a family history of unexplained sudden death.

The resting ECG of a patient with this disorder is usually unremarkable, as are cardiac imaging studies (echocardiogram, angiogram, cardiac MRI, etc.).[62–65] Patients with CPMVT may experience bi-directional or polymorphic ventricular tachycardia with exercise stress testing, with emotional stress, or during infusion of adrenaline (isoproterenol).[64,65] Up to 30% of such patients have been initially misdiagnosed as having LQTS in one study.[61] Autopsy findings in subjects with CPMVT are generally normal.

10.1.3.3 Pathophysiology

Defective calcium channels formed as a result of the mutations in the ryanodine receptor gene *RyR2* lead to abnormal conduction, which predispose the heart to ventricular tachycardia and sudden death.[59–62,66] *RyR2*, the gene encoding the cardiac calcium channel, is responsible for mediating the coupling of the cell's electrical excitation and mechanical contraction. Cellular depolarization leads to release of Ca^{2+} from the sarcoplasmic reticulum via RyR2 and mechanical contraction. Sudden death is hypothesized to occur as the result of torsades de pointes or ventricular fibrillation due to the abnormal calcium channel handling.

10.1.3.4 Genetics

CPMVT is due to a defect in the cardiac ryanodine receptor (RyR2) gene, which is inherited in an autosomal dominant fashion.[59–62,66] Ryanodine receptors are intracellular calcium channels that regulate the release of calcium from different cell sites. Three different isoforms of the ryanodine receptor are known, and a different gene encodes each. They are the largest ion channels yet described. RyR2 (encoded by 105 exons) is characteristically found in the heart while RyR1 is found in skeletal muscle.

Because this entity is newly described and the genes encoding the mutant calcium channel are so large, no commercial genetic screening is currently available for CPMVT.

10.1.3.5 Treatment

Beta-blockers form the mainstay of therapy in this condition. In patients who have survived cardiac arrest or are felt to be at particularly high risk for sudden death, an ICD is offered.[61,65]

10.2 DISORDERS OF THE HEART MUSCLE

10.2.1 Arrhythmogenic Right Ventricular Dysplasia

ARVD is a newly recognized disorder that is a cause of unexplained sudden death in otherwise healthy young adults, particularly young athletic men.[67–69] Particularly in the early stages, affected patients may have grossly normal heart function.

10.2.1.1 Epidemiology

The true incidence of ARVD is unknown. In a prospective, detailed autopsy-based study in the Veneto region of northern Italy, 20% of unexplained sudden deaths in subjects under age 35 were found to have ARVD, including 22% of young athletic men who died suddenly in the region.[70] It is unclear if northern Italy simply has an abnormally high incidence of the disease, or if this reflects the true incidence of the disease. However, it is likely a much more common entity than initially appreciated, as most cases go undetected.

10.2.1.2 Clinical Features

Unfortunately, the initial presentation of ARVD clinically is often the unexplained sudden death in a healthy, athletic male. Patients experience ventricular arrhythmias from the diseased right

PATHOLOGY, TOXICOGENETICS, AND CRIMINALISTICS OF DRUG ABUSE

Table 10.2   ARVD Diagnostic Criteria

ECG findings
Epsilon wave of QRS in leads V1–V3
Late potentials on signal-averaged ECG
Arrhythmias
Right ventricular tachycardia or premature beats
Family history
Confirmed at autopsy
Structural findings
RV global hypokinesis with preserved LV function

ventricle. These range from benign premature ventricular complexes (PVCs) to ventricular tachycardia or even ventricular fibrillation and cardiac arrest.[71–74] ARVD was first described briefly in 1961, and in greater detail in 1977.[75,76] The Study Group on ARVD/C has defined specific criteria to aid in the diagnosis of ARVD (Table 10.2).[77]

ECG findings include a complete or incomplete right bundle branch block during normal sinus rhythm with T wave inversion in leads V_1 to V_3. An epsilon wave, a terminal notch in the QRS, may also be present.[67–69,71–73] A signal-averaged ECG (SAECG) is also characteristically abnormal.[77]

Echocardiographic findings may be normal or reveal a variety of abnormalities in the right ventricle including RV wall thinning, dilatation, or dysfunction.[67–69,71–73,78] Cardiac MRI can sometimes be useful as it may reveal the fibrofatty infiltration of the RV free wall.[79,80] Biopsy of the RV septum (done in the septum and not in the free wall, due to free wall thinning) is often not helpful because involvement of the septum in ARVD is sporadic.

ARVD represents one of the few genetically based causes of sudden death that can be identified at autopsy, at least in grossly abnormal cases. The pathologist may find diffuse or segmental loss of myocardium in the right ventricular free wall, with concomitant replacement with fibrofatty tissue.[67–69] Two-thirds of such patients have patchy, acute myocarditis-type of findings with lymphocytic infiltration and cell death.[71–73] Up to 50% of patients with ARVD have right ventricular aneurysms at autopsy.[71–73,77]

Patients can have progressive dilatation and failure of the right ventricle over time, which can also occasionally involve the left ventricle, leading to a diffuse cardiomyopathy. One study found that 76% of ARVD subjects had histologic involvement of the left ventricle.[77]

10.2.1.3 Pathophysiology

The pathophysiology of ARVD is unclear. It likely represents a complex interplay among genetic predisposition, cellular mechanisms, and unknown environmental factors.[67–69,77] Several consistent features of ARVD can be noted: apoptosis (programmed cell death), a component of inflammatory heart disease (e.g., acute myocarditis), and myocardial dystrophy. The disease is progressive over decades in some patients, whereas it is relatively quiescent, for unknown reasons, in others.

10.2.1.4 Genetics

At least seven distinct chromosomal loci for ARVD have so far been located.[81–85] These loci include two on chromosome 10, two on chromosome 14, and one each on chromosomes 1, 2, and 3. One autosomal recessive form of ARVD is associated with palmoplantar keratoderma and woolly hair.[86] It is due to a mutation in the gene for plakoglobin. Another syndrome found in Ecuador involves a recessive mutation in the gene for desmoplakin.[87] Both are components of desmosomes, which form the major cell adhesion junctions. Currently, there is no commercial genetic testing available to diagnose ARVD.

For most cases of ARVD, the genetic linkage is unclear. Up to 30 to 50% of the cases will have an associated family history consistent with ARVD (including sudden death).[71–73,77]

10.2.1.5 Treatment

There is no consensus for how to treat ARVD.[77] In those patients who have survived cardiac arrest, implantation of an ICD is generally recommended to avoid sudden death.[88] Pharmacologic therapy with beta-blocker or antiarrhythmic medications has also been suggested.[77] Radiofrequency ablation during electrophysiology study of ventricular arrhythmias has also been attempted.[89]

10.2.2 Hypertrophic Cardiomyopathy

HCM is one of the oldest known non-atherosclerotic causes of sudden death. It was first described in 1958.[90] It has been called HOCM (hypertrophic obstructive cardiomyopathy) and also IHSS (idiopathic hypertrophic subaortic stenosis) despite that 75% of affected patients do not have a sizable resting outflow gradient.[91,92] It is a polygenic, relatively common, genetic cause of sudden death, particularly in young athletes.

10.2.2.1 Epidemiology

HCM is actually the most common genetically associated form of sudden cardiac death. It is estimated that 1 in 500 people (0.2% of the general population) carry an HCM genetic mutation.[93,94] However, the phenotypic presentation or clinical penetrance of the disease is much lower. Most patients with an HCM mutation will not demonstrate clinical manifestations of the disease during life.

10.2.2.2 Clinical Features

The hallmark feature of HCM, when present, is myocyte disarray.[92,95,96] The clinical diagnosis of HCM during life is made most reliably by echocardiography. Severe ventricular wall thickening can be noted. A normal left ventricular wall thickness is generally <12 mm, but thicknesses >30 mm are not unusual in severe cases of HCM.[97–101] Marked septal hypertrophy is often an age-dependent effect and may not be seen initially in young patients. In most cases, the left ventricle is affected diffusely, or it may demonstrate ASH (asymmetric septal hypertrophy).[95–101] In contrast, in the Japanese variant of HCM, the apical left ventricle is primarily affected and shows abnormal thickening.[92,95–101]

At autopsy using detailed pathologic examination, one can frequently see hypertrophied myocytes with bizarre shapes, chaotic cellular alignment, and gross cellular disarray in the left ventricle.[102–106] The disarray is most evident in the mid-portion of the septum. Patchy areas of myocardial scarring and fibrosis can be seen, a lesion that is thought to be due to the presence of abnormal intramural coronary arteries.[107,108]

10.2.2.3 Pathophysiology

Syncope in these subjects may occur due to arrhythmias, or it may be the result of outlet obstruction due to ventricular hypertrophy and cavitary obliteration.[90,97,98] Dehydration can trigger syncopal events in such patients. Sudden death in HCM is primarily due to electrical abnormalities generating ventricular arrhythmias.[92,97,109–112] In support of this view, one large study of patients with HCM, in whom defibrillators were implanted, demonstrated that nearly 25% of the patients had documented ventricular arrhythmias over a 3-year follow-up period.[113]

The disease may be progressive in certain individuals. Cardiomyocytes continue to hypertrophy over years, but in a clinically silent manner that may lead ultimately to an end-stage, dilated cardiomyopathic picture.[92,97,98] Depending on the timeframe during which the patient is evaluated, the HCM-affected heart could appear grossly normal, markedly hypertrophied, or dilated, which makes the diagnosis difficult.

10.2.2.4 Genetics

The polygenic and multicellular nature of HCM makes it a frustratingly difficult disease to diagnose unless gross histopathologic abnormalities are found on ECG or at autopsy. At least ten different genes encoding the cardiac sarcomere have been implicated in HCM.[92,97,98,114] More than 150 unique mutations have been reported since the first genetic cause for HCM was identified in 1990.[115] Most such mutations are missense mutations found in the proteins of the cardiac sarcomere and are located in the β-myosin heavy chain, cardiac troponin T, or myosin binding protein-C.[111–119] Although the disease is autosomal dominant, a family history of syncope or sudden death may be lacking, and the disease has variable clinical penetrance.

Within the β-myosin heavy chain gene (*MYH7*), numerous mutations have been described as malignant mutations associated with a poor clinical prognosis.[118–121] These particular mutations seemed to be associated with a severe clinical phenotype including progression to end-stage heart failure or sudden death, a relatively high penetrance of the disease, and extreme left ventricular wall thickness.[92,97,98,112,117,118]

10.2.2.5 Treatment

There are no formal guidelines for treating asymptomatic patients with HCM.[92,97,98] In symptomatic patients with shortness of breath, treatment with medications that reduce the outflow gradient remains the mainstay of therapy.[92,97,98,122,123] Such medications include beta-blockers or calcium channel blockers. In very symptomatic patients with a large (>50 mm) gradient, the outflow gradient can be reduced by surgical myomectomy or by catheter-based alcohol ablation.[92,97,98,124,125] The latter is a relatively new technique, which causes a controlled myocardial infarction and thus reduces the obstruction to outflow.

In those patients deemed at high risk for an arrhythmic event, an ICD may be implanted to avert sudden death.

10.3 DRUG CAUSES OF SUDDEN DEATH

Clearly, many medications and drugs of abuse can lead to cardiac arrhythmias and sudden death. A detailed description of these topics is beyond the scope of this chapter. However, we consider three major causes of sudden death that should be considered by the pathologist at autopsy: ephedra (or ma huang), methamphetamine, and cocaine.

10.3.1 Ephedra

Ma huang is a popular herb derived from the genus *Ephedra* used for over 5000 years in Chinese folk remedies.[126] It is a natural source of ephedrine taken in various vitamin or other supplements to promote weight loss and boost energy. Ephedrine and its derivatives function in the body by increasing the availability of naturally released catecholamines.[127] Its physiologic effects on the body include increasing the heart rate, raising the cardiac output, and elevating the vascular resistance.[128] It is excreted in the urine and has a serum half-life of 2.7 to 3.6 h.[129]

Before the supplements were withdrawn from the market, it was one of the most widely used herbal supplements in the world. Even though ephedra-containing supplements are no longer for sale, millions of consumers still use ephedrine on a daily basis in the form of over-the-counter asthma preparations. It is puzzling that these asthma preparations, which have been available for more than 50 years, were never associated with any of the complications attributed to the supplements. An estimated 12 million consumers in the U.S. alone purchased over-the-counter ephedra-containing preparations in 1999.[130–132] Caffeine is also a common ingredient in ephedra preparations; the combination of the two drugs, when taken in excess, clearly can cause ventricular arrhythmias, hypertension, or cardiovascular collapse.

Numerous case reports have linked ma huang to cases of cardiovascular disorders, sudden death, and hemorrhagic stroke.[133] One analysis of adverse event reports evaluated 926 possible cases of ephedra toxicity reported to the FDA from 1995 through 1997.[130] The authors identified 37 major cardiovascular events they thought likely to be ma huang related, including 16 strokes, 11 cardiac arrests, and 10 myocardial infarctions. The average age of the 37 patients was only 43 ± 13 years and included 23 women.

Pathologists should consider testing for ephedra/ma huang particularly in young, otherwise healthy subjects who die suddenly with a normal autopsy, or if autopsy reveals early-onset vascular disease such as strokes or myocardial infarction.[134–137] Particular attention should be paid to a history of vitamin supplement ingestion in such patients.

10.3.2 Methamphetamine

Methamphetamine is a central nervous stimulant that was first synthesized by a German chemist in 1887.[138] It is an odorless, crystalline powder that is soluble in alcohol or water. Its precursors are ephedrine and pseudoephedrine.

Its sympathomimetic actions produce hypertension, elevated heart rate, ischemia, vasoconstriction, and other adrenergic-type of stimuli upon the heart. Acute aortic dissection has been described at autopsy in methamphetamine users.[139] Myocardial infarction, chest pain syndromes, and coronary artery disease have been found in such patients, and a direct toxic effect on myocytes has been implicated for methamphetamine.[140–142] Methamphetamine may promote ventricular arrhythmias and sudden death with its use.[143] Chronic use may lead to a dilated cardiomyopathy.[144–147]

Methamphetamine use is increasingly popular and should be considered in the autopsy evaluation when present, but usually there are other stigmata present suggesting the diagnosis, and sudden cardiac death with a negative autopsy is rare in a methamphetamine abuser.

10.3.3 Cocaine

Cocaine (benzoylmethylecgonine) is an alkaloid originally extracted from the leaves of the *Erythroxylon coca* plant.[147] It is estimated that at least 30 million people in the U.S. have used cocaine at some point. Cocaine acts at both the central and peripheral adrenergic nervous system by blocking the reuptake of norepinephrine and dopamine from presynaptic terminals. These effects lead to a net stimulatory effect upon the cardiovascular system.[148,149]

Cocaine causes a variety of cardiac complications. Its basic pathophysiologic effect is to induce an adrenergic overload leading to acceleration of the heart rate, proarrhythmic effects, and even cardiac collapse.[147,148,150,151] Cocaine increases myocardial oxygen demand acutely while concomitantly reducing myocardial oxygen supply with its direct vasoconstrictive effects on the coronary arteries. It promotes intracoronary thrombosis and platelet aggregation in the absence of coronary atherosclerosis, leading to vascular injury.[147,148,150–152] Finally, long-term cocaine use has been associated with premature and accelerated atherosclerosis.[155]

The pathologist should consider cocaine toxicity as an adjunctive diagnosis in the unexplained sudden death of seemingly healthy subjects. However, as is true for methamphetamine abusers, sudden death with a negative autopsy is an uncommon finding in a cocaine abuser.

In addition to its direct cardiac effects (e.g., myocardial infarction, stroke, aortic dissection, cardiac arrhythmias), cocaine has been found to directly block the *HERG* potassium channel.[157] This finding represents yet another way cocaine may cause sudden cardiac death, and is particularly important, since *HERG* blockade would not be associated with any identifiable anatomic markers.

10.4 MOLECULAR DIAGNOSIS OF CARDIOVASCULAR DISEASE

With the explosion of molecular techniques, DNA testing on peripheral blood and tissue has revolutionized the diagnosis of genetic causes of sudden death. We describe the basic methods of tissue preparation and DNA analysis as a useful overview for the clinical pathologist and coroner.

10.4.1 Collection of DNA from Blood Samples

It is easiest to amplify DNA that will be used for genetic testing when it is taken from blood samples.[158,159] Ideally, the medical examiner or pathologist would collect the samples at the time of autopsy. At least 15 ml of blood should be collected in EDTA-containing tubes, in order to prevent coagulation and degradation of the DNA. The tubes are then stored at 4°C until the DNA can be extracted for analysis, which should be within 1 week, although sometimes DNA can be extracted up to 4 months after collection. If the blood samples are collected in tubes that do not contain an anticoagulant, the DNA should be extracted promptly (within days of the initial collection).

10.4.2 Collection of DNA from Tissue Samples

Extraction of high-quality DNA from tissue that can be used for PCR (polymerase chain reaction) amplification is much more problematic than using blood samples. It is often difficult to amplify long fragments of DNA from formalin-fixed and paraffin-embedded tissue because formalin fixation may damage the DNA, as may long storage in the tissue blocks prior to analysis. Formic acid may also form in the sample, making PCR difficult, if not impossible.[160,161] Formic acid hydrolyzes the DNA and creates single-strand nicks in the DNA. In post-mortem tissues fixed in nonbuffered formalin (usually in tissue preserved more than 20 years ago), DNA fragments longer than 90 base pairs cannot be amplified.

There are a variety of published methods to extract DNA from preserved tissue.[162,163] Many involve a phenol-chloroform digestion and washing step. Commercial kits are also available that may simplify the methodology. One recent paper described a "pre-PCR restoration process" in which the single-stranded DNA nicks are repaired with Taq polymerase prior to PCR amplification, greatly enhancing the length of DNA pieces that could be amplified.[164]

An alternative method for obtaining usable DNA from tissue collected at autopsy is to snap-freeze fresh myocardial tissue in liquid nitrogen, and store it at −80°C until DNA extraction is performed. Using this method allows the extraction process to be deferred for many months. Clearly, collection and preservation of tissue or blood samples for future DNA analysis is cumbersome, time-intensive, and costly. However, it may be of great assistance in determining the cause of death if tissue is carefully preserved for future DNA testing, especially in those cases where a genetic cause of sudden death is suspected.

ACKNOWLEDGMENTS

This work was funded in part by an American Heart Association Beginning-Grant-in-Aid, Western States Affiliates, to Dr. Glatter.

REFERENCES

1. Escobedo LG and Zack MM. Comparisons of sudden and nonsudden coronary deaths in the United States. *Circulation* 1996;93:2033–6.
2. Goraya TY, Jacobsen SJ, Kottke TE, et al. Coronary heart disease death and sudden cardiac death. *Am J Epidemiol* 2003;157:763–70.
3. Zheng ZJ, Croft BJ, Giles WH, et al. Sudden cardiac death in the United States, 1989 to 1998. *Circulation* 2001;104:2158–63.
4. Wehrens XH, Vos MA, Doevendans PA, et al. Novel insights in the congenital long QT syndrome. *Ann Intern Med* 2002;137:981–92.
5. Vincent GM. The molecular genetics of the long QT syndrome: genes causing fainting and sudden death. *Annu Rev Med* 1998;49:263–74.
6. Zeltser D, Justo D, Halkin A, et al. Torsade de pointes due to noncardiac drugs: most patients have easily identifiable risk factors. *Medicine* 2003;82:282–90.
7. Al-Khatib SM, LaPointe NM, Kramer JM, et al. What clinicians should know about the QT interval. *JAMA* 2003;289:2120–7.
8. Yang P, Kanki H, Drolet B, et al. Allelic variants in long-QT disease genes in patients with drug-associated torsades de pointes. *Circulation* 2002;105:1943–8.
9. Roden DM. Pharmacogenetics and drug-induced arrhythmias. *Cardiovasc Res* 2001;50;224–31.
10. Schwartz PJ, Priori SG, Spazzolini C, et al. Genotype-phenotype correlation in the long-QT syndrome: gene-specific triggers for life-threatening arrhythmias. *Circulation* 2001;103:89–95.
11. Moss AJ, Schwartz PJ, Crampton RS, et al. The long QT syndrome: a prospective international study. *Circulation* 1985;71:17–21.
12. Moss AJ, Schwartz PJ, Crampton RS, et al. The long QT syndrome. Prospective longitudinal study of 328 families. *Circulation* 1991;84:1136–44.
13. Zareba W, Moss AJ, Schwartz PJ, et al. Influence of genotype on the clinical course of the long-QT syndrome. International Long-QT Syndrome Registry Research Group. *N Engl J Med* 1998;339:960–5.
14. Locati EH, Zareba W, Moss AJ, et al. Age- and sex-related differences in clinical manifestations in patients with congenital long-QT syndrome. *Circulation* 1998;97:2237–44.
15. Moss AJ, Robinson JL, Gessman L, et al. Comparison of clinical and genetic variables of cardiac events associated with loud noise versus swimming among subjects with the long QT syndrome. *Am J Cardiol* 1999;84:876–9.
16. Ali RH, Zareba W, Moss AJ, et al. Clinical and genetic variables associated with acute arousal and nonarousal-related cardiac events among subjects with long QT syndrome. *Am J Cardiol* 2000;85:457–61.
17. Wilde AA, Jongbloed RJ, Doevendans PA, et al. Auditory stimuli as a trigger for arrhythmic events differentiate *HERG*-related (LQTS2) patients from *KVLQT1*-related patients (LQTS1). *J Am Coll Cardiol* 1999;33:327–32.
18. Priori SG, Napolitano C, Schwartz PJ. Low penetrance in the long-QT syndrome: clinical impact. *Circulation* 1999;99:529–33.
19. Swan H, Viitasalo M, Piippo K, et al. Sinus node function and ventricular repolarization during exercise stress test in long QT syndrome patients with *KvLQT1* and *HERG* potassium channel defects. *J Am Coll Cardiol* 1999;34:823–9.
20. Swan H, Toivonen L, Viitasalo M. Rate adaptation of QT intervals during and after exercise in children with congenital long QT syndrome. *Eur Heart J* 1998;19:508–13.
21. Schwartz PJ, Priori SG, Dumaine R, et al. A molecular link between the sudden infant death syndrome and the long-QT syndrome. *N Engl J Med* 2000;343:262–7.
22. Ackerman MJ, Siu BL, Sturner WQ, et al. Postmortem molecular analysis of *SCN5A* defects in sudden infant death syndrome. *JAMA* 2001;286:2264–9.
23. Keating M, Atkinson D, Dunn C, et al. Linkage of a cardiac arrhythmia, the long QT syndrome, and the Harvey ras-1 gene. *Science* 1991;252:704–6.
24. Jiang C, Atkinson D, Towbin JA, et al. Two long QT syndrome loci map to chromosomes 3 and 7 with evidence for further heterogeneity. *Nat Genet* 1994;8:141–7.

25. Abbott GW, Sesti F, Splawski I, et al. *MiRP1* forms I_{Kr} potassium channels with *HERG* and is associated with cardiac arrhythmia. *Cell* 1999;97:175–87.
26. Wang Q, Li Z, Shen J, et al. Genomic organization of the human *SCN5A* gene encoding the cardiac sodium channel. *Genomics* 1996;34:9–16.
27. Mohler PJ, Schott JJ, Gramolini AO, et al. Ankyrin-B mutation causes type 4 long-QT cardiac arrhythmia sudden cardiac death. *Nature* 2003;421:634–9.
28. Chen Q, Zhang D, Gingell RL, et al. Homozygous deletion in KVLQT1 associated with Jervell and Lange-Nielsen syndrome. *Circulation* 1999;99:1344–7.
29. Splawski I, Timothy KW, Vincent GM, et al. Molecular basis of the long-QT syndrome associated with deafness. *N Engl J Med* 1997;336:1562–7.
30. Jervell A, Lange-Nielsen F. Congenital deaf-mutism, functional heart disease with prolongation of the Q-T interval, and sudden death. *Am Heart J* 1957;54:59–68.
31. Crotti L, Lundquist AL, Insolia R, et al. KNCH2-K897T is a genetic modifier of latent congenital long-QT syndrome. *Circulation* 2005;222:1251–8.
32. Chiang CE and Roden DM. The long QT syndromes: genetic basis and clinical implications. *J Am Coll Cardiol* 2000;36:1–12.
33. Groh WJ, Silka MJ, Oliver RP, et al. Use of implantable cardioverter-defibrillators in the congenital long QT syndrome. *Am J Cardiol* 1996;78:703–6.
34. Dorostkar PC, Eldar M, Belhassen B, et al. Long-term follow-up of patients with long-QT syndrome treated with beta-blockers and continuous pacing. *Circulation* 1999;100:2431–6.
35. Antzelevitch C, Brugada P, Brugada J, et al. Brugada syndrome: a decade of progress. *Circ Res* 2002;91:1114–8.
36. Gussak I, Antzelevitch C, Bjerregaard P, et al. The Brugada syndrome: clinical, electrophysiologic, and genetic aspects. *J Am Coll Cardiol* 1999;33:5–15.
37. Antzelevitch C. The Brugada syndrome: ionic basis and arrhythmia mechanisms. *J Cardiovasc Electrophysiol* 2001;12:268–72.
38. Nademanee K, Veerakul G, Nimmannit S, et al. Arrhythmogenic marker for the sudden unexplained death syndrome in Thai men. *Circulation* 1997;96:2595–2600.
39. Wilde AAM, Antzelevitch C, Borggrefe M, et al. The Study Group on the Molecular Basis of Arrhythmias of the European Society of Cardiology. Proposed diagnostic criteria for the Brugada syndrome: consensus report. *Circulation* 2002;106:2514–9.
40. Priori SG, Napolitano C, Gasparini M, et al. Natural history of Brugada syndrome: insights for risk stratification and management. *Circulation* 2002;105:1342–7.
41. Alings M and Wilde A. "Brugada" syndrome: clinical data and suggested pathophysiological mechanism. *Circulation* 1999;99:666–73.
42. Brugada P and Brugada J. Right bundle branch block, persistent ST segment elevation and sudden cardiac death: a distinct clinical and electrocardiographic syndrome. *J Am Coll Cardiol* 1992; 20:1391–6.
43. Brugada J, Brugada R, Antzelevitch C, et al. Long-term follow-up of individuals with the electrocardiographic pattern of right bundle-branch block and ST-segment elevation in precordial leads V1 to V3. *Circulation* 2002;105:73–8.
44. Brugada J, Brugada R, and Brugada P. Right bundle-branch block and ST-segment elevation in leads V1 through V3. *Circulation* 1998;97:457–60.
45. Priori SG, Napolitano C, Gasparini M, et al. Clinical and genetic heterogeneity of right bundle branch block and ST-segment elevation syndrome. *Circulation* 2000;102:2509–15.
46. Smits JP, Eckardt L, Probst V, et al. Genotype-phenotype relationship in Brugada syndrome: electrocardiographic features differentiate *SCN5A*-related patients from non-*SCN5A*-related patients. *J Am Coll Cardiol* 2002;40:350–6.
47. Brugada R, Brugada J, Antzelevitch C, et al. Sodium channel blockers identify risk for sudden death in patients with ST-segment elevation and right bundle branch block but structurally normal hearts. *Circulation* 2000;101:510–5.
48. Priori SG, Napolitano C, Schwartz PJ, et al. The elusive link between LQT3 and Brugada syndrome: the role of flecainide challenge. *Circulation* 2000;102:945–7.
49. Brugada P, Brugada R, Mont L, et al. Natural history of Brugada syndrome: the prognostic value of programmed electrical stimulation of the heart. *J Cardiovasc Electrophysiol* 2003;14:455–7.

TOXICOGENETICS IN DRUG ABUSE: HERITABLE CHANNELOPATHIES AND MYOPATHIES

50. Kanda M, Shimizu W, Matsuo K, et al. Electrophysiologic characteristics and implications of induced ventricular fibrillation in symptomatic patients with Brugada syndrome. *J Am Coll Cardiol* 2002;39:1799–805.

51. Chen Q, Kirsch GE, Zhang D, et al. Genetic basis and molecular mechanism for idiopathic ventricular fibrillation. *Nature* 1998;392:293–6.

52. Balser JR, The cardiac sodium channel: gating function and molecular pharmacology. *J Mol Cell Cardiol* 2001;33:599–613.

53. Kurita T, Shimizu W, Inagaki M, et al. The electrophysiologic mechanism of ST-segment elevation in Brugada syndrome. *J Am Coll Cardiol* 2002;40:330–4.

54. Yan GX and Antzelevitch C. Cellular basis for the Brugada syndrome and other mechanisms of arrhythmogenesis associated with ST-segment elevation. *Circulation* 1999;100:1660–6.

55. Clancy CE and Rudy Y. Na$^+$ channel mutation that causes both Brugada and long-QT syndrome phenotypes: a simulation study of mechanism. *Circulation* 2002;105:1208–13.

56. Burke A, Creighton W, Mont E, et al. Role of SCN5A Y1102 polymorphism in sudden cardiac death in blacks. *Circulation* 2005;112:798–802.

57. Glatter KA, Wang Q, Keating M, et al. Effectiveness of sotalol treatment in symptomatic Brugada syndrome. *Am J Cardiol* 2004;93:1320–2.

58. Kakishita M, Kurita T, Matsuo K, et al. Mode of onset of ventricular fibrillation in patients with Brugada syndrome detected by implantable cardioverter defibrillator therapy. *J Am Coll Cardiol* 2000;36:1646–53.

59. Laitinen PJ, Brown KM, Piippo K, et al. Mutations of the cardiac ryanodine receptor (RyR2) gene in familial polymorphic ventricular tachycardia. *Circulation* 2001;103:485–90.

60. Swan H, Piippo K, Viitasalo M, et al. Arrhythmic disorder mapped to chromosome 1q42-q43 causes malignant polymorphic ventricular tachycardia in structurally normal hearts. *J Am Coll Cardiol* 1999;34:2035–42.

61. Priori SG, Napolitano C, Memmi M, et al. Clinical and molecular characterization of patients with catecholaminergic polymorphic ventricular tachycardia. *Circulation* 2002;106:69–74.

62. Priori SG, Napolitano C, Tiso N, et al. Mutations in the cardiac ryanodine receptor gene (hRyR2) underlie catecholaminergic polymorphic ventricular tachycardia. *Circulation* 2001;103:196–200.

63. Leenhardt A, Lucet V, Denjoy I, et al. Catecholaminergic polymorphic ventricular tachycardia in children. A 7-year follow-up of 21 patients. *Circulation* 1995;91:1512–9.

64. Lahat H, Eldar M, Levy-Nissenbaum E, et al. Autosomal recessive catecholamine- or exercise-induced polymorphic ventricular tachycardia. *Circulation* 2001;103:2822–7.

65. Fisher JD, Krikler D, Hallidie-Smith KA. Familial polymorphic ventricular arrhythmias: a quarter century of successful medical treatment based on serial exercise-pharmacologic testing. *J Am Coll Cardiol* 1999;34:2015–22.

66. Tunwell RE, Wickenden C, Bertrand BM, et al. The human cardiac muscle ryanodine receptor-calcium release channel: identification, primary structure and topological analysis. *Biochem J* 1996;318:477–87.

67. Corrado D, Basso C, Thiene G. Arrhythmogenic right ventricular cardiomyopathy: diagnosis, prognosis, and treatment. *Heart* 2000;83:588–95.

68. Fontaine G, Fontaliran F, Hebert JL, et al. Arrhythmogenic right ventricular dysplasia. *Annu Rev Med* 1999;50:17–35.

69. Thiene G, Basso C. Arrhythmogenic right ventricular cardiomyopathy: an update. *Cardiovasc Pathol* 2001;May–Jun;10:109–17.

70. Thiene G, Nava A, Corrado D, et al. Right ventricular cardiomyopathy and sudden death in young people. *N Engl J Med* 1988;318:129–33.

71. Nava A, Bauce B, Basso C, et al. Clinical profile and long-term follow-up of 37 families with arrhythmogenic right ventricular cardiomyopathy. *J Am Coll Cardiol* 2000;36:2226–33.

72. Corrado D, Basso C, Thiene G, et al. Spectrum of clinicopathologic manifestations of arrhythmogenic right ventricular cardiomyopathy/dysplasia: a multicenter study. *J Am Coll Cardiol* 1997;30:1512–20.

73. McKenna WJ, Thiene G, Nava A, et al. Diagnosis of arrhythmogenic right ventricular dysplasia/cardiomyopathy. *Br Heart J* 1994;71:215–8.

74. Obata H, Mitsuoka T, Kikuchi Y, et al. Twenty-seven-year follow-up of arrhythmogenic right ventricular dysplasia. *Pacing Clin Electrophysiol* 2001;24:510–1.

75. Dalla Volta S, Battaglia G, Zerbini E. "Auricularization" of right ventricular pressure curve. *Am Heart J* 1961;61:25–33.
76. Fontaine G, Guiraudon G, Frank R, et al. Stimulation studies and epicardial mapping in ventricular tachycardia: study of mechanisms and selection for surgery. In: Kulbertus HE, ed. *Reentrant Arrhythmias: Mechanisms and Treatment.* Lancaster: MTP Press;1977:334–50.
77. Corrado D, Fontaine G, Marcus FI, et al. Arrhythmogenic right ventricular dysplasia/cardiomyopathy: need for an international registry. *Circulation* 2000;101:E101–6.
78. Basso C, Thiene G, Corrado D, et al. Arrhythmogenic right ventricular cardiomyopathy. Dysplasia, dystrophy, or myocarditis? *Circulation* 1996;94:983–91.
79. Midiri M, Finazzo M, Brancato M, et al. Arrhythmogenic right ventricular dysplasia: MR features. *Eur Radiol* 1997;7:307–12.
80. Tandri H, Calkins H, Nasir K, et al. Magnetic resonance imaging findings in patients meeting task force criteria for arrhythmogenic right ventricular dysplasia. *J Cardiovasc Electrophysiol* 2003;14:476–82.
81. Danieli GA and Rampazzo A. Genetics of arrhythmogenic right ventricular cardiomyopathy. *Curr Opin Cardiol* 2002;17:218–21.
82. Rampazzo A, Nava A, Danieli GA, et al. The gene for arrhythmogenic right ventricular cardiomyopathy maps to chromosome 14q23-q24. *Hum Mol Genet* 1994;3:959–62.
83. Ahmad F, Li D, Karibe A, et al. Localization of a gene responsible for arrhythmogenic right ventricular dysplasia to chromosome 3p23. *Circulation* 1998;98:2791–5.
84. Li D, Ahmad F, Gardner MJ, et al. The locus of a novel gene responsible for arrhythmogenic right-ventricular dysplasia characterized by early onset and high penetrance maps to chromosome 10p12-p14. *Am J Hum Genet* 2000;66:148–56.
85. Melberg A, Oldfors A, Blomstrom-Lundqvist C, et al. Autosomal dominant myofibrillar myopathy with arrhythmogenic right ventricular cardiomyopathy linked to chromosome 10q. *Ann Neurol* 1999;46:684–92.
86. Protonotarios N, Tsatsopoulou A, Patsourakos P, et al. Cardiac abnormalities in familial palmoplantar keratosis. *Br Heart J* 1986;56:321–6.
87. Norgett EE, Hatsell SJ, Carvajal-Huerta L, et al. Recessive mutation in desmoplakin disrupts desmoplakin-intermediate filament interactions and causes dilated cardiomyopathy, woolly hair and keratoderma. *Hum Mol Genet* 2000;9:2761–6.
88. Link MS, Wang PJ, Haugh CJ, et al. Arrhythmogenic right ventricular dysplasia: clinical results with implantable cardioverter defibrillators. *J Interv Card Electrophysiol* 1997;1:41–8.
89. Fontaine G, Tonet J, Gallais Y, et al. Ventricular tachycardia catheter ablation in arrhythmogenic right ventricular dysplasia: a 16-year experience. *Curr Cardiol Rep* 2000;2:498–506.
90. Teare D. Asymmetrical hypertrophy of the heart in young adults. *Br Heart J* 1958;20:1–18.
91. Braunwald E, Lambrew CT, Rockoff D, et al. Idiopathic hypertrophic subaortic stenosis. *Circulation* 1964;30(suppl IV):3–217.
92. Maron BJ. Hypertrophic cardiomyopathy: A systematic review. *JAMA* 2002;287:1308–20.
93. Maron BJ, Bonow RO, Cannon RO, et al. Hypertrophic cardiomyopathy. Interrelations of clinical manifestations, pathophysiology, and therapy. *N Engl J Med* 1987;316:780–9.
94. Maron BJ, Gardin JM, Flack JM, et al. Prevalence of hypertrophic cardiomyopathy in a general population of young adults. *Circulation* 1995;92:785–9.
95. Maron BJ, Epstein SE. Hypertrophic cardiomyopathy: a discussion of nomenclature. *Am J Cardiol* 1979;43:1242–4.
96. Klues HG, Schiffers A, Maron BJ. Phenotypic spectrum and patterns of left ventricular hypertrophy in hypertrophic cardiomyopathy. *J Am Coll Cardiol* 1995;26:1699–1708.
97. Spirito P, Seidman CE, McKenna WJ, et al. The management of hypertrophic cardiomyopathy. *N Engl J Med* 1997;336:775–85.
98. Maron BJ. Hypertrophic cardiomyopathy. *Lancet* 1997;350:127–33.
99. Spirito P, Bellone P, Harris KM, et al. Magnitude of left ventricular hypertrophy predicts the risk of sudden death in hypertrophic cardiomyopathy. *N Engl J Med* 2000;342:1778–85.
100. Louie EK, Maron BJ. Hypertrophic cardiomyopathy with extreme increase in left ventricular wall thickness. *J Am Coll Cardiol* 1986;8:57–65.
101. Elliott PM, Gimeno Blanes JR, Mahon NG, et al. Relation between severity of left-ventricular hypertrophy and prognosis in patients with hypertrophic cardiomyopathy. *Lancet* 2001;357:420–4.

TOXICOGENETICS IN DRUG ABUSE: HERITABLE CHANNELOPATHIES AND MYOPATHIES

102. Maron BJ and Roberts WC. Quantitative analysis of cardiac muscle cell disorganization in the ventricular septum of patients with hypertrophic cardiomyopathy. *Circulation* 1979;59:689–706.
103. Ferrans VJ, Morrow AG, Roberts WC. Myocardial ultrastructure in idiopathic hypertrophic subaortic stenosis. *Circulation* 1972;45:769–92.
104. St. John Sutton MG, Lie JT, Anderson KR, et al. Histopathological specificity of hypertrophic obstructive cardiomyopathy. *Br Heart J* 1980;44:433–43.
105. Varnava AM, Elliott PM, Mahon N, et al. Relation between myocyte disarray and outcome in hypertrophic cardiomyopathy. *Am J Cardiol* 2001;88:275–9.
106. Maron BJ, Anan TJ, Roberts WC. Quantitative analysis of the distribution of cardiac muscle cell disorganization in the left ventricular wall of patients with hypertrophic cardiomyopathy. *Circulation* 1981;63:882–94.
107. Maron BJ, Epstein SE, Roberts WC. Hypertrophic cardiomyopathy and transmural myocardial infarction without significant atherosclerosis of the extramural coronary arteries. *Am J Cardiol* 1979;43:1086–1102.
108. Basso C, Thiene G, Corrado D, et al. Hypertrophic cardiomyopathy and sudden death in the young: pathologic evidence of myocardial ischemia. *Hum Pathol* 2000;31:988–98.
109. Elliott PM, Poloniecki J, Dickie S, et al. Sudden death in hypertrophic cardiomyopathy: identification of high risk patients. *J Am Coll Cardiol* 2000;36:2212–8.
110. Maron BJ, Olivotto I, Spirito P, et al. Epidemiology of hypertrophic cardiomyopathy-related death: revisited in a large non-referral-based patient population. *Circulation* 2000;102:858–64.
111. McKenna WJ, England D, Doi YL, et al. Arrhythmia in hypertrophic cardiomyopathy. *Br Heart J* 1981;46:168–72.
112. Watkins H. Sudden death in hypertrophic cardiomyopathy. *N Engl J Med* 2000;342:422–4.
113. Maron BJ, Shen WK, Link MS, et al. Efficacy of implantable cardioverter-defibrillators for the prevention of sudden death in patients with hypertrophic cardiomyopathy. *N Engl J Med* 2000;342:365–73.
114. Seidman JG and Seidman C. The genetic basis for cardiomyopathy: from mutation identification to mechanistic paradigms. *Cell* 2001;104:557–67.
115. Geisterfer-Lowrance AA, Kass S, Tanigawa G, et al. A molecular basis for familial hypertrophic cardiomyopathy: a beta-cardiac myosin heavy chain gene missense mutation. *Cell* 1990;62:999–1006.
116. Watkins H, McKenna WJ, Thierfelder L, et al. Mutations in the genes for cardiac troponin T and alpha-tropomyosin in hypertrophic cardiomyopathy. *N Engl J Med* 1995;332:1058–64.
117. Watkins H, Rosenzweig A, Hwang DS, et al. Characteristics and prognostic implications of myosin missense mutations in familial hypertrophic cardiomyopathy. *N Engl J Med* 1992;326:1108–14.
118. Marian AJ. Pathogenesis of diverse clinical and pathological phenotypes in hypertrophic cardiomyopathy. *Lancet* 2000;355:58–60.
119. Moolman JC, Corfield VA, Posen B, et al. Sudden death due to troponin T mutations. *J Am Coll Cardiol* 1997;29:549–55.
120. Enjuto M, Francino A, Navarro-Lopez F, et al. Malignant hypertrophic cardiomyopathy caused by Arg723Gly mutation in beta-myosin heavy chain gene. *J Mol Cell Cardiol* 2000;32:2307–13.
121. Tesson F, Richard P, Charron P, et al. Genotype-phenotype analysis in four families with mutations in the beta-myosin heavy chain gene responsible for familial hypertrophic cardiomyopathy. *Hum Mutat* 1998;12:385–92.
122. Spicer RL, Rocchini AP, Crowley DC, et al. Chronic verapamil therapy in pediatric and young adult patients with hypertrophic cardiomyopathy. *Am J Cardiol* 1984;53:1614–9.
123. Gilligan DM, Chan WL, Joshi J, et al. A double-blind, placebo-controlled crossover trial of nadolol and verapamil in mild and moderately symptomatic hypertrophic cardiomyopathy. *J Am Coll Cardiol* 1993;21:1672–9.
124. Lakkis NM, Nagueh SF, Dunn JK, et al. Nonsurgical septal reduction therapy for hypertrophic obstructive cardiomyopathy: one-year follow-up. *J Am Coll Cardiol* 2000;36:852–5.
125. Qin JX, Shiota T, Lever HM, et al. Outcome of patients with hypertrophic obstructive cardiomyopathy after percutaneous transluminal septal myocardial ablation and septal myectomy surgery. *J Am Coll Cardiol* 2001;38:1994–2000.
126. Tyler VE. *The Honest Herbal: A Sensible Guide to the Use of Herbs and Related Remedies.* 3rd ed. New York: Pharmaceutical Products Press;1993:119–20.

127. Sapru HN and Theoharides TC. Autonomic nervous system. In: Theoharides TC, ed. *Essentials of Pharmacology*. 2nd ed. Boston: Little, Brown;1996:58.

128. Hoffman BB and Lefkowitz RJ. Catecholamines, sympathomimetic drugs, and adrenergic receptor antagonists. In: Hardman JG, Limbird LE, Molinoff PB, Ruddon RW, Gilman AG, eds. *Goodman and Gilman's The Pharmacological Basis of Therapeutics*. 9th ed. New York: McGraw-Hill;1996:221.

129. Pentel P. Toxicity of over-the-counter stimulants. *JAMA* 1984;252:1898–1903.

130. Samenuk D, Link MS, Homoud MK, et al. Adverse cardiovascular events temporally associated with ma huang, an herbal source of ephedrine. *Mayo Clin Proc* 2002;77:12–6.

131. Haller CA, Benowitz NL. Adverse cardiovascular and central nervous system events associated with dietary supplements containing ephedra alkaloids. *N Engl J Med* 2000;343:1833–8.

132. Gurley BJ, Gardner SF, Hubbard MA. Content versus label claims in ephedra-containing dietary supplements. *Am J Health Syst Pharm* 2000;57:963–9.

133. Karch SB. Use of ephedra-containing products and risk for hemorrhagic stroke. *Neurology* 2003;61:724–5.

134. Shekelle PG, Hardy ML, Morton SC, et al. Efficacy and safety of ephedra and ephedrine for weight loss and athletic performance. *JAMA* 2003;289:1537–45.

135. Foxford RJ, Sahlas D, Wingfeld KA. Vasospasm-induced stroke in a varsity athlete secondary to ephedrine ingestion. *Clin J Sport Med* 2003;13:183–5.

136. Wooltorton E, Sibbald B. Ephedra/ephedrine: cardiovascular and CNS effects. *CMAJ* 2002;166:633.

137. Blechman KM, Karch SB, Stephens BG. Demographic, pathologic, and toxicological profiles of 127 decedents testing positive for ephedrine alkaloids. *Forensic Sci Int* 2004;139:61–9.

138. Yu Q, Larson DF, Watson RR. Heart disease, methamphetamine, and AIDS. *Life Sci* 2003;73:129–40.

139. Swalwell CI, Davis GG. Methamphetamine as a risk factor for acute aortic dissection. *J Forensic Sci* 1999;44:23–6.

140. Turnipseed SD, Richards JR, Kirk JD, et al. Frequency of acute coronary syndrome in patients presenting to the emergency department with chest pain after methamphetamine use. *J Emerg Med* 2003;24:369–73.

141. Carson P, Oldroyd K, Phadke K. Myocardial infarction due to amphetamine. *Br Med J* 1987;294:1524–6.

142. Furst SR, Fallon SP, Reznik GN, et al. Myocardial infarction after inhalation of methamphetamine. *N Engl J Med* 1990;323:1147–8.

143. Bashour TT. Acute myocardial infarction resulting from amphetamine abuse: a spasm-thrombus interplay? *Am Heart J* 1994;128:1237–9.

144. Hong R, Matsuyama E, Nur K. Cardiomyopathy associated with the smoking of crystal methamphetamine. *JAMA* 1991;265:1152–4.

145. Call TD, Hartneck J, Dickinson WA, et al. Acute cardiomyopathy secondary to intravenous amphetamine abuse. *Ann Internal Med* 1982;97:559–60.

146. Karch SB, Stephens BG, Ho CH. Methamphetamine-related deaths in San Francisco: demographic, pathologic, and toxicologic profiles. *J Forensic Sci* 1999;44:359–68.

147. Benzaquen BS, Cohen V, Eisenberg MJ. Effects of cocaine on the coronary arteries. *Am Heart J* 2001;142:402–10.

148. Kloner RA, Hale S, Alker K, et al. The effects of acute and chronic cocaine use on the heart. *Circulation* 1992;85:407–19.

149. O'Brien CP. Drug addiction and drug abuse. In: JG Hardman and LE Limbird, eds. *Goodman and Gilman's The Pharmacological Basis of Therapeutics*. 10th ed. New York: McGraw-Hill;2001:621–42.

150. Minor RL, Scott BD, Brown DD, et al. Cocaine-induced myocardial infarction in patients with normal coronary arteries. *Ann Intern Med* 1991;115:797–806.

151. Mittleman RE and Wetli CV. Cocaine and sudden "natural" death. *J Forensic Sci* 1987;32:11–9.

152. Rod JL and Zucker RP. Acute myocardial infarction shortly after cocaine inhalation. *Am J Cardiol* 1987;59:161.

153. Simpson RW and Edwards WD. Pathogenesis of cocaine-induced ischemic heart disease. *Arch Pathol Lab Med* 1986;110:479–84.

154. Cooke CT and Dowling GP. Cocaine-associated coronary thrombosis and myocardial ischemia. *Pathology* 1988;20:242, 305–6.

TOXICOGENETICS IN DRUG ABUSE: HERITABLE CHANNELOPATHIES AND MYOPATHIES 183

155. Kolodgie FD, Virmani R, Cornhill JF, et al. Increase in atherosclerosis and adventitial mast cells in cocaine abusers: an alternative mechanism of cocaine-associated coronary vasospasm and thrombosis. *J Am Coll Cardiol* 1991;17:1553–60.

156. Kogan MJ, Verebey KG, DePace AC, et al. Quantitative determination of benzoylecgonine and cocaine in human biofluids by gas-liquid chromatography. *Anal Chem* 1977;49:1965–9.

157. Zhang S, Rajamani S, Chen Y, et al. Cocaine blocks HERG, but not KvLQT1 + minK, potassium channels. *Mol Pharmacol* 2001;59;1069–76.

158. Higuchi R. Simple and rapid preparation of samples for PCR. In HA Ehrlich, ed. *PCR Technology: Principles and Applications for DNA Amplification.* New York: Stockton Press;1989:31–38.

159. Bajanowski T, Rossi L, Biondo B, et al. Prolonged QT interval and sudden infant death — report of two cases. *Forensic Sci Int* 2001;115:147–53.

160. Sato Y, Sugie R, Tsuchiya B, et al. Comparison of the DNA extraction methods for polymerase chain reaction amplification from formalin-fixed and paraffin-embedded tissues. *Diagn Mol Pathol* 2001;10:265–71.

161. Cao W, Hashibe M, Rao JY, et al. Comparison of methods for DNA extraction from paraffin-embedded tissues and buccal cells. *Cancer Detect Prev* 2003;27:397–404.

162. Mygind T, Ostergaard L, Birkelund S, et al. Evaluation of five DNA extraction methods for purification of DNA from atherosclerotic tissue and estimation of prevalence of *Chlamydia pneumoniae* in tissue from a Danish population undergoing vascular repair. *BMC Microbiol* 2003;3:19.

163. Konomi N, Lebwohl E, Zhang D. Comparison of DNA and RNA extraction methods for mummified tissues. *Mol Cell Probes* 2002;16:445–51.

164. Bonin S, Petrera F, Niccolini B, et al. PCR analysis in archival postmortem tissues. *Mol Pathol* 2003;56:184–6.

Index

A

Acid Extraction Technique, 12
Activan, 35
Acute bacterial endocarditis, 124
Adams studies, 137
Adipex-P, 37
Adulterants
    cocaine, 14
    color tests, 41
    controlled substances, 50–51
Adventitial mast cells, 101
Ahlner, Holmgren and, studies, 159
Alcohol
    aspiration pneumonia, 133
    central nervous system, 137–139, *138–139*
    fetal alcohol syndrome, 138, 159
    synergy, drugs, 104
Allele, 161
Alprazolam, 35
Alurate, 36
Amidone, 36, *see also* Methadone
Amobarbital, 4, 36
Amphetamines
    cerebral hemorrhage, 107
    cerebral vasculitis, 143
    color tests, 41
    counterfeits, 38
    excited delirium, 139
    fundamentals, 37
    fungal cerebritis, 146
    intracranial hemorrhage, 141
    myocardial alteration, 118
Amytal, 36, *see also* Amobarbital
Anabolic steroids
    control, 30–31
    forensic analysis, 33–34
    physiological effects and medical uses, 62
    regulatory history, 30–31, *31*
    structure-activity relationship, 32, *32*
Androgenic activity, 30
Anesthesia, 107
Angiography, 108
Anoxic ischemic encephalopathy, 146
Aorta, 90, *91–92*
Aprobarbital, 36

Arrhythmogenic right ventricular dysplasia (ARVD),
    171–173
Arterial pressure, 141
Arteries, 80–82, *81–82*
Arteriopathy, 132–133, *132–134*
Arterio-venous malformations, 141
Arteritis, cerebral, 105
ARVD, *see* Arrhythmogenic right ventricular dysplasia
    (ARVD)
Aspiration pneumonia, 133–134, *134–135*
Asthma, 131
Atherosclerosis, 102
Atrioventricular valves, 86
Atrophy, cerebral, 138
Autopsy, 74–77, *75–77*
Ayirookuzhi studies, 165–176

B

Babies, *see* Infants
Bacarate, 37
Bacterial endocarditis, 124
Bailey studies, 129–130
Barbier purification, 8
Barbiturates, 38, 41
Base peak, 46
Beckett, G.H., 6
Beer's law, 51
Bell studies, 123–126, 129–134, 137–148
Benzedrine, 38, *see also* Amphetamines
Benzodiazepines, 35, 38
Benzoylecgonine, 13
Benzphetamine, 37
Berry aneurysms, 141
Beta-blocker therapy, 168, 171, 174
Bingeing
    cocaine, 98, 100
    synergy, drugs, 104
Biotransformation, 156
Biphetamine, 37, *see also* Amphetamines
Blood, DNA collection, 176
Blood pressure, 103, *see also* Hypertension
Blotter paper LSD, 39, *see also* Lysergic acid diethylamide
    (LSD)
"Blue velvet," 132

185

Index

Body packers
  heroin, 6
  scene of death, 73, 74
Body position, 72
Bono studies, 1–69
Brevital, 35
Bricks, 12, 15
Brugada syndrome, 169–170
Burke studies, 79–95, 97–108
Butabarbital, 36
Butisol, 35
By-products, 13–14

C

Caffeine, 175
Calcium channel blockers, 174
Calkins studies, 165–176
cAMP response binding protein (CREB), 116–117
Cannabis, 61, *see also* Marijuana
Capillary column gas chromatography (ccGC), 54
Capillary electrophoresis (CE), 44, 48
Capsule imprints, 38–39
Cardiomyopathy, 85–86, *87–88*
Cardiopulmonary paralysis, 138
Cardiovascular disease, 176
Catecholaminergic polymorphic ventricular tachycardia
      (CPMVT), 170–171
Catecholamines, 118, 141
Catha edulis, 29
ccGC, *see* Capillary column gas chromatography (ccGC)
CE, *see* Capillary electrophoresis (CE)
Central cardiopulmonary paralysis, 138
Central nervous system, depressants, 35–36, *36*
Central nervous system, disorders
    alcohol, 137–139, *138–139*
    anoxic ischemic encephalopathy, 146
    cerebral vasculitis, 143, *144,* 145
    cerebrovascular disease, 140–143, *141–143*
    encephalopathy, 146, 148
    excited delirium, 139–140, *140*
    heroin smokers encephalopathy, 148
    infections, 146–148, *147–148*
    movement disorders, 146
    seizure disorder, *145,* 145–146
Central nervous system, stimulants, 37
Central pontine myelinolysis (CPM), 137–138
Cerebral arteritis, 105
Cerebral atrophy, 138
Cerebral degeneration, 138
Cerebral hemorrhage, 107
Cerebral vasculitis, 143, *144,* 145
Cerebritis, fungal, 146–147
Cerebrovascular disease, 140–143, *141–143*
Cerose, 36
Certainty, controlled substances, 48–49
Channelopathies, *see* Heritable channelopathies and
      myopathies
Charcot-Bouchard microaneurysms, 141–142

Chemicals, clandestine laboratories, 58–60
Cheracol, 36
Children, *see* Infants
China White, 21
Chloral hydrate, 35
Chlordiazepoxide, 35
Chlorphentermine, 37
Chromosomes, *see* Genetics
Cinnamoylcocaines, 13
Cis-cinnamoylcocaines, 13
Clandestine laboratories, *see also specific drug*
    chemicals commonly encountered, 58–60
    fundamentals, 55–56
    regulations, 5
    safety concerns, 57–58
Clinical applications, 158–161
Clinical features
    arrhythmogenic right ventricular dysplasia, 171–172,
      172
    Brugada syndrome, 169
    catecholaminergic polymorphic ventricular
      tachycardia, 170–171
    hypertrophic cardiomyopathy, 173
    long QT syndromes, 167, *167*
Clonazepam, 35
Clonidine, 159
Cloretemine, 37
Clostridium spp., 147–148
Cobalt thyocyanate, 41
Cocaine
    adulterants, 14, 50
    aspiration pneumonia, 133
    atherosclerosis, 102
    by-products, 13–14
    catecholamines, 141
    cerebral vasculitis, 143, 145
    color tests, 41
    crack conversion, 12–13
    diluents, 50
    drug synergy, 104–105
    endothelial dysfunction, 102–103
    excited delirium, 139–140
    exhibit comparison, 54–55
    fundamentals, 9–10, 14
    fungal cerebritis, 146
    hemodynamic alterations, 103, *104*
    heritable channelopathies and myopathies, 175
    historical background, 11
    identifying, 48–49
    intracerebral hemorrhage, 141
    intracranial hemorrhage, 141
    isolation, 11–12
    lung disease, 129, 132
    microvascular resistance, 101
    myocardial alteration, 118
    myocardial hypertrophy, 116
    pneumonitis, 130
    purification, 11–12
    quantitating, 48–49
    seizure disorder, 145
    sources, *10,* 10–11

INDEX

187

"street" exhibits, 50
synergy, drugs, 104
thrombosis, 101–102, *102*
vascular effects, 98, 100–105
vasculitis, 103
vasospasticity, 101
Cocaine hydrochloride, 4, 13
Codeine, 36, 159
Color tests, 33, 41
Commonality of source, 53–55
Comparative analysis, 53–55
Conduction system, 91
Confirmatory chemical tests
capillary electrophoresis, 44
gas chromatography, 42–43
gas chromatography/mass spectrometry, 45–46
high-performance liquid chromatography, 43–44
infrared spectrophotometry, 44–45
microcrystal identifications, 42
nuclear magnetic resonance spectroscopy, 46–47
Connolly studies, 126
Consequences of hypertrophy, 117
Contraction band necrosis, 118
Control, anabolic steroids, 30–31
Controlled substances
adulterants, 50–51
anabolic steroids, 30–34
benzodiazepines, 35
blotter paper LSD, 39
capsule imprints, 38–39
Catha edulis, 29
central nervous system depressants, 35–36
central nervous system stimulants, 37
chemicals, clandestine laboratories, 58–60
clandestine laboratories, 55–60
cocaine, 9–14, 54–55
commonality of source, 53–55
comparative analysis, 53–55
confirmatory chemical tests, 42–47
Controlled Substances Analogue and Enforcement Act of 1986, 4–5
defined, 3
depressants, 35–36
diluents, 50–51
examinations, 47–53
exhibit comparisons, 54–55
fentanyl, 21–22
fundamentals, 3
generic product identification, 37
heroin, 5–9, 54
identifying, 48–51
Khat, 29
laboratory drug analysis, 40–53
legitimate pharmaceutical preparations, 35–37
lysergic acid diethylamide, 20, 39
marijuana, 15–17
medical uses table, 60–62
methcathinone, 28
narcotic analgesics, 36–37
packaging logos, 37–38
peyote, 17–18

phencyclidine, 20–21
phenethylamines, 22–23, 28
physiological effects table, 60–62
psilocybin mushrooms, 18–19
quantitating, 48–49, 51–52
reference standards, 52–53
regulations, 4–5
safety concerns, 57–58
schedule number table, 62–69
scheduling, 3–4
screening tests, 40–42
source commonality, 53–55
stimulants, 37
tables, 60–69
tablet markings, 38–39
unique identifying factors, 37–39
Controlled Substances Analogue and Enforcement Act of 1986
clandestine laboratory impact, 48
controlled substances, 4–5
methcathinone, 28
phenethylamines, 28
Cornstarch, 132–133
Coronary arteries, 80–82, *81–82*
Coronary interventions, 82–85, *83–84*
Correlation spectroscopy (COSY), 47
Cosanyl, 36
Counterfeit industry, 38–39
CPM, *see* Central pontine myelinolysis (CPM)
CPMVT, *see* Catecholaminergic polymorphic ventricular tachycardia (CPMVT)
"Crack" cocaine, 12–13, 131
CREB, *see* cAMP response binding protein (CREB)
Crystal tests, 33
CYP3A4 genes, 158–159, 161
CYP3A5 genes, 161
CYP2D6 gene, 158–159

D

Dalmane, 35
Darvocet, 37
Darvon, 37
Death, during sleep, 169, *see also* Scene of death; Sudden death
Decalcification, 82
Degeneration, cerebral, 138
Delirium, *see* Excited delirium
Demerol, 36
Depressants, 35–36, *36,* 61
Depression, 158
"Designer drugs," *see also* Controlled substances
anabolic steroids, 34
regulations, 5
scene of death, 72
specificity, 48
Desoxyn, 4, 37, *see also* Methamphetamine
Dexedrine, 38
Dextroamphetamine, 37

Dextropropoxyphene, 37
Diazepam, 35, *see also* Valium
Didrex, 37
Diethylpropion, 37
Differential scanning calorimeter (DSC), 52–53
Dilaudid, 36
Dille-Koppanyi reagent, 41
Diluents, 41, 50–51
Diuretics, 106
DNA
   collection, 176
   fundamentals, 154–155
   opiate toxicity, 176
Documentation, 48
Dolene, 37
Dolophine, 36, *see also* Methadone
Doriden, 36
Doyle, Sir Arthur Conan, 11
Dressler and Robert studies, 123
Drug Abuse Warning Network (DAWN), 97
Drug postmortem redistribution, 77
Drug synergy and interactions, 104–105, 159–160
DSC, *see* Differential scanning calorimeter (DSC)
Duquenoise-Levine test, 16–17, 41, 42
Duquenoise reagent, 41
Dyspnea, 126, 133

E

ECG, *see* Electrocardiogram (ECG)
Ecgonine, 13
Ecstasy, 23, 105
Ehrlich's reagent, 41
EI/MS, *see* Electron impact gas chromatogragphy/mass
        spectrometry (EI/MS)
Elad and Ginsburg studies, 8
Electrocardiogram (ECG), 169, 170, 172
Electron capture gas chromatography (GC/ECD), 55
Electron impact gas chromatogragphy/mass spectrometry
        (EI/MS), 45
Elimination, 157–158
Emphysema, 133
Empirin with Codeine, 36
Encephalopathy, 138–139, 146, 148
Endocarditis, fungal, 124
Endothelial dysfunction, 102–103
Eosinophilia-myalgia syndrome, 108
Ephedra, 174–175
Ephedrine
   cerebral vasculitis, 143
   myocardial hypertrophy, 116
   vascular effects, 107
Epidemic ergotism, 106
Epidemiology
   arrhythmogenic right ventricular dysplasia, 171
   Brugada syndrome, 169
   catecholaminergic polymorphic ventricular
      tachycardia, 170
   hypertrophic cardiomyopathy, 173

long QT syndromes, 167
   myocardial alterations, 116
Epidural anesthesia, 107
Equanil, 36
Ergot alkaloids, 106–107, *107*
Ergotism, 106
Examinations, controlled substances, 47–53
Excited delirium
   central nervous system, 139–140, *140*
   scene of death, 73
Exercise, 167, 170
Exhibit comparisons, 54–55

F

False screening tests, 40–41
Farb studies, 79–95
Fastin, 37
Fenfluramine, 37, 126
Fentanyl
   drug interactions, 159
   fundamentals, 21–22, *24–25*
Fetal alcohol syndrome, 138, 159, *see also* Infants
Fibrosis, 119
FID, *see* Flame ionization detector (FID)
Fiorinal with Codeine, 36
Flame ionization detector (FID), 43
Flame ionization gas chromatography (GC-FID), 54–55
Flunitrazepam, 35
Fluoxetine, 159
Flurazepam, 35
Forensic analysis, anabolic steroids, 33–34
Forensic toxicology, 159, *160, 161*
Fourier analysis, 48–49
Framingham Study, 117
Freud studies, 11
Fungal cerebritis, 146–147
Fungal endocarditis, 124

G

Gallium scanning, 132
Gas chromatography (GC)
   anabolic steroids, 33
   capillary electrophoresis comparison, 44
   cocaine adulterants, 14
   confirmatory chemical tests, 42–43
   psilocybin mushrooms, 19
   quantitating, 50–51
   reference standards, 52–53
Gas chromatography/mass spectrometry (GC/MS)
   anabolic steroids, 33
   confirmatory chemical tests, 45–46
   heroin, 49
   methamphetamine, 49
   methyl ecgonidine, 13

INDEX

phencyclidine, 49
psilocybin mushrooms, 19
Gates and Tschudi studies, 8
GC, *see* Gas chromatography (GC)
GC-ECD, *see* Electron capture gas chromatography (GC/ECD)
GC-FID, *see* Flame ionization gas chromatography (GC-FID)
GC/MS, *see* Gas chromatography/mass spectrometry (GC/MS)
Gemonil, 36
Generic products, identifying, 37
Genetics
    arrhythmogenic right ventricular dysplasia, 172
    Brugada syndrome, 170
    catecholaminergic polymorphic ventricular tachycardia, 171
    hypertrophic cardiomyopathy, 174
    long QT syndromes, 168
Genotypes, 161
Ginsburg, Elad and, studies, 8
Glassine envelopes, 38
Glatter studies, 165–176
Glomerular injury, 105
Glue sniffing, 106
Glutethimide, 36
Granulomatous pneumonitis, 132–133, *132–134*

H

Halcion, 35
Hallucinogens, 61
Hands inspection, 73
Hash and hashish oil, 15, 42
HCM, *see* Hypertrophic (obstructive) cardiomyopathy (HCM/HOCM)
Heart
    cocaine, 141
    muscle disorders, 171–174
    weight, 117
Heart disease examination
    aorta, 90, *91–92*
    arteries, 80–82, *81–82*
    cardiomyopathy, 85–86, *87–88*
    fundamentals, 79–80, 95
    hypertrophy, 94
    interventions, 82–85, *83–84*
    myocardium, 85, *86*
    prosthetic valves, 90
    removal, 80
    sudden deaths, 90–94, *92–94*
    valves, 86, *87–89*, 89–90
Heffter, A., 17
Heim, Roger, 18
Helpern, Siegel and, studies, 115
Hemodynamic alterations, 103, *104*
Hemorrhage, cerebral, 107
Hemosiderin-laden macrophages, 129–130
Hemp, *see* Marijuana

Heritable channelopathies and myopathies
    arrhythmogenic right ventricular dysplasia, 171–173
    blood, DNA collection, 176
    Brugada syndrome, 169–170
    cardiovascular disease, 176
    catecholaminergic polymorphic ventricular tachycardia, 170–171
    cocaine, 175
    DNA collection, 176
    ephedra, 174–175
    fundamentals, 166
    heart muscle disorders, 171–174
    hypertrophic cardiomyopathy, 173–174
    ion channel disorders, 167–171
    long QT syndrome, 167–169
    methamphetamine, 175
    sudden death, 174–175
    tissue, DNA collection, 176
Heroin
    adulterants, 50
    asthma, 131
    diluents, 50
    encephalopathy, 148
    exhibit comparison, 54
    fundamentals, 5–6
    fungal cerebritis, 146
    hearts, 117
    identifying, 49
    morphine isolation, 7–9, *9*
    myocardial disease, 115
    nuclear magnetic resonance spectroscopy, 47
    production, 7–9, *9*
    quantitating, 49
    smokers encephalopathy, 148
    sources, 6–7
    "street" exhibits, 50
    synthetic (fentanyl), 21
    vascular effects, 105
Heterozygote, 161
Heumann purification, 8
Hexobarbital, 35
High-performance liquid chromatography (HPLC)
    adulterants, 50
    capillary electrophoresis comparison, 44
    confirmatory chemical tests, 43–44
    diluents, 50
    heroin comparison, 54
    psilocybin mushrooms, 19
    quantitating, 50–51
    reference standards, 52–53
Historical backgrounds
    anabolic steroids, 30–31
    cocaine, 11
    marijuana, 15
HIV, *see* Human immunodeficiency virus (HIV)
HOCM, *see* Hypertrophic (obstructive) cardiomyopathy (HCM/HOCM)
Hofmann, Albert, 18, 20
Holmes, Sherlock, 11
Holmgren and Ahlner studies, 159
Homozygote, 161

HPLC, *see* High-performance liquid chromatography (HPLC)
Human immunodeficiency virus (HIV)
    fungal cerebritis, 147
    heroin, 105
    myocardial disease, 119
Hydrocodone, 36
Hydromorphone, 36
Hypersensitivity vasculitis, 103
Hypertension
    cocaine, 141
    hemodynamic alterations, 103
    pulmonary artery thromboses, 132
Hypertrophic (obstructive) cardiomyopathy (HCM/HOCM), 173–174
Hypertrophy, 94, 117
Hypotension, 106–107

I

Identification
    adulterants and diluents, 50–51
    and quantitating, 48–49
    unique factors, 37–39
Imprints and markings, 38–39
Impulse collection, 91
Infants
    ephedrine, 107
    fetal alcohol syndrome, 138, 159
    sudden death, 91
    sudden infant death syndrome (SIDS), 167
Infections, central nervous system, 146–148, *147–148*
Infective endocarditis, 123–126, *124–126*
Infrared spectrophotometry (IR)
    adulterants, 50
    cocaine, 14, 49
    confirmatory chemical tests, 44–45
    diluents, 50
    fentanyl, 21
    methamphetamine, 49
    phenethylamines, 23
    psilocybin mushrooms, 19
    reference standards, 52
    specificity, 48
Injection sites, autopsy, 74
Inspection of body, scene of death, 72–73
Interventions, coronary, 82–85, *83–84*
Intracerebral hemorrhage, 141–142
Intracoronary stents, 84–85
Intracranial hemorrhage, 141
Intravenous drug use complications, 132–133, *132–134*
Ionamin, 37
Ion channel disorders, 167–171
IR, *see* Infrared spectrophotometry (IR)
Isolation of drugs, 7–9, 11–12, *see also specific method*

J

Jervell and Lange-Nielsen syndrome, 168

K

Karch studies, 115–119
Khat, 29
Kilos, 15, *see also* Bricks
Klebsiella pneumoniae, 134
Klonipin, 35
Koch's triangle, 91
Koller, Karl, 11
Kolodgie studies, 97–108
Korsakoff psychosis, 138–139

L

Laboratory analysis, 16–17, 40–53
Lai Tai, 168
Laminar necrosis, 146
Lawrence, Judy, 69
Leenhardt studies, 170
Legitimate pharmaceutical preparations
    benzodiazepines, 35
    depressants, 35–36, *36*
    fundamentals, 35
    generic products, 37
    narcotic analgesics, 36–37
    stimulants, 37
    vascular effects, 106–107
Librium, 35
Lipohyalinosis, 142, *see also* Charcot-Bouchard microaneurysms
Logos
    blotter paper LSD, 39
    packaging, 37–38
    sources, 35
    tablets and capsules, 38–39
Long QT syndrome, 167–169
Lorazepam, 35
Lotusate, 36
Louria studies, 115
LSD, *see* Lysergic acid diethylamide (LSD)
L-tryptophan, 108
Luminal, 36
Lung disease
    arteriopathy, 132–133, *132–134*
    aspiration pneumonia, 133–134, *134–135*
    granulomatous pneumonitis, 132–133, *132–134*
    smoked illicit drugs, 129–132, *130–131*
Lysergic acid diethylamide (LSD)
    blotter paper, 39
    color tests, 41
    fundamentals, 20, *20*

INDEX

191

M

Magnetic resonance imaging (MRI), 148
Ma huang, *see* Ephedra
Mandrax, 36, 39
Marchiafava-Bignami disease, 137
Mariani, Angelo, 11
Marijuana
    color tests, 41
    Duquenoise-Levine test, 42
    historical background, 15
    laboratory analysis, 16–17
    lung disease, 131
    screening tests, 41
    terminology, 15
    thin-layer chromatography, 42
Markings and imprints, 38–39
Marquis reagents, 41
Mass spectrometry (MS)
    cocaine adulterants, 14
    fentanyl, 21
    phenethylamines, 23
    reference standards, 52
    specificity, 48
Mazanor, 37
Mazindol, 37
MDA, *see* 3,4-Methylenedioxyamphetamine (MDA)
MDMA, *see* 3,4-Methylenedioxymethamphetamine (MDMA)
Mebaral, 36
MECC, *see* Micellar electrokinetic capillary chromatography (MECC)
Mechanism of hypertrophy, 116–117
Medical uses table, 60–62
Melifat, 37
Melting point analysis, 52
Meperidine, 36
Mephobarbital, 36
Meprobamate, 36
Mequin, 36, *see also* Methaqualone
Merck, 11
Mescaline, *see* Peyote
Messenger RNA (mRNA), 154
Metabolism, 156, 159
Methadone
    drug interactions, 159
    fundamentals, 36
    intravenous drug use, 132
Methamphetamine
    central nervous system, 23
    cerebral vasculitis, 145
    counterfeits, 38
    fundamentals, 37
    heritable channelopathies and myopathies, 175
    identifying, 49
    myocardial hypertrophy, 116
    quantitating, 49
    scheduling, 4
    vascular effects, 105–108
Methaqualone, 36, 38
Metharbital, 36

Methcathinone, 28, *28–29*
Methergine, 20
Methohexital, 35
Methylecgonine, 13
3,4-Methylenedioxyamphetamine (MDA)
    myocardial hypertrophy, 116
    phenethylamine, 23
    popularity, 105
3,4-Methylenedioxymethamphetamine (MDMA)
    myocardial hypertrophy, 116
    phenethylamine, 23
    population, 105
Methylphenidate
    drug interactions, 159
    fundamentals, 37
    intracranial hemorrhage, 141
    pulmonary emphysema, 133
    pulmonary hypertension, 132
Methylphenobarbital, 36
Micellar electrokinetic capillary chromatography (MECC), 44
Microcrystal identifications, 42
Microvascular resistance, 101
Migraine headaches, 106
Miltown, 36
Molecular ions, 46
Moliteno studies, 104
Mooney, James, 17
Morning glory seeds, 20
Morphine
    isolation, 7–9, *9*
    screening tests, 41
    synergy, drugs, 104
Mortimer, W.G., 11
Mouth inspection, 73
Movement disorders, 146
MRI, *see* Magnetic resonance imaging (MRI)
mRNA, *see* Messenger RNA (mRNA)
MS, *see* Mass spectrometry (MS)
Mullick studies, 97–108
Murray studies, 129
Mushrooms, *see* Psilocybin mushrooms
Myocardial alterations
    consequences of hypertrophy, 117
    epidemiology, 116
    fundamentals, 115
    mechanism of hypertrophy, 116–117
    opiate users, 119
    stimulant-related disorders, 117–118
Myocardium, 85, *86*
Myocyte disarray, 173
Myopathies, *see* Heritable channelopathies and myopathies

N

Narcotics
    aspiration pneumonia, 133
    legitimate pharmaceutical preparations, 36–37
    physiological effects and medical uses, 60–61

Narula studies, 97–108
Nembutal, 35
Neuroleptic malignant syndrome (NMS), 140
Nicotine, 104, 106
NMR, *see* Nuclear magnetic resonance spectroscopy (NMR)
Noctec, *see* Chloral hydrate
Non-operational clandestine laboratories, 56, *see also* Clandestine laboratories
Norfluoxetine, 159
Nuclear magnetic resonance spectroscopy (NMR)
   anabolic steroids, 33
   cocaine adulterants, 14
   confirmatory chemical tests, 46–47
   fentanyl, 21
   phenethylamines, 23
   quantitating, 51
   reference standards, 52
Nuclear overhauser effect spectroscopy (NOESY), 47

O

Obstetrics, 107
Odors, 57, 76
Open bypass surgery, 82
Operational clandestine laboratories, 55, *see also* Clandestine laboratories
Opiates, opium, and opioids
   color tests, 41
   myocardial alterations, 119
   pharmacogenomics, 158–159
   scheduling, 4
Optical crystallography, 52
Optimil, 36, *see also* Methaqualone
Oxidation, 156–157
Oxycodone, 36

P

Packaging logos, 37–38
Paracelsus, 153–154
Paralysis, central cardiopulmonary, 138
Paraphernalia at scene of death, 72
Paregoric, 132
Parest, 36, *see also* Methaqualone
Parkinson's syndrome, 146
Patel studies, 130
Pathophysiology
   arrhythmogenic right ventricular dysplasia, 172
   Brugada syndrome, 169–170
   catecholaminergic polymorphic ventricular tachycardia, 171
   hypertrophic cardiomyopathy, 173
   long QT syndromes, 168
PCI, *see* Percutaneous coronary interventions (PCI)
PCP, *see* Phencyclidine (PCP)
Pediacof, 36

Pemberton, John, 11
Pentazocine, 36
Pentobarbital, 35
Pentothal, 35
Percodan, 36
Percutaneous coronary interventions (PCI), 82
Perflurotributylamine (PFTBA), 46
Perfusion fixation, 80–81
Peyote, 17–18, *18*, 41
PFTBA, *see* Perflurotributylamine (PFTBA)
Pharmaceutical preparations, legitimate
   benzodiazepines, 35
   depressants, 35–36, *36*
   fundamentals, 35
   generic products, 37
   narcotic analgesics, 36–37
   stimulants, 37
Pharmacogenomics
   clinical applications, 158–161
   depression, 158
   forensic toxicology, 159, *160, 161*
   fundamentals, 153–158, *154, 156, 161*
   opiate toxicity, 158–159
Phencyclidine (PCP)
   color tests, 41
   fundamentals, 20–21, *22–23*
   identifying, 49
   intracranial hemorrhage, 141
   scheduling, 4
Phendimetrazine, 37
Phenethylamines, 22–23, *25–28,* 28, 41
Phenmetrazine, 37
Phenobarbital, 36
Phenophen, 36
Phenothiazines, 106
Phenotypes, 161
Phentermine, 37
Phenylpropanolamine
   cerebral hemorrhage, 107–108
   intracranial hemorrhage, 141
   vascular effects, 108
Physical characteristics, 40–41
Physician's Desk Reference, 35
Physiological effects table, 60–62
Plegine, 37
Pneumonia, 133–134, *134–135*
Pneumonitis, 130
Polymorphism
   Brugada syndrome, 170
   drug interactions, 159
   fundamentals, 161
Pondimin, 37, *see also* Fenfluramine
Position of body, 72
Postmortem drug redistribution, 77
Precursors, clandestine laboratories, 58–60
Preludin, 37
Pre-packaged syringes, 39
Pre-Sate, 37
Prescription drugs, *see* Legitimate pharmaceutical preparations
Production, heroin, 7–9

INDEX

193

Propacet, 37
Propoxyphene, 132
Prosthetic valves, 90
Proteins, 155–156
Pseudoephedrine, 107, 141
Psilocybin mushrooms, 18–19, 41
Psychosis, Karosakof, 138–139
Pulmonary emphysema, 133
Pulmonary hypertension, 132
Purification, 11–12
Pyribenzamine, 132

Q

Quaalude, 36, 39
Quantitating controlled substances, 48–49, 51–52

R

Rapoport studies, 8
Redistribution, drugs, 77
Reference standards, 52–53
Regulations and regulatory history
    anabolic steroids, 30–31, *31*
    cocaine, 9–10
    controlled substances, 4–5
    heroin, 6
Regurgitant valve disease, 126
Renal failure, 105
Restoril, 35
Retention times, 43
RGP, *see* Robertson and Gregory Process (RGP)
Rhizopus spp., 146
Rice studies, 8
Ritalin, *see also* Methylphenidate
    fundamentals, 37
    pulmonary emphysema, 133
    pulmonary hypertension, 132
RNA, 154–155
Robert, Dressler and, studies, 123
Robertson and Gregory Process (RGP), 8
Robitussin A-C, 36
Rohypnol, 35
Round atrophic scars, 76
Rusby, H.H., 11
Ryanodine receptor (RyR2) gene, 171

S

Safety concerns, 57–58
Sajantila studies, 159
Sanorex, 37
Scene of death
    body packers, 74
    excited delirium, 73
    fundamentals, 71–73, *72*

Scheduling and schedule number tables
    anabolic steroids, 31
    controlled substances, 3–4
    schedule I, 62–64
    schedule II, 64–65
    schedule III, 65–67
    schedule IV, 67–68
    schedule V, 69
Schwyzer purification, 8
SCN5A gene, 169–170
Screening tests, 40–42
Secobarbital, 4, 35–36
Seconal, 35–36
Seizure disorder, *145*, 145–146
Semilunar valves, 86, 89–90
SIDS, *see* Sudden infant death syndrome (SIDS)
Siegel and Helpern studies, 115
Sinsemilla, 15
SK-Bamate, 36
Smoked illicit drugs, 129–132, *130–131*
Solvent Extraction Technique, 11–12
Solvents, 106
Sombulex, 35
Somnafac, 36, *see also* Methaqualone
Sopor, 36, *see also* Methaqualone
Sources
    cocaine, *10*, 10–11
    commonality, 53–55
    heroin, 6–7
Späth, E., 17
Spinal anesthesia, 107
Spongiform encephalopathy, 148
St. Anthony's fire, 106
Staphylococcus aureus, 124, 147
Statobex, 37
Stimulant-related disorders, 117–118
Stimulants, 37, 61
Streptococcus pneumoniae, 134
Structure-activity relationship, 32, *32*
Sudden death
    arrhythmogenic right ventricular dysplasia, 171
    cocaine, 175
    conduction system, 89
    drug causes, 174–175
    ephedra, 174–175
    epidemiology, 116
    excited delirium, 73, 139
    heart disease examination, 90–94, *92–94*
    HERG potassium channel, 175
    heritable channelopathies and myopathies, 174–175
    long QT syndrome, 167
    lung disease, 131
    major cause of death, 166
    methamphetamine, 175
    myocardial alteration, 118
Sudden infant death syndrome (SIDS), 167, *see also* Infants
Surital, 35
Syncope, 173
Synthetic heroin, 21
Syringes, 39

T

Tables, controlled substances, 60–69
Tablet markings, 38–39
Tachycardia, 141
Talbutal, 36
Talc, 132–133
Talwin, 36
Tanorex, 37
Temazepam, 35
Tenuate, 37
Tepanil, 37
Terminal hepatic veins, 105
Terminology, marijuana, 15
Thai sticks, 15
The Sign of Four, 11
Thiamylal, 35
Thiboumery and Mohr Process (TMP), 7
Thin-layer chromatography (TLC)
    anabolic steroids, 33
    marijuana, 17
    psilocybin mushrooms, 19
    screening tests, 41–42
Thiopental, 35
Thrombosis, 101–102, *102*
Tissue, DNA collection, 176
TMP, *see* Thiboumery and Mohr Process (TMP)
Tolliver, James, 34
Toxicogenetics, heritable channelopathies and myopathies
    arrhythmogenic right ventricular dysplasia, 171–173
    blood, DNA collection, 176
    Brugada syndrome, 169–170
    cardiovascular disease, 176
    catecholaminergic polymorphic ventricular
        tachycardia, 170–171
    cocaine, 175
    DNA collection, 176
    ephedra, 174–175
    fundamentals, 166
    heart muscle disorders, 171–174
    hypertrophic cardiomyopathy, 173–174
    ion channel disorders, 167–171
    long QT syndrome, 167–169
    methamphetamine, 175
    sudden death, 174–175
    tissue, DNA collection, 176
Toxicogenetics, pharmacogenomics
    clinical applications, 158–161
    depression, 158
    forensic toxicology, 159, *160,* 161
    fundamentals, 153–158, *154, 156,* 161
    opiate toxicity, 158–159
Tracks, autopsy, 75
Trans-cinnamoylcocaines, 13
Treatment
    arrhythmogenic right ventricular dysplasia, 173
    Brugada syndrome, 170
    catecholaminergic polymorphic ventricular
        tachycardia, 171

    hypertrophic cardiomyopathy, 174
    long QT syndromes, 168–169
Triazolam, 35
Tricuspid valve, 89, 134
Tricyclic antidepressants, 106, 159
Tripelennamine, 132
Truxillines, 13
L-tryptophan, 108
Tschudi, Gates and, studies, 8
Tussinex, 36
Tylenol with Codeine, 36

U

Ultraviolet/visible detector (UV/VIS), 43–44, 51
Unique identifying factors, 37–39

V

Valium, 35, 39
Valsalva maneuver, 131
Valves, heart disease examination, 86, *87–89,* 89–90
Valvular heart disease, 123–126, *124–126,* 126
Vascular effects
    accelerated atherosclerosis, 102
    cocaine, 98, 100–105
    drug synergy, 104–105
    endothelial dysfunction, 102–103
    ephedrine, 107
    ergot alkaloids, 106–107, *107*
    fundamentals, 97–98, *99–101*
    glue sniffing, 106
    hemodynamic alterations, 103, *104*
    heroin, 105
    legitimate medications, 106–107
    l-tryptophan, 108
    methamphetamine, 105–108
    microvascular resistance, 101
    nicotine, 106
    phenylpropanolamine, 108
    pseudoephedrine, 107
    solvents, 106
    thrombosis, 101–102, *102*
    vasculitis, 103
    vasospasticity, 101
Vasculitis, 103, 108
Vasculitis, cerebral, 143, *144,* 145
Vasoconstriction, 98, 106
Vasodilators, 106
Vasospasm, 108
Vasospasticity, 101
Vicodin, 36
Virmani studies, 79–95, 97–108
Visceral polyarteritis, 105
Vitamin supplementation, 175
Voranil, 37

INDEX

W

Wernicke's encephalopathy, 138–139
Wassen, R.G., 18
Wassen, V.P., 18
Wetli studies, 71–77, 115
White studies, 153–161
Wild type, 161
Willstatter, Richard, 11
Wong studies, 153–161

Wright, C.P. Alder, 6

X

Xanax, 35
Xenobiotic, 161
X-ray crystallography, 52
X/y coordinate axis, 45–46